Third Workshop on Resources and Representatives for Under-Resourced Languages and Domains (RESOURCEFUL 2025)

Tallinn, Estonia
2 March 2025

Editors:

Špela Arhar Holdt
Nikolai Ilinykh
Barbara Scalvini
Micaella Bruton
Iben Nyholm Debess
Crina Madalina Tudor

ISBN: 979-8-3313-1889-5

Printed from e-media with permission by:

Curran Associates, Inc.
57 Morehouse Lane
Red Hook, NY 12571

Some format issues inherent in the e-media version may also appear in this print version.

Association for Computational Linguistics
209 N. Eighth Street
Stroudsburg, Pennsylvania 18360

Phone: 1-570-476-8006
Fax: 1-570-476-0860

acl@aclweb.org

Additional copies of this publication are available from:

Curran Associates, Inc.
57 Morehouse Lane
Red Hook, NY 12571 USA
Phone: 845-758-0400
Fax: 845-758-2633
Email: curran@proceedings.com
Web: www.proceedings.com

RESOURCEFUL 2025

The Third Workshop on Resources and Representations for Under-Resourced Languages and Domains (RESOURCEFUL 2025)

Proceedings of the 3rd Workshop

Editors: Špela Arhar Holdt, Nikolai Ilinykh, Barbara Scalvini, Micaella Bruton, Iben Nyholm Debess, Crina Madalina Tudor

The RESOURCEFUL organisers gratefully acknowledge the support from the following organisations:

University *of Ljubljana*

UNIVERSITY OF GOTHENBURG

UNIVERSITY OF THE FAROE ISLANDS

Stockholm University

UNIVERSITY OF HELSINKI

UNIVERSITY OF OSLO

UPPSALA UNIVERSITET

SPRÅKBANKENTEXT

Indexed in the ACL Anthology

This work has been supported by Språkbanken – jointly funded by its 10 partner institutions and the Swedish Research Council (2025–2028; grant no. 2023-00161). It has also been supported by HUMINFRA with funding from the Swedish Research Council (grant no. 2023-00171).

Editors:
Špela Arhar Holdt, Nikolai Ilinykh, Barbara Scalvini, Micaella Bruton, Iben Nyholm Debess, Crina Madalina Tudor

Preface

The third workshop on resources and representations for under-resourced languages and domains was held in Tallinn, Estonia, on March 2nd, 2025. The workshop was conducted in person but also provided an option for online participation. In alignment with the goals of the previous two workshops in 2020 and 2023, RESOURCEFUL-2025 explored the role of resource type and quality available to computational linguists, as well as the challenges and directions for constructing new resources in light of the latest trends in natural language processing, computational linguistics, and artificial intelligence. The workshop provided a forum for discussions between the two communities involved in building data-driven and annotation-driven resources.

The call for papers for RESOURCEFUL-2025 requested work on the following topics:

- The types of linguistic knowledge that should be captured by models across different contexts and tasks
- Practical methods for sampling and extracting knowledge
- The relevance of traditional NLP resources for use in data-driven approaches
- The use of data-driven approaches to enhance expert-driven annotation processes
- Current challenges faced in expert-based annotation
- Crowdsourcing and citizen science initiatives to build and enrich linguistic resources
- Methods for evaluating and mitigating unwanted biases in linguistic models and data
- Creating anonymized and pseudonymized datasets and models
- Evaluating the role of modern LLMs in the creation of new linguistic resources

We invited both archival (long and short papers) and non-archival submissions. In total, 33 submissions were received, of which 23 were archival. The program committee (PC) consisted of 33 members (excluding 13 Program Chairs), who served as reviewers. Based on the PC assessments regarding the content and quality of the submissions, the program chairs decided to accept 26 submissions for presentation and publication. Together with the 4 non-archival submissions, we devised a program consisting of 7 talks and 17 posters. The accepted submissions covered topics related to working with specific linguistic characteristics, investigating and analyzing specific aspects of languages or contexts, and exploiting methods for analyzing, exploring, and improving the quality and quantity of low-resourced and medium-resourced languages, domains, and applications. The topics presented in the accepted submissions led to the emergence of the following themes and questions for the panel discussion:

1. **Analysis and Exploration of Linguistic Characteristics and Features in Specific Languages**. This line of presented work focused on the linguistic characteristics and features of various languages, including Uzbek, Korean, Haitian Creole, Central Australian languages, Faroese, Spanish, Icelandic, Ottoman Turkish, Brazilian Indigenous languages, Latvian, Niger-Congo languages, Swedish, Finnish, Armenian, German, Slovene, Luxembourgish dialects, Kirundi, Komi-Permyak, Komi-Zyrian, Polish, and English.
    - What are the current challenges in expert-based annotation, and how can data-driven approaches facilitate this process?
    - Which resources and corpora, and in which modalities (text, image, video, audio), are missing for the computational modeling of the aforementioned languages?

- What are the real-world problem domains where these corpora and models can be applied, such as healthcare or cultural preservation?

2. **Development and Evaluation of Datasets and Models for Linguistic Analysis and NLP Tasks**. Questions regarding datasets include, but are not limited to, the creation of UD treebanks, phonotactic corpora, and various annotation tools for speakers of Indigenous languages. Tasks encompass part-of-speech tagging, linguistic variation, code-switching, OCR error correction, question-answering, noun classification, annotation of political attitudes, text generation, personal information detection, and benchmarking with large language models.
    - What strategies can be implemented to improve specific tasks with no available training data?
    - How can we ensure fairness and inclusivity in NLP models and datasets?
    - How can we assess biases in created datasets and inform users about them?

3. **Challenges in Expert-Based Annotation vs. Data-Driven Approaches**.
    - What are the current bottlenecks in expert-based annotation, and where do data-driven, semi-supervised, or active learning methods offer improvements?
    - Can hybrid approaches be developed to leverage the strengths of both human expertise and automated techniques?
    - How can we standardize annotation practices to improve cross-dataset compatibility and overall quality?

Completing the program were three invited keynote speakers: Beáta Megyesi from Stockholm University, Jussi Karlgren from Silo AI and Joshua Wilbur from University of Tartu.

Words of appreciation and acknowledgment are due to the program committee, the local NoDaLiDa/Baltic-HLT 2025 organisers, and OpenReview.

The RESOURCEFUL 2025 Program Chairs

Organizing Committee

Organizing Committee

Špela Arhar Holdt, University of Ljubljana, Slovenia
Nikolai Ilinykh, CLASP, University of Gothenburg, Sweden
Barbara Scalvini, University of the Faroe Islands, Faroe Islands
Mattias Appelgren, University of Gothenburg, Sweden
Micaella Bruton, Stockholm University, Sweden
Dana Dannélls, Språkbanken Text, University of Gothenburg, Sweden
Simon Dobnik, CLASP, University of Gothenburg, Sweden
Crina Tudor, Stockholm University, Sweden
Joakim Nivre, RISE and Uppsala University, Sweden
Iben Nyholm Debess, University of the Faroe Islands, Faroe Islands
Sara Stymne, Uppsala University, Sweden
Jörg Tiedemann, University of Helsinki, Finland
Lilja Øvrelid, University of Oslo, Norway

Program Committee

Program Chairs

Mattias Appelgren, Göteborg University
Micaella Bruton, Stockholm University
Dana Dannélls, Göteborg University
Iben Nyholm Debess, University of the Faroe Islands, Faroe Islands
Simon Dobnik, University of Gothenburg
Špela Arhar Holdt, University of Ljubljana
Nikolai Ilinykh, Göteborg University
Joakim Nivre, Uppsala University
Barbara Scalvini, University of the Faroe Islands
Sara Stymne, Uppsala University
Jörg Tiedemann, University of Helsinki
Crina Tudor, Stockholm University
Lilja Øvrelid, Dept. of Informatics, University of Oslo

Reviewers

David Alfter

Micaella Bruton

Peter Ebert Christensen

Dana Dannélls, Simon Dobnik, Luise Dürlich

Emilie Marie Carreau Francis

Evangelia Gogoulou

Carlos Daniel Hernández Mena, Špela Arhar Holdt

Nikolai Ilinykh

Herbert Lange, Staffan Larsson, Ying Li, Ellinor Lindqvist

Arianna Masciolini, John Philip McCrae, Felix Morger, Amanda Muscat, Ricardo Muñoz Sánchez, Petter Mæhlum

Joakim Nivre, Bill Noble

Robert Östling, Lilja Øvrelid

Danila Petrelli

Michael Rießler

Annika Simonsen, Maria Irena Szawerna

Jörg Tiedemann, Tiago Timponi Torrent, Crina Tudor

Thomas Vakili

Table of Contents

Universal Dependencies Treebank for Uzbek

Arofat Akhundjanova and **Luigi Talamo**
Saarland University / Saarbrücken, Germany
arak00001@stud.uni-saarland.de, luigi.talamo@uni-saarland.de

Abstract

We present the first Universal Dependencies treebank for Uzbek, a low-resource language from the Turkic family. The treebank contains 500 sentences (5850 tokens) sourced from the news and fiction genres and it is annotated for lemmas, part-of-speech (POS) tags, morphological features, and dependency relations. We describe our methodology for building the treebank, which consists of a mix of manual and automatic annotation and discuss some constructions of the Uzbek language that pose challenges to the UD framework.

1 Introduction

Although Uzbek ranks as the second Turkic language in terms of speakers after Turkish (Boeschoten, 2021a), computational resources for this language are scarce. We aim to partially fill this gap by introducing the first fully annotated Universal Dependencies (UD) treebank for Uzbek - Uzbek-UT (Uzbek Universal Treebank)[1].

The UD framework facilitates consistent morpho-syntactic annotation across different languages (de Marneffe et al., 2021) and represents an open community initiative aimed at creating annotated corpora for numerous languages. As of v.2.15, UD includes 296 treebanks covering 168 languages[2]. Nowadays treebanks are essential for the development of Natural Language Processing (NLP) tools and are also increasingly used in linguistic research.

The present paper is organized as follows. In Section 2, we provide a brief sketch of the Uzbek language and in Section 3, we review the existing computational resources for Uzbek. Section 4 forms the core of the paper, describing the steps involved in the treebank development, including automatic annotation and manual correction. In Section 5, we analyze some constructions that pose challenges to the UD framework. Section 6 summarizes our work and proposes directions for future research.

2 The Uzbek Language

Uzbek is a member of the Karluk branch of the Turkic language family and has the status of official language in Uzbekistan. With over 40 million speakers, it is primarily used in Uzbekistan and surrounding Central Asian countries, and considered as the second-most widely spoken Turkic language after Turkish (Boeschoten, 2021a).

The official script of the language is Latin, but the old Cyrillic script is still in use (Boeschoten, 2021b, 390). The treebank described in this work only contains Uzbek sentences written in the Latin script.

Uzbek grammar shares similarities with other Turkic languages, but computational resources developed for cognate languages cannot be directly applied. From a typological perspective, Uzbek is a null-subject, highly agglutinative language and lacks gender distinctions and articles. Like other Turkic languages, Uzbek has a basic SOV word order, which is quite flexible and can be easily altered for information structure by fronting the topic (Boeschoten, 2021b, 401-407). Its morphology is highly regular and the standard orthography does not indicate vowel harmony or consonant assimilation. Modifiers precede the head noun and are generally follow the pronoun-quantifier-adjective order. Number agreement in the nominal phrase is not obligatory, and nouns modified by quantifiers are often unmarked for plural. (Boeschoten, 2021b, 392-393)

[1]The treebank is available online at https://github.com/UniversalDependencies/UD_Uzbek-UT.

[2]https://universaldependencies.org/

Proceedings of the Third Workshop on Resources and Representations for Under-Resourced Languages and Domains (RESOURCEFUL-2025), pages 1–6, March 2, 2025 ©2025 Association for Computational Linguistics

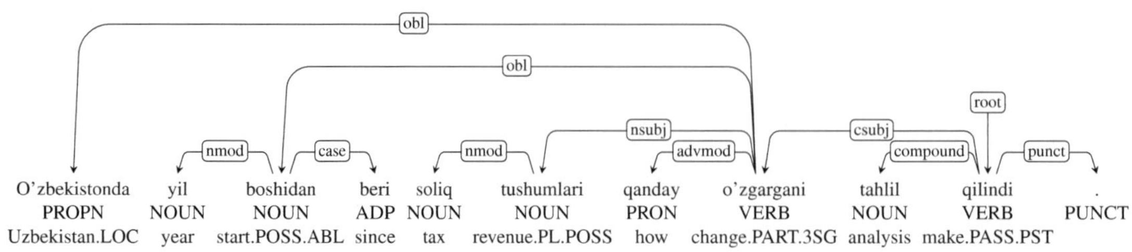

'How tax revenues have changed in Uzbekistan since the beginning of the year was analyzed.'

Figure 1: UD annotation of an Uzbek sentence

3 Related Work

Early computational resources for Uzbek included a morphological parser written in Prolog (Matlatipov and Vetulani, 2009), which however lacked support for complex words. Sharipov et al. (2022) introduced an expanded tagset through deeper morphological and syntactic analysis. This was followed by the creation of UzbekTagger, a rule-based POS tagger (Sharipov et al., 2023), which was based on 12 POS tags and tested on the manually annotated data.

The development of stemmers and lemmatizers (Sharipov and Yuldashov, 2022; Sharipov and Sobirov, 2022) has been another important contribution. UzMorphAnalyzer, introduced by Salaev (2023), represents a more comprehensive tool, integrating a stemmer, lemmatizer, and POS tagger. Additionally, a robust finite-state transducer (FST)-based morphological analyzer, included in the Apertium monolingual package, supports Uzbek text processing[3].

Significant efforts have also been directed toward dataset creation, including WordNet-type synsets (Agostini et al., 2021; Madatov et al., 2022), sentiment analysis datasets (Kuriyozov et al., 2019; Matlatipov et al., 2022), semantic evaluation dataset (Salaev et al., 2022) and text classification datasets (Rabbimov and Kobilov, 2020; Kuriyozov et al., 2023). However, there remains a lack of a fully annotated gold-standard dataset for training automatic taggers and parsers.

In recent years, neural transformer-based language models like UzBERT (Mansurov and Mansurov, 2021) and BERTbek (Kuriyozov et al., 2024) have emerged. These models were pretrained and evaluated against multilingual BERT (Devlin et al., 2019), showing promising results in masked language modeling and other downstream tasks.

4 Treebank Development

4.1 Overview and Data Selection

The treebank building consists of the following steps: (i) word segmentation and lemmatization, (ii) morphological and Universal Parts-of-Speech (UPOS) tagging and (iii) dependency parsing. We cover all the annotation fields in the CoNLL-U format[4], except for the language-specific part-of-speech tagset (XPOS) and the enhanced dependency graph (DEPS). Figure 1 shows an Uzbek sentence to exemplify different UD annotation fields.

Our methodology combines automated processing with manual annotation and revision. Whenever possible, processing tasks were performed automatically using existing tools, and then revised manually by a native Uzbek-speaking author with a background in Uzbek linguistics. The entire treebank underwent manual verification and correction to resolve ambiguities, eliminate errors and ensure consistency. Ambiguous cases were solved through extensive discussions with other linguists and UD experts.

The treebank contains 500 sentences (5,850 tokens), 250 of which are collected from news articles and 250 from fiction books. The news sentences are taken from the UzCrawl dataset (Mamasaidov and Shopulatov, 2023), which collected data from major news sites[5] covering diverse topics and representing modern Uzbek language usage. The fiction sentences are selected from the publicly available 20th- and 21st-century Uzbek literary works found online. To ensure data qual-

[3]https://github.com/apertium/apertium-uzb

[4]https://universaldependencies.org/format.html

[5]https://kun.uz/ and https://daryo.uz/

	Sentences	Tokens	Unique words	POS tags	Features	Dependencies
No.	500	5850	3523	17	42	32

Table 1: Basic statistics for the UT treebank.

Model run No.	No. of sentences			Tokenizer	Lemmatizer	UPOS Tagger	Parser
	train	**test**	**dev**				
1st run	100	-	50	99.86	86.78	69.39	46.26
2nd run	240	30	30	96.72	86.88	68.22	48.98
3nd run	400	50	50	98.30	92.11	73.08	52.43

Table 2: Model evaluation with F1 score for the three runs.

ity, all sentences were manually selected. The inclusion of both news and fiction ensures coverage of different domains, levels of formality, and stylistic variations. The two genres are distinguishable by sentence IDs: the first half of the treebank corresponds to news, while the second half belongs to fiction. Table 1 provides basic statistics for the treebank.

4.2 Word Segmentation and Lemmatization

The segmentation of sentences into words was performed automatically with the NLTK tokenizer[6] (Loper and Bird, 2002). The tokenized data amounts to 5,850 tokens. Currently, UD does not permit words containing spaces. Although multiword expressions (MWEs) are conceptually treated as single words, they are annotated using specific dependency relations rather than being merged into a single token. For example, the proper noun *Tog'li Qorabog'* 'Nagorno-Karabakh' is segmented into two tokens and annotated with `flat` relation. Punctuation marks that are attached to a word are tokenized as separate words; exceptions are full stop marking an abbreviation, which are tokenized together, e.g. *mln.* 'million', *A. Navoiy* 'A. Navoi'.

Lemmatization was performed automatically with the UzMorphAnalyzer tool (Salaev, 2023). However, since UzMorphAnalyzer does not disambiguate between identical tokens with different lemmas, manual disambiguation was required.

4.3 UPOS and Morphological Tagging

UPOS tagging is notably a tedious and time-consuming task. In order to speed up the annotation process, we tagged the tokens with the UzMorpAnalyser. Before starting the tagging process, we first mapped traditional Uzbek word classes (Rahmatullayev, 2006) to 17 UPOS tags, adhering to the UD guidelines[7].UPOS-tagged tokens were then manually checked and corrected, as the tagger did not reach a satisfactory level of accuracy.

For morphological features, which are referred to as 'Universal features'[8] in the UD framework, we first selected 42 Universal features and annotated 150 sentences manually. We then used these sentences as training data to build a parser for automatically tagging the remaining sentences. For this task, we used Stanford Stanza [9] (Qi et al., 2020), a Python-based NLP library with neural network components. This significantly reduced manual work, as some Universal features were predicted with near-perfect accuracy. As the final step of this task, we manually revised and corrected the annotations for 350 sentences.

4.4 Dependency Parsing

To train a dependency parser, Stanford Stanza requires a pipeline with three interconnected processors: a tokenizer, lemmatizer and POS tagger. Therefore, we left dependency parsing as the last step in building the treebank. We first selected 32 UD syntactic relations and manually annotated 150 sentences with the help of Grew tools (Guillaume, 2021). Together with Uzbek word vectors from the fastText collection (Grave et al., 2018), we used these sentences to train an initial Stanza dependency parsing model (1st run). This model was then used to parse an additional 200 sentences, which were manually corrected for dependency relations and used to train a second model

[6] http://www.nltk.org/api/nltk.tokenize.html

[7] https://universaldependencies.org/u/pos/index.html

[8] https://universaldependencies.org/u/feat/index.html

[9] https://stanfordnlp.github.io/stanza/

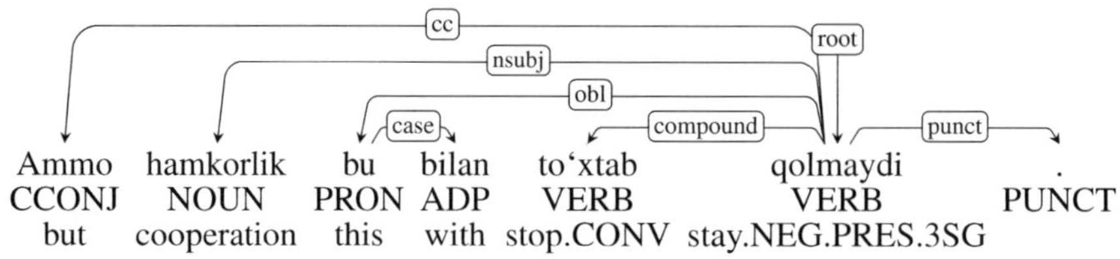

'But the cooperation does not end with this.'

Figure 2: Annotation for the postverbial construction *to'xtab qol*.

(2nd run) Finally, we re-iterated the training and correction process with the remaining sentences to train a final model (3rd run). Table 2 shows the performance improvements over the three runs.

5 Challenging Constructions

In this section, we address some of the challenges we have encountered in building the UT treebank for different annotation fields: UPOS, Universal Features and syntactic relations.

As for UPOS tagging, the Particle + Verb pattern used in verbal multi-word expressions (MWEs) is particularly challenging, as the Particle does not have a standalone meaning and does not occur outside of a verbal MWE. For example, *tashkil* in the MWE *tashkil qil* 'establish' does not belong to any POS in Uzbek and the whole phrase is considered a verb in traditional Uzbek grammar. However, UD requires to analyze this phrase as two tokens tagged `PART` and `VERB`, respectively. The main challenge is the lack of a comprehensive list of such MWEs, requiring frequent dictionary lookups to verify if the first element of the verb phrase belongs to a different POS category.

With regard to Universal Features, Uzbek verbs can be morphologically marked for the Voice category by more than one value. In such cases, the actual value is determined by the most external voice suffix. For instance, *ko'ch-ir-il-ish-i* 'relocate-CAU-PASS-VNOUN-3SG' has a causative and a passive morpheme, but the verb is ultimately considered as having a passive voice. This ambiguity should be resolved manually, as the parser has no representation for the order of the morphemes.

As for syntactic relations, postverbial constructions with auxiliary verbs, which are defined by Johanson (2021, 36-37) as "converb[s] of a lexical verb and a second auxiliary verb form[ing] a verbal phrase with strong semantic fusion", are notoriously challenging to analyze. There are about 27 verbs in Uzbek that can be used as auxiliaries to form such constructions, e.g. *to'xtab* 'stop' as in *to'xtab qol* ('lit.: stopping stay) 'end, finish' (see Figure 2) (Boeschoten, 2021b, 396).

Postverbial constructions are common in the Turkic family, but their annotation lacks consistency across the UD treebanks for Turkic languages. In the Uyghur treebank, auxiliaries are analyzed as the head of an open clausal complement relation (`xcomp`)[10], although this does not fully align with the UD guidelines. In the Kyrgyz treebank, converbs are treated as the head of the relation, with the postverbial element assigned an auxiliary relation (`aux`)[11]. However, this seems inaccurate, as verbal features like person, tense and mood are marked on the postverbial element. In Uzbek, words used as auxiliaries also have non-auxiliary uses, and `aux` is only assigned to modal and copular verbs. This inconsistency across languages highlights the need for a standardized approach. One potential solution is to introduce a new subtype for compound relations, pending discussion among Turkic UD contributors and approval by the UD coordinators. In the meantime, we analyze such Uzbek verb constructions with a `compound` relation, in which the postverbial element serves as the head.

6 Conclusion

In this work, we presented the first UD treebank for Uzbek – Uzbek-UT. The annotation methodology was semi-automatic, starting from manual annotation of training data to automatic parsing with freely available tools, followed by human post-editing. Additionally, we analyzed constructions that are particularly challenging in the UD framework. Despite its small size, the treebank serves

[10] `https://universaldependencies.org/ug/index.html`

[11] `https://github.com/UniversalDependencies/UD_Kyrgyz-TueCL`

as a quality resource for linguistic research and model training in several NLP tasks, which we intend to conduct in future work. In the future, this treebank can be extended in size, covering more registers and enriched with additional tags and improved solutions for MWEs.

References

Alessandro Agostini, Timur Usmanov, Ulugbek Khamdamov, Nilufar Abdurakhmonova, and Mukhammadsaid Mamasaidov. 2021. UZWORDNET: A lexical-semantic database for the Uzbek language. In *Proceedings of the 11th Global Wordnet Conference*, pages 8–19, University of South Africa (UNISA). Global Wordnet Association.

Hendrik Boeschoten. 2021a. The speakers of Turkic languages. In Lars Johanson and Éva Á. Csató, editors, *The Turkic languages*, pages 1–12. Routledge.

Hendrik Boeschoten. 2021b. Uzbek. In Lars Johanson and Éva Á. Csató, editors, *The Turkic languages*, pages 388–408. Routledge.

Jacob Devlin, Ming-Wei Chang, Kenton Lee, and Kristina Toutanova. 2019. BERT: pre-training of deep bidirectional transformers for language understanding. In *Proceedings of the 2019 Conference of the North American Chapter of the Association for Computational Linguistics: Human Language Technologies, NAACL-HLT 2019, Minneapolis, MN, USA, June 2-7, 2019, Volume 1 (Long and Short Papers)*, pages 4171–4186. Association for Computational Linguistics.

Edouard Grave, Piotr Bojanowski, Prakhar Gupta, Armand Joulin, and Tomas Mikolov. 2018. Learning word vectors for 157 languages. In *Proceedings of the International Conference on Language Resources and Evaluation (LREC 2018)*.

Bruno Guillaume. 2021. Graph matching and graph rewriting: GREW tools for corpus exploration, maintenance and conversion. In *Proceedings of the 16th Conference of the European Chapter of the Association for Computational Linguistics: System Demonstrations*, pages 168–175, Online. Association for Computational Linguistics.

Lars Johanson. 2021. The structure of Turkic. In Lars Johanson and Éva Á. Csató, editors, *The Turkic languages*, pages 26–59. Routledge.

Elmurod Kuriyozov, Sanatbek Matlatipov, Miguel A. Alonso, and Carlos Gómez-Rodríguez. 2019. Construction and evaluation of sentiment datasets for low-resource languages: The case of Uzbek. In *Human Language Technology. Challenges for Computer Science and Linguistics: 9th Language and Technology Conference, LTC 2019, Poznan, Poland, May 17–19, 2019, Revised Selected Papers*, page 232–243, Berlin, Heidelberg. Springer-Verlag.

Elmurod Kuriyozov, Ulugbek Salaev, Sanatbek Matlatipov, and Gayrat Matlatipov. 2023. Text classification dataset and analysis for Uzbek language. *CoRR*, abs/2302.14494.

Elmurod Kuriyozov, David Vilares, and Carlos Gómez-Rodríguez. 2024. BERTbek: A pretrained language model for Uzbek. In *Proceedings of the 3rd Annual Meeting of the Special Interest Group on Under-resourced Languages @ LREC-COLING 2024*, pages 33–44, Torino, Italia. ELRA and ICCL.

Edward Loper and Steven Bird. 2002. NLTK: the natural language toolkit. In *Proceedings of the ACL-02 Workshop on Effective tools and methodologies for teaching natural language processing and computational linguistics*, volume 1, page 63–70. Association for Computational Linguistics.

Kh. A. Madatov, D. J. Khujamov, and B. R. Boltayev. 2022. Creating of the Uzbek WordNet based on Turkish WordNet. In *AIP Conference Proceedings*, volume 2432. AIP Publishing.

Mukhammadsaid Mamasaidov and Abror Shopulatov. 2023. Uzcrawl dataset.

B. Mansurov and A. Mansurov. 2021. UzBERT: pretraining a BERT model for Uzbek. *CoRR*, abs/2108.09814.

Marie-Catherine de Marneffe, Christopher D. Manning, Joakim Nivre, and Daniel Zeman. 2021. Universal Dependencies. *Computational Linguistics*, 47(2):255–308.

Gayrat Matlatipov and Zygmunt Vetulani. 2009. *Representation of Uzbek Morphology in Prolog*, page 83–110. Springer-Verlag, Berlin, Heidelberg.

Sanatbek Matlatipov, Hulkar Rahimboeva, Jaloliddin Rajabov, and Elmurod Kuriyozov. 2022. Uzbek sentiment analysis based on local restaurant reviews. In *Proceedings of the ALTNLP The International Conference and workshop on Agglutanative Language Technologies as a challenge of Natural Language Processing, Virtual Event, Koper, Slovenia, June, 7th and 8th, 2022*, volume 3315 of *CEUR Workshop Proceedings*, pages 126–136. CEUR-WS.org.

Peng Qi, Yuhao Zhang, Yuhui Zhang, Jason Bolton, and Christopher D. Manning. 2020. Stanza: A python natural language processing toolkit for many human languages. In *Proceedings of the 58th Annual Meeting of the Association for Computational Linguistics: System Demonstrations*. Association for Computational Linguistics.

I. M. Rabbimov and S. S. Kobilov. 2020. Multi-class text classification of Uzbek news articles using machine learning. *Journal of Physics: Conference Series*, 1546(1):012097.

Shavkat Rahmatullayev. 2006. *Hozirgi Adabiy O'zbek Tili [Contemporary Literary Uzbek Language (textbook)]*. Universitet.

Ulugbek Salaev. 2023. Modeling morphological analysis based on word-ending for Uzbek language. *Science and innovation*, 2(C11):29–34.

Ulugbek Salaev, Elmurod Kuriyozov, and Carlos Gómez-Rodríguez. 2022. SimRelUz: Similarity and relatedness scores as a semantic evaluation dataset for Uzbek language. In *Proceedings of the 1st Annual Meeting of the ELRA/ISCA Special Interest Group on Under-Resourced Languages*, pages 199–206, Marseille, France. European Language Resources Association.

Maksud Sharipov, Elmurod Kuriyozov, Ollabergan Yuldashev, and Ogabek Sobirov. 2023. Uzbektagger: The rule-based POS tagger for Uzbek language. *arXiv preprint arXiv:2301.12711*.

Maksud Sharipov, Jamolbek Mattiev, Jasur Sobirov, and Rustam Baltayev. 2022. Creating a morphological and syntactic tagged corpus for the Uzbek language. In *Proceedings of the ALTNLP The International Conference and workshop on Agglutanative Language Technologies as a challenge of Natural Language Processing, Virtual Event, Koper, Slovenia, June, 7th and 8th, 2022*, volume 3315 of *CEUR Workshop Proceedings*, pages 93–98. CEUR-WS.org.

Maksud Sharipov and Ogabek Sobirov. 2022. Development of a rule-based lemmatization algorithm through finite state machine for Uzbek language. In *Proceedings of the ALTNLP The International Conference and workshop on Agglutanative Language Technologies as a challenge of Natural Language Processing, Virtual Event, Koper, Slovenia, June, 7th and 8th, 2022*, volume 3315 of *CEUR Workshop Proceedings*, pages 154–159. CEUR-WS.org.

Maksud Sharipov and Ollabergan Yuldashov. 2022. Uzbekstemmer: Development of a rule-based stemming algorithm for Uzbek language. In *Proceedings of the ALTNLP The International Conference and workshop on Agglutanative Language Technologies as a challenge of Natural Language Processing, Virtual Event, Koper, Slovenia, June, 7th and 8th, 2022*, volume 3315 of *CEUR Workshop Proceedings*, pages 137–144. CEUR-WS.org.

Fine-Tuning Cross-Lingual LLMs for POS Tagging in Code-Switched Contexts

Shayaan Absar
School of Informatics
University of Edinburgh, United Kingdom
m.s.absar@sms.ed.ac.uk

Abstract

Code-switching (CS) involves speakers switching between two (or potentially more) languages during conversation and is a common phenomenon in bilingual communities. The majority of NLP research has been devoted to mono-lingual language modelling. Consequentially, most models perform poorly on code-switched data. This paper investigates the effectiveness of Cross-Lingual Large Language Models on the task of POS (Part-of-Speech) tagging in code-switched contexts, once they have undergone a fine-tuning process. The models are trained on code-switched combinations of Indian languages and English. This paper also seeks to investigate whether fine-tuned models are able to generalise and POS tag code-switched combinations that were not a part of the fine-tuning dataset.

Additionally, this paper presents a new metric, the S-index (Switching-Index), for measuring the level of code-switching within an utterance.

1 Introduction

1.1 Background

At present, approximately half of the world's population is bilingual and increased globalisation and migration is creating more multilingual communities. (Stavans and Porat, 2019). Consequently, code-switching is becoming an increasingly common form of communication, especially in online media.

Code-switching in digital and face-to-face communication can arise for a multitude of reasons including quoting someone, excluding a particular person or group from a conversation and emphasising group identity (Grosjean, 1997).

1.2 Code Switching

Code Switching is not simply alternating between two languages. Instead, it involves the fusion of two different languages which gives rise to unique grammatical constructs that are not present in either of the original languages (Attia and Elkahky, 2019). This means that mono-lingual models cannot simply be combined to produce models that are capable of dealing with CS. Additionally, CS can occur at the level of individual morphemes within a single word. This can result in frequent out-of-vocabulary words.

Often in CS, asymmetry arises (Joshi, 1982) whereby one language is more dominant compared to the other. The dominant language is referred to as the Matrix Language (ML) and the other as the Embedded Language (EL). It has been proposed (Joshi, 1982) that CS can be modelled with two grammars representing the ML and EL where a mechanism can be used to shift control from the ML to EL but not vice-versa (Martinez, 2020).

Alternatively, CS between two specific languages can be modelled as its own language (Çetinoğlu et al., 2016). For inter-sentential CS, the model can be trained on mono-lingual data from both languages. For intra-sentential CS, specific CS datasets must be obtained as the language of tokens may change within a sentence.

1.3 POS Tagging

POS (Part-of-Speech) Tagging is the task of predicting the part-of-speech of a word given its context. Complexity arises due to the fact that the same token can have different meanings and different parts of speech when used in different contexts.

This paper uses the base version of XLM-RoBERTa (Conneau et al., 2020), a cross-lingual language model trained on data from 100 different languages. The model was fine-tuned to predict part-of-speech tags. Previous attempts at this idea (Maksutov et al., 2021) involve modelling the task as a sequence-to-sequence task to generate a tag for each word in the input sequence. It is important to note here that the output vocabulary for the transformer is incredibly small compared to the

Proceedings of the Third Workshop on Resources and Representations for Under-Resourced Languages and Domains (RESOURCEFUL-2025), pages 7–12, March 2, 2025 ©2025 Association for Computational Linguistics

input vocabulary. The output vocabulary is the set of possible part of speech tags, whereas the input vocabulary is the set of all words that appear in the training dataset.

The BERT architecture (Devlin et al., 2019) is highly appropriate for this as the Masked Language Model objective used during pre-training, allows the model to learn bi-directional context. This should enable the model to more easily understand the sequences passed to it.

2 Measuring Code-Switching

2.1 Current Metrics

As previously mentioned, the Matrix Language is the dominant language in a code-switched text.

$$L_{matrix}(s) = \arg\max_{L_i \in \mathbb{L}} \{t_{L_i}\}(s) \tag{1}$$

($L_i \in \mathbb{L}$ iterates through each language in the corpus, $\{t_{L_i}\}(s)$ returns the number of tokens of language L_i in sequence s, L_{matrix} is the matrix language)

The Code-Mixing Index metric (Gambäck and Das, 2016) can be used to measure the level of code switching in a sequence s-

$$CMI(s) = \frac{\lambda(N(s) - \{t_{L_{matrix}}\}(s)) + \mu P(s)}{N(s)} \tag{2}$$

($N(s)$ is the number of tokens in the sequence, $\{t_{L_{matrix}}\}(s)$ is the number of tokens in the matrix language, $P(s)$ is the number of code alteration points and λ and μ are weights that sum to 1)

If a sequence has a high number of tokens not in the matrix language, it has a high amount of code-switching. The sequence also has a high amount of code-switching if there are a large number of alteration points. This measurement manages to capture both of these metrics.

This metric can exaggerate the level of code-switching in short sequences since it divides by the length of the sequence. This is particularly prominent in sequences with a single word followed by punctuation. This arises since punctuation is often listed as a language of its own (e.g. 'universal'). Therefore a sequence such as 'What?' is calculated as having a high-level of code-switching since there is one alteration point and one token not in the matrix language in a sequence with only two tokens.

2.2 Proposed New Metric

To solve this problem, this paper introduces the S-index measure ($\mathcal{S}$) using the same two metrics as the CMI.

$$\mathcal{S}(s) = \lambda \tanh(\mu P(s)) \times \log\left(\frac{N(s)}{\{t_{L_{matrix}}\}(s)}\right) \tag{3}$$

(λ and μ are arbitrary constants. The values in this paper use $\lambda = 1$ and $\mu = 0.5$)

Since this metric does not divide by the number of tokens in the sequence and a logarithm is applied to the ratio of tokens to tokens in the matrix language, the exaggeration for short sequences is prevented. The use of the hyperbolic tangent, limits the influence of $P(s)$ for very long sequences (preventing the opposite form of exaggeration), since it naturally saturates for large values. The constants λ and μ can be used to adjust when and to what value the $P(s)$ term saturates.

Token	**Language**
Matlab	Hindi
?	Universal
Translation	Meaning?
$N(s)$	2
$\{t_{L_{max}}\}(s)$	1
$P(s)$	1
$CMI(s)$	0.5
$\mathcal{S}(s)$	0.32

Table 1: CMI exaggerates the level of code-switching here.

It is clear that the sequence in Table 2 has a higher level of code-switching than the sequence in Table 1. However, the CMI metric fails to capture this but the S-index does.

3 Training

3.1 Dataset

We utilise a dataset consisting of code-switched social media posts and messages in three different language combinations (Jamatia et al., 2015) that was used for the ICON 2016 shared NLP task. Table 3 details the make-up of the dataset and the Code-Mixing Index and S-Index for each language pair. For the entire dataset, Pearson's Correlation Coefficient (r) (Lee Rodgers and Nicewander, 1988) between the CM-Index and S-Index was 0.85. This indicates that there is a generally strong positive

Token	Language
I	English
mean	English
.	Universal
Ye	Hindi
bol	Hindi
ri	Hindi
thi	Hindi
ki	Hindi
unki	Hindi
pics	English
do	Hindi
Translation	I mean. She was saying to give her pictures.
$N(s)$	11
$\{t_{L_{max}}\}(s)$	7
$P(s)$	3
$CMI(s)$	0.36
$\mathcal{S}(s)$	0.41

Table 2: CMI undervalues the level of code-switching here.

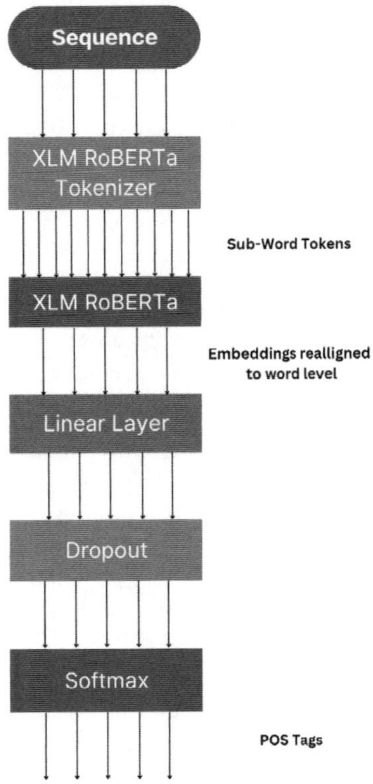

Figure 1: Model Architecture

correlation between the two measures, yet also shows that there is significant cases where they differ and where we believe the S-index resolves some of the flaws of the CM-Index.

3.2 POS-Tagging with BERT models

The tokenizers used by BERT models (and many other Large Language Models) often produce multiple tokens per word (Schuster and Nakajima, 2012). This means that when assigning POS-tags, complexity arises, as each POS-tag can be associated with multiple tokens. Some simple solutions to this problem (Saidi et al., 2021) include assigning the POS tag to the first sub-word token of each word and assigning the same POS tag to each sub-word token. The solution implemented here is to pass each sub-word token into the model, producing a context-aware embedding for each sub-word token. These are then re-aligned to the word level by taking the average embedding for words that consist of more than one token (Lauren, 2022).

The use of sub-word tokenizers can be viewed as a benefit in the case of code-switching as it enables the model to more effectively deal with out-of-vocabulary words (Nayak et al., 2020).

Here, the POS-tagging task is modelled as a sequence-to-sequence task. Upon passing a sequence to the model, a tag is generated for each token in the input sequence.

3.3 Model

The sequences are tokenized using the XLM-RoBERTa tokenizer and then passed into XLM-RoBERTa which produces a high-dimensional embedding of each token in the input sequence. This embedding passes through a linear layer and finally, a softmax operation to transform it into a low-dimensional probability distribution, indicating the likelihood of each token belonging to different part-of-speech tags.

We utilise dropout layers between the output of XLM-RoBERTa and the linear layer to reduce the effects of overfitting during training.

3.4 Fine-Tuning

We fine-tuned four XLM-RoBERTa models on different language pair combinations: (1) HI-EN, TE-EN, and BE-EN; (2) HI-EN and TE-EN; (3) HI-EN and BE-EN; and (4) TE-EN and BE-EN. The purpose of this was to investigate whether the models were capable of generalising the POS-tagging process to language combinations that were not present in the dataset used for fine-tuning. Previous studies (Blum, 2022) have evaluated the effectiveness of

Languages	Mean CM-Index	Mean S-Index	Count
English-Hindi	0.405	0.583	1867
English-Bengali	0.507	0.776	625
English-Telugu	0.503	0.792	1487
Overall	0.458	0.692	3979

Table 3: Statistics for each language combination in the dataset.

fine-tuned multilingual language models for POS tagging in languages that were absent from the fine-tuning dataset, specifically in contexts without code-switching.

We employ the use of a learning rate scheduler and the AdamW (Loshchilov and Hutter, 2019) optimiser during the fine-tuning process.

3.5 Performance on Unseen Combinations during Fine-Tuning

Figure 3 shows the performance of the models on the hidden language combination during training. Despite the fine-tuning dataset containing no data from the respective languages, it is clear that the performance improves significantly during the fine-tuning process.

One cause of this property is the overlap between the subword tokens found in the training dataset and the hidden language datasets. Therefore, the model is still indirectly exposed to some of the same tokens, improving its performance. Experiments (Pires et al., 2019) show that when tested in this way, fine-tuned multilingual models do not solely rely on an overlap between tokens (which would indicate learning through simple vocabulary memorisation) and that the pretraining process has enabled more robust multilingual representations.

However, the loss values for the hidden languages do not reach as low as the validation loss (only containing the language combinations visible in the fine-tuning process) as shown in Figure 2. It is unclear whether this is due to the small size of the model and the lack of data (Kaplan et al., 2020) or if there is a hypothetical limit on the performance on hidden languages when models are fine-tuned in this way.

A cause of this limit could be catastrophic forgetting (McCloskey and Cohen, 1989) whereby the model loses some of its ability to understand the languages that appeared during pre-training when fine-tuned on the other languages.

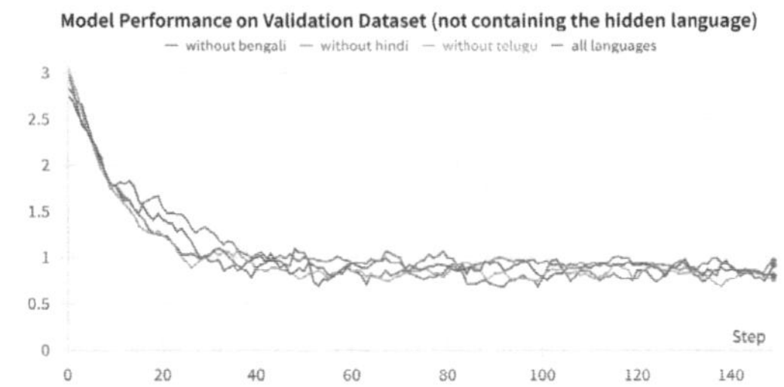

Figure 2: The performance of the model on the validation dataset (containing data from the languages the model is fine-tuned on) during the fine-tuning process.

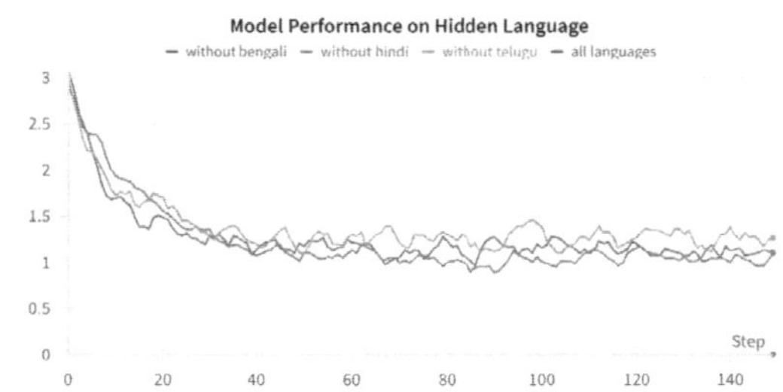

Figure 3: The performance of the model on the data from the language that is not contained in the fine-tuning dataset.

4 Results

The fine-tuned models were tested on a portion of the dataset. The results are shown in Table 4. The testing shows that the models were able to predict POS-tags with a reasonable degree of accuracy. We feel that the performance of the models is highly promising given that the language model used only has 279 million trainable parameters and only a small dataset was used.

4.1 Performance on Unseen Code-Switched Combinations

The testing shows that the models are capable of predicting POS-tags in unseen language combinations to a similar level of accuracy as to when these combinations are included in the fine-tuning dataset.

The fact that Bengali, Hindi, and Telugu are all

Combinations Trained On	% of tokens correctly predicted			
	HI-EN	TE-EN	BE-EN	Overall
HI-EN, TE-EN, BE-EN	76.54	71.86	73.75	74.53
HI-EN, TE-EN	78.67	74.32	67.68	70.28
HI-EN, BE-EN	77.80	67.90	75.32	69.60
TE-EN, BE-EN	72.14	73.15	77.90	72.40

Table 4: The % of tokens in the test dataset that each model correctly predicted.

Indian languages with shared grammatical features likely contributes to this ability. Moreover, the consistent subject-object-verb (SOV) word order across these languages helps in POS tagging by providing a similar syntactic structure.

However, Telugu belongs to a different language family (Dravidian) than Bengali and Hindi (Indo-European) which introduces some variance. This would suggest that the models are capable of learning more general syntactic patterns that appear across different languages. To determine whether this ability persists in other code-switched language combinations would require further experiments. Unfortunately, the current lack of suitable datasets presents a challenge to conducting such investigations.

When the HI-EN data is removed, the performance on this language combination improves significantly compared to when other language pairs are removed. This is likely because Hindi, being the most widely spoken language in India, is often mixed into other language pairs. This pattern was observed by the creators of the dataset[1].

5 Conclusion and Future Work

Although the performance of the models trained here is not comparable to those of today's state-of-the-art POS taggers, we feel that our models are highly promising.

The ability of models to POS-tag in unseen code-switched combinations is evident and more research needs to be performed to analyse whether this property extends to other code-switched language combinations that are not so closely related.

Additionally, the ability of multilingual models to be fine-tuned to perform other NLP tasks such as Sentiment Analysis and Named Entity Recognition is also an area that needs to be researched.

[1]https://amitavadas.com/Code-Mixing.html

Limitations

This study was limited to a small number of code-switched combinations between English and three Indian languages, due to a lack of widely available datasets.

Furthermore, we noted a small yet significant discrepancy between the performance of the models on code-switched combinations that were included in the fine-tuning dataset and those that were not. We feel that more research needs to be done on the causes of this discrepancy and how they can be limited.

References

Mohammed Attia and Ali Elkahky. 2019. Segmentation for domain adaptation in Arabic. In *Proceedings of the Fourth Arabic Natural Language Processing Workshop*, pages 119–129, Florence, Italy. Association for Computational Linguistics.

Frederic Blum. 2022. Evaluating zero-shot transfers and multilingual models for dependency parsing and POS tagging within the low-resource language family tupían. In *Proceedings of the 60th Annual Meeting of the Association for Computational Linguistics: Student Research Workshop*, pages 1–9, Dublin, Ireland. Association for Computational Linguistics.

Özlem Çetinoğlu, Sarah Schulz, and Ngoc Thang Vu. 2016. Challenges of computational processing of code-switching. In *Proceedings of the Second Workshop on Computational Approaches to Code Switching*, pages 1–11, Austin, Texas. Association for Computational Linguistics.

Alexis Conneau, Kartikay Khandelwal, Naman Goyal, Vishrav Chaudhary, Guillaume Wenzek, Francisco Guzmán, Edouard Grave, Myle Ott, Luke Zettlemoyer, and Veselin Stoyanov. 2020. Unsupervised cross-lingual representation learning at scale. In *Proceedings of the 58th Annual Meeting of the Association for Computational Linguistics*, pages 8440–8451, Online. Association for Computational Linguistics.

Jacob Devlin, Ming-Wei Chang, Kenton Lee, and Kristina Toutanova. 2019. BERT: Pre-training of deep bidirectional transformers for language understanding. In *Proceedings of the 2019 Conference of the North American Chapter of the Association for Computational Linguistics: Human Language Technologies, Volume 1 (Long and Short Papers)*, pages 4171–4186, Minneapolis, Minnesota. Association for Computational Linguistics.

Björn Gambäck and Amitava Das. 2016. Comparing the level of code-switching in corpora. In *Proceedings of the Tenth International Conference on Language Resources and Evaluation (LREC'16)*, pages 1850–1855, Portorož, Slovenia. European Language Resources Association (ELRA).

François Grosjean. 1997. The bilingual individual. *Interpreting*, 2:163–187.

Anupam Jamatia, Björn Gambäck, and Amitava Das. 2015. Part-of-speech tagging for code-mixed English-Hindi Twitter and Facebook chat messages. In *Proceedings of the International Conference Recent Advances in Natural Language Processing*, pages 239–248, Hissar, Bulgaria. INCOMA Ltd. Shoumen, BULGARIA.

Aravind K. Joshi. 1982. Processing of sentences with intra-sentential code-switching. In *Coling 1982: Proceedings of the Ninth International Conference on Computational Linguistics*.

Jared Kaplan, Sam McCandlish, Tom Henighan, Tom B. Brown, Benjamin Chess, Rewon Child, Scott Gray, Alec Radford, Jeffrey Wu, and Dario Amodei. 2020. Scaling laws for neural language models.

Paula Lauren. 2022. Reconstructing word representations from pre-trained subword embeddings. In *2022 International Conference on Computational Science and Computational Intelligence (CSCI)*, pages 35–40.

Joseph Lee Rodgers and W Alan Nicewander. 1988. Thirteen ways to look at the correlation coefficient. *The American Statistician*, 42(1):59–66.

Ilya Loshchilov and Frank Hutter. 2019. Decoupled weight decay regularization.

Artem A. Maksutov, Vladimir I. Zamyatovskiy, Viacheslav O. Morozov, and Sviatoslav O. Dmitriev. 2021. The transformer neural network architecture for part-of-speech tagging. In *2021 IEEE Conference of Russian Young Researchers in Electrical and Electronic Engineering (ElConRus)*, pages 536–540.

Victor Soto Martinez. 2020. *Identifying and modeling code-switched language*. Columbia University.

Michael McCloskey and Neal J Cohen. 1989. Catastrophic interference in connectionist networks: The sequential learning problem. In *Psychology of learning and motivation*, volume 24, pages 109–165. Elsevier.

Anmol Nayak, Hariprasad Timmapathini, Karthikeyan Ponnalagu, and Vijendran Gopalan Venkoparao. 2020. Domain adaptation challenges of BERT in tokenization and sub-word representations of out-of-vocabulary words. In *Proceedings of the First Workshop on Insights from Negative Results in NLP*, pages 1–5, Online. Association for Computational Linguistics.

Telmo Pires, Eva Schlinger, and Dan Garrette. 2019. How multilingual is multilingual BERT? In *Proceedings of the 57th Annual Meeting of the Association for Computational Linguistics*, pages 4996–5001, Florence, Italy. Association for Computational Linguistics.

Rakia Saidi, Fethi Jarray, and Mahmud Mansour. 2021. A bert based approach for arabic pos tagging. In *Advances in Computational Intelligence: 16th International Work-Conference on Artificial Neural Networks, IWANN 2021, Virtual Event, June 16–18, 2021, Proceedings, Part I 16*, pages 311–321. Springer.

Mike Schuster and Kaisuke Nakajima. 2012. Japanese and korean voice search. In *2012 IEEE International Conference on Acoustics, Speech and Signal Processing (ICASSP)*, pages 5149–5152.

Anat Stavans and Ronit Porat. 2019. Codeswitching in multilingual communities. *Multidisciplinary Perspectives on Multilingualism: The Fundamentals*, 19:123.

Second language Korean Universal Dependency treebank v1.2: Focus on data augmentation and annotation scheme refinement

Hakyung Sung
Department of Linguistics
University of Oregon
hsung@uoregon.edu

Gyu-Ho Shin
Department of Linguistics
University of Illinois Chicago
ghshin@uic.edu

Abstract

We expand the second language (L2) Korean Universal Dependencies (UD) treebank with 5,454 manually annotated sentences. The annotation guidelines are also revised to better align with the UD framework. Using this enhanced treebank, we fine-tune three Korean language models—Stanza, spaCy, and Trankit—and evaluate their performance on in-domain and out-of-domain L2-Korean datasets. The results show that fine-tuning significantly improves their performance across various metrics, thus highlighting the importance of using well-tailored L2 datasets for fine-tuning first-language-based, general-purpose language models for the morphosyntactic analysis of L2 data.

1 Introduction

The Universal Dependencies (UD) framework, designed to facilitate accessible morphosyntactic annotations (de Marneffe et al., 2021), has been applied increasingly in linguistics, particularly to annotate learner corpora. This approach supports tasks such as modeling the trajectories of second language (L2) acquisition, which often require treebanks for fine-tuning language models or evaluating their performance on L2 data. Such data are typically characterized by simpler and/or nontarget-like lexico-grammatical usages compared to those produced by first-language speakers, although these characteristics vary across L2 proficiency. Previous research has increasingly adopted the UD framework to automatically handle learner corpora in various languages, including English (Berzak et al., 2016; Kyle et al., 2022; Lyashevskaya and Panteleeva, 2017; Huang et al., 2018), Chinese (Lee et al., 2017), Italian (Di Nuovo et al., 2019, 2022), Russian (Rozovskaya, 2024), and Swedish (Masciolini et al., 2024; Masciolini, 2023; Masciolini et al., 2023), demonstrating its utility in L2 studies.

Among these efforts, recent studies in Korean have developed L2-Korean UD treebanks with language-specific morphemes and dependency tags (Sung and Shin, 2023a,b, 2024). However, two research gaps remain. First, while continuing to expand the amount of data, annotation guidelines should be iteratively updated to balance cross-linguistic standardization with the preservation of language-specific features (de Marneffe et al., 2021; Manning, 2011). Second, the effectiveness of L2-Korean-optimized models should be assessed using out-of-domain data to improve their reliability in broader contexts for which they are designed (Plank, 2016; Joshi et al., 2018).

The present study addresses these gaps with three key contributions: (1) augmenting the existing L2-Korean UD treebank (v1.1, 7,530 sentences) by adding 5,454 manually annotated sentences with Korean-specific morphemes and UD annotations; (2) revising dependency annotation guidelines extensively to better align with the language-general UD framework, while implementing minor adjustments to the guidelines to better reflect the linguistic properties of Korean; and (3) fine-tuning and evaluating three Korean language models in both in-domain and out-of-domain contexts using the updated L2-Korean UD treebank (v1.2, 12,984 sentences, see Appendix for XPOS and DEPREL tag distributions).

2 Related works

A line of studies have established approaches for morpheme and dependency annotations in L2 Korean. Sung and Shin (2023b) provided preliminary guidelines for Korean morpheme annotations, addressing the need to parse morphemes taking into account the agglutinative nature of Korean morphosyntax, where a single word often combines lexical morphemes (e.g., noun, verb) and func-

Proceedings of the Third Workshop on Resources and Representations for Under-Resourced Languages and Domains (RESOURCEFUL-2025), pages 13–19, March 2, 2025 ©2025 Association for Computational Linguistics

tional morphemes (e.g., postpositions, tense-aspect-modality markers). Expanding this work, Sung and Shin (2024) introduced detailed UD annotation guidelines to handle Korean-specific dependency cases such as particles and coordination.

Sung and Shin (2023a) fine-tuned morpheme parsers optimized for L2 Korean and evaluated them on in-domain and out-of-domain datasets, demonstrating the importance of high-quality input for fine-tuning L2-Korean language models. However, those studies did not include training or evaluating dependency tags. Additionally, their fine-tuning strategy was relatively simple, relying solely on one Korean pre-trained model.

3 Dataset

Building upon the previous L2-Korean UD annotation projects (Sung and Shin, 2023b, 2024), we continued annotating L2-Korean sentences using a subset of data from the same source (Park and Lee, 2016).[1] For the out-of-domain testing, we annotated additional data from the KoLLA dataset (Lee, 2022), which was designed to analyze Korean learner language with a focus on particle error annotations.[2]

Along with the annotations, we refined the annotation guidelines, implementing major revisions to better align with the language-general UD annotation scheme and minor adjustments to morpheme annotations. Together, the updated L2-Korean UD treebank (v1.2) comprises (# sents = 12,984): (1) additional data augmented and annotated using the revised scheme (# sents = 4,532); (2) revised data from the previous project (Sung and Shin, 2024), updated with the new annotation scheme (# sents = 7,530); (3) data sourced from the KoLLA dataset (Lee, 2022), annotated with the revised scheme for the out-of-domain testing (# sents = 922).

3.1 Refining annotation guidelines

Carefully curated linguistic annotations balance two key challenges: maintaining consistency and ensuring accuracy. Manning (2011) highlighted the challenges involving POS labeling, noting the inherent ambiguities and unclear boundaries between word classes, which complicate the definitive assignment of labels. Such intrinsic ambiguities can degrade the performance of taggers when training language models. Therefore, systematic checks and guideline refinements are essential for achieving optimal annotations.

For L2-Korean annotations, Sung and Shin (2024) emphasized dependency annotations grounded in language-specific justifications, building upon earlier studies of Korean dependency annotations (Lee et al., 2019; Kim et al., 2018; Seo et al., 2019). However, the previous annotation scheme did not fully conform to the language-general UD framework and exhibited notable mismatches between tags, particularly `conj`, `flat`, and `aux`. To address these issues, we revised the previous dependency annotation guidelines to better align with the language-general UD conventions, thus enhancing global applicability. Below, we outline two key areas of major changes implemented.

3.1.1 Following the left-to-right rule

The UD framework enforces a strict left-to-right rule for coordination to ensure consistency and cross-linguistic applicability in morphosyntactic annotations (Nivre et al., 2016; de Marneffe et al., 2021). This approach originates from the Stanford-typed dependencies for English (de Marneffe et al., 2006), which serve as the foundation for the universal dependency representation (McDonald et al., 2013).

Coordination Coordination (`conj`) is handled by consistently attaching the coordinating conjunction to the head of the first conjunct. The leftmost conjunct is designated as the head, with subsequent conjuncts and the coordinating conjunction depending on it.[3]

Initially, Sung and Shin (2024) assigned the head to the right-headed structure in complex clauses or noun phrase conjunctions. For instance, in complex clauses, the head was assigned to the predicate, often resulting in a right-headed structure. This approach was driven by the nature of the Korean connective marker (e.g., -고 [*-ko*]), which signifies conjunction and is logically tagged as `conj` (p. 3748). However, in line with the current UD guidelines, we revised the previous approach to strictly follow the left-to-right head structure, consistent with the UD's left-headed coordination. Now, the connective marker -고 (*-ko*) is tagged as `root`, and

[1]The source data became unavailable as of September 2024.

[2]The dataset is publicly available at: `https://cl.indiana.edu/~kolla/`

[3]This approach, while widely adopted, has raised some questions, as noted by Gerdes and Kahane (2016), where the selection of the first conjunct as the head is made without extensive justifications (p. 7).

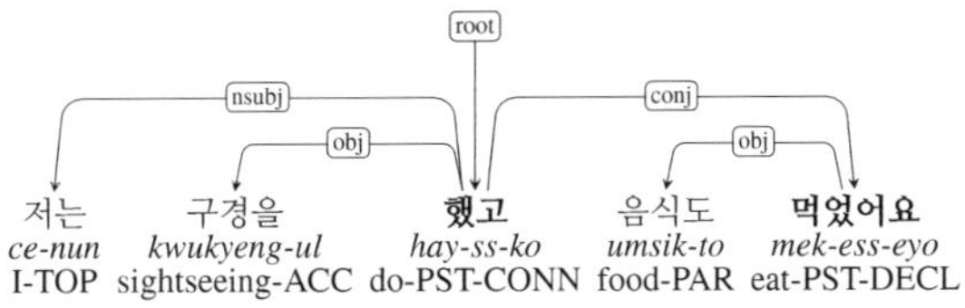

Figure 1: Coordination (Left-headed)
'I looked around and ate some foods.'

the final predicate receives the `conj` tag (Figure 1).[4]

Flat Flat (`flat`) is used when no single element in an expression can be clearly identified as the head. Similar to the case of coordination, in this structure, the leftmost element is treated as the head, with all subsequent components attached to it as equals. This applies to expressions such as "John Smith" or "San Francisco," where no one part dominates the meaning of the whole.

In the previous L2-Korean UD annotation scheme, the core principle for assigning the head was based on the presence of particles, reflecting how they function in determining the grammatical roles of nouns in Korean—core arguments (subject, object) or non-core arguments (obliques) within a clause (Sohn, 1999). However, to conform to the UD framework's left-to-right rule, we rigorously revised all flat relations to follow this directionality. This revision affected the majority of naming conventions and combinations of names with titles in our annotated data, as described in Figure 2.

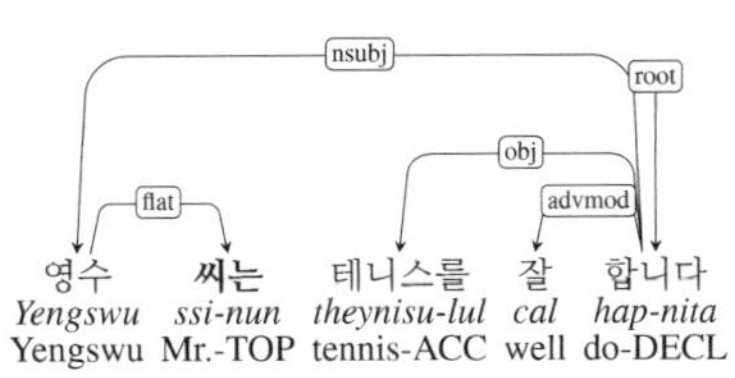

Figure 2: Flat (Left-headed)
'Youngsoo is good at tennis.'

3.1.2 Treatment of auxiliary verbs

The revised annotation scheme strictly adheres to the UD guidelines for Korean, limiting the annotation of auxiliary verbs to five specific forms.[5] These forms include (1) the affirmative copula 이- (*i-*, "to be"), which is treated as a separate auxiliary even when it functions as a suffix to a nominal predicate;[6] (2) the negative copula 않- (*anh-*, "to not be"), annotated as `AUX` in negative clauses; (3) the affirmative auxiliary 있- (*iss-*, "to be"), used as an auxiliary in affirmative clauses or to indicate progressive aspect; (4) the necessitative modal 하- (*ha-*, "must, should"), which functions as a modal auxiliary expressing necessity; and (5) the desiderative modal 싶- (*sip-*, "will, want"), which serves as a modal auxiliary expressing a desire or intention. Verbs with auxiliary-like meanings outside this set were tagged as adverbial clause modifiers (`advcl`).

3.2 Annotation process

The annotation was conducted by five native Korean speakers, each holding at least an undergraduate degree in Korean linguistics. To manage the workload and ensure comprehensive coverage, the annotators were divided into two groups, with each sentence independently annotated by a pair from one group. The annotators worked independently to minimize bias and preserve the integrity of their individual assessments, without interim adjudication meetings to resolve disagreements. When discrepancies arose between the initial pair of annotators, a third annotator, and if necessary, a fourth, were involved sequentially. Inter-annotator reliability was assessed for the initial annotation pairs (before the adjudication process) using the augmented dataset (# sents = 4,532, Table 1).

Annotation	Cohen's *Kappa*
LEMMA	0.964
XPOS	0.908
HEAD	0.892
DEPREL	0.927

Table 1: Inter-annotator reliability

4 Experiment

4.1 Model training

We evaluated four language models against L2-Korean morphosyntactic annotation tasks, drawing upon user-friendly NLP toolkits designed for multilingual applications in fundamental NLP tasks:

[4]We also revised noun phrase conjunctions, as in examples such as 사과와 바나나 (*sakwa-wa panana*, "apple and banana"), where 사과 (*sakwa*, "apple") is the head and 바나나 (*panana*, "banana") depends on it, with the coordinating conjunction -와 (*-wa*, "and") linking the two.

[5]`https://universaldependencies.org/ko/index.html`

[6]When 이- follows a noun and precedes a sentence-final functional morpheme (e.g., -다 *-ta*, as in 친구이다 *chinkwu-i-ta, "is a friend"*), we assigned it the `root` tag, simplifying the earlier practice of using a special `root:cop` tag.

(1) **Baseline:** Stanza-Korean (GSD package) (Qi et al., 2020) was used as a benchmark without fine-tuning. It aligns with both the Sejong tag set and the UD framework; (2) ***Stanza*:** We fine-tuned Stanza-Korean (GSD), which employs a biLSTM architecture (Huang et al., 2015) to model sequential dependencies. Fine-tuning allows the model to better capture localized morphosyntactic patterns in L2-Korean data by leveraging the tagging scheme and linguistic patterns encoded in the pre-existing GSD package; (3) ***spaCy*:** We fine-tuned spaCy (Honnibal et al., 2020), which uses its `tok2vec` layer to generate token-level embeddings from sub-word features. Fine-tuning in spaCy benefits from pre-trained word vectors and built-in lexical resources, making it well-suited for modeling specific lexico-grammatical nuances; (4) ***Trankit*:** We fine-tuned Trankit (Van Nguyen et al., 2021), which uses a transformer-based architecture (XLM-RoBERTa, Conneau et al., 2020) pre-trained on 100 languages. Fine-tuning a custom pipeline in *Trankit* using the *TPipeline* class enables the model to capture long-range dependencies and complex syntactic structures. All models were trained using their default hyperparameter settings to ensure a fair comparison.

4.2 Dataset split

The updated L2-Korean UD treebank (v1.2) was divided into subsets for training and evaluation. The training set contained 9,649 sentences, while the development set, comprising 1,208 sentences, was used for fine-tuning and model optimization. The test set, which included 1,205 sentences, was used to evaluate in-domain performance. Additionally, an out-of-domain test set comprising 922 sentences was designated to assess the models' robustness and generalizability to data beyond the training space.

4.3 Evaluation Metrics

To evaluate these models, we measured F1 scores across the following metrics: XPOS, LEMMA, UAS (Unlabeled Attachment Score), and LAS (Labeled Attachment Score).

4.4 Results

The fine-tuned models effectively improved their performance across various metrics for both in-domain and out-of-domain datasets. For the in-domain L2K-UD-test set, Trankit outperformed other models in XPOS, UAS, and LAS, while

Dataset	Metric	Baseline	Stanza	spaCy	Trankit
L2K-UD-test (in-domain)	XPOS	82.44	89.72	83.15	**91.81**
	LEMMA	89.61	**95.64**	87.97	88.84
	UAS	76.72	85.53	82.21	**92.28**
	LAS	60.69	80.36	75.21	**89.13**
KoLLA (out-of-domain)	XPOS	77.79	81.87	71.21	**84.51**
	LEMMA	88.03	**91.01**	79.64	86.90
	UAS	72.30	81.17	74.48	**88.93**
	LAS	58.53	75.14	63.56	**85.45**

Table 2: Evaluation metrics

Stanza achieved the best LEMMA score despite trailing overall. In the out-of-domain KoLLA treebank, Trankit again excelled in XPOS, UAS, and LAS, demonstrating its generalizability beyond the traning space. Stanza consistently performed best in the LEMMA metric, indicating its strong lexical capabilities even with domain shifts.

5 Discussion and future directions

We expanded the L2-Korean UD treebank with refined annotation schemes to improve model performance after fine-tuning. Using this treebank, we fine-tuned three models—Stanza, spaCy, and Trankit—and evaluated their performance in both in-domain and out-of-domain contexts. The evaluation results showed significant performance improvements across various metrics, underscoring the value of using an L2 dataset for fine-tuning. Among the models, Trankit's transformer-based architecture outperformed the others in XPOS, UAS, and LAS across both test datasets, demonstrating its effectiveness of capturing morphosyntactic features in L2-Korean data. The fine-tuned models and relevant documentations are available at `https://github.com/NLPxL2Korean/UD-KSL`. The treebank will be updated at `https://github.com/UniversalDependencies/UD_Korean-KSL`.

Although both Trankit and Stanza employ a character-based seq2seq model (Van Nguyen et al., 2021), Stanza's superior lemmatization performance compared to Trankit can be attributed to two primary factors. First, Stanza includes a dictionary-based lemmatizer (Qi et al., 2020), which may have strengthened its ability to handle a wide variety of morphological patterns. Second, as noted earlier, Stanza uniquely leverages a model that was pre-trained on L1 data (UD-Korean GSD) before being fine-tuned on the current L2 data, which appears to enable it to capitalize on prior lemmatization knowledge for more accurate predictions.

To fully harness the potential of transformer-based architectures in fine-tuning L2-Korean models, future L2-Korean UD treebanks could adopt two complementary strategies. One approach involves combining L2-Korean data drawn from various genres or diverse learner backgrounds. The other centers on refining the match between universal UPOS tags and language-specific XPOS tags through expert revisions to enhance UPOS to boost their effectiveness for lemmatization within the seq2seq framework.

Acknowledgments

The authors gratefully acknowledge Hee-June Koh, Chanyoung Lee, Youkyung Sung for their contributions to manual annotations and discussions for the enhancement of annotation guidelines. This research was supported by the 2024 Korean Studies Grant Program of the Academy of Korean Studies (AKS-2024-R-012).

References

Yevgeni Berzak, Jessica Kenney, Carolyn Spadine, Jing Xian Wang, Lucia Lam, Keiko Sophie Mori, Sebastian Garza, and Boris Katz. 2016. https://aclanthology.org/P16-1070.pdf Universal dependencies for learner english. In *Proceedings of the 54th Annual Meeting of the Association for Computational Linguistics (Volume 1: Long Papers)*, pages 737–746.

Alexis Conneau, Alexei Baevski, Ronan Collobert, Abdelrahman Mohamed, and Michael Auli. 2020. Unsupervised cross-lingual representation learning for speech recognition. *arXiv preprint arXiv:2006.13979*.

Elisa Di Nuovo, Cristina Bosco, Alessandro Mazzei, Manuela Sanguinetti, et al. 2019. Towards an italian learner treebank in universal dependencies. In *CEUR workshop proceedings*, volume 2481, pages 1–6. CEUR-WS.

Elisa Di Nuovo, Manuela Sanguinetti, Alessandro Mazzei, Elisa Corino, and Cristina Bosco. 2022. Valico-ud: Treebanking an italian learner corpus in universal dependencies. *IJCoL. Italian Journal of Computational Linguistics*, 8(8-1).

Kim Gerdes and Sylvain Kahane. 2016. Dependency annotation choices: Assessing theoretical and practical issues of universal dependencies. In *LAW X (2016) The 10th Linguistic Annotation Workshop: 131.*

Matthew Honnibal, Ines Montani, Sofie Van Landeghem, and Adriane Boyd. 2020. spacy: Industrial-strength natural language processing in python.

Yan Huang, Akira Murakami, Theodora Alexopoulou, and Anna Korhonen. 2018. https://www.jbe-platform.com/content/journals/10.1075/ijcl.16080.hua Dependency parsing of learner english. *International Journal of Corpus Linguistics*, 23(1):28–54.

Zhiheng Huang, Wei Xu, and Kai Yu. 2015. Bidirectional lstm-crf models for sequence tagging. *arXiv preprint arXiv:1508.01991*.

Vidur Joshi, Matthew Peters, and Mark Hopkins. 2018. https://doi.org/10.18653/v1/P18-1110 Extending a parser to distant domains using a few dozen partially annotated examples. In *Proceedings of the 56th Annual Meeting of the Association for Computational Linguistics (Volume 1: Long Papers)*, pages 1190–1199, Melbourne, Australia. Association for Computational Linguistics.

Hansaem Kim et al. 2018. *2018년 국어 말뭉치 연구 및 구축 [2018 Korean language corpus research and construction]*. National Institute of Korean Language, Republic of Korea.

Kristopher Kyle, Masaki Eguchi, Aaron Miller, and Theodore Sither. 2022. https://aclanthology.org/2022.bea-1.7/ A dependency treebank of spoken second language english. In *Proceedings of the 17th Workshop on Innovative Use of NLP for Building Educational Applications (BEA 2022)*, pages 39–45.

Chanyoung Lee, Tae hwan Oh, and Hansam Kim. 2019. 한국어 보편 의존 구문 분석 (universal dependencies) 방법론 연구 [a study on universal dependency annotation for korean]. *언어사실과 관점 [Language Facts and Perspectives]*, 47:141–175.

John Lee, Herman Leung, and Keying Li. 2017. https://aclanthology.org/W17-0408/ Towards universal dependencies for learner chinese. In *Proceedings of the NoDaLiDa 2017 Workshop on Universal Dependencies (UDW 2017)*, pages 67–71.

Sun-Hee Lee. 2022. Corpus-based research and ksl. In *The Routledge Handbook of Korean as a Second Language*, pages 257–276. Routledge.

Olga Lyashevskaya and Irina Panteleeva. 2017. Realec learner treebank: annotation principles and evaluation of automatic parsing. In *Proceedings of the 16th International Workshop on Treebanks and Linguistic Theories*, pages 80–87.

Christopher D Manning. 2011. Part-of-speech tagging from 97% to 100%: is it time for some linguistics? In *International conference on intelligent text processing and computational linguistics*, pages 171–189. Springer.

Marie-Catherine de Marneffe, Bill MacCartney, Christopher D Manning, et al. 2006. Generating typed dependency parses from phrase structure parses. In *Lrec*, volume 6, pages 449–454.

Marie-Catherine de Marneffe, Christopher D Manning, Joakim Nivre, and Daniel Zeman. 2021. Universal dependencies. *Computational linguistics*, 47(2):255–308.

Arianna Masciolini. 2023. A query engine for l1-l2 parallel dependency treebanks. In *Proceedings of the 24th Nordic Conference on Computational Linguistics (NoDaLiDa)*, pages 574–587.

Arianna Masciolini, Emilie Francis, and Maria Irena Szawerna. 2024. Synthetic-error augmented parsing of swedish as a second language: Experiments with word order. In *Proceedings of the Joint Workshop on Multiword Expressions and Universal Dependencies (MWE-UD)@ LREC-COLING 2024*, pages 43–49.

Arianna Masciolini, Elena Volodina, and Dana Dannlls. 2023. Towards automatically extracting morphosyntactical error patterns from l1-l2 parallel dependency treebanks. In *Proceedings of the 18th Workshop on Innovative Use of NLP for Building Educational Applications (BEA 2023)*, pages 585–597.

Ryan McDonald, Joakim Nivre, Yvonne Quirmbach-Brundage, Yoav Goldberg, Dipanjan Das, Kuzman Ganchev, Keith Hall, Slav Petrov, Hao Zhang, Oscar Täckström, et al. 2013. https://aclanthology.org/P13-2017/ Universal dependency annotation for multilingual parsing. In *Proceedings of the 51st Annual Meeting of the Association for Computational Linguistics (Volume 2: Short Papers)*, pages 92–97.

Joakim Nivre, Marie-Catherine De Marneffe, Filip Ginter, Yoav Goldberg, Jan Hajic, Christopher D Manning, Ryan McDonald, Slav Petrov, Sampo Pyysalo, Natalia Silveira, et al. 2016. Universal dependencies v1: A multilingual treebank collection. In *Proceedings of the Tenth International Conference on Language Resources and Evaluation (LREC'16)*, pages 1659–1666.

Jungyeul Park and Jung Hee Lee. 2016. A korean learner corpus and its features. *En-e-hak [Linguistics]*, (75):69–85.

Barbara Plank. 2016. What to do about non-standard (or non-canonical) language in nlp. *arXiv preprint arXiv:1608.07836*.

Peng Qi, Yuhao Zhang, Yuhui Zhang, Jason Bolton, and Christopher D Manning. 2020. https://aclanthology.org/2020.acl-demos.14/ Stanza: A python natural language processing toolkit for many human languages. In *Proceedings of the 58th Annual Meeting of the Association for Computational Linguistics: System Demonstrations*, pages 101–108.

Alla Rozovskaya. 2024. Universal dependencies for learner russian. In *Proceedings of the 2024 Joint International Conference on Computational Linguistics, Language Resources and Evaluation (LREC-COLING 2024)*, pages 17112–17119.

Saetbyol Seo et al. 2019. 한국어 보편 의존 관계 분석에 관한 제언 [a proposal on universal dependencies (v.2) annotation for korean]. *언어와 정보 [Language and Information]*, 23(1):91–122.

Ho-Min Sohn. 1999. *The Korean language*. New York, NY: Cambridge University Cambridge University Press.

Hakyung Sung and Gyu-Ho Shin. 2023a. Diversifying language models for lesser-studied languages and language-usage contexts: A case of second language korean. In *Findings of the Association for Computational Linguistics: EMNLP 2023*, pages 11461–11473.

Hakyung Sung and Gyu-Ho Shin. 2023b. Towards l2-friendly pipelines for learner corpora: A case of written production by l2-korean learners. In *Proceedings of the 18th Workshop on Innovative Use of NLP for Building Educational Applications (BEA 2023)*, pages 72–82.

Hakyung Sung and Gyu-Ho Shin. 2024. Constructing a dependency treebank for second language learners of korean. In *Proceedings of the 2024 Joint International Conference on Computational Linguistics, Language Resources and Evaluation (LREC-COLING 2024)*, pages 3747–3758.

Minh Van Nguyen, Viet Dac Lai, Amir Pouran Ben Veyseh, and Thien Huu Nguyen. 2021. Trankit: A light-weight transformer-based toolkit for multilingual natural language processing. In *Proceedings of the 16th Conference of the European Chapter of the Association for Computational Linguistics: System Demonstrations*, pages 80–90.

Appendix

XPOS	v1.1	v1.2	DEPREL	v1.1	v1.2
NNG	25338	40001	nsubj	8767	13781
VV	10219	16714	punct	8287	14066
EC	8600	13282	obl	7332	12034
EF	7541	12994	root	6866	12989
SF	7525	12948	obj	5572	9203
ETM	6694	9831	advmod	4995	7829
JKB	6366	10450	advcl	4703	8425
JX	5406	8656	acl	4501	6400
NNB	4748	7454	nmod	2059	3882
JKO	4735	7717	aux	1963	2312
MAG	4312	6774	conj	1860	2782
JKS	4136	6668	amod	1413	2176
VA	3380	5905	cc	1306	2154
XSV	3278	4761	nmod:poss	1299	1877
VX	3237	4555	det	933	1373
EP	2850	5215	case	894	1477
NNP	2847	4810	flat	854	1172
NP	2145	3548	ccomp	642	897
VCP	2083	3098	dislocated	576	1035
MM	1672	2689	mark	509	838
XSN	1467	2179	list	303	444
JKG	1329	1921	goeswith	203	235
NF	1312	2208	nummod	179	342
XSA	1199	1815	appos	128	95
MAJ	1160	1921	compound	52	112
SN	1017	1475	vocative	46	49
ETN	830	1213	parataxis	37	39
NA	818	1215	csubj	22	22
JC	685	1269	discourse	6	6
SP	607	864	fixed	6	24
XR	424	684	dep	3	5
SS	266	378			
NV	262	516			
VCN	174	251			
XPN	167	208			
NR	157	228			
SL	133	268			
JKC	122	177			
JKQ	58	86			

Table 3: Comparison of XPOS and DEPREL tag distributions in L2-Korean UD v.1.1 and v.1.2

Recommendations for Overcoming Linguistic Barriers in Healthcare: Challenges and Innovations in NLP for Haitian Creole

Ludovic Mompelat
Department of Modern Languages and Literatures
University of Miami
Miami, FL, USA
lvm861@miami.edu

Abstract

Haitian Creole, spoken by millions in Haiti and its diaspora, remains underrepresented in Natural Language Processing (NLP) research, limiting the availability of effective translation tools. In Miami, a significant Haitian Creole-speaking population faces healthcare disparities exacerbated by language barriers. Existing translation systems fail to address key challenges such as linguistic variation within the Creole language, frequent code-switching, and the lack of standardized medical terminology. This work proposes a structured methodology for the development of an AI-assisted translation and interpretation tool tailored for patient-provider communication in a medical setting. To achieve this, we propose a hybrid NLP approach that integrates fine-tuned Large Language Models (LLMs) with traditional machine translation methods. This combination ensures accurate, context-sensitive translation that adapts to both formal medical discourse and conversational registers while maintaining linguistic consistency. Additionally, we discuss data collection strategies, annotation challenges, and evaluation metrics necessary for building an ethically designed, scalable NLP system. By addressing these issues, this research provides a foundation for improving healthcare accessibility and linguistic equity for Haitian Creole speakers.

Keywords: Haitian Creole, NLP, Healthcare, Low-resource Languages, LLM, Code-switching, Variation

1 Introduction

Creole languages have historically been underrepresented—and often outright ignored—in Natural Language Processing (NLP) research (Joshi et al., 2020; Lent et al., 2021). Many are classified as low-resource languages due to the scarcity of annotated datasets and corpora. This is largely attributed to several factors: the limited availability of speakers for endangered Creole languages, pervasive negative attitudes and stigmatization that discourage research investment, and the overall lack of theoretical and applied linguistic engagement with these languages (Mompelat, 2023). This neglect is particularly striking given that Creole languages, as a group, are spoken by millions of people worldwide. Their exclusion from NLP research increases linguistic inequalities and can limit access to crucial technologies, including healthcare-related applications.

Despite these challenges, there has been a growing effort to develop NLP solutions for Creole languages, leading to advancements in part-of-speech tagging, syntactic parsing, named-entity recognition, and machine translation (Cortegoso and Viktor, 2021; Ramsurrun et al., 2024; Robinson et al., 2024; Schieferstein, 2018; Dabre and Sukhoo, 2022; Lent et al., 2021; Macaire et al., 2022). Researchers have increasingly adopted hybrid approaches that combine traditional machine learning with more data-intensive neural and large language model (LLM) techniques to address data scarcity (Fekete et al., 2024; Smart et al., 2024). This hybrid approach has proven crucial for advancing NLP capabilities in low-resource contexts like Creole languages. However, most existing models fail to account for linguistic variation within Creoles, code-switching patterns, and domain-specific terminology—three key issues critical for real-world deployment, particularly in healthcare.

Proceedings of the Third Workshop on Resources and Representations for Under-Resourced Languages and Domains (RESOURCEFUL-2025), pages 20–31, March 2, 2025 ©2025 Association for Computational Linguistics

Due to the rapid expansion of NLP and AI research, Creole researchers face a race against time and technological advances. This urgency often leads to an overemphasis on dominant varieties within specific Creoles, while linguistic variation—present in all natural languages, including Creoles—receives insufficient attention. Variation, whether diatopic, diachronic, diastratic, or diaphasic, is frequently overlooked, resulting in general LLMs and machine translation systems failing to account for this diversity (Joshi et al., 2024). This issue, described as *translationese* by Volansky et al. (2015), can negatively impact the very language communities these technologies aim to serve.

A unique challenge shared by most Creole languages stems from their origins and ongoing language contact situations. Creole-speaking communities often exist in environments of constant interaction with another language. This contact leads to significant linguistic interference, manifesting as diglossia in some contexts or bilingualism in others. The propensity for interlingual interference results in phenomena like code-switching, borrowing, and other forms of multilingual restructuring. These dynamics highlight the critical need to incorporate linguistic variation into NLP research for Creole languages, ensuring that technologies reflect their rich diversity and complex sociolinguistic realities.

One domain where language access is critical is healthcare. Haitian Creole, the most widely spoken Creole language, is vastly underrepresented in NLP, contributing to severe healthcare disparities for Haitian Creole-speaking communities in multilingual environments like Miami. In these settings, patients frequently switch between Haitian Creole, French, English, and Spanish, a phenomenon that existing translation systems fail to handle effectively. Additionally, formal medical discourse differs significantly from everyday conversational Haitian Creole, further complicating automatic translation efforts.

The lack of medical translation tools tailored to Haitian Creole leads to miscommunication between healthcare providers and patients, which has been linked to misdiagnoses, non-compliance with treatment plans, and preventable health complications. Addressing this issue requires NLP models that accurately capture Creole linguistic variation, handle multilingual and code-switched text, and integrate standardized medical terminology—none of which are adequately covered by current Haitian Creole language models.

This work proposes a structured methodology for developing an AI-assisted translation and interpretation tool specifically designed for healthcare communication. Our approach prioritizes linguistic variation, code-switching, and domain-specific adaptation to create a culturally and context-sensitive NLP system.

To achieve this, we:

1. Develop strategies to collect domain-specific data, leveraging community engagement, partnerships with local organizations, and web scraping while adhering to ethical and legal guidelines for medical data.

2. Design advanced annotation methods, involving linguists, medical professionals, and native speakers to ensure accurate and culturally appropriate translations.

3. Adopt a hybrid NLP approach, integrating fine-tuned Large Language Models (LLMs) with traditional machine translation methods and Retrieval-Augmented Generation (RAG) to handle complex sentence structures and specialized medical language.

4. Define evaluation metrics that assess linguistic variety, code-switching accuracy, and domain adaptation performance while incorporating human evaluation to measure real-world usability.

By addressing these linguistic and computational challenges, this project contributes to both NLP research and healthcare equity. It also provides a scalable framework for other low-resource languages facing similar issues in medical translation, multilingual communication, and linguistic variation.

2 Background and Related Work

Haitian Creole exhibits significant linguistic variation, including basilectal and mesolectal varieties influenced by French and other languages. The basilect-mesolect-acrolect continuum in Creole-speaking territories describes the range of language varieties, from the most Creole-like variety (the basilect) to the variety most closely resembling the European lexifier language (in this case, French), referred to as the acrolect. The mesolect, or mesolectal zone, serves as an intermediary area encompassing a blend of phonological, lexical, morphosyntactic, and semantic features from both the basilect and acrolect (Bernabé, 1982).

In this context, linguists have characterized the mesolect as containing a Creole-based variety influenced by the acrolect, sometimes described as a "Frenchified Creole." In Haiti, this variety is known as Kréyòl swa (Tezil, 2022). Conversely, the continuum also includes a local French variety influenced by the basilect, often termed "Creolized French." Of particular interest to this work is the relationship between the basilectal variety, known as Krèyòl rèk, and Kréyòl swa within the linguistic continuum.

Krèyòl rèk is predominantly spoken by monolingual Haitian Creole speakers in Haiti and possesses distinctive features that set it apart from Kréyòl swa, which is primarily used by bilingual Haitian Creole-French speakers in Haiti and its diaspora. Due to their numerous structural differences, these two varieties need to be treated as two distinct linguistic units. Krèyòl rèk is often associated with lower prestige and is viewed as the most authentic representation of the basilectal variety, while Kréyòl swa carries higher prestige due to its proximity to French. These dynamics reflect deeper sociolinguistic patterns tied to language, identity, and power in Haitian society (Tezil, 2022; Tézil, 2024).

Among NLP initiatives and LLM developments for Haitian Creole and other Creole languages, several notable contributions stand out. Lent et al. (2024) introduced Creoleval, a multilingual benchmark for Creole languages and Lent et al. (2022) proposed guidelines for developing NLP technologies for Creole languages. Older but equally important initiatives include the Haitian Creole language data by Carnegie Mellon [1], which contains medical domain phrases and sentences; the Universal Dependencies (UD) Haitian Creole Autogramm Treebank (Jagodzińska et al.)[2], with sentences sourced from the Bible, novels, and newspapers; and the Leipzig Corpora Collection[3] a scraped Haitian Creole corpus primarily composed of Wikipedia articles. Additionally, mainstream multilingual LLMs, such as mBERT (Devlin et al., 2018), XLM-R (Conneau et al., 2019), mT5 (Xue et al., 2020), and M2M-100 (Fan et al., 2020), include Haitian Creole as part of their training data.

Despite these contributions, no existing model sufficiently addresses the specific challenges of our task. Variation is a critical component of NLP tasks for Haitian Creole due to the complexity of its linguistic landscape, which spans multiple varieties and contact languages. Current models often fail to encompass the linguistic diversity of Haitian Creole, whether within Haiti or the broader diaspora. While linguistic variation can theoretically be "learned" by systems through extensive data, the scarcity of annotated resources for underrepresented languages like Haitian Creole renders this approach ineffective.

Another significant limitation of existing models is their lack of robust accuracy in handling code-switching effectively for language pairs containing low-resource languages in particular (Çetinoğlu et al., 2016; Sitaram et al., 2019; Winata et al., 2022). This issue is also particularly pronounced in multilingual environments like Miami, where Haitian Creole speakers frequently switch between Haitian Creole, French, English, and Spanish.

Finally, there is a lack of resources and models specifically designed for Haitian Creole in domain-specific contexts, such as healthcare. This gap is compounded by broader challenges in extending Creole languages beyond their traditionally established functions, particularly in scientific and technical domains. A notable effort in this regard is the MIT-Ayiti lab's initiative to create new vocabulary for STEM materials[4]. However, this project faced criticism from linguists for its reliance on the lexifier language (French) to generate new Haitian Creole terms, which sparked debates about linguistic authenticity and community acceptance[5].

This project therefore requires a series of targeted steps to address the multifaceted challenges of developing an accurate and culturally sensitive machine translation (MT) model for Haitian Creole speakers in Miami's healthcare context.

[1] http://www.speech.cs.cmu.edu/haitian/

[2] https://github.com/UniversalDependencies/UD_Haitian_Creole-Autogramm - Accessed:2024-12-07

[3] https://corpora.uni-leipzig.de?corpusId=hat_community_2017 - Accessed:2024-12-07

[4] https://haiti.mit.edu/glossaryglose/

[5] https://rezonodwes.com/?p=314768

By leveraging existing research and creating new task-specific NLP resources, we aim to tackle the following critical issues:

1. Addressing linguistic variation in Haitian Creole to ensure the model can encode and decode language reflective of the target community's usage. This includes accurately representing Kreyòl swa and Kreyòl rèk varieties.

2. Managing code-switching in this multilingual environment. The model must handle (a) frequent switching between Haitian Creole and French, and (b) more complex switching among Haitian Creole, English, and Spanish, which is common in Miami's diverse linguistic landscape.

3. Translating specialized medical terminology accurately, which is crucial to facilitating effective communication between patients and healthcare providers. This requires not only linguistic precision but also cultural sensitivity.

4. Involving Haitian Creole-speaking communities in Miami throughout the development process is key to ensuring cultural relevance and linguistic authenticity. This includes collaboration with healthcare professionals, linguists, and native speakers to guide resource creation, annotation, and evaluation.

5. At a later stage, prioritizing ethical issues, such as ensuring patient confidentiality and addressing potential biases in the MT model. Additionally, practical concerns, such as deploying the model in real-time healthcare settings, should be addressed to ensure usability.

To achieve these objectives, we propose evaluating existing and new models across the following tasks:

- Task 1: Classification and identification of Kreyòl swa and Kreyòl rèk varieties.

- Task 2: Accuracy in producing texts in Kreyòl swa and Kreyòl rèk.

- Task 3: Language identification for code-switched texts, specifically Haitian Creole-French and Haitian Creole-English-Spanish.

- Task 4: Domain-specific machine translation for Haitian Creole-English and Haitian Creole-Spanish.

- Task 5 : Context-aware evaluation to ensure that translations align with cultural norms and healthcare-specific needs in real-world situations.

By integrating these steps, the project aims to address linguistic, cultural, and practical challenges, ensuring the resulting MT model is not only accurate but also relevant and beneficial to the Haitian Creole-speaking community in Miami's healthcare system.

3 Methodology and Guidelines

3.1 Linguistic Variation and Code-Switching

Addressing linguistic variation requires collecting data that represent the diverse varieties of Haitian Creole for classification tasks. Table 1 outlines existing corpora that form the basis of our investigation.

Corpora	Genre	Quantity
(Munro, 2010)	SMS	80k messages
CMU (1997-1998)	multi	2k sentences, 33k tokens, 1.2m. words
UD-HC	multi	144 sentences, 3k tokens
Leipzig	Wikipedia	23k sentences, 32k tokens, 290k words

Table 1: Corpora for Haitian Creole

While these corpora represent valuable resources, they provide limited coverage of Haitian Creole's linguistic diversity. For example, Munro (2010) compiled an 80k SMS corpus translated into English, offering insights into informal, casual Creole. However, its spelling has been normalized by the authors, diverging from Haiti's standard orthographic norms. For instance, Lewis (2010) noted the alternation between the personal pronouns *mwen* and *m* as reflecting high and low registers, respectively. The corpus homogenized this feature by replacing all instances of *m* with *mwen*, thereby prioritizing the high register. However,Valdman (2015) attributes this variation to phonological processes or free variation rather than solely register distinctions. This demonstrates the need to include linguistics research and developments in NLP.

The CMU corpus encompasses multiple genres, including novels, political speeches, and training manuals, and provides parallel Haitian Creole-English texts, including a medical domain subset. It also includes audio recordings of 150 Haitian Creole speakers from diverse locations (Pittsburgh, New York City, and Paris) recorded in 1997-1998 while reading various texts. However, it does not offer authentic oral data that can adequately represent diaphasic and diastratic variation.

The UD-HC treebank contains annotated data from literature and newspapers, providing part-of-speech, lemma, and dependency information. However, its limited size —144 sentences and 3k tokens—limits its scalability to more genres or everyday language use.

Lastly, the Leipzig corpus consists of 290k words scraped from Haitian Creole Wikipedia articles. While useful for understanding formal and encyclopedic language, it lacks representation of informal or spoken varieties.

Overall, the existing freely available corpora each have their strengths and limitations, but none explicitly represent the distinctions between Kréyòl rèk and Kréyòl swa—whether in written or spoken form—or include instances of code-switching. Despite these limitations, these corpora will provide a valuable and foundational baseline for training and fine-tuning multilingual language models to account for linguistic variation and code-switching in Haitian Creole.

Now looking specifically at the medical field, we collected pedagogical and instructional materials meant to facilitate patient-provider communication and information sharing (see examples in Figures 1 and 2 from EMSC (2023) and USSAAC (2023)). These documents provide, most of the time, a medical term in English and its equivalent in Haitian Creole, with or without the support of pictures. These resources have clear limitations as they show very limited and simplified medical terminology and therefore fail to represent the vast diversity of communicative situations a patient and a provider might find themselves in.

3.2 Data Collection and Augmentation Methods

Due to the limitations of the existing corpora of Haitian Creole, data collection and augmentation will be a necessary step to this project. For this, we will engage linguists, educators, healthcare professionals, and community leaders to help with data collection, ensuring ethical representation, and aligning linguistic standardization efforts with community needs. Their expertise may also help distinguish Kréyòl rèk from Kréyòl swa and refine domain-specific terminology. To address the specific needs of this project, we outline four key strategies for augmenting the existing corpora.

3.2.1 Community Engagement

Engaging with the Haitian Creole-speaking community and the linguistics community is essential for ensuring the cultural relevance and linguistic authenticity of the collected data. Community-driven initiatives such as focus groups, surveys, and storytelling workshops can help capture linguistic nuances that might otherwise go undocumented. For instance, via oral interviews, we propose collecting data on regional phonological and syntactic variations and documenting informal language use and code-switching patterns in real-life scenarios. Via crowdsourcing, we aim to draw on successful methods like those from Abraham et al. (2020), where mobile applications and community events can be employed to gather diverse speech samples, particularly from underrepresented speakers. Collaborating with the community also fosters trust and ensures that the data collected reflect the use of the language in the real world.

3.2.2 Web Scraping

Web scraping serves as a complementary strategy to gather written data from online sources such as blogs, forums, social media, and news websites. The newly collected data shall update language use as of today to augment the data collected 10 to over 20 years ago. Platforms popular within the Haitian diaspora, especially those catering to Miami's multilingual community, are particularly valuable. These sources can provide insights into both formal registers, such as news articles, and informal registers, such as casual online discussions.

This will allow us to develop a model that is sensitive to spelling variations in everyday communications.

3.2.3 Collaborations with Local Organizations

Partnering with local organizations offers a practical and impactful avenue for gathering and evaluating domain-specific data. To train our model, rather than using direct patient-provider interactions, we will rely on publicly available health resources, including patient education materials, public health campaign documents, and instructional content developed specifically for the Haitian Creole-speaking community. We will collaborate with medical professionals and interpreters to validate terminology, ensuring that translated materials reflect the nuances of real-world medical discourse. This expert-validated data will also serve as feedback for reinforcement learning, allowing us to fine-tune Large Language Models (LLMs) by iteratively improving translations based on linguistic accuracy and domain relevance.

Beyond medical content, linguistic diversity will be reinforced by incorporating educational materials, children's literature, and oral narratives from schools and cultural institutions. These additional sources will provide valuable insights into age-specific language use, different speech registers, and regional variations within Haitian Creole.

3.2.4 Machine Learning Methods for Augmentation

The UD-HC treebank provides valuable syntactic insights into Haitian Creole and is a key resource for improving NLP models. However, its small size limits the ability of language models to generalize effectively, making data augmentation necessary for robust parsing. One effective method is to leverage structurally similar languages with larger datasets to enhance the parsing performance of a Creole-specific syntactic parser. This method was previously explored in Mompelat et al. (2022) for parsing Martinican Creole (MC), another French-based Creole closely related to Haitian Creole. The approach involved using UD-French treebanks in Fine-tuning and Multitask Learning methods to compensate for the lack of annotated Martinican Creole data, resulting in promising improvements in parsing performance.

For Haitian Creole, we propose a similar strategy, combining the UD-HC treebank with our UD-formatted Martinican Creole treebank while also leveraging existing UD-French treebanks. By applying multitask learning and fine-tuning techniques, we aim to enhance syntactic parsing accuracy, ensuring that models trained on Haitian Creole can generalize more effectively across diverse linguistic structures.

3.3 Annotation and Data Curation

Accurate and consistent annotation is fundamental for training effective NLP models, especially for low-resource languages like Haitian Creole. Given Haitian Creole's linguistic complexity—including its regional variations, code-switching phenomena, and diverse registers, careful curation and processing of available corpora are essential. This process involves cleaning, annotating, and standardizing data to ensure it can be effectively used for both training and evaluation tasks.

3.3.1 Annotation Process

Capturing linguistic nuances such as phonological variation, syntactic structures, and lexical distinctions requires the involvement of both linguists and native speakers for both written and spoken forms of Haitian Creole. To ensure consistency and reliability across datasets, we will develop annotation guidelines tailored specifically to Haitian Creole. These guidelines will integrate feedback from linguistic experts, native speakers, and community stakeholders to address the diversity and sociolinguistic dynamics of the language.

3.3.2 Data Cleaning and Preprocessing

To prepare the data for model training and fine-tuning, we will implement a multi-step cleaning and preprocessing pipeline that will include a normalization stage to resolve inconsistencies in spelling, punctuation, and capitalization across datasets. This step is particularly important for reconciling informal and formal as well as interlectal variations in the language. Data will also be annotated for Part-of-Speech (POS) and dependency Parsing. This will help leverage existing tools in performing tasks that require detailed syntactic understanding, such as those involved in code-switching decoding and domain-specific utterance decoding and encoding.

With the current datasets available, this will include the augmentation of the UD treebank corpus, the normalization of the parallel text corpus Haitian-English by the CMU, and the transcription of the oral corpus to be collected within the community.

To ensure the reliability and utility of the preprocessed data, annotators will undergo rigorous training to minimize errors and adhere to standardized annotation guidelines. We will regularly use calculated metrics to assess consistency among annotators and identify areas needing further clarification or refinement. Finally, a continuous feedback system between linguists and annotators will address ambiguities in the data and refine annotation practices over time.

4 Modeling Approach

The modeling approach for this project builds upon recommendations from Zampieri et al. (2020), combining traditional machine learning methods with modern transformer-based techniques. They point out that traditional classifiers, such as support vector machines (SVMs), have proven effective in distinguishing closely related languages but that advancements in contextual embedding models, particularly BERT, have outperformed traditional methods in tasks requiring nuanced language understanding.

For Haitian Creole, multilingual transformer-based models (e.g., mBERT, XLM-R) offer significant potential to handle linguistic complexity and code-switching. This section outlines strategies to adapt and fine-tune these models to the unique challenges of Haitian Creole in healthcare contexts.

4.1 Leveraging Large Language Models

LLMs based on architectures like GPT have proven particularly effective for language generation tasks driven by a given query or prompt. These models, trained on vast datasets, excel in language understanding, generation, and even reasoning and have been used to create synthetic data used to fine tune models (Long et al., 2024). Advances in Retrieval-Augmented Generation (RAG) have further enhanced their utility, allowing general-purpose models to be specialized for specific tasks and domains, such as those encountered in the medical sphere (Amugongo et al., 2024; Yu et al., 2024; Anandavally, 2024). For instance, Wang et al. (2023) propose a framework to align LLMs with conversational patterns characteristic of medical consultations, enabling models to generate domain-specific, context-aware responses. This strategy provides a pathway for designing models that are not only accurate in their domain knowledge but also culturally sensitive in their output.

The goal of the Haitian Creole translator/interpreter model is to deliver contextually appropriate and linguistically accurate responses to queries, particularly when bridging Haitian Creole and other languages like English and Spanish in healthcare communication scenarios. This requires a model capable of translating and interpreting domain-specific content accurately while addressing linguistic nuances and sociolinguistic dynamics.

The application of LLMs in medical contexts has already demonstrated promising results across various use cases. For example, models have been employed to assist in diagnostics and provide clinical decision support, yielding improved outcomes in patient care (Nazary et al., 2024). LLMs have also been fine-tuned to offer medical diagnostic advice and personalized patient information (Panagoulias et al., 2024). Finally, frameworks aligning LLMs with medical consultation scenarios have successfully captured the nuances of patient-provider interactions, enhancing the relevance and accuracy of generated responses (Wang et al., 2023).

While these advancements lay a strong foundation, the specific linguistic and sociolinguistic characteristics of Haitian Creole require specialized adaptations of LLMs. Pre-trained multilingual models such as BERT, GPT, XLM-R, and mT5 will be fine-tuned on Haitian Creole corpora. This adaptation allows the models to capture unique linguistic features, including morphosyntactic patterns, phonological distinctions, and lexical variations inherent to Haitian Creole. By combining the generative capabilities of LLMs with retrieval mechanisms, the model will integrate external domain-specific knowledge. This includes medical terminology, patient-provider communication conventions, and sociolinguistic context, ensuring responses are both accurate and culturally appropriate. To address the challenges of healthcare communication, the model will be trained on authentic and synthetically generated scenarios requiring high precision in translation between Haitian Creole and English or Spanish. This includes translating specialized medical terms and interpreting patient narratives or provider instructions.

4.2 Handling Code-Switching

Handling code-switching effectively is essential for building a translator and interpreter model that aligns with the linguistic realities of Haitian Creole speakers. This capability is particularly important in multilingual healthcare settings, where accurate understanding and translation of mixed-language input can directly impact patient outcomes.

By addressing code-switching through tailored datasets and fine-tuned multilingual architectures, this project not only advances NLP for Haitian Creole but also contributes to the broader field of multilingual NLP by providing scalable solutions for similar low-resource languages and mixed-language contexts. Strategies involve incorporating loss functions that emphasize language boundary detection and coherence, ensuring that the embeddings capture the relationships between languages, particularly between Haitian Creole and French, and including examples from healthcare and other formal domains to improve the model's performance in professional contexts.

5 Evaluation and Mitigation of Bias in Domain-Specific Tasks

Ensuring fairness and accuracy in NLP models tailored for Haitian Creole, particularly in domain-specific tasks like healthcare communication, requires a comprehensive evaluation framework. This framework must address linguistic variation, code-switching, and the unique demands of domain-specific applications. By carefully designing evaluation criteria and incorporating iterative improvements, this section outlines a strategy to assess model performance while identifying and mitigating biases that may affect the utility and inclusivity of the system.

5.1 Evaluation Metrics

To evaluate linguistic variety, the dataset must include basilectal forms such as Kréyòl rèk and mesolectal forms like Kréyòl swa. Evaluation metrics in this context should assess the model's ability to accurately recognize and process these distinct varieties. Precision and recall metrics should be employed to determine how well the model identifies key linguistic features unique to each variety, while qualitative assessments should gauge the naturalness and cultural appropriateness of outputs.

For code-switching contexts, the dataset must incorporate authentic instances of language switching between Haitian Creole and other languages, particularly French, English, and Spanish, as these are the most commonly intertwined in multilingual settings like Miami. Evaluation metrics here should measure the coherence and fluency of the model's outputs when processing mixed-language inputs. BLEU and METEOR scores can quantify translation quality in these contexts, while human evaluators can provide insights into the semantic and syntactic coherence of the outputs.

In addressing registers, the dataset should span a range of formal and informal language uses. Formal registers may include medical documents or professional communications, while informal registers could consist of conversational Haitian Creole found in social interactions or casual settings. The evaluation for registers should measure the model's ability to align outputs with the expected level of formality or informality. Metrics like domain-specific accuracy and register appropriateness scores can help quantify the model's adaptability across varying communication styles.

5.2 Mitigation bias

Haitian Creole speakers, particularly those from diverse sociolinguistic backgrounds, will play a central role in the evaluation process. Regular consultations with community members will help identify biases that may not be apparent through automated metrics alone. For example, the model's treatment of linguistic variation, such as its handling of Kréyòl rèk versus Kréyòl swa, will be closely examined for equitable representation. Healthcare professionals, linguists, and cultural experts will provide critical insights to ensure that the model aligns with real-world usage patterns, particularly in sensitive contexts like medical communication. Their feedback will help refine the system to avoid potentially harmful inaccuracies or cultural missteps.

6 Scalability and Generalization to NLP Field

To ensure the scalability and adaptability of the methodologies developed, the model must be tested with Haitian Creole-speaking populations in various contexts, including Haiti, the wider Caribbean, and diaspora communities across North America and beyond.

Testing across these diverse linguistic and cultural environments will help validate the tool's flexibility in capturing regional and sociolinguistic nuances. The outcomes of this testing will also provide valuable insights into the scalability of the framework to other under-resourced languages. Many such languages share challenges similar to those faced by Haitian Creole, such as limited availability of annotated datasets, significant regional variation, and a lack of domain-specific corpora.

7 Conclusion

7.1 Contributions to NLP

By demonstrating the effectiveness of these approaches for Haitian Creole, this research shows the blueprints for a replicable framework for addressing these issues in other low-resource languages. This generalization is particularly important for the global NLP field, as it paves the way for scalable solutions that can address linguistic diversity and underrepresentation on a larger scale. By prioritizing inclusivity and contextual accuracy, this project seeks to inspire advancements in multilingual NLP, empowering researchers and communities worldwide.

7.2 Future Work

To achieve the large-scale objectives of this project, the next phases will focus on parallel priorities: (1) expanding data collection and (2) developing hybrid NLP experiments to determine the most effective methods given the available data. Running these two priorities simultaneously will allow for progressive model refinement and scalable dataset expansion, ensuring that each iteration improves both real-world and synthetic data quality. Our proposed timeline is as follows:

1. Short-term (0-12 months):
   - Collect additional data through community engagement, web-based sources, and expert annotation to increase linguistic coverage across Haitian Creole varieties.
   - Develop and evaluate hybrid NLP models, comparing traditional machine learning approaches with fine-tuned LLMs
   - Generate initial synthetic data to augment low-resource datasets, using real-world data to fine-tune LLMs and mitigate biases in synthetic outputs.
2. Mid-term (12-24 months):
   - Scale up the dataset by integrating validated synthetic data and iteratively improve data augmentation pipelines
   - Conduct user studies with Haitian Creole speakers and healthcare professionals to assess usability, cultural appropriateness, and translation accuracy.
3. Long-term (24+ months)
   - Deploy the AI-assisted translation tool in clinical settings, community health programs, and mobile applications.
   - Refine real-time translation capabilities, integrating adaptive learning mechanisms to continuously improve model accuracy based on new data and real-world usage.
   - Expand research to other Creole languages, applying the methodology to support low-resource language NLP beyond Haitian Creole.

To foster open research and collaboration, all datasets, fine-tuned models, and evaluation frameworks will be made publicly available, supporting ongoing advancements in NLP for Haitian Creole and other under-resourced languages.

Acknowledgments

I would like to express my sincere gratitude to Dr. David Tézil and Dr. Marie Denise Gervais for their invaluable contribution and shared dedication to this project. Their expertise and commitment to addressing linguistic issues and healthcare disparities are instrumental in shaping this work. I deeply appreciate their ongoing collaboration in advancing this important initiative.

References

Basil Abraham, Danish Goel, Divya Siddarth, Kalika Bali, Manu Chopra, Monojit Choudhury, Pratik Joshi, Preethi Jyoti, Sunayana Sitaram, and Vivek Seshadri. 2020. Crowdsourcing speech data for low-resource languages from low-income workers. In *Proceedings of the Twelfth Language Resources and Evaluation Conference*, pages 2819–2826.

Lameck Mbangula Amugongo, Pietro Mascheroni, Steven Geoffrey Brooks, Stefan Doering, and Jan Seidel. 2024. Retrieval augmented generation for large language models in healthcare: A systematic review.

Biju Baburajan Anandavally. 2024. Improving clinical support through retrieval-augmented generation powered virtual health assistants. *Journal of Computer and Communications*, 12(11):86–94.

Jean Bernabé. 1982. Contribution à une approche glottocritique de l'espace littéraire antillais. *La linguistique*, 18(Fasc. 1):85–109.

Özlem Çetinoğlu, Sarah Schulz, and Ngoc Thang Vu. 2016. Challenges of computational processing of code-switching. *arXiv preprint arXiv:1610.02213*.

Alexis Conneau, Kartikay Khandelwal, Naman Goyal, Vishrav Chaudhary, Guillaume Wenzek, Francisco Guzmán, Edouard Grave, Myle Ott, Luke Zettlemoyer, and Veselin Stoyanov. 2019. Unsupervised cross-lingual representation learning at scale. *CoRR*, abs/1911.02116.

Vissio Nicolás Cortegoso and Zakharov Viktor. 2021. Towards a part-of-speech tagger for sranan tongo. *International Journal of Open Information Technologies*, 9(12):99–103.

Raj Dabre and Aneerav Sukhoo. 2022. Kreolmorisienmt: A dataset for mauritian creole machine translation. In *Findings of the Association for Computational Linguistics: AACL-IJCNLP 2022*, pages 22–29.

Jacob Devlin, Ming-Wei Chang, Kenton Lee, and Kristina Toutanova. 2018. BERT: pre-training of deep bidirectional transformers for language understanding. *CoRR*, abs/1810.04805.

Florida EMSC. 2023. Medical Communication Cards 2023 Haitian Creole and English Version.

Angela Fan, Shruti Bhosale, Holger Schwenk, Zhiyi Ma, Ahmed El-Kishky, Siddharth Goyal, Mandeep Baines, Onur Celebi, Guillaume Wenzek, Vishrav Chaudhary, Naman Goyal, Tom Birch, Vitaliy Liptchinsky, Sergey Edunov, Edouard Grave, Michael Auli, and Armand Joulin. 2020. Beyond english-centric multilingual machine translation. *CoRR*, abs/2010.11125.

Marcell Fekete, Ernests Lavrinovics, Nathaniel Robinson, Heather Lent, Raj Dabre, and Johannes Bjerva. 2024. Leveraging adapters for improved cross-lingual transfer for low-resource creole mt. In *Proceedings of the Fourth Workshop on Multilingual Representation Learning (MRL 2024)*, pages 212–215.

Sandra Jagodzińska, Claudel Pierre-Louis, Sylvain Kahne, Agata Savary, and Emmanuel Schang. Le premier corpus arboré en créole haïtien. Accessed: 2024-12-05.

Aditya Joshi, Diptesh Kanojia, Heather Lent, Hour Kaing, and Haiyue Song. 2024. Connecting ideas in'lower-resource'scenarios: Nlp for national varieties, creoles and other low-resource scenarios. *arXiv preprint arXiv:2409.12683*.

Pratik Joshi, Sebastin Santy, Amar Budhiraja, Kalika Bali, and Monojit Choudhury. 2020. The state and fate of linguistic diversity and inclusion in the nlp world. *arXiv preprint arXiv:2004.09095*.

Heather Lent, Emanuele Bugliarello, Miryam De Lhoneux, Chen Qiu, and Anders Søgaard. 2021. On language models for creoles. *arXiv preprint arXiv:2109.06074*.

Heather Lent, Kelechi Ogueji, Miryam de Lhoneux, Orevaoghene Ahia, and Anders Søgaard. 2022. What a creole wants, what a creole needs. *arXiv preprint arXiv:2206.00437*.

Heather Lent, Kushal Tatariya, Raj Dabre, Yiyi Chen, Marcell Fekete, Esther Ploeger, Li Zhou, Ruth-Ann Armstrong, Abee Eijansantos, Catriona Malau, et al. 2024. Creoleval: Multilingual multitask benchmarks for creoles. *Transactions of the Association for Computational Linguistics*, 12:950–978.

William Lewis. 2010. Haitian creole: How to build and ship an mt engine from scratch in 4 days, 17 hours, & 30 minutes. In *Proceedings of the 14th Annual conference of the European Association for Machine Translation*.

Lin Long, Rui Wang, Ruixuan Xiao, Junbo Zhao, Xiao Ding, Gang Chen, and Haobo Wang. 2024. On llms-driven synthetic data generation, curation, and evaluation: A survey. *arXiv preprint arXiv:2406.15126*.

Cécile Macaire, Didier Schwab, Benjamin Lecouteux, and Emmanuel Schang. 2022. Automatic speech recognition and query by example for creole languages documentation. In *Findings of the Association for Computational Linguistics: ACL 2022*.

Ludovic Mompelat, Daniel Dakota, and Sandra Kübler. 2022. How to parse a creole: When martinican creole meets french. In *Proceedings of the 29th International Conference on Computational Linguistics*, pages 4397–4406.

Ludovic Vetea Mompelat. 2023. *To Infinitive and Beyond, or Revisiting Finiteness in Creoles: A Contrastive Study of the Complementation Systems of Martinican Creole and Haitian Creole*. Ph.D. thesis, Indiana University.

Robert Munro. 2010. Crowdsourced translation for emergency response in haiti: the global collaboration of local knowledge. In *Proceedings of the Workshop on Collaborative Translation: technology, crowdsourcing, and the translator perspective*.

Fatemeh Nazary, Yashar Deldjoo, Tommaso Di Noia, and Eugenio di Sciascio. 2024. Xai4llm. let machine learning models and llms collaborate for enhanced in-context learning in healthcare. *arXiv preprint arXiv:2405.06270*.

Dimitrios P Panagoulias, Maria Virvou, and George A Tsihrintzis. 2024. Augmenting large language models with rules for enhanced domain-specific interactions: The case of medical diagnosis. *Electronics*, 13(2):320.

Neha Ramsurrun, Rolando Coto-Solano, and Michael Gonzalez. 2024. Parsing for mauritian creole using universal dependencies. In *Proceedings of the 2024 Joint International Conference on Computational Linguistics, Language Resources and Evaluation (LREC-COLING 2024)*, pages 12622–12632.

Nathaniel R Robinson, Raj Dabre, Ammon Shurtz, Rasul Dent, Onenamiyi Onesi, Claire Bizon Monroc, Loïc Grobol, Hasan Muhammad, Ashi Garg, Naome A Etori, et al. 2024. Krey\ol-mt: Building mt for latin american, caribbean and colonial african creole languages. *arXiv preprint arXiv:2405.05376*.

Sarah Schieferstein. 2018. *Improving neural language models on low-resource creole languages*. Ph.D. thesis, University of Illinois at Urbana-Champaign.

Sunayana Sitaram, Khyathi Raghavi Chandu, Sai Krishna Rallabandi, and Alan W Black. 2019. A survey of code-switched speech and language processing. *arXiv preprint arXiv:1904.00784*.

Andrew Smart, Ben Hutchinson, Lameck Mbangula Amugongo, Suzanne Dikker, Alex Zito, Amber Ebinama, Zara Wudiri, Ding Wang, Erin van Liemt, João Sedoc, et al. 2024. Socially responsible data for large multilingual language models. *arXiv preprint arXiv:2409.05247*.

David Tezil. 2022. On the influence of kreyòl swa: Evidence from the nasalization of the haitian creole determiner/la/in non-nasal environments. *Journal of Pidgin and Creole Languages*, 37(2):291–320.

David Tézil. 2024. Sociolinguistic challenges and new perspectives on determining french speakers in creole communities: the case of haiti. *International Journal of the Sociology of Language*, 2024(288):177–207.

USSAAC. 2023. Patient-Provider Bilingual Tools Haitian Creole and English Version.

Albert Valdman. 2015. *Haitian Creole: structure, variation, status, origin*. Equinox Sheffield.

Vered Volansky, Noam Ordan, and Shuly Wintner. 2015. On the features of translationese. *Digital Scholarship in the Humanities*, 30(1):98–118.

Wen Wang, Zhenyue Zhao, and Tianshu Sun. 2023. Gpt-doctor: Customizing large language models for medical consultation. *arXiv preprint arXiv:2312.10225*.

Genta Indra Winata, Alham Fikri Aji, Zheng-Xin Yong, and Thamar Solorio. 2022. The decades progress on code-switching research in nlp: A systematic survey on trends and challenges. *arXiv preprint arXiv:2212.09660*.

Linting Xue, Noah Constant, Adam Roberts, Mihir Kale, Rami Al-Rfou, Aditya Siddhant, Aditya Barua, and Colin Raffel. 2020. mt5: A massively multilingual pre-trained text-to-text transformer. *CoRR*, abs/2010.11934.

Huizi Yu, Jiayan Zhou, Lingyao Li, Shan Chen, Jack Gallifant, Anye Shi, Xiang Li, Wenyue Hua, Mingyu Jin, Guang Chen, et al. 2024. Aipatient: Simulating patients with ehrs and llm powered agentic workflow. *arXiv preprint arXiv:2409.18924*.

Marcos Zampieri, Preslav Nakov, and Yves Scherrer. 2020. Natural language processing for similar languages, varieties, and dialects: A survey. *Natural Language Engineering*, 26(6):595–612.

A Appendix A: Example Patient-Provider Communication Cards

To illustrate the challenges of medical translation and register adaptation in Haitian Creole, we provide sample patient-provider communication cards below.

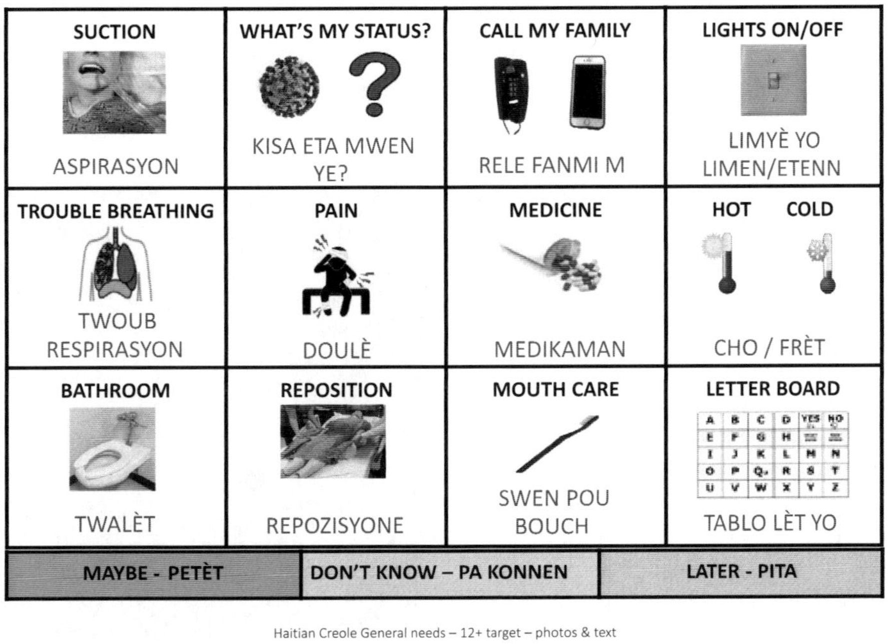

Figure 1: Example patient-provider communication cards in Haitian Creole and English for Adults.

For a more comprehensive set of Haitian-English medical communication cards, see USSAAC (2023).

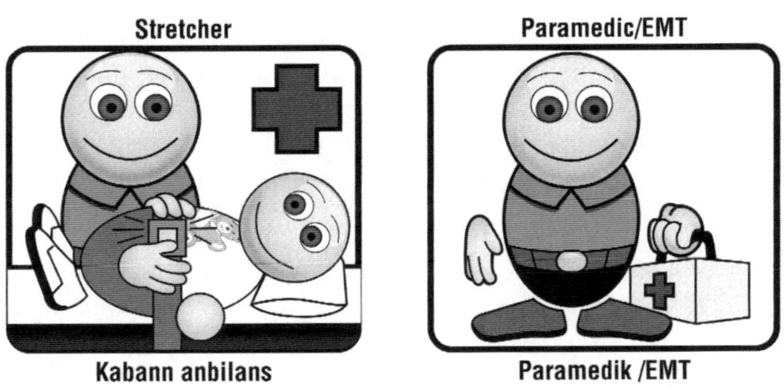

Figure 2: Example patient-provider communication cards in Haitian Creole and English for Children and Families.

For a more comprehensive set of Haitian-English medical communication cards, see EMSC (2023).

Beyond a means to an end: A case study in building phonotactic corpora for Central Australian languages

Saliha Muradoğlu James Gray Jane Simpson Michael Proctor Mark Harvey
The Australian National University (ANU) University of Newcastle
Macquarie University Independent Scholar
Firstname.Lastname@ {anu.edu.au, newcastle.edu.au,
mq.edu.au, @alumni.anu.edu.au}

Abstract

Linguistic datasets are essential across fields: computational linguists use them for NLP development, theoretical linguists for statistical arguments supporting hypotheses about language, and documentary linguists for preserving examples and aiding grammatical descriptions. Transforming raw data (e.g., recordings or dictionaries) into structured forms (e.g., tables) requires non-trivial decisions within processing pipelines. This paper highlights the importance of these processes in understanding linguistic systems. Our contributions include: (1) an interactive dashboard for four central Australian languages with custom filters, and (2) demonstrating how data processing decisions influence measured outcomes.

1 Introduction

With ubiquitous use of advanced NLP systems for language technology and linguistics (often by proxy), linguistic corpora and the processing it entails are often treated as a means to an end.

In this paper, we show that the process is vital in enhancing our understanding of linguistic systems. Each step in the processing pipeline embodies a linguistic decision that can be non-trivial. For example, when building a phonotactic corpus, we want each entry to be a root. But how do we judge what constitutes a root? Should the decision be structural or semantic? The definition of how to classify a root has been a subject of numerous literature (Harley, 2014; Embick, 2021; Gouskova, 2023). To help guide this decision making we present an interactive web interface, to highlight the flow-on effects of analysis decisions.

This system was designed with the following questions in mind: (1) Are vowels distributed evenly across syllable positions? (2) Does the vowel distribution by syllable position change across different parts of speech (POS)? (3) Do some vowels occur more frequently in the root final position? (4) Does the characteristic of the following consonant affect the distribution of vowels? (5) If the initial vowel is /a/, then what is the distribution of vowels in syllable 2; if the initial vowel is /i/, then what is the distribution of vowels in syllable 2; if the initial vowel is /u/, then what is the distribution of vowels in syllable 2?

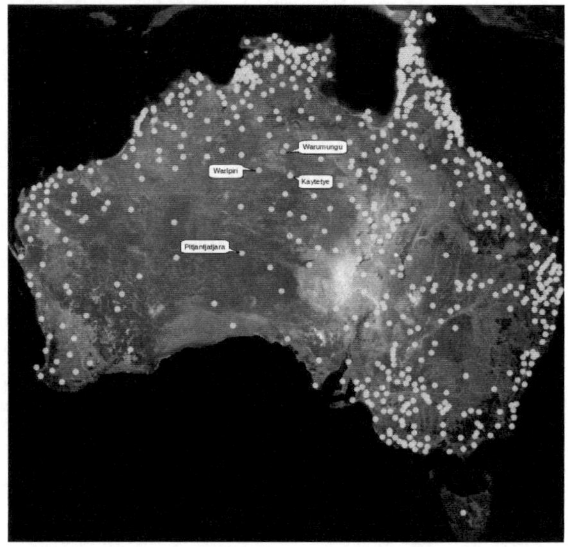

Figure 1: First Languages map of Australia with indicative locations for speakers of Kaytetye, Pitjantjatjara, Warlpiri and Warumungu. Image adapted from Gambay.

Our contributions are two-fold; first, we present an interactive dashboard for four central Australian languages with custom filter functions; second, we show that the processing of raw data into a desired format is embedded with decisions that alter the measured outcomes.

Proceedings of the Third Workshop on Resources and Representations for Under-Resourced Languages and Domains (RESOURCEFUL-2025), pages 32–37, March 2, 2025 ©2025 Association for Computational Linguistics

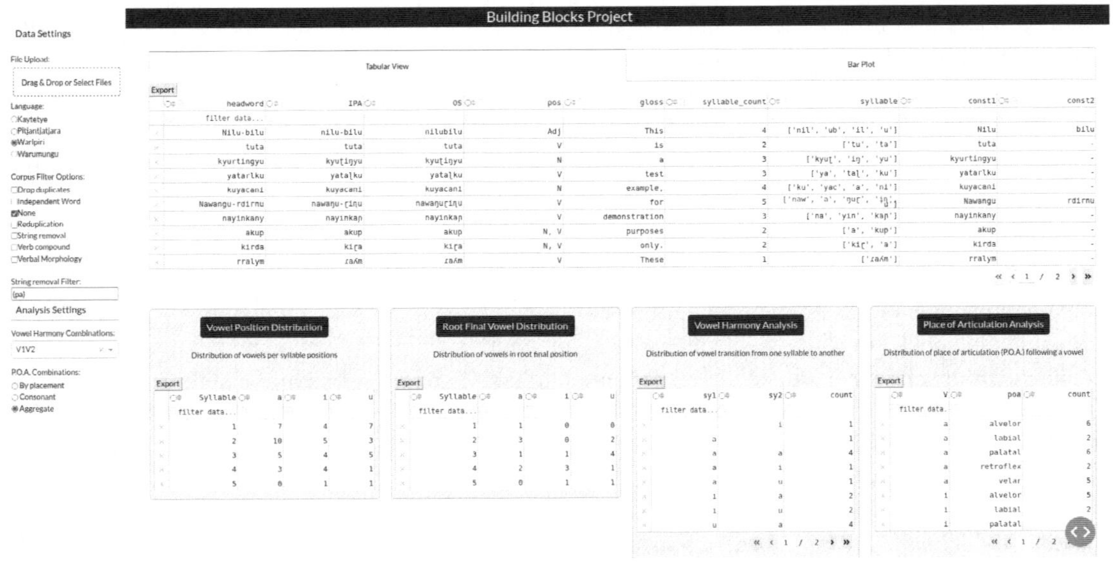

Figure 2: *Interface and system design.* The left-aligned side bar entails a settings control panel, starting with upload options, followed by options for language and filtering function to be applied. In the bottom half of the side bar, two analysis settings are presented: the vowel positions for vowel harmony, and the level of detail required for place of articulation distribution. The center console entails two tabs: 'Tabular View' shows an interactive table of the data uploaded post-filtering, 'Bar Plot' shows the distribution of words with respect to word length (see Figure 3). Depicted beneath the console are four distributions calculated from the dataset: vowel distribution per syllable, root final vowel distribution, vowel harmony, and place of articulation distributions. (Note: examples shown are made-up, for demonstration purposes only).

2 Related Work

Anthony (2022) outlines the differences between online, offline and DIY corpus tools. Online tools are hosted on a cloud and accessible via the internet (such as *english-corpora.org, sketchengine.eu.* Offline are tools such as AntConc, WordSmith Tool or LancsBox (Brezina and Platt, 2023) which run on a local device. Finally, Do-It-Yourself (DIY) describes scripts developed by researchers. The major drawback of DIY tools is the programming skills needed, but are otherwise largely successful in providing tailored, innovative solutions for niche, language-specific concerns.

The majority of corpus tools are built to examine word-level statistics, such as frequency or concordance. While it is possible to adapt these to analyse intra-word components, it can be intricate. Addressing these concerns are often not possible with standard tools (Anthony, 2012). Biber (1988) advocates for DIY tools, given their adaptability and efficiency to phenomena and corpus size. Further, DIY circumnavigate propriety software. In our design, we propose a local web-based interface to ensure data privacy and longevity.

Previous studies have presented online calculators for phonotactic distributions: English (Vitevitch and Luce, 2004; Storkel and Hoover, 2010), Modern Standard Arabic (Aljasser and Vitevitch, 2018) and Czech (Čechová et al., 2023). Most of these resources appear to be hosted on external servers and some are no longer available.

Phonotactic structures in Australian languages have been studied through the lenses of historical linguistics and typology (Macklin-Cordes and Round, 2020, 2022), and it is advantageous for researchers to be able to bring insights from historical, areal and typological phenomena to inform analyses at different stages of the workflow.

3 Languages

Australian languages are characterised by small vowel inventories – often three distinctions in place and quality (Fletcher, 2014; Baker, 2014). Over three quarters of Australian languages have a vowel inventory between three and six vowels (Round, 2023a). Consonant inventories exhibit elaborate place contrasts, but comparatively few manners of articulation (Fletcher, 2014; Round, 2023b). Vowel harmony is observed more than 50% of the time across adjacent syllables in several Australian languages (Round, 2023b).

The phonetic inventories of the languages considered here are listed in Table 1.

Kaytetye Kaytetye (ISO 639-3: gbb) is part of the Arandic branch of the Pama-Nyungan family. It is primarily spoken in Kaytetye country, which is approximately 300km north of Alice Springs (see figure 1 for approximate geographic region) (Turpin, 2000). Vowel inventory in Kaytetye has been a subject of discussion, with accounts varying from two (/a/ and /ə/) and four ([i], [a], [ə], [u]) (Harvey et al., 2023). In this paper we follow the four vowel analysis as we utilised the root corpus developed by (Panther, 2021)[1].

Pitjantjatjara Pitjantjatjara (ISO639-3: pjt) is a dialect of the Western Desert Language (Douglas et al., 1964) and is a part of the Pama-Nyungan family. In 2016, over 3,000 speakers were recorded (Wilmoth, 2022). It is closely related to the Yankunytjatjara dialect (Goddard, 1983, 2001). It follows the norm for Australian languages, with a three vowel system and a consonant inventory that spans many places of articulation but fewer manners of articulation (Tabain et al., 2014; Tabain and Butcher, 2014).

Warlpiri Warlpiri (ISO 639-3: wbp) is spoken in the northwest of Alice Springs by a few thousand people. It is a Pama-Nyungan language. It has one of the largest speaker populations of the Australian languages (Nash, 1980). It aligns with the typical inventory of Australian languages, featuring a three-vowel system and a consonant inventory with diverse articulation points but few articulation manners (Loakes et al., 2008). Warlpiri has been a subject of extensive study, particularly in the domain of syntax, given its free word order (Nash, 1980; Simpson, 1983, 2012).

Warumungu Warumungu (ISO 639-3: wrm) is spoken by a few hundred people in the central part of the Northern Territory of Australia around Tennant Creek. It is a member of the Desert Nyungic branch of the Pama-Nyungan family. It is closely related to Warlpiri (Simpson, 2017). The Warumungu sound system is typical of Australian languages. A three-way vowel system, five places of articulation and eight different possible manners of articulation. Warumungu differs by having a second stop series.

Language	Consonant Inventory	Vowel Inventory
Pitjantjatjara	{c, j, k, l, m, n, p, r, t, w, ŋ, ɭ, ɲ, ɳ, ɻ, ʈ, ʎ}	{a, i, u}
Warlpiri	{c, k, l, m, n, p, r, t, w, y, ŋ, ɭ, ɭʈ, ɲ, ɲc, ɳ, ɳʈ, ɽ, ɾ, ʈ, ʎ, ʎc}	{a, i, u}
Warumungu	{c, k, l, m, n, p, r, t, w, y, ŋ, ɭ, ɲ, ɳ, ɾ, ʈ, ʎ}	{a, i, u}
Kaytetye	{c, cɲ, k, l, l̪, m, n, n̪, p, r, t, t̪, t̪n̪, w, y, ɰ, ŋ, ɭ, ɳ, ɲ, ɾ, ʈ, ʈɳ, ʎ}	{a, i, u, ə}

Table 1: Vowel and consonant inventories of the four languages included in the analysis.

4 System

A key consideration for this project is flexibility in working with the various forms of available data and different approaches to encoding similar phenomena. For example, one linguist might choose to encode a gloss field with additional notes, while another does not. Corollary to this, custom filters and calculations can be added to the system.

An additional consideration is privacy, given the non-public nature of some of these databases. For this reason, the system is designed to be run locally via a Jupyter notebook on the operators computer.

We use Plotly dash module (Albini et al., 2022; Schroeder et al., 2022) to generate an interactive dashboard[2] .

4.1 Pre-processing

The system we present consists of two sections. The first, a preprocessing step that involves transforming hierarchical dictionary data into a tabular form. While the transformation can be extended to extract additional fields, for the purposes of building a root database this step extracts the **headword**, **POS** and **gloss**. Limiting to these three fields also allows for flexibility across various legacy sources and documentation styles.

An additional step is needed for the Warumungu data, since the pos and gloss fields in the dictionary file contained additional notes. It is language- and linguist-specific, but can be taken as an example for other such considerations.

[1]For an overview of Kaytetye phonetics and phonology see Harvey et al. (2015); Turpin and Ross (2012); Panther (2021).

[2]All code is available at `https://github.com/smuradoglu/phc`

4.2 Dashboard design

4.2.1 Tabular View

Once the tabular data consisting of the **headword**, **POS** and **gloss** triplet is uploaded into the system, six additional columns are added.

The headword is mapped to IPA based on language-specific vowel and consonant inventories. To allow for traceability, we have kept the headword entry as it is found in the original file (dictionary). The 'OS' column reflects the operational string that is used for consequent calculations. This field becomes more relevant as the filter options are added. Syllable count is calculated by counting the vowels in each word. This is meant as an independent operation from the adjacent syllable column, to validate the predictions.

The syllable column reflects predictions of syllable structure based on the NLTK legality principle module (Bird, 2006). This module is implemented using the Legality Principle, which states that syllable onsets and codas are only legal if they are found as word onsets or codas in the language. Since onsets are most likely maximised, the longest legal onset is prioritized.

The last two columns show the constituents of the headword entry separated by hyphens ('-'). This column is later used for filtering reduplications and verb compounds.

4.2.2 Bar Plot

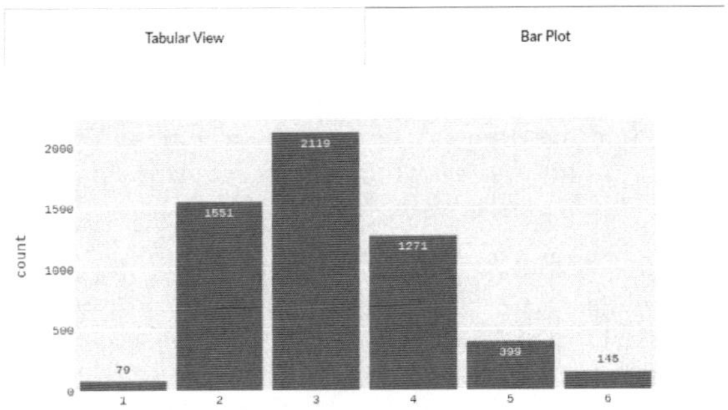

Figure 3: Bar plot showing distribution of words with respect to word length (syllables).

Using the syllable count from the table, a bar plot is produced (shown in Figure 3). This is a quick way to examine the distribution of word length (in syllables) with respect to number of words.

4.2.3 Filter options

String removal This is a straightforward function that filters the string sequence inputted by the user. It is motivated by the occurrence of '(pa)' in Warlpiri and Warumungu dictionary entries. '(pa)' is a semantically meaningless element which is sometimes added word finally to avoid illicit phonotactic consonant final words. As such, the default value is set to '(pa)'. However, it can be used to be a filter for any other string.

Reduplication This filter utilises the '-' marking out different sections of the word (separated out as **const 1** and **const 2** as shown in 2). It compares these two columns. If they match it only considers the first column for the subsequent calculations of syllable count and syllable structure. We remove the second occurrence to avoid a bias in the data towards those sound combinations.

Verb Compound In a similar manner to the reduplication filter, this option utilises **const 1** and **const 2** . It checks whether the second constituent is an entry in it's own right. If it is, it is not considered for the following calculations.

Verbal Morphology This filter is language-specific and as the name suggests, deals with the verbal morphology. In effect it strips verbs of their inflection. In the languages considered here, only suffixes are applicable.

Independent Word When checked, this option removed dependent words like clitics. These are typically marked as beginning with '-' in dictionaries. As such this function simply filters out words beginning with '-'.

Drop duplicates This option removes duplicates based on the proposed syllable structure. It is mainly useful after other filters have been applied (although it can be used to deal with duplicates in the uploaded file as well).

Drop English Loans This is only applicable to Pitjantjatjara for the languages we consider. It filters entries which can readily be identified as English loan words by the presence of "From English" in the gloss field.

Light Verbs This option is similar to the 'Verb Compound' option but because some of these constructions are not separated by space or hyphen, we list out the available constructions in Pitjantjatjara to filter them out.

Verb Analysis This option only pertains to Pitjantjatjara. The reason for this is that the constituents are not marked like Warlpiri and Warumungu, and striping verbs of the suffixes yields some questionable analyses for the root. Given that it requires further input by linguists, we have instead introduced this option to provide a hypothesis that can be verified by a linguist/language expert.

4.3 Analysis

Vowel Distribution The modelled syllables are taken as the input for this function. The syllable length is calculated[3]. The syllables are sorted according to position. Vowels are counted for each syllable position (i.e., for Pitjantjatjara, Warlpiri and Warumungu {a,i,u} is enumerated, for Kaytetye {a,i,u,ə}).

This function is aimed to address the question of how vowels are distributed across different syllable positions.

Root Final Vowel Distribution This is similar to the Vowel Distribution function, except instead of sorting based on syllable position, we sort based on on word length. Here the input is both the modelled syllables and their respective lengths.

Vowel Harmony The list of predicted syllables is taken as an input for this operation. A 'syllable matrix' is constructed where each word is considered in a new row and each column represents a syllable. For example, the sound sequence *kitji*[4] would be two columns [ki] and [tji]. This extends to the maximum syllable length observed in the corpus. For shorter words, the remaining columns are left empty. Vowels are counted across each column.

For this analysis, our interface provides the option of choosing the transition between vowel one and two (V1V2), vowel two and three (V2V3) and so on.

Place of Articulation For this calculation, the language selected (to determine the possible consonants) and the 'OS' column is taken as input. Each vowel and consonant is converted to a 'V' or 'C' to construct a word template. From the word template, all VC structures are pooled together and sorted based on placement (i.e., coda or onset).

[3]This can be cross-checked with the syllable counts provided by counting the number of vowels.

[4]Part of the Pitjantjatjara word for tickle: *kitji-kitjini*.

Once we collect all VCs and their syllable position, we labelled the consonant according to the place of articulation. We consider five places of articulation (labial, alvelor, retroflex, palatal and velar).

Here the dashboard provides several options: to provide an aggregate count across vowel and place of articulation, a more detailed view by accounting for placement. Lastly, a frequency table of vowel and consonant combinations in all extracted VCs.

5 Conclusion

We introduce a local web-based interactive dashboard designed for targeted analysis of phonotactic patterns, and illustrate its application to four Central Australian languages. This is a customizable tool which can be adapted for a variety of search and data conditioning tasks in a wide range of linguistic data, supporting interactive analyses of morpho-phonological phenomena. The toolkit works on the principle that an iterative interactive approach is required for robust linguistically-informed processing and analysis of complex and potentially inconsistent lexical datasets, especially in corpus composition decisions.

References

Gabriele Albini, Shane Mattner, Marcel Zeuch, Arne Petter, and Joel Ostblom. 2022. The Dash Open-Source Curriculum. `https://open-resources.github.io/dash_curriculum/preface/about.html`. [Accessed 07-12-2024].

Faisal Aljasser and Michael S Vitevitch. 2018. A web-based interface to calculate phonotactic probability for words and nonwords in modern standard arabic. *Behavior research methods*, 50:313–322.

Laurence Anthony. 2012. Of software tools for corpus studies: The case for collaboration. *Contemporary Corpus Linguistics*, pages 87–104.

Laurence Anthony. 2022. What can corpus software do? In *The Routledge Handbook of Corpus Linguistics*, 2 edition, pages 103–125. Routledge.

Brett Baker. 2014. 4. word structure in australian languages. In *The Languages and Linguistics of Australia*, pages 139–214. DE GRUYTER, Berlin, Boston.

Douglas Biber. 1988. *Variation across Speech and Writing*. Cambridge University Press.

Steven Bird. 2006. NLTK: The Natural Language Toolkit. In *Proceedings of the COLING/ACL*

2006 Interactive Presentation Sessions, pages 69–72, Sydney, Australia. Association for Computational Linguistics.

Vaclav Brezina and William Platt. 2023. Lancsbox [software]. *online: http://corpora. lancs. ac. uk/lancsbox.*

Petra Čechová, Luca Cilibrasi, Jan Henyš, Jaroslav Čecho, et al. 2023. Introducing a phonotactic probability calculator for Czech. *Naše řeč (Our Speech)*, 1:72–83.

Wilfrid Henry Douglas, Arthur Capell, and Stephen Adolphe Wurm. 1964. *An introduction to the Western Desert language*. University of Sydney.

David Embick. 2021. The motivation for roots in distributed morphology. *Annual Review of Linguistics*, 7(Volume 7, 2021):69–88.

Janet Fletcher. 2014. 3. sound patterns of australian languages. In *The Languages and Linguistics of Australia*, pages 91–138. DE GRUYTER, Berlin, Boston.

Cliff Goddard. 1983. *A semantically-oriented grammar of the Yankunytjatjara dialect of the Western Desert language*. The Australian National University (Australia).

Cliff Goddard. 2001. *Pitjantjatjara/Yankunytjatjara to English Dictionary*, 2 edition. IAD Press, Alice Springs, NT, Australia.

Maria Gouskova. 2023. Phonological asymmetries between roots and affixes. *The Willey Blackwell Companion to Morphology*.

Heidi Harley. 2014. On the identity of roots. *Theoretical Linguistics*, 40(3-4):225–276.

Mark Harvey, Susan Lin, Myfany Turpin, Ben Davies, and Katherine Demuth. 2015. Contrastive and non-contrastive pre-stopping in Kaytetye. *Australian Journal of Linguistics*, 35(3):232–250.

Mark Harvey, Nay San, Michael Proctor, Forrest Panther, and Myfany Turpin. 2023. The Kaytetye segmental inventory. *Australian Journal of Linguistics*, 43(1):33–68.

Deborah Loakes, Andrew Butcher, Janet Fletcher, and Hywel Stoakes. 2008. Phonetically prestopped laterals in Australian languages: a preliminary investigation of Warlpiri. In *INTERSPEECH*, pages 90–93.

Jayden L Macklin-Cordes and Erich R Round. 2020. Re-evaluating phoneme frequencies. *Frontiers in psychology*, 11:570895.

Jayden L Macklin-Cordes and Erich R Round. 2022. Challenges of sampling and how phylogenetic comparative methods help: with a case study of the pama-nyungan laminal contrast. *Linguistic Typology*, 26(3):533–572.

David George Nash. 1980. *Topics in Warlpiri grammar.* Ph.D. thesis, Massachusetts Institute of Technology.

Forrest Panther. 2021. *Topics in Kaytetye Phonology and Morpho-Syntax*. Ph.D. thesis, Doctoral dissertation. University of Newcastle, NSW, Australia.

Erich R Round. 2023a. 10. segment inventries. In Claire Bowern, editor, *The Oxford Guide to Australian languages*. Oxford University PressOxford.

Erich R Round. 2023b. 11. phonotactics. In Claire Bowern, editor, *The Oxford Guide to Australian languages*. Oxford University PressOxford.

Adam Schroeder, Christian Mayer, and Ann Marie Ward. 2022. *The Book of Dash: Build Dashboards with Python and Plotly*. No Starch Press.

Jane Simpson. 2012. *Warlpiri morpho-syntax: A lexicalist approach*, volume 23. Springer Science & Business Media.

Jane Simpson. 2017. *Warumungu (Australian – Pama-Nyungan)*, chapter 32. John Wiley & Sons, Ltd.

Jane Helen Simpson. 1983. *Aspects of Warlpiri morphology and syntax*. Ph.D. thesis, Massachusetts Institute of Technology.

Holly L Storkel and Jill R Hoover. 2010. An online calculator to compute phonotactic probability and neighborhood density on the basis of child corpora of spoken american english. *Behavior research methods*, 42(2):497–506.

Marija Tabain and Andrew Butcher. 2014. Pitjantjatjara. *Journal of the International Phonetic Association*, 44(2):189–200.

Marija Tabain, Janet Fletcher, and Andrew Butcher. 2014. Lexical stress in Pitjantjatjara. *Journal of Phonetics*, 42:52–66.

Myfany Turpin. 2000. *A learner's guide to Kaytetye*, volume 2. Iad Press.

Myfany Turpin and Alison Ross. 2012. *Kaytetye to English dictionary*. IAD Press.

Michael S Vitevitch and Paul A Luce. 2004. A web-based interface to calculate phonotactic probability for words and nonwords in english. *Behavior Research Methods, Instruments, & Computers*, 36(3):481–487.

S L Wilmoth. 2022. *The Dynamics of Contemporary Pitjantjatjara: An Intergenerational Study*. Ph.D. thesis, The University of Melbourne.

OCR Error Post-Correction with LLMs in Historical Documents: No Free Lunches

Jenna Kanerva, Cassandra Ledins, Siiri Käpyaho, and Filip Ginter
TurkuNLP, Department of Computing
University of Turku, Finland
{jmnybl, caledi, siakap, figint}@utu.fi

Abstract

Optical Character Recognition (OCR) systems often introduce errors when transcribing historical documents, leaving room for post-correction to improve text quality. This study evaluates the use of open-weight LLMs for OCR error correction in historical English and Finnish datasets. We explore various strategies, including parameter optimization, quantization, segment length effects, and text continuation methods. Our results demonstrate that while modern LLMs show promise in reducing character error rates (CER) in English, a practically useful performance for Finnish was not reached. Our findings highlight the potential and limitations of LLMs in scaling OCR post-correction for large historical corpora.

1 Introduction

Digitizing and transcribing historical documents and literature is vital for preserving our cultural heritage and making it accessible for modern digital research methods. The transcription process relies on OCR, which naturally introduces noise into the output. The noise varies in severity depending on the quality of the source material and the OCR technology used, impacting the research usage of the data (Chiron et al., 2017b). The OCR output at two noise levels is illustrated in Figure 1. Although modern OCR systems are becoming increasingly accurate (Li et al., 2023), reprocessing large collections of historical literature remains a significant challenge, as the resources available to the institutions maintaining these collections are often insufficient for such an undertaking. Consequently, OCR error post-correction has been suggested as means of improving the historical collections without the need to repeat the whole transcription process (Nguyen et al., 2021).

Mild noise (0.04 CER):

```
A work of art, (be it what it may, house,
pi&ure, book, or  garden,) however
beautiful in it's underparts, loses half
it's value, if the gneralfcope
of it be not obvio',s to conception.
```

Severe noise (0.19 CER):

```
bke up at Sx in the Mo.r aig.  11 the
eauing Withr he went from Cbaud to Cbhh
every Suday, «d from Play. bote~PIOoaB
cu evi Niuht m the Week, but  vd
```

Figure 1: Example extracts of texts at two different OCR noise levels from the ECCO dataset of 18th century literature.

Recent studies (Boros et al., 2024; Bourne, 2024) have proposed the application of LLMs to the task, with varying degrees of success. Currently, there is no clear consensus as to how LLMs can be applied to the task and how to deal with the various methodological challenges it poses. Our objective is to address some of these challenges as well as to assess several open LLMs to correct OCR-generated text when prompted to. We study hyperparameter optimization, quantization levels, input lengths, output post-processing and several novel correction methods so as to benchmark and improve the LLM performance on this task.

As our long-term goal is to post-correct two large historical datasets, one in English and the other in Finnish, we focus on these two languages as well as open-weight LLMs, since post-correction of large datasets with commercial models is infeasible cost-wise.

2 Related work

Despite decades of active research, post-correction of historical documents remains a challenge. The ICDAR 2017 and 2019 shared tasks (Chiron et al.,

Proceedings of the Third Workshop on Resources and Representations for Under-Resourced Languages and Domains (RESOURCEFUL-2025), pages 38–47, March 2, 2025 ©2025 Association for Computational Linguistics

2017a; Rigaud et al., 2019) addressed the lack of adequate benchmarks for evaluating OCR performance across several languages, introducing two tracks: detecting OCR errors, and correcting previously detected errors. This setting has naturally guided the development towards two-stage systems, and the best performing models in the ICDAR 2019 edition were based on the BERT model fine-tuned separately for each task (Rigaud et al., 2019). Such two-step approaches are still actively pursued, with e.g. Beshirov et al. (2024) applying a BERT classifier for error detection, and an LSTM-based seq2seq model for error correction in Bulgarian.

Recently, LLMs have been effectively applied to text correction problems, for example, Penteado and Perez (2023) and Östling et al. (2024) demonstrated that LLMs perform well in grammatical error correction. Naturally, LLMs have been proposed also to the OCR post-correction task, in line with the two broad paradigms of LLM use: fine-tuning for the post-correction task and purely prompt-based zero-shot generation. Fine-tuning was applied e.g. by Soper et al. (2021) who fine-tune the BART model on the English subset of the ICDAR 2017 data and apply it to English Newspaper text. Veninga (2024) fine-tunes the character-based ByT5 model on the ICDAR 2019 data, with a prompt-based Llama model as a baseline. Similarly, Madarász et al. (2024) apply the mT5 model to historical Hungarian scientific literature, and Dereza et al. (2024) applies the BART model to historical Irish–English bilingual data.

In the zero-shot, prompt-based line of work, Boros et al. (2024) evaluated a variety of models and prompts on several multilingual historical datasets. Interestingly, the results of the study were mostly negative, concluding that LLMs (including the commercial GPT-4 model) are not effective at correcting transcriptions of historical documents, in many cases the LLM actually decreasing the quality instead of improving it. Bourne (2024) conducted a similar study on three historical English datasets, arriving at the opposite conclusion. They achieved over 60% reduction of character error rate at best, with most of the evaluated models improving the data quality.

Finally, several studies also pursue approaches that include the original image as an input, together with the OCR output to be post-corrected. Here, e.g. Chen and Ströbel (2024) combine a state-of-the-art transformer-based OCR system with the character-based CharBERT model for handwritten text recognition, and Fahandari et al. (2024) propose a model iterating between OCR and post-correction steps for Farsi. Such image-text approaches are, nevertheless, beyond the scope of the present study.

3 Data

In our study, we utilize manually corrected samples of two large historical datasets, one for English and the other for Finnish.

3.1 English ECCO-TCP

Eighteenth Century Collections Online (ECCO) (Gale) is a dataset of over 180,000 digitized publications (books and pamphlets) originally printed in the 18th century Britain and its overseas colonies, Ireland, as well as the United States. While mainly in English, some texts appear in other languages. The collection was created by the software and education company Gale by scanning and OCRing the publications. ECCO has significantly impacted 18th-century historical research despite its known limitations (Gregg, 2021; Tolonen et al., 2021).

While ECCO contains only OCR engine output, the ECCO-TCP initiative[1] provides highly accurate, human-made text versions for 2,473 publications from the original collection (Gregg, 2022). In this study, we use a dataset from the Helsinki Computational History Group[2], where clean ECCO-TCP texts are paired with their corresponding ECCO OCR publications, creating an OCR ground truth dataset (Hill and Hengchen, 2019). The data is paired on page level, resulting in a dataset of 338K pages.

To prepare data for post-correction evaluation, we applied several filtering steps. First, we excluded 1,436 pages (0.4%) marked as blank in ECCO-TCP, ECCO OCR, or both. We also removed 5,782 pages (1.7%) containing fewer than 150 non-whitespace characters in either collection. Further filtering was necessary in cases of substantial mismatch between OCR and GT pages, typically with large chunks of text missing in either OCR or GT, or otherwise an obvious lack of correspondence. A brief manual analysis identified as typical causes (1) very noisy OCR output with a large amount of non-alphanumerical characters, likely from OCR engine transcribing an image; (2)

[1] https://textcreationpartnership.org/tcp-texts/ecco-tcp-eighteenth-century-collections-online/

[2] https://github.com/COMHIS

Dataset	Language	Pages	OCR words	GT words	OCR w./pg.	CER	WER
ECCO-TCP	English	301,937	67,549,822	64,519,266	223.72	0.07	0.22
NLF GT	Finnish	449	449,088	461,305	1000.20	0.09	0.28

Table 1: Dataset statistics after preprocessing in terms of whitespace delimited words. *OCR w./pg.* denotes for mean OCR words per page, and CER and WER are average page-level character and word error rates in the data, weighted by the page length. For details about the metrics, see Section 4.1.

OCR and GT containing approximately the same text, but in different order due to misidentified reading order or column layout; and (3) significant length differences between pages, possibly from errors in automated page alignments, unrecognized regions left out in the OCR process, or omissions in the ECCO-TCP data.

To identify such instances, we align each OCR and GT page pair on their non-whitespace characters[3] and slide a 100-character window across the alignment. If in any window less than 10% of characters were aligned as a match, the page was discarded from the dataset. In total, 28,907 (8.6%) pages were removed by this process.

Our filtering produced a dataset of 301,937 well-aligned pages (89.3% of the initial ECCO-TCP pages). While we do not filter by language, nearly all the data is in English, with other languages appearing only very rarely.

3.2 Finnish NLF Ground Truth Data

For Finnish, we use the National Library of Finland (NLF) OCR ground truth dataset[4] of Kettunen et al. (2018, 2020), specifically intended for OCR quality evaluation. The data draws from the National Library's collection of digitized newspapers, and consists of 479 pages randomly chosen from 188 different Finnish newspapers and journals published between 1836–1918, all printed in the Fraktur font.

The ground truth was created by manually correcting the OCR system output with reference to the original scans. The dataset contains texts produced by three different OCR software (ABBYY FineReader 7/8, ABBYY FineReader 11, and Tesseract) along with the ground truth. In this work, we use output produced by ABBYY FineReader 7/8, which is the OCR engine that has been used to digitize the majority of the NLF collection and therefore gives most useful information for a possible future post-correction effort targeting it.

We applied the same filtering procedure as for the ECCO-TCP data, resulting in the removal of 29 pages (6%), and we further removed one page written in Swedish. The final dataset consists of 449 pages, with 449,088 OCR words, and 461,305 GT words of text. The key statistics for both datasets are shown in Table 1.

4 Experiments

First, we set out to evaluate the basic performance of different LLMs on the OCR error correction task and establish how the generation and model hyperparameters (e.g. sampling parameters and quantization) affect the results.

The page lengths in our data vary, with the ECCO-TCP pages on average at 200 words, and the Finnish newspaper pages at about 1,000 words. To improve comparability of the results, we split the pages to segments of 200 OCR words for English and 100 OCR words for Finnish, both corresponding to roughly 300 sub-words in OpenAI's GPT-4 tokenization for the language in question. The length of roughly 300 sub-words was established as suitable in our initial experiments, however, we will carry out a more detailed evaluation of segment lengths as a separate experiment in Section 6.

Since the Finnish data is originally word-aligned, obtaining these shorter-than-page segments is trivial. For the English data, which is only page-aligned, we utilize the character-level OCR-GT alignments produced during data filtering (described in Section 3.1), allowing us to find corresponding points. In cases where the segment boundary falls within a region of poor alignment, we shift the boundary to the next reliable word (the word starting the next aligned region). Therefore, the exact segment length may vary depending on how well the OCR and GT strings could be aligned.

Given the substantial volume of our data, and the number of LLM runs necessary in our experiments, we randomly sample for each language a development and a test set, each containing 200

[3] Using global string alignment as implemented in the PairwiseAligner module in biopython.

[4] http://digi.nationallibrary.fi

examples (i.e. segments of about 300 sub-words in length). These constitute 244K+243K GT characters for English, and 162K+165K GT characters for Finnish. The development set is used to set the generation parameters and the test set is used to report all results, unless otherwise stated.

4.1 Evaluation Metric

As a primary evaluation metric, we use Character Error Rate (CER) defined as the sum of character substitutions, deletions and insertions, divided by the length of the ground truth string. In line with the common practice in OCR post-correction literature, we mainly report relative CER reduction defined for one examples as $\text{CER\%} = (\text{CER}_{\text{orig}} - \text{CER}_{\text{post}})/\text{CER}_{\text{orig}} \times 100$ where *orig* and *post* refer to before and after correction, respectively. The overall CER% is calculated as an average of example-wise CER% weighted by example lengths in terms of OCR character count. The example-wise CER% values are further clipped not to go below -100% to prevent extremely large negative scores in cases where most of the text is omitted. The CER% therefore works on a range between -100% and 100%.

Many downstream applications utilizing historical corpora, such as various literature search interfaces, operate at the level of words rather than characters. Therefore, the main results are reported also in terms of Word Error Rate (WER) and its relative improvement (WER%). This metric is much like CER, but on the level of words.[5]

Finally, we apply few normalization steps before the evaluation. First, all unicode whitespace characters (\s+) are normalized into a single whitespace. Secondly, in line with similar works (Duong et al., 2021; Kettunen and Pääkkönen, 2016), we apply two normalization steps to address systematic differences between historical and modern spellings. In the English ECCO-TCP ground truth data, the long-s character ſ appears in places where modern English would use s. Similarly, in older Finnish historical texts w is often used where modern Finnish uses v. These spelling variations do not alter meaning, and we choose to disregard them by applying Unicode NFKC normalization, which handles both canonically equivalent and compatible transformations (including converting ſ to s) for both languages. Additionally, for Finnish, we replace all occurrences of w with v before evaluation, as modern Finnish does not use w except in loanwords or proper names, which occur only very rarely, making the difference negligible.

4.2 Models and Generation Parameters

We evaluate several top-tier open-weight models as well as OpenAI's GPT-4o (v. 2024-08-06). The latter is included mostly for comparison, since it would not be cost-wise feasible to apply it to post-correction at a large scale, unlike open-weight models which can be applied on academic supercomputing infrastructure. The evaluated open models are: Llama-3-8B-Instruct, Llama-3.1-8B-Instruct, and Llama-3.1-70B-Instruct from Meta (AI@Meta, 2024a,b), Mixtral-8x7B-Instruct-v0.1 from MistralAI (Jiang et al., 2024), and Gemma-2-9B-it and Gemma-2-27B-it from Google (Mesnard et al., 2024). It is noteworthy that while several of the open models are multilingual, none officially report supporting Finnish.

All models are run on the Ollama framework[6] (v. 0.3.8) for fast inference, using the default 4-bit quantization unless otherwise stated. Other quantization levels are experimented separately, and reported in Section 5.2. All parameters of the framework and models are set to default except for the ones explored in Section 4.4. Note that we will not repeat the "Instruct" in model names in tables and figures for space considerations.

4.3 LLM Overgeneration Removal

LLM outputs often include undesired content in addition to the requested output. In most cases, the undesired text appears either before the corrected text (e.g. *"Here is your corrected text:"*), or after the corrected text has been provided (e.g. hallucinated continuation, or an additional commentary). This was noted also by Boros et al. (2024), who applied simple heuristics for removing any unwanted text, such as removal of whitespace, parts of the prompt, and specific phrases commonly appearing in the model's output, together with trimming the predicted text if it exceeded 1.5 times the original.

Therefore, we base our overgeneration removal on automatically aligning the generated output against the original input on character level, and filtering out leading and trailing texts which do not align well to the input. For this purpose, we utilize

[5]We use the HuggingFace *evaluate* package implementation of both CER and WER.

[6]`https://ollama.com/`

Model	English CER %	English WER %	Finnish CER %	Finnish WER %
Llama-3-8B	7.3	31.4	-68.8	-28.2
Llama-3.1-8B	19.5	37.7	-65.7	-30.1
Llama-3.1-70B	38.7	46.3	-47.0	-8.9
Mixtral-8x7B	-14.9	19.1	-76.5	-40.5
Gemma-2-9B	28.2	38.4	-24.0	-4.1
Gemma-2-27B	35.6	37.8	-19.1	0.0
GPT-4o	58.1	59.1	11.9	33.5

Table 2: Overall CER and WER relative improvement.

character-level local sequence alignment[7] of the model's output and the OCR text, and recover the region between the first and the last aligned characters. The alignment is configured to ignore whitespace and the '-' character, to avoid text formatting discrepancies having an impact on the outcome of the alignment.

4.4 Parameter Optimization

The model generation parameters naturally affect the quality of the output and we therefore optimize the most critical parameters of the open-weight model generation on a held-out development set. As discussed earlier, this set is not used in any subsequent experiments.

Using the Optuna hyperparameter optimization library (Akiba et al., 2019), we set the temperature, top_k and top_p parameters. For each model and each language, we test 100 runs with different parameter combinations. Subsequently, the 10 best runs in terms of CER were selected, creating a range of possible best parameters. These ranges generally overlap across models but not across languages, therefore we pick a set of parameters for each language. The final parameters are chosen as the median value of the 10 best runs of every model. For English, the parameters are temperature 0.26, top_k 65, and top_p 0.66. For Finnish, the final parameters are temperature 0.14, top_k 30, and top_p 0.60.

5 Results

The main results are shown in Table 2. For English, six out of seven models achieve positive improve-

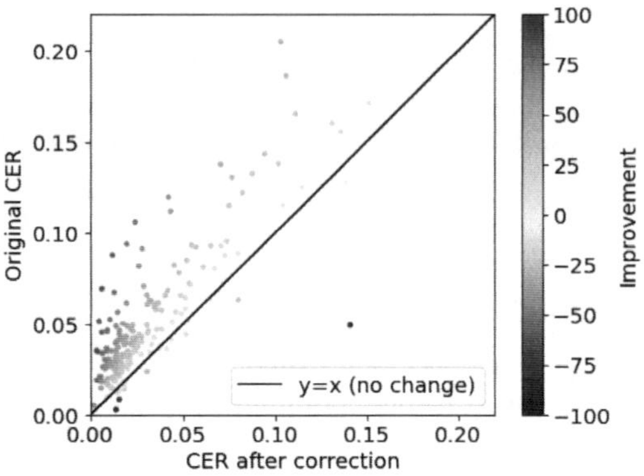

Figure 2: CER before and after correction on English test data (Llama-3.1-70B).

ment, ranging from 7.3% (Llama-3-8B) to 58.1% (GPT-4o) in terms of CER%. GPT-4o outperforms all open models by a large margin, the next best model (Llama-3.1-70B) being almost 20pp worse. However, the Llama-3.1-70B still shows a notable improvement of 38.7%. In Figure 2 we illustrate the CER values for English test examples before and after the Llama-3.1-70B correction. Most examples demonstrate improved CER scores, regardless of whether they initially had mild or severe noise levels.

In terms of WER%, all models show positive improvement on English, the two best models achieving an improvement of 59.1% (GPT-4o) and 46.3% (Llama-3.1-70B). The relative order of the models seems to mostly follow the number of model parameters, bigger models generally performing better, expect for Mixtral which is clearly worse than the others, and the two Gemma models performing almost equally in terms of WER%, although the Gemma-2-27B version clearly outperforms the 8B model in terms of CER%.

For Finnish, on the other hand, GPT-4o is the only model achieving a positive improvement in either metric, albeit considerably smaller in absolute terms than for English with 11.9 CER% and 33.5 WER%. Seeing these entirely negative results for Finnish, we are forced to conclude that prompt-based OCR post-correction is presently infeasible for this language using any of the tested open-weight models. This is disappointing, but not surprising since none of the models officially support Finnish.[8]

[7]Unlike global sequence alignment, its local counterpart does not penalize leading and trailing misalignments. We use the implementation in the *biopython* package, with open-gap-score -1 and extend-gap-score -0.5

[8]We made also preliminary experiments with the well-known Finnish Poro model of Luukkonen et al. (2024), but the results were considerably worse than the models in our

```
OCR: … mirkamalta on mahmgoNmen   , mntta ei ole musasta sekään että mallion mallaa ja armoa mäbennetään.
GPT: … virkavalta on vahingollinen, mutta ei ole viisasta sekään että vallan  valtaa ja armoa vähennetään.
GT : … wirkawalta on wahingollinen, mutta ei ole wiisasta sekään että waltion waltaa ja arwoa wähennetään.

OCR: Mr.. Powv.'s   mind wvas R aid  upon God in to stoadil:a m:;:'.cir, that after wv. had sung an hymn, …
GPT: Mr.  Powell's  mind was  stayed upon God in so steadfast a manner,  that after we  had sung a  hymn, …
GT : Mr.  Powell's  mind was  ſtaid  upon God in ſo ſteadfaſt a manner,  that after we  had ſung an hymn, …

OCR error  GPT modernization  GPT error
```

Figure 3: An example in both languages illustrating historical language artifacts alongside the corresponding GPT-4o generated output.

Model	Overg. removal w/o	Overg. removal with
Llama-3-8B	-74.1	7.3
Llama-3.1-8B	-57.4	19.5
Llama-3.1-70B	-53.6	38.7
Gemma-2-9B	28.1	28.2
Gemma-2-27B	35.3	35.6
GPT-4o	53.7	58.1

Table 3: The CER improvement on English test data with and w/o the overgeneration removal step.

The striking effect of a common but meaning-preserving difference between historical and modern language becomes apparent when measuring the effect of modern spelling produced by the LLMs such as the ſ vs. s and w vs. v variation discussed in Section 4.1. A typical example for both languages is illustrated in Figure 3. Without the applied normalization, the results of GPT-4o would have been 34.9 CER% and 35.5 WER% (compared to 58.1% and 59.1% with normalization) for English, and -10.1 CER% and -4.8 WER% (compared to 11.9% and 33.5%) for Finnish. This demonstrates a substantial impact on the reported scores, and while the relative model ranking is unlikely to change, we can see that the conclusion w.r.t. this model's performance on Finnish would have been the opposite, and the improvements seen in English would have been lot smaller.

Given the entirely negative results for Finnish with the open-weight models, we carry out all further analyses on English only. Furthermore, we also remove the Mixtral-8x7B from follow-up experiments as it performs notably worse than the other models.

5.1 LLM Overgeneration Removal

Next we measure the effect of the alignment-based overgeneration removal method described in Section 4.3, i.e. we evaluate the raw model-generated output against the post-processed version of the generated output. The results are shown in Table 3. For the Llama family models, the results without this post-processing step are highly negative, whereas all Llama models achieve positive improvements when this step is applied. This highlights the necessity of post-processing for the Llama models, which very systematically generate an additional explanation together with the requested output. An example of a typical Llama generation is:

```
Here is the corrected text: {{answer}}
I corrected the following errors:
* "pi\&ure" -> "picture"
* "it's" -> "its"  (multiple instances)
* "gneralfcope" -> "general scope"
...
```

On the other hand, Gemma models seem to be largely unaffected, as they generally tend to not produce any additional text. For the GPT-4o model, we also notice a small gain when applying the post-processing, as it occasionally generates explanatory phrases like *"Here is the corrected text:"*.

5.2 Quantization and Performance

Since the historical text collections to which post-correction would potentially be applied comprise millions of pages of text, it is necessary to strike balance between accuracy and computational resources. Among the most important factors here is model quantization, i.e. real number representation with fewer bits. High degrees of quantization substantially reduce model memory footprint and increase inference speed, but can be assumed to potentially degrade model performance. We therefore evaluate the models at the 4 bit Q4_0 quantization (default setting in Ollama), and at the standard 16 bit fp16 floating point representation.

The results are reported in Table 4. As expected, the fp16 quantization performs better for all the evaluated models, with a gain of 2.5-4.7pp, except for Llama-3.1-8B where we do not experience a

study, and we did not pursue it any further.

Model	CER%		Memory (Gb)	
	q4	fp16	q4	fp16
Llama-3-8B	7.3	12.0	6.3	16.1
Llama-3.1-8B	19.5	19.4	6.3	16.1
Llama-3.1-70B	38.7	42.6	43.6	132.1*
Gemma-2-9B	28.2	30.7	8.9	20.9
Gemma-2-27B	35.6	38.1	19.2	58.9

Table 4: CER improvement on English test data using 4bit quantized (q4) and fp16 models, alongside peak memory usage. * in the memory consumption indicates the number was obtained using the HuggingFace library, as we were not able to run the Llama-3.1-70B model with fp16 through Ollama.

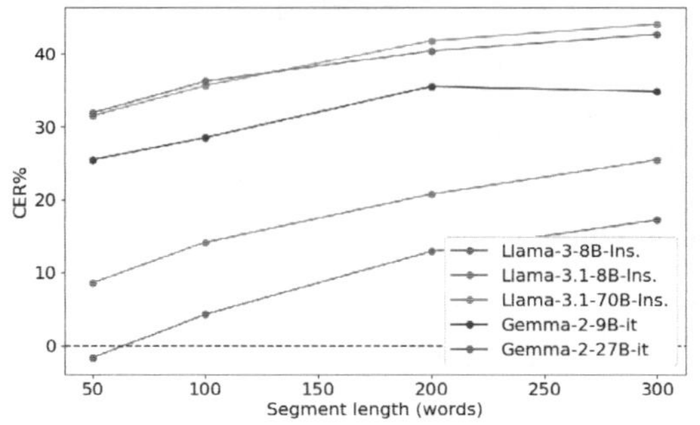

Figure 4: CER% improvement for English when using different segment lengths.

significant difference between 4bit and fp16 models. The relative ranking of the selected models is preserved regardless the quantization level, and using fp16 does not help less performing models to outrank any of the originally best performing 4bit quantized models. The improvement comes at a high cost in terms of memory footprint. As seen in the table, the best improvement is unsurprisingly achieved by the largest model, where the memory requirement increases from 43Gb to 132Gb. It is of consideration that even with 4bit quantization, using the largest Llama-3.1-70B model would necessitate 2 GPUs (assuming 32GB GPU memory), instantly doubling the GPU hours required to complete the task compared to other models which can fit on one GPU.

6 Segment Length and Continuation

The results in the previous sections were reported for text segments about 300 sub-words in length. The actual texts in the historical collections are naturally substantially longer, necessitating splitting the input into segments of appropriate length. This raises two related questions: (1) how long the input segments should optimally be for best post-correction accuracy, and (2) how should the outputs be combined to minimize degradation on segment boundaries.

Our English data is on the level of pages, which we cannot simply naively concatenate, we need other means to obtain sufficiently long documents. For this experiment, we sample long pages of at least 600 whitespace delimited OCR words in length from the development data, taking at maximum two pages from any one book. This resulted in a sample of 53 development set pages.

These sampled pages are then divided into non-overlapping segments of 50, 100, 200, and 300 words, using the same alignment-based splitting strategy as described in Section 4. The segments are corrected individually and the CER% improvement over the segments is calculated. The results are shown in Figure 4. Shorter segments (50–100 words) get notably worse CER% score for all models, with the gains diminishing past about 200–300 words, but our page-level data does not have long-enough examples to allow us to reach the point where the performance would start consistently decreasing as the segments become too long. In the future, we plan to develop a book-level version of the data, and study the correction performance on even longer segments.

6.1 Post-correction on Segment Boundaries

Presently, post-correction studies either do not address segment-wise correction of longer texts as it is not necessary for the datasets they study, or split the input into non-overlapping segments, whose corrections are simply concatenated. This may potentially disrupt text continuity since neither word nor sentence boundaries can be reliably adhered to in the noisy OCR input. Furthermore, it also means that no left context is available for the correction of the beginning of each segment. This may potentially have a negative effect on the correction in the region around segment boundary. Here we quantify this effect and explore several straightforward methods for its mitigation.

For the prompt optimization, we use the same sample of 53 pages as in the previous section, and the final results are reported on a similar sample of 50 pages from the test data. In order to maximize the number of examples of segment boundaries for evaluation, we generate—from each page—pairs of segments 200+200 words long, with stride of 100 words. With this method, each page of at least 600 words produces a minimum of 3 examples of neighboring segment pairs. The final development and test samples include 194 and 208 such examples, respectively.

On these examples, we evaluate the following methods of post-correction on segment boundaries: (1) *Baseline*: Each segment is corrected independently with the same prompt and the outputs are concatenated; (2) *Left-corrected-concatenate (LCC)*: The left segment is corrected first and given as prior context for the correction of the right segment, the model is instructed to only correct the right segment; and (3) *Left-uncorrected-concatenate (LUC)*: The uncorrected left segment is provided for context in the correction of the right segment. The primary advantage of this method is that correcting the right segment does not need the left segment to be corrected first, making parallelization of the process much simpler technically.

The overall results across these strategies are shown in Table 5 and suggest that at present only the two largest models are able to follow the more complex prompts necessitated when merging neighboring segment corrections. The smaller models occasionally suffer from omitting part of the text to correct, which did not seem to occur if only one text was given at a time. For the two models improving on performance, we inspect the boundary effect more closely in Table 6 where we report CER% calculated on ±10 words around the boundary of the two segments.[9] Here we see that both methods effectively incorporate the provided additional context, substantially improving the post-correction of the right segment at the boundary, whereas the baseline system's performance on the right side is notably worse compared to its performance on the left side.

	Method		
Model	Bas.	LCC	LUC
Llama-3-8B	-0.2	-2.9	-2.8
Llama-3.1-8B	13.7	8.4	10.6
Llama-3.1-70B	33.2	36.0	34.6
Gemma-2-9B	29.2	27.9	28.3
Gemma-2-27B	38.1	39.9	39.7

Table 5: CER improvement on English test data with different correction methods.

	Method			
	Baseline		LCC	LUC
Model	L	R	R	R
Llama-3.1-70B	29.1	9.8	21.4	21.7
gemma-2-27b	34.5	18.7	29.7	33.7

Table 6: CER% around segment boundaries with different correction methods. L and R stand for left and right of the boundary.

7 Conclusion

We set out to establish the ability of recent open-weight models to post-correct OCR errors in a zero-shot, prompt-based setting. In the first set of experiments, we established that for historical English these models achieved notable improvements (Llama-3.1-70B-Instruct reaching a CER improvement of 38.7%), even though still far behind the commercial GPT-4o model (58.1 CER%). We also demonstrate the necessity of post-processing to remove any additional, model generated text, and present an effective string alignment technique to address this. We also highlight the effect of segment length, which may have a substantial negative impact on the outcome if set too short.

Unlike for English, for Finnish we find poor performance across the board and need to conclude that zero-shot post-correction with open-weight models remains currently out of reach for historical Finnish.

In a separate set of experiments we examine how segment-wise correction of long documents should be approached. We devise and evaluate a number of methods to incorporate additional context for the correction of individual segments. We find that some of these methods have a strong positive effect in the immediate proximity of segment boundaries, however, for smaller models the more complicated prompt may cause unexpected degradation in performance when the whole text is considered. Further work will be necessary to resolve these issues.

As future work, we will pursue a large correction run of the ECCO collection as well as a fine-tuned model for Finnish post-correction. All datasets and evaluation scripts used in this study are available at `https://github.com/TurkuNLP/ocr-postcorrection-lm` to support result replication and comparability.

[9]The ±10 word boundaries were human-verified to ensure that the evaluation occurred at the same boundary, even in more complex examples where words were omitted and/or added.

Limitations

Our work includes certain limitations, which we will discuss next. First, during data preprocessing, we discarded a proportion of documents (~10% for English, ~6% for Finnish) that our correction methods may not be able to address. These documents include cases with severe alignment issues between OCR output and ground truth. We acknowledge that our post-correction method, which relies entirely on the OCR system's output, cannot recover text where significant portions are missing, therefore setting an upper-boundary for the method. Further analysis is needed to investigate the causes of these gaps and to determine how much, if any, of this missing information could potentially be addressed through post-correction.

We also find that OCR post-correction evaluation suffers from various dataset and metric issues, some of which we have already discussed (e.g. normalization). In related work (including our own study conducted directly on our long-term target corpora), results are reported on varying datasets and evaluations metrics. These challenges make it difficult to achieve comparable results across studies and languages, potentially contributing to some of the contradictory conclusions reported in prior work. Clearly, more work will be needed to establish a set of standard benchmarks that resolve most of the data and evaluation issues.

Finally, reporting pure numeric improvements does not address all aspects of downstream data usability. While an improved word error rate has a direct, positive effect on certain applications (e.g. lexical search), its impact on others (e.g. close reading) may be less straightforward or proportional.

Acknowledgments

This work was carried out in the *Human Diversity* University profilation programme (PROFI-7) of the Research Council of Finland, as well as in the context of several other research projects supported by the Research Council of Finland. Computational resources were provided by CSC — the Finnish IT Center for Science.

References

AI@Meta. 2024a. https://github.com/meta-llama/llama3/blob/main/MODEL_CARD.md Llama 3 model card.

AI@Meta. 2024b. https://github.com/meta-llama/llama-models/blob/main/models/llama3_1/MODEL_CARD.md Llama 3.1 model card.

Takuya Akiba, Shotaro Sano, Toshihiko Yanase, Takeru Ohta, and Masanori Koyama. 2019. Optuna: A next-generation hyperparameter optimization framework. In *Proceedings of the 25th ACM SIGKDD International Conference on Knowledge Discovery and Data Mining*.

Angel Beshirov, Milena Dobreva, Dimitar Dimitrov, Momchil Hardalov, Ivan Koychev, and Preslav Nakov. 2024. Post-OCR text correction for Bulgarian historical documents. *ArXiv preprint arXiv:2409.00527*.

Emanuela Boros, Maud Ehrmann, Matteo Romanello, Sven Najem-Meyer, and Frédéric Kaplan. 2024. Post-correction of historical text transcripts with large language models: An exploratory study. In *Proceedings of the 8th Joint SIGHUM Workshop on Computational Linguistics for Cultural Heritage, Social Sciences, Humanities and Literature (LaTeCH-CLfL 2024)*, pages 133–159. Association for Computational Linguistics.

Jonathan Bourne. 2024. CLOCR-C: Context leveraging OCR correction with pre-trained language models. *ArXiv preprint arXiv:2408.17428*.

Yung-Hsin Chen and Phillip B. Ströbel. 2024. TrOCR meets language models: An end-to-end post-correction approach. In *Proceedings of the Document Analysis and Recognition – ICDAR 2024 Workshops*, pages 12–26. Springer Nature Switzerland.

Guillaume Chiron, Antoine Doucet, Mickaël Coustaty, and Jean-Philippe Moreux. 2017a. ICDAR 2017 competition on post-OCR text correction. In *Proceedings of the 14th IAPR International Conference on Document Analysis and Recognition (ICDAR 2017)*, volume 1, pages 1423–1428. IEEE.

Guillaume Chiron, Antoine Doucet, Mickael Coustaty, Muriel Visani, and Jean-Philippe Moreux. 2017b. Impact of OCR errors on the use of digital libraries: Towards a better access to information. In *Proceedings of the 2017 ACM/IEEE Joint Conference on Digital Libraries (JCDL)*, pages 1–4.

Oksana Dereza, Deirdre Ní Chonghaile, and Nicholas Wolf. 2024. "To have the 'million' readers yet": Building a digitally enhanced edition of the bilingual Irish-English newspaper An Gaodhal (1881-1898). In *Proceedings of the Third Workshop on Language Technologies for Historical and Ancient Languages (LT4HALA) @ LREC-COLING-2024*, pages 65–78. ELRA and ICCL.

Quan Duong, Mika Hämäläinen, and Simon Hengchen. 2021. An unsupervised method for OCR post-correction and spelling normalisation for Finnish. In *Proceedings of the 23rd Nordic Conference on Computational Linguistics (NoDaLiDa)*, pages 240–248. Linköping University Electronic Press.

Ali Fahandari, Fatemeh Asadi Zeydabadi, Elham Shabaninia, and Hossein Nezamabadi-pour. 2024. Enhancing Farsi text recognition via iteratively using a language model. In *Proceedings of the 20th CSI International Symposium on Artificial Intelligence and Signal Processing (AISP)*.

Gale. https://www.gale.com/intl/primary-sources/eighteenth-century-collections-online Eighteenth Century Collections Online.

Stephen H. Gregg. 2021. *Old Books and Digital Publishing: Eighteenth-Century Collections Online*. Elements in Publishing and Book Culture. Cambridge University Press.

Stephen H. Gregg. 2022. The nature of ECCO-TCP. *Digital Defoe: Studies in Defoe & His Contemporaries*, 14(1).

Mark J. Hill and Simon Hengchen. 2019. Quantifying the impact of dirty OCR on historical text analysis: Eighteenth Century Collections Online as a case study. *Digital Scholarship in the Humanities*, 34(4):825–843.

Albert Q. Jiang, Alexandre Sablayrolles, Antoine Roux, Arthur Mensch, Blanche Savary, Chris Bamford, Devendra Singh Chaplot, Diego de las Casas, Emma Bou Hanna, Florian Bressand, et al. 2024. Mixtral of experts. *arXiv preprint arXiv:2401.04088*.

Kimmo Kettunen, Jukka Kervinen, and Mika Koistinen. 2018. Creating and using ground truth OCR sample data for Finnish historical newspapers and journals. In *Proceedings of the Digital Humanities in the Nordic Countries Conference*.

Kimmo Kettunen, Mika Koistinen, and Jukka Kervinen. 2020. Ground truth OCR sample data of Finnish historical newspapers and journals in data improvement validation of a re-OCRing process. *LIBER Quarterly: The Journal of the Association of European Research Libraries*, 30(1):1–20.

Kimmo Kettunen and Tuula Pääkkönen. 2016. Measuring lexical quality of a historical Finnish newspaper collection — analysis of garbled OCR data with basic language technology tools and means. In *Proceedings of the Tenth International Conference on Language Resources and Evaluation (LREC'16)*, pages 956–961. European Language Resources Association (ELRA).

Minghao Li, Tengchao Lv, Jingye Chen, Lei Cui, Yijuan Lu, Dinei Florencio, Cha Zhang, Zhoujun Li, and Furu Wei. 2023. TrOCR: Transformer-based optical character recognition with pre-trained models. In *Proceedings of The Thirty-Seventh AAAI Conference on Artificial Intelligence (AAAI-23)*.

Risto Luukkonen, Jonathan Burdge, Elaine Zosa, Aarne Talman, Ville Komulainen, Väinö Hatanpää, Peter Sarlin, and Sampo Pyysalo. 2024. Poro 34b and the blessing of multilinguality. *ArXiv preprint arXiv:2404.01856*.

Gábor Madarász, Noémi Ligeti-Nagy, András Holl, and Tamás Váradi. 2024. OCR cleaning of scientific texts with LLMs. In *Natural Scientific Language Processing and Research Knowledge Graphs*, pages 49–58. Springer Nature Switzerland.

Thomas Mesnard, Cassidy Hardin, Robert Dadashi, Surya Bhupatiraju, Laurent Sifre, Morgane Rivière, Mihir Sanjay Kale, Juliette Love, Pouya Tafti, Léonard Hussenot, et al. 2024. https://www.kaggle.com/m/3301 Gemma.

Thi Tuyet Hai Nguyen, Adam Jatowt, Mickael Coustaty, and Antoine Doucet. 2021. Survey of post-OCR processing approaches. *ACM Comput. Surv.*, 54(6).

Robert Östling, Katarina Gillholm, Murathan Kurfalı, Marie Mattson, and Mats Wirén. 2024. Evaluation of really good grammatical error correction. In *Proceedings of the 2024 Joint International Conference on Computational Linguistics, Language Resources and Evaluation (LREC-COLING 2024)*, pages 6582–6593, Torino, Italia. ELRA and ICCL.

Maria Carolina Penteado and Fábio Perez. 2023. Evaluating GPT-3.5 and GPT-4 on grammatical error correction for Brazilian Portuguese. In *Proceedings of the LatinX in AI Workshop at ICML 2023*.

Christophe Rigaud, Antoine Doucet, Mickaël Coustaty, and Jean-Philippe Moreux. 2019. ICDAR 2019 competition on post-OCR text correction. In *Proceedings of the 15th International Conference on Document Analysis and Recognition (ICDAR 2019)*, pages 1588–1593. IEEE.

Elizabeth Soper, Stanley Fujimoto, and Yen-Yun Yu. 2021. BART for post-correction of OCR newspaper text. In *Proceedings of the Seventh Workshop on Noisy User-generated Text (W-NUT 2021)*, pages 284–290. Association for Computational Linguistics.

Mikko Tolonen, Eetu Mäkelä, Ali Ijaz, and Leo Lahti. 2021. Corpus linguistics and Eighteenth Century Collections Online (ECCO). *Research in Corpus Linguistics*, 9:19–34.

Martijn Veninga. 2024. LLMs for OCR post-correction. Master's thesis, University of Twente.

FoQA: A Faroese Question-Answering Dataset

Annika Simonsen
University of Iceland
ans72@hi.is

Dan Saattrup Nielsen
Alexandra Institute
dan.nielsen@alexandra.dk

Hafsteinn Einarsson
University of Iceland
hafsteinne@hi.is

Abstract

We present FoQA, a Faroese extractive question-answering (QA) dataset with 2,000 samples, created using a semi-automated approach combining Large Language Models (LLMs) and human validation. The dataset was generated from Faroese Wikipedia articles using GPT-4-turbo for initial QA generation, followed by question rephrasing to increase complexity and native speaker validation to ensure quality. We provide baseline performance metrics for FoQA across multiple models, including LLMs and BERT, demonstrating its effectiveness in evaluating Faroese QA performance. The dataset is released in three versions: a validated set of 2,000 samples, a complete set of all 10,001 generated samples, and a set of 2,395 rejected samples for error analysis.

1 Introduction

Recent NLP advancements, driven by the transformer architecture (Vaswani et al., 2017), have led to large-scale models that excel in understanding (Devlin et al., 2018) and generating (Brown et al., 2020) human language. While many models are "massively multilingual" (Conneau et al., 2019; He et al., 2021a; Brown et al., 2020) they often perform better on high-resource languages, leaving low-resource languages undersupported. Furthermore, low-resource languages typically have limited access to native speakers who can serve as data annotators, making it difficult to create high-quality evaluation datasets. High-quality evaluation datasets are crucial for assessing and improving models for these languages, helping to measure performance and guide language technology development.

Extractive QA datasets (Srivastava and Memon, 2024) are especially useful, as they simulate real-world applications like retrieval-augmented generation (Gao et al., 2023). Creating these datasets traditionally requires substantial human effort, often involving multiple annotators for question generation and answer validation. Standardising methods for creating these datasets can significantly advance technology for low-resource languages.

Our research addresses these challenges and makes the following key contributions:

- **An efficient, single-annotator methodology for producing high-quality extractive QA datasets** using a semi-automated approach that significantly reduces the human effort required for dataset creation, provided as an open-source Python codebase[1]
- **The first extractive QA dataset for Faroese** using this method[2].

2 Related Work

QA systems are divided into extractive and abstractive types (Fan et al., 2019). This work focuses on extractive QA, also known as reading comprehension, where text passages are paired with questions, and answers are directly extracted from the text. A well-known example of an extractive QA dataset is the Stanford Question Answering Dataset (SQuAD), which includes over 100,000 QA pairs from Wikipedia articles (Rajpurkar et al., 2016). In the case of Icelandic, a language closely related to Faroese, several QA datasets have been developed. Snæbjarnarson and Einarsson (2022a) introduced a cross-lingual open-domain QA system using machine-translated data, and the Natural Questions in Icelandic, an extractive QA

[1] https://github.com/alexandrainst/foqa

[2] https://huggingface.co/datasets/alexandrainst/foqa

Proceedings of the Third Workshop on Resources and Representations for Under-Resourced Languages and Domains (RESOURCEFUL-2025), pages 48–57, March 2, 2025 ©2025 Association for Computational Linguistics

dataset, which demonstrates approaches applicable to other low-resource languages such as Faroese (Snæbjarnarson and Einarsson, 2022b). Similarly, Skarphedinsson et al. (2023) developed a method to gamify QA dataset creation. However, both approaches relied heavily on human question generation, which bottlenecked the dataset creation process.

At the time of writing, few benchmark datasets exist for Faroese. Snæbjarnarson et al. (2023) introduced named entity recognition[3] and semantic text similarity datasets[4]. The FLORES-200 dataset (Costa-Jussà et al., 2022) is another significant contribution to Faroese benchmarks, being a multilingual parallel corpus covering over 200 languages, including Faroese. Additionally, Nielsen (2023) introduced ScaLA-Fo, a linguistic acceptability dataset for Faroese. Despite these resources, a dedicated Faroese QA dataset is still lacking, which this work aims to address.

3 Methodology

3.1 Generation of Tentative Dataset

The process of generating an extractive question-answering dataset begins with several key components: a vocabulary, a text corpus, a generative model, and specialised functions for generating questions and answers and for question reformulation. Using these components, we create a tentative dataset through a two-step process. First, we apply a QA generation function to our text corpus to create initial QA pairs. Then, we refine these pairs by rewriting the questions while keeping the answers unchanged.

The QA generation function operates by utilising our generative model to create multiple questions for each document in the corpus, along with corresponding answers that must be found verbatim within the source document. To ensure consistency and maintainability, we implement strict formatting requirements for the model's output. Specifically, we require the model to generate responses in a structured JSON format, following the approach described by Willard and Louf (2023). Each output must be a dictionary containing a "results" key, which maps to a list of dictionaries. These inner dictionaries must contain exactly two keys: "question" and "answer." Any outputs that deviate from this precise format are automatically filtered out of the dataset.

A significant limitation of the initially generated questions lies in their close adherence to the source documents' original phrasing. These questions often merely restructure existing statements from the text into interrogative forms, diminishing their effectiveness as evaluation tools. Consider a document containing the statement "Jane Smith is an executive and her bike is red." The initial generation might produce "What colour is Jane Smith's bike?"—a question that could be answered through simple text matching algorithms, requiring minimal linguistic or reasoning capabilities. To address this limitation, we employ a question reformation process that introduces additional complexity. By transforming the previous example to "What colour is the executive's bicycle?", we create questions that demand more sophisticated comprehension abilities, including synonym recognition and multi-hop reasoning in this example. This reformulation process is implemented through our question-rewriting function, which utilises the generative model to produce modified questions.

We release our code base implementing this generation process open-source[5].

3.2 Manual Filtering of Tentative Dataset

To ensure high-quality dataset creation, we implemented a human validation phase using a custom annotation interface built with Gradio (Abid et al., 2019), a Python library for web-based interfaces. The tool presents annotators with each generated question and its answer, offering three classification options: CORRECT (both question and answer are grammatically and contextually appropriate), INCORRECT (question is grammatically incorrect or contextually inappropriate), and INCORRECT ANSWER (answer is irrelevant, inaccurate, or grammatically incorrect). An annotator reviews each QA pair and assigns the appropriate classification, ensuring linguistic quality and filtering out inadequate samples. The annotation tool is available open-source[6].

[3] https://huggingface.co/datasets/vesteinn/sosialurin-faroese-ner

[4] https://huggingface.co/datasets/vesteinn/faroese-sts

[5] https://github.com/alexandrainst/foqa

[6] https://huggingface.co/spaces/saattrupdan/foqa-validation

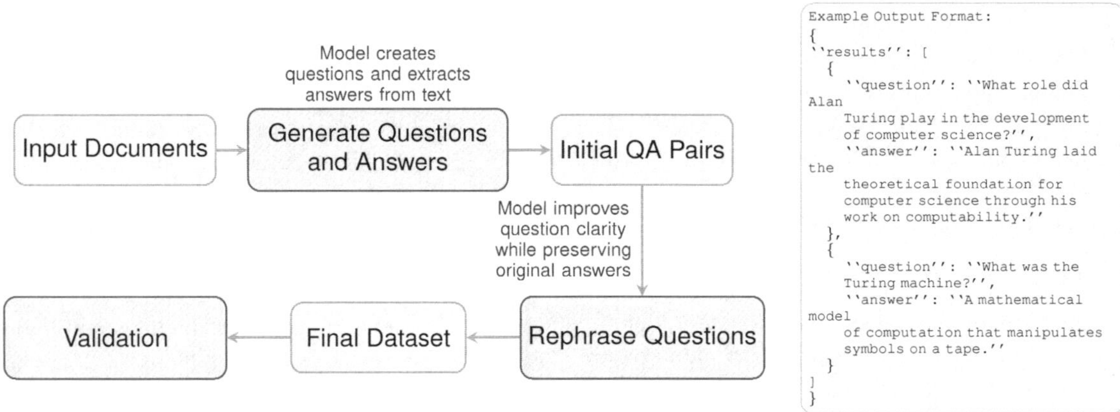

Figure 1: Overview of the QA dataset generation pipeline. The system processes input documents to generate initial QA pairs, followed by a question rewriting phase that improves clarity while maintaining the original answers. All outputs follow a structured JSON format to ensure consistency. Note that while the outputs are in Faroese, the example shown in this figure uses an English example for illustrative purposes.

3.3 Annotation Guidelines

This section outlines the complete annotation guidelines for evaluating QA pairs in Faroese. The annotator will follow a three-tier classification system when analysing each sample.

Tier 1: Grammatical Assessment The annotator should begin by evaluating the grammatical correctness of both the question and answer in Faroese. The annotator must check for proper agreement between subjects and verbs, correct case marking on nouns and pronouns, standard Faroese word order, accurate spelling and so on. If any grammatical errors are found in the question, the annotator should mark the entire sample as INCORRECT. If the grammatical errors only appear in the answer, the sample should be marked as INCORRECT ANSWER.

Tier 2: Semantic and Contextual Assessment After confirming grammatical correctness, the annotator should examine the relationship between the question and answer, as well as their connection to the source text. The answer must directly address the question being asked. Additionally, the annotator should ensure the answer demonstrates logical consistency within its context. If any issues with relevance, accuracy, or consistency are found, the sample should be marked as INCORRECT ANSWER.

Tier 3: Final Classification When a sample passes both the grammatical and semantic assessments, the annotator should mark it as CORRECT. The annotator will also be asked to correct a selection of questions marked as INCORRECT. When performing these corrections, the annotator should focus only on samples where the question itself contains errors, not the answer. This is crucial because modifying answers would compromise the extractive nature of the QA task, as answers should appear verbatim in the source text.

Quality Control Process All samples marked as CORRECT can undergo a secondary review by another annotator who is also a native Faroese speaker. This second annotator will apply the same three-tier evaluation process described above.

4 Faroese Setup

We applied our methodology (Section 3) to the Faroese Wikipedia[7] as the text source and `gpt-4-turbo-2024-04-09` (OpenAI, 2023) as the generative model, selected for its top performance on Faroese tasks in the ScandEval benchmark (Nielsen, 2023; Nielsen et al., 2024). To ensure non-trivial contexts, only articles with over 1,000 characters were included, i.e., 1675 articles in total and 655 articles used for the validated dataset. We set the model temperature to 1.0 and generated a maximum of 1,024 tokens, with a consistent random seed (4242) to maintain re-

[7]This dump: https://hf.co/datasets/alexandrainst/scandi-wiki.

producibility. The system prompt we use is the following:

> You are a helpful Faroese question answering dataset generator. The only language you know is Faroese.

While we did not explore Faroese-language prompting or prompt variations in this study, such modifications could potentially improve the effectiveness of our approach. As our primary focus was developing a question-answering dataset for Faroese, we leave prompt optimisation for future work. The following prompt was used for generating QA pairs:

> The following is a Wikipedia article in Faroese.
>
> ¡article¿
> {article}
> ¡/article¿
>
> Generate 2 to 10 questions about the article, depending on the length of the article, all of which answered in the article.
>
> You also have to supply answers to the questions, and the answers have to appear exactly as written in the article (including same casing).
>
> The answers should only contain the answers themselves, and not the surrounding sentence - keep the answers as short as possible.
>
> The answers have to be different from each other.
>
> All your questions and answers must be in Faroese.
>
> Your answer must be a JSON dictionary with the key "results", with the value being a list of dictionaries having keys "question" and "answer".

Lastly, we use the following prompt to re-write the questions:

> The following is a Faroese question.
>
> ¡question¿
> {question}
> ¡/question¿
>
> Re-write the question, preserving the meaning, using synonyms or a different (valid) word order.
>
> Your question must be in Faroese.
>
> Your answer must be a JSON dictionary with the key "question".

In both prompts, we replace {article} and {question} with the actual Wikipedia article and the generated question, respectively.

5 The Dataset

5.1 Format

The validated QA pairs are stored in a structured format, with each entry containing a unique identifier (`id`), the source article's URL (`url`), the article title (`title`), the full text (`context`), the generated and rephrased question (`question`), and an answers dictionary (`answers`) that includes the answer text and its character index (`answer_start`) within the context. This structure ensures compatibility with standard extractive QA formats like SQuAD (Rajpurkar et al., 2016), enabling seamless integration with existing NLP frameworks and models.

5.2 Statistics

The tentative dataset in our Faroese case consisted of **10,001** samples, which were randomly selected from the Wikipedia articles meeting our length criteria (¿1,000 characters). From these samples, **4,130** were annotated by a human annotator. Out of the annotated samples, **1,759** were annotated as CORRECT, **1,908** were INCORRECT[8] and **222** had an INCORRECT ANSWER. While the initial validation was performed by a single annotator, we conducted a second validation phase specifically for the samples marked as CORRECT, where these samples were evenly split between two annotators: the original annotator and a second native Faroese speaker. During this step, **41** out of the **1,759** CORRECT samples were found to have been incorrectly labelled as CORRECT by the annotator, which was then corrected. Additionally, **241** samples have the label CORRECTED where the original question has been corrected by the human annotator (this includes the 41 incorrectly labelled samples which were corrected). These corrected samples are intended to both measure and mitigate potential biases introduced by GPT-4-turbo during the initial sample creation. By comparing model performance on the corrected versus uncorrected samples of the dataset, we can assess whether the model exhibits any bias toward its own generated questions.

5.3 Dataset Versions

We are releasing three versions of the FoQA dataset on the Hugging Face Hub[9]. The format of the dataset is compatible with standard extractive QA formats like SQuAD. The primary version, **default**, contains 2,000 validated examples (comprising 1,759 initially correct examples and 241 examples that were corrected during re-

[8] While more than half of all generated question/answer pairs were marked as incorrect, we release the full dataset to enable researchers to study GPT-4's error patterns in Faroese.

[9] Available at `https://huggingface.co/datasets/alexandrainst/foqa`.

view), including 848 for training, 128 for validation, and 1,024 for testing, with shortened contexts for improved usability. The second version, **all-samples**, includes all 10,001 examples from the initial dataset, retaining full, unshortened contexts, even those that were rejected or not validated. The final version, **incorrect-samples**, comprises 2,395 examples that were rejected during the manual review process.

5.3.1 Question Types

We used the `gpt-4o-2024-05-13` model from OpenAI to annotate the questions into categories and we used the following system prompt:

> Categorize the question (written in Faroese) based on the type of question it is. The question types are "time" for questions that ask about the time of something, "place" if they ask for a place, "people" if they ask about a person, "object" if they ask about an object or a non-person entity. If the question does not fit any of these categories, respond with "other".

Most questions received the people label (679, 33.95%), followed by object (516, 25.80%), time (367, 18.35%), place (290, 14.50%) and other (148, 7.40%).

To assess the quality of the automatic question categorisation, the annotator manually validated 200 randomly sampled questions from the dataset. The validation methodology included assigning binary scores: 1 for correct categorization and 0 for incorrect categorisation. The validation followed an inclusive approach, accepting multiple valid category assignments where applicable. For instance, questions about a person's birthplace (e.g., "Where was Turi Sigurardóttir born?") were considered correctly categorised if labelled as either "person" or "place," as both categories are contextually relevant to the question's intent. This flexible validation framework acknowledges the inherent ambiguity in question categorisation, where multiple interpretations may be equally valid.

The manual validation revealed an error rate of 7.5% (15 incorrect categorisations out of 200 validated samples), suggesting that the GPT-4o categorisation system achieved 92.5% accuracy on the validated subset.

The annotator also conducted a qualitative error type analysis. Here it was found that common error types in the QA dataset include grammatical gender mistakes, such as using neuter instead of masculine forms in questions about pool length (e.g., "Hvussu langur er svimjihyli.NEUT í kappingunum"). Incorrect phrasing surrounding years, like omitting the preposition "í" (in) when asking about dates (e.g., "Hvørjum ári doyi Stephen Hawking?"), is also prevalent. Icelandicisms appear as words that are partially or fully Icelandic (e.g., the use of "hrai" (speed) inflected as a Faroese noun in "Hvør er hrain á jørini í kilometrum hvønn tíma?"). The questions and answers also contained errors in punctuation, spelling, and capitalization, as seen in the improper capitalization of "Smyril" (merlin) when referring to the bird rather than the ferry (e.g., "Hvat ger Smyril?"). Lastly, some incorrect terms are used consistently (e.g., "høvusbýur" (main city) used instead of "høvusstaur" (capital) when asking about capital cities).

Model Name	F1 Score	Exact Match
GPT-4-turbo[10]	77.6 ± 1.0	55.6 ± 1.8
GPT-4o[11]	77.1 ± 1.0	54.1 ± 1.6
GPT-4o-mini[12]	75.2 ± 1.0	51.2 ± 1.5
Llama-3.1-8B[13]	73.6 ± 1.2	51.9 ± 1.5
GPT-SW3-6.7B[14]	63.4 ± 2.2	45.2 ± 2.1
Mistral-7B[15]	62.4 ± 1.7	45.0 ± 1.6
FoBERT[16]	36.0 ± 1.7	26.8 ± 1.5
mDeBERTa-v3[17]	30.6 ± 1.6	21.0 ± 1.2
ScandiBERT[18]	30.9 ± 2.7	21.9 ± 2.3

Table 1: Evaluation results on FoQA according to F1 scores and exact match.

6 Evaluation

We evaluated several models on the dataset. Since we ensured that all answers appear exactly as in the documents, this allows us to evaluate both encoder models and decoder models on the dataset. We evaluate both Faroese and massively multilingual models on FoQA, the results of which can be found in Table 1.

We also evaluated the model used to generate the dataset, `gpt-4-turbo-2024-04-09`, on

[10]Full OpenAI model ID: `gpt-4-1106-preview`

[11]Full OpenAI model ID: `gpt-4o-2024-05-13`

[12]Full OpenAI model ID: `gpt-4o-mini-2024-07-18`

[13]`https://hf.co/meta-llama/Llama-3.1-8B`

[14]`https://hf.co/AI-Sweden-Models/gpt-sw3-6.7b-v2`

[15]`https://hf.co/mistralai/Mistral-7B-v0.3`

[16]`https://hf.co/vesteinn/FoBERT`

[17]`https://hf.co/microsoft/mdeberta-v3-base`

[18]`https://hf.co/vesteinn/ScandiBERT-no-faroese`

the corrected samples, before and after the correction. This was to test whether the model is biased towards its own generated questions, or whether it generalises to the corrected ones as well. Surprisingly, the model ended up performing significantly better[19] on the corrected samples, rather than the samples it had generated itself.

7 Discussion and Future Work

Our evaluation of the FoQA dataset reveals insights into the performance of various language models on Faroese QA tasks. GPT-4-turbo and GPT-4o achieved the highest performance scores in our evaluation, though further research would be needed to understand whether this indicates genuine Faroese language comprehension or other factors like strong general question-answering capabilities. This finding suggests promising directions for low-resource language processing, while highlighting the need for more detailed investigation into how these models handle Faroese specifically.

An important observation from our annotator indicates that most errors in the generated questions were grammatical in nature rather than contextual. This suggests a need for dedicated benchmarks specifically measuring grammatical correctness of LLMs in Faroese, which would complement FoQA's focus on QA capabilities.

Early question answering datasets like SQuAD faced criticism that their questions were too simplistic, often directly mirroring the source text structure. Later datasets like TyDi QA (Clark et al., 2020) and Natural Questions in Icelandic (Snæbjarnarson and Einarsson, 2022b) addressed this by having annotators create natural questions first, which were later matched to source material. This approach prevented the tight coupling between question phrasing and source text that can make questions artificially easy. Following this insight, we implemented question rephrasing in our methodology. However, we acknowledge that we did not specifically measure performance differences between original and rephrased questions, which would require separate evaluation sets.

We found that encoder models like mDeBERTa-v3 (He et al., 2021a,b), FoBERT and ScandiBERT (Snæbjarnarson and Einarsson, 2022a) perform significantly worse than the decoder models, but that could simply be explained by the fact that these models differ in sizes by several orders of magnitude. A controlled experiment will need to reveal whether architectural choices are the real cause for difference in performance or whether it is due to other reasons such as parameter count. A performance gap has been observed between encoder-type models and decoder-type models across other languages and (Nielsen et al., 2024) suggests that certain architectures may be inherently better suited for specific language processing tasks.

For future work, we propose evaluating larger open models, such as 70B parameter models and even larger ones like Llama 3.1 405B (Dubey et al., 2024). Additionally, assessing the performance of Claude 3.5 Sonnet (Anthropic, 2024) would be valuable, given its strong performance on Icelandic NLP tasks[20] since Icelandic is a language closely related to Faroese.

8 Conclusion

We introduced FoQA, the first Faroese extractive question-answering dataset, containing 2,000 QA pairs. All samples underwent initial validation by one annotator, followed by a second validation phase where the correct samples were split equally between the original annotator and a second annotator. Our evaluation reveals significant performance gaps between decoder-based LLMs and encoder models, with GPT-4-turbo achieving the highest F1 score of 77.6, while encoder models like mDeBERTa-v3 and ScandiBERT scored around 30. Notably, our analysis of question types shows a diverse distribution across categories, with people-related questions comprising the largest portion at 33.95%. The dataset's manual validation process identified common error patterns, including grammatical gender mistakes and Icelandicisms, providing valuable insights for future Faroese language model development. The FoQA dataset serves as valuable benchmark for evaluating Faroese language understanding. Additionally, our contributions include a semi-automated methodology for creating extractive QA datasets for low-resource languages.

[19] $p = 0.0007$ for F1-score and $p = 0.0185$ for exact match, using a two-tailed t-test.

[20] https://huggingface.co/spaces/mideind/icelandic-llm-leaderboard

Limitations

A significant limitation of our dataset is that our current annotation process does not differentiate between grammatical errors and contextual errors in the generated questions. This granular error categorisation would provide valuable insights for improving model performance and understanding specific challenges in Faroese language generation.

The use of GPT-4-turbo for dataset generation introduces potential biases in the linguistic patterns of the generated text. Despite native speaker validation, there remains a risk that the generated questions may not fully capture natural Faroese language patterns and could subtly reflect machine-generated language characteristics.

Our methodology relied on a single annotator for the initial validation phase, which means we could not perform traditional inter-annotator agreement measurements. While this limitation was intentional, as our approach aimed to demonstrate the feasibility of creating useful datasets with minimal human resources, it does impact our ability to measure annotation consistency quantitatively. Another limitation is our lack of evaluation on the non-rephrased questions. This missing comparison makes it difficult to quantify the impact of our question rephrasing strategy and determine whether it actually increased question difficulty as intended.

Furthermore, Faroese Wikipedia, while a valuable resource, is relatively small and occasionally contains ungrammatical content due to a limited pool of contributors. This occasionally led to incorrect-answer errors, since the answers are extracted directly from the source text. And lastly, the current size of 2,000 validated QA pairs, while a solid starting point, is relatively small compared to QA datasets for high-resource languages, which may limit its capacity to train or fine-tune LLMs effectively.

Ethical Statement

The creation of language resources for low-resource languages like Faroese raises important ethical considerations, particularly when utilising LLMs. Our dataset generation process involved processing approximately 1,675 Faroese Wikipedia articles through GPT-4-turbo. While this automated approach enabled efficient initial data generation, we acknowledge the computational resources required and their environmental impact, and we conservatively estimate that the processing spanned 48 GPU hours. We note that OpenAI's infrastructure runs on Azure, and Azure will be running on 100% renewable energy by 2025 and has been carbon neutral since 2012[21].

A primary ethical concern in using LLMs for low-resource language content generation is the potential introduction of non-native language patterns and cultural misrepresentations. This risk is particularly relevant for Faroese, where preserving authentic linguistic patterns and cultural context is crucial. To address these concerns, we implemented a comprehensive validation protocol requiring native speaker review of all generated content. This human-in-the-loop approach helped identify and correct systematic errors while ensuring linguistic authenticity.

To maximise the dataset's benefit to the Faroese language technology community, we have made it freely available under an open-source license. We are committed to ongoing maintenance and error correction, ensuring the dataset remains a valuable resource for Faroese language technology development while maintaining high standards of linguistic quality and cultural authenticity.

Acknowledgments

AS was supported by the European Commission under grant agreement no. 101135671. We thank the reviewers for their constructive and helpful comments, which have significantly improved the quality and clarity of our manuscript.

[21]See more information on Azure's sustainability page.

References

Abubakar Abid, Ali Abdalla, Ali Abid, Dawood Khan, Abdulrahman Alfozan, and James Zou. 2019. Gradio: Hassle-Free Sharing and Testing of ML Models in the Wild. *arXiv preprint arXiv:1906.02569*.

Anthropic. 2024. Claude 3.5 Sonnet. `https://www.anthropic.com`. Proprietary software, closed-source.

Tom Brown, Benjamin Mann, Nick Ryder, Melanie Subbiah, Jared D Kaplan, Prafulla Dhariwal, Arvind Neelakantan, Pranav Shyam, Girish Sastry, Amanda Askell, Sandhini Agarwal, Ariel Herbert-Voss, Gretchen Krueger, Tom Henighan, Rewon Child, Aditya Ramesh, Daniel Ziegler, Jeffrey Wu, Clemens Winter, Chris Hesse, Mark Chen, Eric Sigler, Mateusz Litwin, Scott Gray, Benjamin Chess, Jack Clark, Christopher Berner, Sam McCandlish, Alec Radford, Ilya Sutskever, and Dario Amodei. 2020. Language Models are Few-Shot Learners. In *Advances in Neural Information Processing Systems*, volume 33, pages 1877–1901. Curran Associates, Inc.

Jonathan H. Clark, Eunsol Choi, Michael Collins, Dan Garrette, Tom Kwiatkowski, Vitaly Nikolaev, and Jennimaria Palomaki. 2020. TyDi QA: A Benchmark for Information-Seeking Question Answering in Typologically Diverse Languages. *Transactions of the Association for Computational Linguistics*, 8:454–470.

Alexis Conneau, Kartikay Khandelwal, Naman Goyal, Vishrav Chaudhary, Guillaume Wenzek, Francisco Guzmán, Edouard Grave, Myle Ott, Luke Zettlemoyer, and Veselin Stoyanov. 2019. Unsupervised Cross-lingual Representation Learning at Scale. *arXiv preprint arXiv:1911.02116*. *Equal contribution for first two authors.

Marta R. Costa-Jussà, James Cross, Onur Çelebi, Maha Elbayad, Kenneth Heafield, Kevin Heffernan, Elahe Kalbassi, Janice Lam, Daniel Licht, Jean Maillard, Anna Sun, Skyler Wang, Guillaume Wenzek, Al Youngblood, Bapi Akula, Loic Barrault, Gabriel Mejia Gonzalez, Prangthip Hansanti, John Hoffman, Semarley Jarrett, Kaushik Ram Sadagopan, Dirk Rowe, Shannon Spruit, Chau Tran, Pierre Andrews, Necip Fazil Ayan, Shruti Bhosale, Sergey Edunov, Angela Fan, Cynthia Gao, Vedanuj Goswami, Francisco Guzmán, Philipp Koehn, Alexandre Mourachko, Christophe Ropers, Safiyyah Saleem, Holger Schwenk, and Jeff Wang. 2022. No Language Left Behind: Scaling Human-Centered Machine Translation. *arXiv preprint arXiv:2207.04672*.

Jacob Devlin, Ming-Wei Chang, Kenton Lee, and Kristina Toutanova. 2018. BERT: Pre-training of Deep Bidirectional Transformers for Language Understanding. *arXiv preprint arXiv:1810.04805*.

Abhimanyu Dubey, Abhinav Jauhri, Abhinav Pandey, Abhishek Kadian, Ahmad Al-Dahle, Aiesha Letman, Akhil Mathur, Alan Schelten, Amy Yang, Angela Fan, Anirudh Goyal, Anthony Hartshorn, Aobo Yang, Archi Mitra, Archie Sravankumar, Artem Korenev, Arthur Hinsvark, Arun Rao, Aston Zhang, Aurelien Rodriguez, Austen Gregerson, Ava Spataru, Baptiste Roziere, Bethany Biron, Binh Tang, Bobbie Chern, Charlotte Caucheteux, Chaya Nayak, Chloe Bi, Chris Marra, Chris McConnell, Christian Keller, Christophe Touret, Chunyang Wu, Corinne Wong, Cristian Canton Ferrer, Cyrus Nikolaidis, Damien Allonsius, Daniel Song, Danielle Pintz, Danny Livshits, David Esiobu, Dhruv Choudhary, Dhruv Mahajan, Diego Garcia-Olano, Diego Perino, Dieuwke Hupkes, Egor Lakomkin, Ehab AlBadawy, Elina Lobanova, Emily Dinan, Eric Michael Smith, Filip Radenovic, Frank Zhang, Gabriel Synnaeve, Gabrielle Lee, Georgia Lewis Anderson, Graeme Nail, Gregoire Mialon, Guan Pang, Guillem Cucurell, Hailey Nguyen, Hannah Korevaar, Hu Xu, Hugo Touvron, Iliyan Zarov, Imanol Arrieta Ibarra, Isabel Kloumann, Ishan Misra, Ivan Evtimov, Jade Copet, Jaewon Lee, Jan Geffert, Jana Vranes, Jason Park, Jay Mahadeokar, Jeet Shah, Jelmer van der Linde, Jennifer Billock, Jenny Hong, Jenya Lee, Jeremy Fu, Jianfeng Chi, Jianyu Huang, Jiawen Liu, Jie Wang, Jiecao Yu, Joanna Bitton, Joe Spisak, Jongsoo Park, Joseph Rocca, Joshua Johnstun, Joshua Saxe, Junteng Jia, Kalyan Vasuden Alwala, Kartikeya Upasani, Kate Plawiak, Ke Li, Kenneth Heafield, Kevin Stone, Khalid El-Arini, Krithika Iyer, Kshitiz Malik, Kuenley Chiu, Kunal Bhalla, Lauren Rantala-Yeary, Laurens van der Maaten, Lawrence Chen, Liang Tan, Liz Jenkins, Louis Martin, Lovish Madaan, Lubo Malo, Lukas Blecher, Lukas Landzaat, Luke de Oliveira, Madeline Muzzi, Mahesh Pasupuleti, Mannat Singh, Manohar Paluri, Marcin Kardas, Mathew Oldham, Mathieu Rita, Maya Pavlova, Melanie Kambadur, Mike Lewis, Min Si, Mitesh Kumar Singh, Mona Hassan, Naman Goyal, Narjes Torabi, Nikolay Bashlykov, Nikolay Bogoychev, Niladri Chatterji, Olivier Duchenne, Onur Çelebi, Patrick Alrassy, Pengchuan Zhang, Pengwei Li, Petar Vasic, Peter Weng, Prajjwal Bhargava, Pratik Dubal, Praveen Krishnan, Punit Singh Koura, Puxin Xu, Qing He, Qingxiao Dong, Ragavan Srinivasan, Raj Ganapathy, Ramon Calderer, Ricardo Silveira Cabral, Robert Stojnic, Roberta Raileanu, Rohit Girdhar, Rohit Patel, Romain Sauvestre, Ronnie Polidoro, Roshan Sumbaly, Ross Taylor, Ruan Silva, Rui Hou, Rui Wang, Saghar Hosseini, Sahana Chennabasappa, Sanjay Singh, Sean Bell, Seohyun Sonia Kim, Sergey Edunov, Shaoliang Nie, Sharan Narang, Sharath Raparthy, Sheng Shen, Shengye Wan, Shruti Bhosale, Shun Zhang, Simon Vandenhende, Soumya Batra, Spencer Whitman, Sten Sootla, Stephane Collot, Suchin Gururangan, Sydney Borodinsky, Tamar Herman, Tara Fowler, Tarek Sheasha, Thomas Georgiou, Thomas Scialom, Tobias Speckbacher, Todor Mihaylov, Tong Xiao,

Ujjwal Karn, Vedanuj Goswami, Vibhor Gupta, Vignesh Ramanathan, Viktor Kerkez, Vincent Gonguet, Virginie Do, Vish Vogeti, Vladan Petrovic, Weiwei Chu, Wenhan Xiong, Wenyin Fu, Whitney Meers, Xavier Martinet, Xiaodong Wang, Xiaoqing Ellen Tan, Xinfeng Xie, Xuchao Jia, Xuewei Wang, Yaelle Goldschlag, Yashesh Gaur, Yasmine Babaei, Yi Wen, Yiwen Song, Yuchen Zhang, Yue Li, Yuning Mao, Zacharie Delpierre Coudert, Zheng Yan, Zhengxing Chen, Zoe Papakipos, Aaditya Singh, Aaron Grattafiori, Abha Jain, Adam Kelsey, Adam Shajnfeld, Adithya Gangidi, Adolfo Victoria, Ahuva Goldstand, Ajay Menon, Ajay Sharma, Alex Boesenberg, Alex Vaughan, Alexei Baevski, Allie Feinstein, Amanda Kallet, Amit Sangani, Anam Yunus, Andrei Lupu, Andres Alvarado, Andrew Caples, Andrew Gu, Andrew Ho, Andrew Poulton, Andrew Ryan, Ankit Ramchandani, Annie Franco, Aparajita Saraf, Arkabandhu Chowdhury, Ashley Gabriel, Ashwin Bharambe, Assaf Eisenman, Azadeh Yazdan, Beau James, Ben Maurer, Benjamin Leonhardi, Bernie Huang, Beth Loyd, Beto De Paola, Bhargavi Paranjape, Bing Liu, Bo Wu, Boyu Ni, Braden Hancock, Bram Wasti, Brandon Spence, Brani Stojkovic, Brian Gamido, Britt Montalvo, Carl Parker, Carly Burton, Catalina Mejia, Changhan Wang, Changkyu Kim, Chao Zhou, Chester Hu, Ching-Hsiang Chu, Chris Cai, Chris Tindal, Christoph Feichtenhofer, Damon Civin, Dana Beaty, Daniel Kreymer, Daniel Li, Danny Wyatt, David Adkins, David Xu, Davide Testuggine, Delia David, Devi Parikh, Diana Liskovich, Didem Foss, Dingkang Wang, Duc Le, Dustin Holland, Edward Dowling, Eissa Jamil, Elaine Montgomery, Eleonora Presani, Emily Hahn, Emily Wood, Erik Brinkman, Esteban Arcaute, Evan Dunbar, Evan Smothers, Fei Sun, Felix Kreuk, Feng Tian, Firat Ozgenel, Francesco Caggioni, Francisco Guzmán, Frank Kanayet, Frank Seide, Gabriela Medina Florez, Gabriella Schwarz, Gada Badeer, Georgia Swee, Gil Halpern, Govind Thattai, Grant Herman, Grigory Sizov, Guangyi, Zhang, Guna Lakshminarayanan, Hamid Shojanazeri, Han Zou, Hannah Wang, Hanwen Zha, Haroun Habeeb, Harrison Rudolph, Helen Suk, Henry Aspegren, Hunter Goldman, Ibrahim Damlaj, Igor Molybog, Igor Tufanov, Irina-Elena Veliche, Itai Gat, Jake Weissman, James Geboski, James Kohli, Japhet Asher, Jean-Baptiste Gaya, Jeff Marcus, Jeff Tang, Jennifer Chan, Jenny Zhen, Jeremy Reizenstein, Jeremy Teboul, Jessica Zhong, Jian Jin, Jingyi Yang, Joe Cummings, Jon Carvill, Jon Shepard, Jonathan McPhie, Jonathan Torres, Josh Ginsburg, Junjie Wang, Kai Wu, Kam Hou U, Karan Saxena, Karthik Prasad, Kartikay Khandelwal, Katayoun Zand, Kathy Matosich, Kaushik Veeraraghavan, Kelly Michelena, Keqian Li, Kun Huang, Kunal Chawla, Kushal Lakhotia, Kyle Huang, Lailin Chen, Lakshya Garg, Lavender A, Leandro Silva, Lee Bell, Lei Zhang, Liangpeng Guo, Licheng Yu, Liron Moshkovich, Luca Wehrstedt, Madian Khabsa, Manav Avalani, Manish Bhatt, Maria Tsimpoukelli, Martynas Mankus, Matan Hasson, Matthew Lennie, Matthias Reso, Maxim Groshev, Maxim Naumov, Maya Lathi, Meghan Keneally, Michael L. Seltzer, Michal Valko, Michelle Restrepo, Mihir Patel, Mik Vyatskov, Mikayel Samvelyan, Mike Clark, Mike Macey, Mike Wang, Miquel Jubert Hermoso, Mo Metanat, Mohammad Rastegari, Munish Bansal, Nandhini Santhanam, Natascha Parks, Natasha White, Navyata Bawa, Nayan Singhal, Nick Egebo, Nicolas Usunier, Nikolay Pavlovich Laptev, Ning Dong, Ning Zhang, Norman Cheng, Oleg Chernoguz, Olivia Hart, Omkar Salpekar, Ozlem Kalinli, Parkin Kent, Parth Parekh, Paul Saab, Pavan Balaji, Pedro Rittner, Philip Bontrager, Pierre Roux, Piotr Dollar, Polina Zvyagina, Prashant Ratanchandani, Pritish Yuvraj, Qian Liang, Rachad Alao, Rachel Rodriguez, Rafi Ayub, Raghotham Murthy, Raghu Nayani, Rahul Mitra, Raymond Li, Rebekkah Hogan, Robin Battey, Rocky Wang, Rohan Maheswari, Russ Howes, Ruty Rinott, Sai Jayesh Bondu, Samyak Datta, Sara Chugh, Sara Hunt, Sargun Dhillon, Sasha Sidorov, Satadru Pan, Saurabh Verma, Seiji Yamamoto, Sharadh Ramaswamy, Shaun Lindsay, Shaun Lindsay, Sheng Feng, Shenghao Lin, Shengxin Cindy Zha, Shiva Shankar, Shuqiang Zhang, Shuqiang Zhang, Sinong Wang, Sneha Agarwal, Soji Sajuyigbe, Soumith Chintala, Stephanie Max, Stephen Chen, Steve Kehoe, Steve Satterfield, Sudarshan Govindaprasad, Sumit Gupta, Sungmin Cho, Sunny Virk, Suraj Subramanian, Sy Choudhury, Sydney Goldman, Tal Remez, Tamar Glaser, Tamara Best, Thilo Kohler, Thomas Robinson, Tianhe Li, Tianjun Zhang, Tim Matthews, Timothy Chou, Tzook Shaked, Varun Vontimitta, Victoria Ajayi, Victoria Montanez, Vijai Mohan, Vinay Satish Kumar, Vishal Mangla, Vítor Albiero, Vlad Ionescu, Vlad Poenaru, Vlad Tiberiu Mihailescu, Vladimir Ivanov, Wei Li, Wenchen Wang, Wenwen Jiang, Wes Bouaziz, Will Constable, Xiaocheng Tang, Xiaofang Wang, Xiaojian Wu, Xiaolan Wang, Xide Xia, Xilun Wu, Xinbo Gao, Yanjun Chen, Ye Hu, Ye Jia, Ye Qi, Yenda Li, Yilin Zhang, Ying Zhang, Yossi Adi, Youngjin Nam, Yu, Wang, Yuchen Hao, Yundi Qian, Yuzi He, Zach Rait, Zachary DeVito, Zef Rosnbrick, Zhaoduo Wen, Zhenyu Yang, and Zhiwei Zhao. 2024. The Llama 3 Herd of Models. *arXiv preprint arXiv:2407.21783*.

Angela Fan, Yacine Jernite, Ethan Perez, David Grangier, Jason Weston, and Michael Auli. 2019. ELI5: Long Form Question Answering. In *Proceedings of the 57th Annual Meeting of the Association for Computational Linguistics*, pages 3558–3567, Florence, Italy. Association for Computational Linguistics.

Yunfan Gao, Yun Xiong, Xinyu Gao, Kangxiang Jia, Jinliu Pan, Yuxi Bi, Yi Dai, Jiawei Sun, and Haofen Wang. 2023. Retrieval-Augmented Generation for Large Language Models: A Survey. *arXiv preprint arXiv:2312.10997*.

Pengcheng He, Jianfeng Gao, and Weizhu Chen. 2021a. DeBERTaV3: Improving DeBERTa using ELECTRA-Style Pre-Training with Gradient-Disentangled Embedding Sharing. *arXiv preprint arXiv:2111.09543*.

Pengcheng He, Xiaodong Liu, Jianfeng Gao, and Weizhu Chen. 2021b. DeBERTa: Decoding-enhanced BERT with Disentangled Attention. In *International Conference on Learning Representations*.

Dan Nielsen. 2023. Scandeval: A Benchmark for Scandinavian Natural Language Processing. In *Proceedings of the 24th Nordic Conference on Computational Linguistics (NoDaLiDa)*, pages 185–201.

Dan Saattrup Nielsen, Kenneth Enevoldsen, and Peter Schneider-Kamp. 2024. Encoder vs Decoder: Comparative Analysis of Encoder and Decoder Language Models on Multilingual NLU Tasks. *arXiv preprint arXiv:2406.13469*.

OpenAI. 2023. New models and developer products announced at DevDay.

Pranav Rajpurkar, Jian Zhang, Konstantin Lopyrev, and Percy Liang. 2016. SQuAD: 100,000+ Questions for Machine Comprehension of Text. In *In Proceedings of the 2016 Conference on Empirical Methods in Natural Language Processing*, pages 2383–2392, Austin, Texas. Association for Computational Linguistics.

Njall Skarphedinsson, Breki Gudmundsson, Steinar Smari, Marta Kristin Larusdottir, Hafsteinn Einarsson, Abuzar Khan, Eric Nyberg, and Hrafn Loftsson. 2023. GameQA: Gamified Mobile App Platform for Building Multiple-Domain Question-Answering Datasets. In *Proceedings of the 17th Conference of the European Chapter of the Association for Computational Linguistics: System Demonstrations*, pages 152–160, Dubrovnik, Croatia. Association for Computational Linguistics.

Vésteinn Snæbjarnarson and Hafsteinn Einarsson. 2022a. Cross-Lingual QA as a Stepping Stone for Monolingual Open QA in Icelandic. In *Proceedings of the Workshop on Multilingual Information Access (MIA)*, pages 29–36, Seattle, USA. Association for Computational Linguistics.

Vésteinn Snæbjarnarson and Hafsteinn Einarsson. 2022b. Natural Questions in Icelandic. In *Proceedings of the Thirteenth Language Resources and Evaluation Conference*, pages 4488–4496, Marseille, France. European Language Resources Association.

Vésteinn Snæbjarnarson, Annika Simonsen, Goran Glavaš, and Ivan Vulić. 2023. Transfer to a Low-Resource Language via Close Relatives: The Case Study on Faroese. In *Proceedings of the 24th Nordic Conference on Computational Linguistics (NoDaLiDa)*, pages 728–737, Tórshavn, Faroe Islands. University of Tartu Library.

Akchay Srivastava and Atif Memon. 2024. Towards Robust Evaluation: A Comprehensive Taxonomy of Datasets and Metrics for Open Domain Question Answering in the Era of Large Language Models. *IEEE Access*.

Ashish Vaswani, Noam Shazeer, Niki Parmar, Jakob Uszkoreit, Llion Jones, Aidan N. Gomez, Łukasz Kaiser, and Illia Polosukhin. 2017. Attention Is All You Need. *Advances in Neural Information Processing Systems*, 30.

Brandon T Willard and Rémi Louf. 2023. Efficient Guided Generation for Large Language Models. *arXiv preprint arXiv:2307.09702*.

Automatic Validation of the Non-Validated Spanish Speech Data of Common Voice 17.0

Carlos Daniel Hernández Mena[a], **Barbara Scalvini**[b], **Dávid í Lág**[b]
[a]Barcelona Supercomputing Center
carlos.hernandez@bsc.es
[b]University of the Faroe Islands
{barbaras,davidl}@setur.fo

Abstract

Mozilla Common Voice is a crowdsourced project that aims to create a public, multilingual dataset of voice recordings for training speech recognition models. In Common Voice, anyone can contribute by donating or validating recordings in various languages. However, despite the availability of many recordings in certain languages, a significant percentage remains unvalidated by users. This is the case for Spanish, where in version 17.0 of Common Voice, 75% of the 2,220 hours of recordings are unvalidated. In this work, we used the Whisper recognizer to automatically validate approximately 784 hours of recordings which are more than the 562 hours validated by users. To verify the accuracy of the validation, we developed a speech recognition model based on a version of NVIDIA-NeMo's Parakeet, which does not have an official Spanish version. Our final model achieved a WER of less than 4% on the test and validation splits of Common Voice 17.0. Both the model and the speech corpus are publicly available on Hugging Face.

1 Introduction

Developing Automatic Speech Recognition (ASR) systems requires extensive labeled speech data, which is costly and time-consuming to annotate manually. Crowdsourcing and automated methods help address these challenges by enabling efficient and consistent validation of data quality. For instance, Hernandez et al. (2018) used the Kaldi toolkit (Povey et al., 2011) to prepare the TED-LIUM corpus, while Krizaj et al. (2022) introduced a toolkit for automatic validation based on criteria like audio quality and transcription accuracy. Automated pipelines have also been applied in domain-specific scenarios (Romanovskyi et al., 2021), audio-visual speech recognition (Ma et al., 2023), and multilingual ASR systems from parliamentary archives (Nouza and Safarik, 2017; Kulebi et al., 2022; Helgadóttir et al., 2017). In this work, we employ OpenAI's Whisper ASR model to automatically validate the data by comparing the automatic transcription to a reference, which may or may not accurately reflect the content of the speech recording.

1.1 Objectives

Mozilla Common Voice (Ardila et al., 2019) is a multilingual, crowdsourced dataset of voice recordings that are validated based on user votes. Recordings are labeled as "validated" if they receive at least two more positive votes than negative ones. Recordings rejected by the community are labeled as "invalidated," while those with inconclusive results are categorized as "other."

We focus on the "other" category in Common Voice 17.0 (CV17), using Whisper-based ASR to validate recordings by matching transcriptions with references, as done in similar efforts for Icelandic data (Hernández Mena et al., 2024).

We evaluated our method with NVIDIA's Parakeet architecture (Galvez et al., 2024), comparing models fine-tuned on original CV17 validated data ($\sim$500 hours) and our validated data ($\sim$784 hours), both achieving a Word Error Rate (WER) $< 5\%$. Combining both subsets ($\sim$1284 hours) further reduced WER. Our validated dataset and best-performing model are publicly available on Hugging Face.

1.2 Paper Organization

This paper is organized as follows: Section 2 presents the final version of *The Corpus* shared in this work. Section 3 details the *Validation Methodology* used to automatically verify the

Proceedings of the Third Workshop on Resources and Representations for Under-Resourced Languages and Domains (RESOURCEFUL-2025), pages 58–63, March 2, 2025 ©2025 Association for Computational Linguistics

CV17 speech recordings, which later became part of the corpus. In Section 4, we describe the development and fine-tuning of the *Acoustic Models* used to assess the effectiveness of the validation methodology. Finally, Section 5 concludes the paper with a summary of our contributions and suggestions for future work.

2 The Corpus

The corpus "Spanish Common Voice V17.0 Split Other Automatically Verified,"[1] as its name suggests, is the result of the automatic validation of the split called "other," which is part of the Spanish version of the Common Voice 17.0 corpus (CV17 for short). The corpus contains 784 hours and 50 minutes of audio across 581,680 recordings, surpassing the size of the "validated" category in CV17, which contains only 562 hours. Of these, 53 hours are allocated to the "test" and "dev" splits, while the remaining 509 hours belong to the "train" split. In comparison to the original CV17, our corpus contains only a single split called "other."

2.1 Audio Format

The audio files are distributed in the same format as the original CV17, with a sample rate of 48 kHz, a single channel, a bitrate of 64 kbps, and the MPEG-1 Layer 3 (MP3) codec.

2.2 Data Loader

In general, Hugging Face allows users to share datasets with others through dataset cards. A dataset card is a web page that contains the profile of the dataset. On this "web page," users can typically find documentation for the dataset, speech files, transcriptions, and metadata, as is the case with our corpus. Since the repository chosen to share our corpus is Hugging Face, the implications are that 1) the corpus has its own dataset card and, 2) the speech data can be accessed through the "datasets" Python library (Lhoest et al., 2021). In datasets, the object responsible for downloading the data from the dataset card, loading it into memory, and allowing Python to iterate over each recording in a for-loop is a "data loader." The data loader communicates with code executed by the Hugging Face website via the dataset card of the corpus. We programmed our data loader to download the data directly from the original CV17 repository, which means that our dataset card does not contain any audio files. The only information provided is a TSV file containing metadata for each recording in the corpus. Consequently, before downloading our corpus through the datasets library, it is important to agree to the terms and conditions shown on the dataset card for Mozilla Common Voice.[2]

2.3 Corpus Metadata

As explained in Section 2.2, the corpus metadata is contained in a TSV file that is stored in the dataset card. The information in the TSV was taken from the original CV17 with no changes; however, the rows in the TSV correspond only to the speech files validated by us. The columns of this TSV file are as follows: The `client_id` is a hexadecimal ID identifying the client (voice) that made the recording. The `path` field specifies the ID of the audio file followed by the extension ".mp3". The `sentence_id` is a hexadecimal ID of the speaker. The `sentence` field contains the sentence the user was prompted to speak. The `sentence_domain` indicates the context or scope to which the sentence belongs (this field is empty in all cases). The `up_votes` and `down_votes` fields represent the number of upvotes and downvotes, respectively, received by the audio file from reviewers. The `age` field denotes the age group of the speaker (e.g., teens, twenties, fifties), while the `gender` field specifies the speaker's gender (`male_masculine` or `female_feminine`). The `accents` field lists the speaker's accent(s) (e.g., España, México, Caribe, América Central), and the `variant` field refers to specific types of accents or pronunciation patterns associated with the speaker (this field is empty in all cases). The `locale` field indicates the locale of the speaker (the value is "es" in all cases). Finally, the `segment` field can either be empty or have the value "Benchmark."

3 Validation Methodology

Whisper (Radford et al., 2023) is one of the state-of-the-art multilingual speech recognition and translation models, available under the MIT license. It utilizes a Transformer-based architec-

[1] https://huggingface.co/datasets/projecte-aina/cv17_es_other_automatically_verified

[2] https://huggingface.co/datasets/mozilla-foundation/common_voice_17_0

ture with an encoder-decoder structure, trained via weak supervision on a massive dataset of multilingual speech (680 000 hours). The Whisper architecture supports both transcription and translation tasks.

As part of our validation methodology, we use OpenAI's Whisper to transcribe the speech recordings in the "other" category of CV17. If Whisper produces the same transcription as the reference, the recording is considered validated and added to the final corpus; otherwise, the recording is rejected. A total of 1,138,631 recordings were transcribed through this process, of which 581,680 (784 hours and 50 minutes) matched the reference transcription. This subset represents the total size of the corpus shared in this work. However, the reference transcriptions used in this process are not the original ones found in CV17 but have been normalized.

3.1 Normalization of the Transcripts

Reference transcriptions in CV17 include capitalization and punctuation. However, CV17 is used in experiments with a wide variety of ASR models and architectures, some of which do not accept punctuation marks as inputs. Additionally, we have detected that the Spanish portion of CV17 contains some characters not belonging to the Spanish alphabet (e.g., ä, ë, ô, ö). For this reason, the version of CV17 that we store is normalized as follows: 1) lowercase, 2) punctuation marks removed, and 3) letters not belonging to the Spanish alphabet are replaced with white spaces. In consequence, the same normalization is applied to the output transcriptions of Whisper during the validation process described in Section 3.

4 Acoustic Models

An indirect way to assess the correctness of our validation process is to evaluate how our validated recordings perform when training a real ASR model, as faulty data would hinder the production of a good acoustic model. For this purpose, we fine-tuned distinct models based on NVIDIA's Parakeet architecture, as described in Section 4.1.

It is important to note that, to the best of our knowledge, the official model (trained by NVIDIA) based on the specific Parakeet architecture we use in this work is only available in English; so, we chose this Parakeet architecture with the hope of making a meaningful contribution to the language technologies community.

4.1 NVIDIA's Parakeet

The Parakeet ASR models (Galvez et al., 2024), developed by NVIDIA as part of the NeMo framework (Kuchaiev et al., 2019), are state-of-the-art speech recognition systems offering high-accuracy English transcription. The Parakeet family includes four models: two with RNNT decoders and two with CTC decoders. This study employs the nvidia/parakeet-rnnt-1.1b model, ranked third on the Hugging Face speech recognition leaderboard.[3]

Built on the Fast Conformer architecture (Rekesh et al., 2023), an optimized version of the Conformer (Gulati et al., 2020), Parakeet features efficient downsampling, enhanced convolutional kernels, and local attention mechanisms. These improvements reduce memory use while enabling accurate transcription of audio segments up to 11 hours long (Koluguri et al., 2024).

4.2 Results

Table 1 shows WER and Character Error Rate (CER) results for models based on the "Parakeet RNNT 1.1B" architecture, evaluated on the "test" and "dev" splits of CV17. The "CV17 Validated" model was fine-tuned on user-validated CV17 data (~500 hours), the "CV17 Other" model on data validated by our methodology (~784 hours), and the "CV17 Combined" model on the combined dataset (~1284 hours).

All models were fine-tuned for 48 hours using NVIDIA H100 GPUs. The "CV17 Validated" and "CV17 Other" models used 12 GPUs each, while the "CV17 Combined" model used 32 GPUs. Checkpoint 17, corresponding to epoch 18, was selected for all models to ensure comparability.

Additionally, Table 1 shows results using the first version of OpenAI's Whisper and the latest version Whisper-large-v3. As can be seen, the official Whisper models tend to outperform the models "CV17 Validated" and "CV17 Other"; however, our "CV17 Combined"[4] model outperforms all other models in the table, demonstrating the effectiveness of our validation method.

[3]https://huggingface.co/spaces/hf-audio/open_asr_leaderboard

[4]https://huggingface.co/projecte-aina/parakeet-rnnt-1.1b_cv17_es_ep18_1270h

Model	Split	WER (%)	CER (%)
CV17 Validated	Test	5.13	1.69
	Dev	4.66	1.41
CV17 Other	Test	5.23	1.80
	Dev	4.85	1.53
CV17 Combined	Test	**3.93**	**1.29**
	Dev	**3.55**	**1.05**
OpenAI Whisper large	Test	4.97	1.81
	Dev	4.21	1.45
Whisper-large-v3	Test	5.15	1.84
	Dev	4.34	1.48

Table 1: Performance of the models trained with distinct subsets of Common Voice compared to the performance of two different versions of Whisper.

It is important to note that we distinguish between OpenAI's Whisper (sourced from GitHub) and Whisper-large-v3 (sourced from Hugging Face). In various experiments conducted for this and other studies, we have observed that the Whisper model available on GitHub and the Whisper model available on Hugging Face yield different results, even when they are the same size (tiny, base, small, etc.).

4.3 The Use of a Unique ASR System.

One potential criticism of this work is that we did not use multiple ASR systems for the validation process, as was done in the previously cited study by Hernández Mena et al. (2024). In that study, a recording was considered validated if at least one of their four ASR systems produced the same transcription as the reference, or a "perfect match" as they termed it. With this in mind, we can infer that involving additional ASR systems in our validation process would result in more validated recordings, though it would not invalidate those already verified by our single ASR system. Due to constraints in time and computational resources, we made the decision to use only one ASR system; however, we believe our results remain valid and valuable under the current experimental conditions.

4.4 The Use of Normalized Transcriptions

Another aspect worth discussing is the normalization of the transcripts. Given that the original CV17 references include punctuation and capitalization, and Whisper is capable of generating transcriptions with those same features, why not compare the transcripts without normalization? The answer lies partly in Section 3.1, where we explain that our laboratory experiment with a wide variety of ASR systems. Ultimately, we seek data that is compatible with both current and future experiments, adaptable to the latest technology as well as systems that have already proven reliable. In this regard, normalized transcriptions enable compatibility with a broader spectrum of ASR systems, many of which are not designed to handle punctuation, as is the case of Parakeet.

4.5 Performance of Acoustic Models

Results in Table 1 demonstrate the Whisper's impressive performance, as it outperforms two out of the three models we developed for this study. This reinforces the capability of Whisper to handle diverse datasets effectively, a result likely tied to the extensive training hours and resources invested in its development. Whisper's robustness in handling varied linguistic inputs, coupled with its high accuracy across CV17's "test" and "dev" splits, highlights its value as a benchmark model in automatic validation processes.

However, our best model, "CV17 Combined," achieves lower WER and CER than Whisper, suggesting that our validation method successfully curated a high-quality dataset for Spanish ASR. Although Whisper's performance is consistent with expectations given its extensive training set, and it was likely trained on a version of Mozilla Common Voice in Spanish that may introduce a bias enhancing its transcription accuracy on our test data, our results demonstrate that a carefully validated, language-specific corpus can yield models that not only compete closely with but even surpass larger-scale models.

These findings underscore the importance of targeted, language-specific model training, even in an era where large-scale, multilingual models dominate ASR.

5 Conclusions and Further Work

Crowdsourcing platforms are vital for ASR development, offering affordable and diverse data collection. However, manual validation limits their efficiency. This study demonstrated the potential of automatic validation for the Spanish subset of Common Voice 17.0 (CV17) using a Whisper-based ASR system. Our best Parakeet model trained with the extended dataset, "CV17 Combined", outperformed both OpenAI's Whisper and Whisper-large-v3, showcasing the benefits of automated validation. Future work could explore applying this approach to other datasets (e.g., Voxforge[5]) and languages, especially low-resource ones, which could gain significantly from automated dataset expansion despite potential model performance challenges.

Acknowledgments

This work is funded by the Ministerio para la Transformación Digital y de la Función Pública and Plan de Recuperación, Transformación y Resiliencia - Funded by EU – NextGenerationEU within the framework of the project ILENIA with reference 2022/TL22/00215337.

References

Rosana Ardila, Megan Branson, Kelly Davis, Michael Henretty, Michael Kohler, Josh Meyer, Reuben Morais, Lindsay Saunders, Francis M Tyers, and Gregor Weber. 2019. Common voice: A massively-multilingual speech corpus. *arXiv preprint arXiv:1912.06670*.

Daniel Galvez, Vladimir Bataev, Hainan Xu, and Tim Kaldewey. 2024. Speed of light exact greedy decoding for rnn-t speech recognition models on gpu. *arXiv preprint arXiv:2406.03791*.

Anmol Gulati, James Qin, Chung-Cheng Chiu, Niki Parmar, Yu Zhang, Jiahui Yu, Wei Han, Shibo Wang, Zhengdong Zhang, Yonghui Wu, et al. 2020. Conformer: Convolution-augmented transformer for speech recognition. *arXiv preprint arXiv:2005.08100*.

Inga Rún Helgadóttir, Róbert Kjaran, Anna Björk Nikulásdóttir, and Jón Gudnason. 2017. Building an asr corpus using althingi's parliamentary speeches. In *Interspeech*, pages 2163–2167.

François Hernandez, Vincent Nguyen, Sahar Ghannay, Natalia Tomashenko, and Yannick Esteve. 2018. Ted-lium 3: Twice as much data and corpus repartition for experiments on speaker adaptation. In *Speech and Computer: 20th International Conference, SPECOM 2018, Leipzig, Germany, September 18–22, 2018, Proceedings 20*, pages 198–208. Springer.

Carlos Daniel Hernández Mena, Thorsteinn Dadi Gunnarsson, and Jón Gudnason. 2024. Samrómur milljón: An asr corpus of one million verified read prompts in icelandic. In *Proceedings of the 2024 Joint International Conference on Computational Linguistics, Language Resources and Evaluation (LREC-COLING 2024)*, pages 14305–14312.

Nithin Rao Koluguri, Samuel Kriman, Georgy Zelenfroind, Somshubra Majumdar, Dima Rekesh, Vahid Noroozi, Jagadeesh Balam, and Boris Ginsburg. 2024. Investigating end-to-end asr architectures for long form audio transcription. In *ICASSP 2024-2024 IEEE International Conference on Acoustics, Speech and Signal Processing (ICASSP)*, pages 13366–13370. IEEE.

Janez Krizaj, Jerneja Zganec Gros, and Simon Dobrisek. 2022. Validation of speech data for training automatic speech recognition systems. In *2022 30th European Signal Processing Conference (EUSIPCO)*, pages 1165–1169. IEEE.

Oleksii Kuchaiev, Jason Li, Huyen Nguyen, Oleksii Hrinchuk, Ryan Leary, Boris Ginsburg, Samuel Kriman, Stanislav Beliaev, Vitaly Lavrukhin, Jack Cook, et al. 2019. Nemo: a toolkit for building ai applications using neural modules. *arXiv preprint arXiv:1909.09577*.

Baybars Kulebi, Carme Armentano-Oller, Carlos Rodríguez-Penagos, and Marta Villegas. 2022. Parlamentparla: A speech corpus of catalan parliamentary sessions. In *Proceedings of the Workshop ParlaCLARIN III within the 13th Language Resources and Evaluation Conference*, pages 125–130.

Quentin Lhoest, Albert Villanova Del Moral, Yacine Jernite, Abhishek Thakur, Patrick Von Platen, Suraj Patil, Julien Chaumond, Mariama Drame, Julien Plu, Lewis Tunstall, et al. 2021. Datasets: A community library for natural language processing. *arXiv preprint arXiv:2109.02846*.

Pingchuan Ma, Alexandros Haliassos, Adriana Fernandez-Lopez, Honglie Chen, Stavros Petridis, and Maja Pantic. 2023. Auto-avsr: Audio-visual speech recognition with automatic labels. In *ICASSP 2023-2023 IEEE International Conference on Acoustics, Speech and Signal Processing (ICASSP)*, pages 1–5. IEEE.

Jan Nouza and Radek Safarik. 2017. Parliament archives used for automatic training of multi-lingual automatic speech recognition systems. In *Text, Speech, and Dialogue: 20th International Conference, TSD 2017, Prague, Czech Republic, August 27-31, 2017, Proceedings 20*, pages 174–182. Springer.

Daniel Povey, Arnab Ghoshal, Gilles Boulianne, Lukas Burget, Ondrej Glembek, Nagendra Goel, Mirko Hannemann, Petr Motlicek, Yanmin Qian, Petr Schwarz, et al. 2011. The kaldi speech recognition toolkit. In *IEEE 2011 workshop on automatic speech recognition and understanding*. IEEE Signal Processing Society.

Alec Radford, Jong Wook Kim, Tao Xu, Greg Brockman, Christine McLeavey, and Ilya Sutskever. 2023.

[5] `https://www.voxforge.org/`

Robust speech recognition via large-scale weak supervision. In *International conference on machine learning*, pages 28492–28518. PMLR.

Dima Rekesh, Nithin Rao Koluguri, Samuel Kriman, Somshubra Majumdar, Vahid Noroozi, He Huang, Oleksii Hrinchuk, Krishna Puvvada, Ankur Kumar, Jagadeesh Balam, et al. 2023. Fast conformer with linearly scalable attention for efficient speech recognition. In *2023 IEEE Automatic Speech Recognition and Understanding Workshop (ASRU)*, pages 1–8. IEEE.

O Romanovskyi, I Iosifov, O Iosifova, V Sokolov, F Kipchuk, and I Sukaylo. 2021. Automated pipeline for training dataset creation from unlabeled audios for automatic speech recognition. In *International Conference on Computer Science, Engineering and Education Applications*, pages 25–36. Springer.

WikiQA-IS: Assisted Benchmark Generation and Automated Evaluation of Icelandic Cultural Knowledge in LLMs

Þórunn Arnardóttir
Miðeind
thorunn@mideind.is

Elías Bjartur Einarsson
Miðeind
elias@mideind.is

Garðar Ingvarsson Juto
Miðeind
gardar@mideind.is

Þorvaldur Páll Helgason
Miðeind
thorvaldur@mideind.is

Hafsteinn Einarsson
University of Iceland
hafsteinne@hi.is

Abstract

This paper presents WikiQA-IS, a novel question-answering dataset focusing on Icelandic culture and history, along with an automated pipeline for dataset generation and evaluation. Leveraging GPT-4 to create questions and answers based on Icelandic Wikipedia articles and news sources, we produced a high-quality corpus of 2,000 question-answer pairs. We introduce an automatic evaluation method using GPT-4o as a judge, which shows strong agreement with human evaluations. Our benchmark reveals varying performances across different language models, with closed-source models generally outperforming open-weights alternatives. This work contributes a resource for evaluating language models' knowledge of Icelandic culture and offers a replicable framework for creating similar datasets in other cultural contexts.

1 Introduction

Recent advancements in natural language processing (NLP) have led to significant improvements in question-answering systems, particularly through large language models (LLMs) (Brown, 2020). While these models show impressive capabilities, they can generate incorrect or fabricated information, a phenomenon known as hallucination (Bender et al., 2021; Huang et al., 2024). This makes it crucial to systematically measure how much factual knowledge these models actually possess about specific domains, such as individual cultures or topics. Current evaluation methods often lack domain-specific benchmarks, making it difficult to assess models' true understanding of particular cultural contexts. This paper presents an automated approach to generate and evaluate questions and answers, using Icelandic culture and history as a case study.

Icelandic, despite its small speaker base, has a rich literary and historical heritage. However, creating comprehensive QA datasets for such domains is resource-intensive if done manually. While prior work on Icelandic QA datasets has focused on language and reading comprehension (Snæbjarnarson and Einarsson, 2022b; Skarphedinsson et al., 2023; Snæbjarnarson and Einarsson, 2022a; Geirsson, 2013; De Bruyn et al., 2021), there remains a need for a dataset testing knowledge of culture and history in an open-ended fashion.

Our research introduces a method leveraging an LLM to automate the generation of high-quality questions and answers based on Icelandic Wikipedia articles, inspired by previous work extracting knowledge from Wikipedia (Yang et al., 2015; Auer et al., 2007) and work on automatic QA dataset creation (Lewis et al., 2019). This approach addresses the challenge of creating large-scale datasets for low-resource languages and extends the application of language models to cultural and historical knowledge evaluation.

The main contribution of this paper is the WikiQA-IS corpus[1] along with the pipeline used to generate the corpus and the automatic evaluation approach[2]. This research not only contributes to create benchmarks focusing on Icelandic cultural knowledge but also offers a replicable framework adaptable to other languages and cultural contexts.

[1] Dataset released under a CC BY license: https://repository.clarin.is/repository/xmlui/handle/20.500.12537/347

[2] Code: https://github.com/icelandic-lt/AutomaticQAPipeline and https://github.com/mideind/lm-evaluation-harness/blob/add-icelandic-evals/lm_eval/tasks/icelandic_qa/icelandic_wiki_qa.yaml

Proceedings of the Third Workshop on Resources and Representations for Under-Resourced Languages and Domains (RESOURCEFUL-2025), pages 64–73, March 2, 2025 ©2025 Association for Computational Linguistics

2 Methods

2.1 Dataset Preparation

The questions in this work are based on the Icelandic Wikipedia and on the news from RÚV in the Icelandic Gigaword corpus (Steingrímsson et al., 2018). From Wikipedia, the 41,569 articles that contained at least 250 characters were used, and from the RÚV news, because the data is extensive, only a portion of articles that contained at least 500 characters were used. For each page used in a given source, we kept track of the "url", "title" and "text" as fields in a JSONL file. The text field serves as the basis for question generation.

2.2 Question Generation Pipeline

2.2.1 Document to Request Conversion

We first convert the documents into requests suitable for the GPT model. This process involves creating a JSON object for each document, which includes a system prompt and a user prompt, both in Icelandic. The system prompt is: *Þú ert vandvirk aðstoðarmanneskja* which translates to *You are a meticulous assistant.*

The complete prompt structure pairs document text with an instruction component that guides the model in generating questions and performing dual evaluations: it must score both the quality and relevance of each generated question and assess the document's connection to Icelandic culture and history, using a scale from 0 to 1 for both metrics. These scores enable automatic filtering of questions and documents that would likely be rejected by human annotators. The instruction component underwent several rounds of refinement until it reliably produced high-quality questions from the input texts, and is provided below in both Icelandic and English.

```
Semdu almenna spurningu upp úr
 ↪ þessu skjali og svaraðu
 ↪ henni ef skjalið fjallar að
 ↪ einhverju leyti um íslenska
 ↪ menningu og/eða íslenska
 ↪ sögu.
Spurningin á að vera um innihald
 ↪ skjalsins, ekki skjalið
 ↪ sjálft. Ekki vísa í skjalið
 ↪ í spurningunni.
Hafðu svarið eins hnitmiðað og
 ↪ hægt er.
Ef spurning og/eða svar vísar
 ↪ til tíma þarf sá tími eða
 ↪ ártal að vera tekið fram í
 ↪ bæði spurningu og svari.
Spurning og/eða svar má ekki
 ↪ vísa til hluta sem eru
 ↪ núverandi, heldur þarf
 ↪ tímasetning að vera til
 ↪ staðar.
Skilaðu niðurstöðunni á
 ↪ eftirfarandi json sniði:

{"question": [question],
 ↪ "answer": [answer], "id":
 ↪ [doc["url"] OR
 ↪ doc["xml_id"]],
 ↪ "question_score": [score
 ↪ 0.0-1.0], "document_score":
 ↪ [score 0.0-1.0], "source":
 ↪ [doc["source"]]}

Spurningin á að vera almenn og
 ↪ tengjast íslenskri menningu
 ↪ og/eða íslenskri sögu.
 ↪ "question_score" á að meta
 ↪ hversu mikið spurning
 ↪ tengist íslenskri menningu
 ↪ og/eða íslenskri sögu og
 ↪ hversu góð og almenn hún er
 ↪ en "document_score" á að
 ↪ meta hversu gott skjalið er
 ↪ og hversu mikið það tengist
 ↪ íslenskri menningu og/eða
 ↪ íslenskri sögu.
Ef skjalið er stutt, slæmt eða
 ↪ ekki er hægt að skapa
 ↪ spurningu upp úr skjalinu,
 ↪ skilaðu þá sama json sniði
 ↪ með engu innihaldi fyrir
 ↪ "question" og "answer".
Ef skjalið fjallar ekki um
 ↪ íslenska menningu eða
 ↪ íslenska sögu, skilaðu þá
 ↪ sama json sniði með engu
 ↪ innihaldi fyrir "question"
 ↪ og "answer".
```

An English translation of the prompt is given below.

```
Generate a general question from this document and answer it if the document relates in any way to Icelandic culture and/or Icelandic history.
The question should be about the content of the document, not the document itself. Don't reference the document in the question.
Keep the answer as concise as possible.
If the question and/or answer refers to time, that time or year must be specified in both question and answer.
Question and/or answer must not refer to current things, rather a timestamp must be present.
Return the result in the following json format:

{"question": [question], "answer": [answer], "id": [doc["url"] OR doc["xml_id"]], "question_score": [score 0.0-1.0], "document_score": [score 0.0-1.0], "source": [doc["source"]]}

The question should be general and relate to Icelandic culture and/or Icelandic history. "question_score" should evaluate how much the question relates to Icelandic culture and/or Icelandic history and how good and general it is, while "document_score" should evaluate how good the document is and how much it relates to Icelandic culture and/or Icelandic history.
If the document is short, poor, or it's not possible to create a question from the document, then return the same json format with no content for "question" and "answer".
If the document does not discuss Icelandic culture or Icelandic history, then return the same json format with no content for "question" and "answer".
```

Note that if the document is inadequate or unrelated to Icelandic culture/history, an empty response should be returned in the same JSON format.

2.2.2 API Calls to GPT

We make API calls to OpenAI's `gpt-4-turbo` model using the prepared requests. The model generates questions, answers, and scores based on the input documents.

2.2.3 Filtering Generated Questions

The generated questions and answers are filtered based on the scores provided by the LLM. We selected only questions that had both a document score of at least 0.7 and a question score of at least 0.7. Note that these thresholds were chosen based on intuition after inspecting the documents and questions. We discarded 29,450 questions created from the 41,569 Wikipedia articles through this approach, meaning that 29% of the automatically created questions were deemed adequate. For the RÚV news data, 5,350 questions, created from 6,672 articles, were discarded, which means that 20% of questions were adequate. The difference in adequacy can be explained by the fact that the question and document had to relate to Icelandic culture and/or history. The question-answer pairs that were not discarded were then eligible for manual question-answer pair review (see below), but note that not all pairs were manually reviewed.

2.2.4 Spelling and Grammar Correction

While `gpt-4-turbo` demonstrates strong comprehension of Icelandic, its generative capabilities in the language exhibit some limitations. The model produces generally intelligible output, but frequently requires grammatical corrections, particularly in terms of nominal inflection, which is a crucial feature of Icelandic morphology[3].

We use a Byte-Level Neural Error Correction Model for Icelandic to correct spelling and grammar in the generated questions and answers (Ingólfsdóttir et al., 2023). During this process, 26.49% of questions were corrected and 41.99% of answers.

2.2.5 Dataset Format

The dataset is available in different formats compatible with BIG-bench (Srivastava et al., 2022), OpenAI-evals and the Language Model Evaluation Harness (Gao et al., 2023).

2.3 Manual Question-Answer Pair Review

Question-answer pairs generated with the pipeline were reviewed by a single human annotator, a native speaker of Icelandic with a B.A. degree in general linguistics. Due to time restraints, only a portion of the generated question-answer pairs were manually reviewed. All pairs are, however, published as part of the dataset. In this process, the annotator had access to the context used to generate the question-answer pair. The annotator was instructed to work based on the following annotation guidelines and to discard or improve questions and answers if they did not meet some of these points. As a result, the majority of question-answer pairs were manually corrected so that they met the points in the guidelines.

- Questions and answers must be in Icelandic.
- Questions and answers must relate to Icelandic culture and/or history.
- A question can only include one question, and the answer must answer that question unambiguously and contain no information beyond that.
- A question and answer cannot include any spelling or grammar errors, and the text must be natural.

2.4 Automatic Evaluation

To evaluate the performance of language models on our dataset, we employed an automated evaluation process using `gpt-4o-2024-08-06` as a judge model. This process involves presenting the model under evaluation with a question, collecting its generated answer, and then providing the question, generated answer, and correct answer to the judge model for assessment. The judge model evaluates the correctness and relevance of the generated answer, providing a rating of "poor" (0 points), "fair" (0.5 points), or "excellent" (1 point). The instructions for the LLM are given below:

```
Please act as an impartial judge
 ↪ and evaluate the quality of
 ↪ the response provided by an
 ↪ AI assistant to the user
 ↪ question displayed below.
 ↪ Your evaluation should
 ↪ consider correctness. You
 ↪ will be given the question
 ↪ which was asked, a correct
 ↪ reference answer, and the
 ↪ assistant's answer. Begin
 ↪ your evaluation by briefly
 ↪ comparing the assistant's
 ↪ answer with the correct
 ↪ answer. Identify any
 ↪ mistakes. Be as objective as
 ↪ possible. Additional
 ↪ information beyond the
 ↪ reference answer's content
 ↪ should not be considered. If
 ↪ the assistant's answer is
 ↪ not in Icelandic but the
 ↪ reference answer is, you
 ↪ should rate the answer
 ↪ poorly. After providing your
 ↪ short explanation, you must
 ↪ rate the assistant's answer
 ↪ using the following scale:
 ↪ [[poor]]: Incorrect,
 ↪ off-topic or in a different
 ↪ language; [[fair]]:
 ↪ Partially aligns with the
 ↪ reference answer with some
 ↪ inaccuracies or irrelevant
 ↪ information; [[excellent]]:
 ↪ Accurate and relevant,
 ↪ matching the reference
 ↪ answer in content and
 ↪ language.
```

[3]The current ranking of models on the Icelandic inflection benchmark is shown on the Icelandic LLM leaderboard

2.5 Manual Evaluation

To validate the performance of the automatic evaluation process, three annotators also perform manual evaluation. In the manual evaluation phase, a human annotator receives the question and compares the generated answer to the reference answer. The human annotator is tasked with providing a rating of "poor" (0 points), "fair" (0.5 points), or "excellent" (1 point) and receives the same instructions as the LLM. We compute the agreement between the annotators and the LLM as a judge using Cohen's Kappa (Cohen, 1960).

2.6 Question Classification

We used `gpt-4o-2024-08-06` to classify the questions into five classes we considered to be representative of the majority of questions in the dataset. The prompt is given below and we used structured output so the model could only respond with one of the five given categories.

```
Categorize the question (written
↪ in Icelandic) based on the
↪ type of question it is. The
↪ question types are 'time'
↪ for questions that ask about
↪ the time of something,
↪ 'place' if they as for a
↪ place, 'people' if they ask
↪ about a person, 'object' if
↪ they ask about an object or
↪ a non-person entity. If the
↪ question does not fit any of
↪ these categories, respond
↪ with 'other'.
```

An annotator was tasked with evaluating whether the categorization was correct or not. They received instructions stating how the questions were categorized, along with the prompt, and were asked to judge whether the categorization was correct or not for 200 questions chosen uniformly at random.

3 Results

3.1 Dataset Generation and Curation

Our data generation and curation process produced a dataset of high-quality question-answer pairs focusing on Icelandic culture and history. The automatically generated pairs were reviewed to ensure their quality and relevance.

For the Wikipedia-based dataset, we examined 2,116 question-answer pairs, ultimately including 1,900 in the final set. This high retention rate of 89.8% demonstrates the effectiveness of our automated generation process. In contrast, the IGC-RÚV (Icelandic Gigaword Corpus – RÚV) dataset yielded a lower retention rate. Out of 274 reviewed pairs, only 100 met our inclusion criteria, resulting in a 36.5% retention rate. The observed difference can be attributed to the distinct focus of each corpus: while the RÚV corpus consists primarily of contemporary news content, the Wikipedia corpus contains a higher proportion of articles dedicated to Icelandic culture and history.

It is worth noting that most retained pairs required some level of correction. These ranged from minor spelling adjustments missed by our automatic correction tool to more substantial revisions of questions and answers based on the source documents. This manual refinement process was crucial in ensuring the dataset's overall quality, naturalness and accuracy. For the resulting dataset, the questions varied in length ranging from 15 to 210 characters and the answers varied from 2 to 233 characters. The distributions of question and answer lengths are shown in Figure 1.

3.2 Evaluation of Automatic Evaluation

To assess the reliability of our automatic evaluation method, we conducted a human evaluation study. Our automatic evaluation uses GPT-4o as a judge to evaluate responses from other LLMs, categorizing them as "Excellent", "Fair", or "Poor". To validate this approach, we sampled 100 responses each from `gpt-4o-2024-08-06` and `claude-3-5-sonnet-20240620`, that were then evaluated manually as described in Section 2.5. Tables 1 and 2 present the confusion matrices for GPT-4o and Claude 3.5 Sonnet, respectively.

The results demonstrate high agreement between our automatic evaluation method and human judgments. For GPT-4o judging GPT-4o responses, we observed an a Cohen's kappa score with human annotators ranging from 0.81 to 0.91. The evaluation of GPT-4o judging Claude 3.5 Sonnet responses showed slightly lower agreement but still strong agreement with Cohen's kappa ranging from 0.75 to 0.82. These results suggest that our judge based on GPT-4o provides a robust and effi-

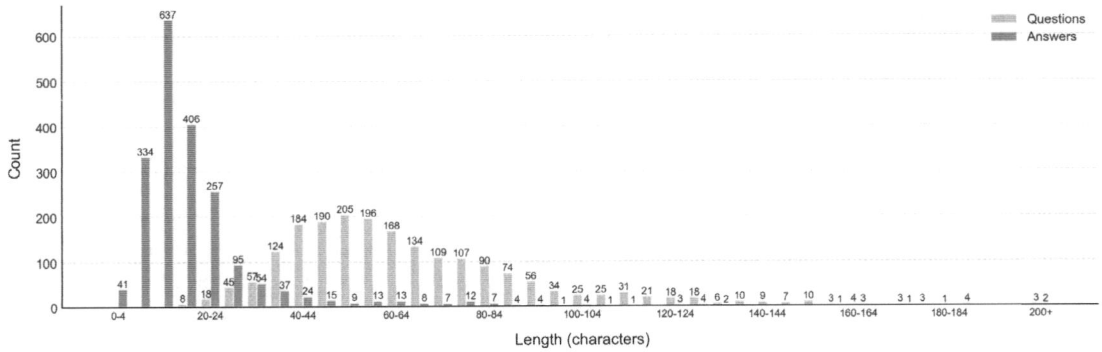

Figure 1: Distribution of question and answer lengths.

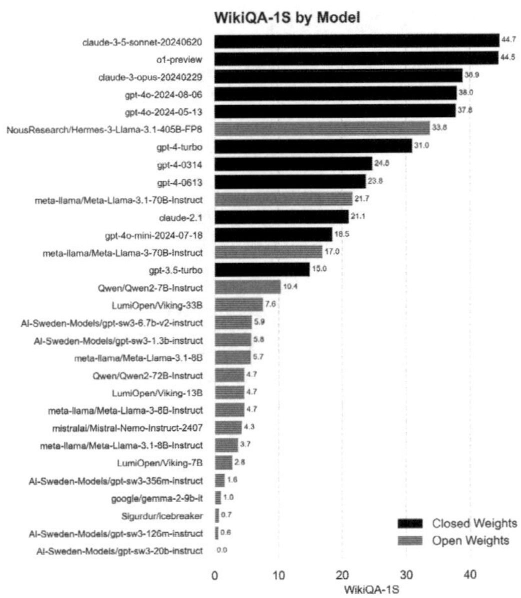

Figure 2: Performance comparison of various models on the WikiQA-IS dataset. The plot illustrates the accuracy of different models, with black bars representing closed weight models and gray bars representing open weight models.

cient means of evaluating LLM responses, closely aligning with human judgments.

In an effort to reveal systemic biases in the evaluation, we manually inspected the few examples where human and GPT-4o annotations differed. We see that in almost all cases where a human rated an answer higher than GPT-4o, the answer was either partially or fully correct, but contained some additional information which the LLM judge penalized it for more severely than the human. We also notice an opposite trend where in half of the cases where GPT-4o scored an answer as "fair" but a human as "poor", the answer was factually correct but required more domain knowledge to verify than the human could be expected to infer from the reference answer. This suggests that GPT-4o might be biased towards rewarding answers that align with its own factual knowledge, instead of comparing the answer against the reference answer in isolation. The LLM judge, however, never awarded an answer with the "excellent" score if it did not semantically match the reference answer, even when it was factually correct, indicating that this slight bias has limited impact.

3.3 LLM Performance

Figure 2 presents the performance of various language models on the WikiQA-IS benchmark. The results demonstrate a clear performance hierarchy among the evaluated models. The top-performing models are predominantly large, closed-source language models developed by major AI research companies. `Claude-3.5-sonnet-20240620` and `o1-preview` achieve the highest scores of 44.7 and 44.5, respectively, closely followed by `claude-3-opus-20240229` with 38.9. The GPT-4o variants also perform well, scoring 38.0 and 37.8, respectively.

Among the open-weights models, Llama 3.1 (405B) (Dubey et al., 2024) stands out with a score of 33.8, demonstrating competitive performance with some of the closed-weights models. This suggests that well-trained open-weights models can approach the capabilities of proprietary models in specialized tasks like answering questions about Icelandic culture and history.

There is a noticeable performance gap between

the top-tier models and the rest of the field. Models such as GPT-4 variants show moderate performance, with scores ranging from 23.8 to 31.0. The performance then drops significantly for smaller models and earlier versions, with scores falling below 20 for models like Llama 3.1 (70B) and `claude-2.1`.

Open-weights models generally perform less well than their closed-source counterparts, with most scoring below 10 on the WikiQA-IS benchmark. However, there is significant variation among open-weights models, with some (like the top Llama models) performing much better than others. We specifically chose to include models from AI-Sweden (Ekgren et al., 2022) as they were amongst the only models trained specifically for Nordic languages at the time of the evaluation.

	Human Rating		
Judge Rating	Poor	Fair	Excellent
Poor	117	3	0
Fair	3	39	21
Excellent	0	0	117

Table 1: Agreement between three human annotators and GPT-4o judge for responses generated by GPT-4o.

	Human Rating		
Judge Rating	Poor	Fair	Excellent
Poor	79	5	0
Fair	7	15	12
Excellent	1	1	80

Table 2: Agreement between two human annotators and GPT-4o judge for responses generated by Claude 3.5 Sonnet

3.4 Question Difficulty Analysis

The analysis of model performance across questions revealed substantial variation in question difficulty (Figure 3). Most notably, 761 questions (roughly 38% of the dataset) received no "Excellent" rated responses from any of the 30 models tested, indicating that these questions were particularly challenging. The distribution of high-quality responses shows a rapid decline, with progressively fewer questions receiving multiple "Excellent" rated responses. Only a small subset of questions were answered excellently by more than 7 models, suggesting that most models tested struggle with consistent high-quality performance on questions related to Icelandic culture and history.

The gap between questions receiving "Excellent" rated responses and those receiving either "Fair" or "Excellent" rated responses remains relatively constant across the distribution, indicating that for most questions, several models typically provided "Fair" rather than "Excellent" responses. This pattern suggests that while models often capture some relevant information, they frequently include unnecessary details or minor inaccuracies in their responses. The rapid decline in both distributions also highlights that achieving a majority consensus among models on correct answers is rare, pointing to the continuing challenges in providing factful responses in this domain. 761 questions received no "Excellent" ratings, while 488 questions garnered neither "Excellent" nor "Fair" ratings. These findings indicate that a substantial portion of our dataset consists of questions that pose significant challenges for LLMs. To further investigate the nature of these challenging questions, we employed an LLM to systematically categorize each question into one of five types (object, people, place, time, and other). An annotator manually reviewed 200 questions to estimate the performance of this categorization and they were judged to be appropriate in 95.5% of cases. The confusion occurred where the category "other" should have been used instead of "object".

Table 3 presents a comparative distribution of these question types, contrasting the overall dataset with the subset of questions that no LLM could answer correctly. We observe that among the most difficult questions for LLMs, nearly half (48.05%) pertain to people or individuals, a marked increase from the 34.74% in the overall dataset. This disparity reflects the hallucination tendency of LLMs (Kalai and Vempala, 2024) since the names in the questions and the facts asked about rarely appear in the pretraining data.

4 Discussion

Our study demonstrates the effectiveness of leveraging LLMs for creating specialized question-answering datasets. The significant difference in retention rates between Wikipedia-based questions (89.8%) and news articles (36.5%) underscores the importance of source material selection

Question Set	People	Time	Object	Place	Other
All Questions	660 (34.7%)	576 (30.3%)	310 (16.3%)	229 (12.1%)	125 (6.6%)
Difficult Questions	234 (48.0%)	136 (27.9%)	53 (10.9%)	55 (11.3%)	10 (2.0%)

Table 3: Distribution of question types.

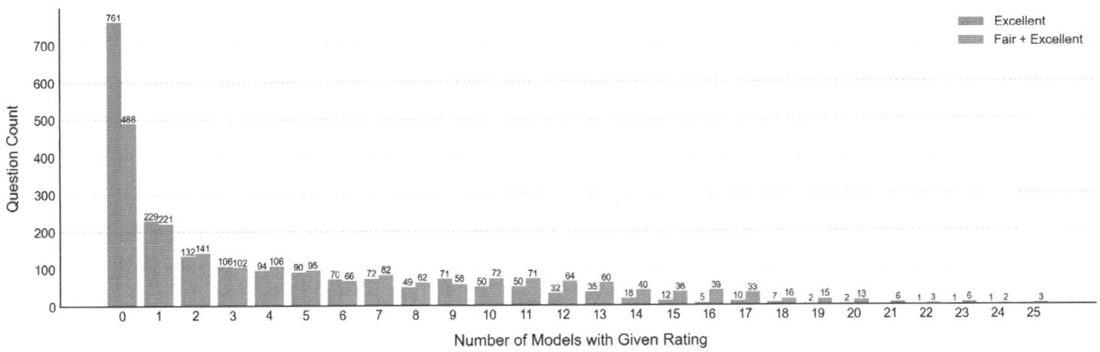

Figure 3: Distribution of question difficulty based on large language model performance. The histogram shows how many questions (y-axis) received a specific number of high-quality responses (x-axis). The blue bars represent questions receiving "Excellent" rated responses from LLMs, while the orange bars show questions receiving either "Fair" or "Excellent" rated responses. 488 questions received zero combined "Fair" or "Excellent" rated responses, indicating these questions were particularly challenging.

in QA dataset creation.

The performance analysis reveals a clear hierarchy among models, with closed-source models generally outperforming open-weights alternatives. This gap highlights ongoing challenges in democratizing advanced language understanding capabilities for specialized domains. Our automatic evaluation method shows promise for efficient, large-scale assessment, though it may be influenced by the judge model's capabilities and biases.

Future work could explore expanding source materials to reduce potential biases, and develop more comprehensive categorization of questions to uncover specific areas of model strength and weakness. While our method provides valuable insights into models' cultural knowledge, it represents just one facet of measuring world knowledge, and complementary approaches could offer a more holistic assessment of cultural understanding.

Ethics Statement

Experiments were conducted via OpenAI's API services, Anthropic's API services and on a local machine with eight A100 GPUs. While the exact computational infrastructure is not publicly disclosed, we estimate the carbon footprint based on the assumption that computation was performed in Microsoft Azure datacenters in Western Europe, with an estimated grid carbon intensity of 0.57 $kgCO_2eq/kWh$. Given OpenAI's non-disclosure of infrastructure details, we estimate that the experiments consumed in the order of 10 GPU hours, presumably on NVIDIA A100 PCIe 40/80GB GPUs with a Thermal Design Power of 250W.

The total estimated emissions for 10 GPU hours amount to 1.4 $kgCO_2eq$. For context, these emissions are equivalent to driving approximately 5.7 kilometers in a conventional internal combustion engine vehicle. We also note that OpenAI's infrastructure runs on Azure, and Azure will be running on 100% renewable energy by 2025 and has been carbon neutral since 2012[4].

We similarly estimate conservatively that answer generation and evaluation of other models is at most 20 GPU hours amounting to at most 2.8 $kgCO_2eq$.

Estimations were conducted using the Machine-Learning Impact calculator presented in (Lacoste et al., 2019).

[4]See more information on Azure's sustainability page.

Limitations

While our approach demonstrates promising results in creating and evaluating culturally-specific QA datasets, several limitations should be acknowledged. First, our reliance on Wikipedia and RÚV news articles as source material may introduce coverage biases. These sources, while authoritative, may not fully represent the breadth of Icelandic cultural knowledge, particularly oral traditions, contemporary cultural developments, or specialized academic research not covered in these venues.

The use of GPT-4 Turbo for question generation, while efficient, may introduce systematic biases in question formulation and potentially limit the diversity of question types. Although our manual review process helps mitigate these issues, it may not completely eliminate them. Using GPT-4 Turbo also introduces limitations on using the generated dataset based on OpenAI's terms of use,[5] particularly the clause on using output to develop models that compete with OpenAI. The generated dataset is published under a CC BY license but as its intended use is for benchmarking, we do not consider its publication to violate the terms of use.

Our automated evaluation method, despite showing strong correlation with human judgments, relies on large language models as judges, which may perpetuate certain biases or limitations inherent to these systems. The nature of our scoring system (poor/fair/excellent) may not fully capture nuanced differences in answer quality, particularly for questions about cultural interpretations or historical perspectives where multiple valid viewpoints might exist.

Finally, while our dataset size of 2,000 questions is substantial for a language with limited resources like Icelandic, it may not be comprehensive enough to fully evaluate an LLM's knowledge of Icelandic culture and history. The current version of the dataset also lacks explicit categorization of different aspects of cultural knowledge (e.g., literature, folklore, social customs), which could provide more granular insights into model performance across different cultural domains.

Acknowledgments

Þórunn and Elías were supported by the Icelandic Language Technology Programme and Garðar was supported by the European Commission under grant agreement no. 101135671. We thank the reviewers for their constructive feedback that helped us improve the manuscript.

[5] `https://openai.com/policies/terms-of-use/`

References

Sören Auer, Christian Bizer, Georgi Kobilarov, Jens Lehmann, Richard Cyganiak, and Zachary Ives. 2007. Dbpedia: A nucleus for a web of open data. In *international semantic web conference*, pages 722–735. Springer.

Emily M Bender, Timnit Gebru, Angelina McMillan-Major, and Shmargaret Shmitchell. 2021. On the dangers of stochastic parrots: Can language models be too big? In *Proceedings of the 2021 ACM conference on fairness, accountability, and transparency*, pages 610–623.

Tom B Brown. 2020. Language models are few-shot learners. *arXiv preprint arXiv:2005.14165*.

Jacob Cohen. 1960. A coefficient of agreement for nominal scales. *Educational and psychological measurement*, 20(1):37–46.

Maxime De Bruyn, Ehsan Lotfi, Jeska Buhmann, and Walter Daelemans. 2021. MFAQ: a multilingual FAQ dataset. In *Proceedings of the 3rd Workshop on Machine Reading for Question Answering*, pages 1–13, Punta Cana, Dominican Republic. Association for Computational Linguistics.

Abhimanyu Dubey, Abhinav Jauhri, Abhinav Pandey, Abhishek Kadian, Ahmad Al-Dahle, Aiesha Letman, Akhil Mathur, Alan Schelten, Amy Yang, Angela Fan, et al. 2024. The llama 3 herd of models. *arXiv preprint arXiv:2407.21783*.

Ariel Ekgren, Amaru Cuba Gyllensten, Evangelia Gogoulou, Alice Heiman, Severine Verlinden, Joey Öhman, Fredrik Carlsson, and Magnus Sahlgren. 2022. Lessons learned from GPT-SW3: Building the first large-scale generative language model for Swedish. In *Proceedings of the Thirteenth Language Resources and Evaluation Conference*, pages 3509–3518, Marseille, France. European Language Resources Association.

Leo Gao, Jonathan Tow, Baber Abbasi, Stella Biderman, Sid Black, Anthony DiPofi, Charles Foster, Laurence Golding, Jeffrey Hsu, Alain Le Noac'h, Haonan Li, Kyle McDonell, Niklas Muennighoff, Chris Ociepa, Jason Phang, Laria Reynolds, Hailey Schoelkopf, Aviya Skowron, Lintang Sutawika, Eric Tang, Anish Thite, Ben Wang, Kevin Wang, and Andy Zou. 2023. A framework for few-shot language model evaluation.

Ólafur Páll Geirsson. 2013. Iceqa: Developing a question answering system for icelandic.

Lei Huang, Weijiang Yu, Weitao Ma, Weihong Zhong, Zhangyin Feng, Haotian Wang, Qianglong Chen, Weihua Peng, Xiaocheng Feng, Bing Qin, and Ting Liu. 2024. A survey on hallucination in large language models: Principles, taxonomy, challenges, and open questions. *ACM Trans. Inf. Syst.* Just Accepted.

Svanhvít Lilja Ingólfsdóttir, Petur Ragnarsson, Haukur Jónsson, Haukur Simonarson, Vilhjalmur Thorsteinsson, and Vésteinn Snæbjarnarson. 2023. Byte-level grammatical error correction using synthetic and curated corpora. In *Proceedings of the 61st Annual Meeting of the Association for Computational Linguistics (Volume 1: Long Papers)*, pages 7299–7316, Toronto, Canada. Association for Computational Linguistics.

Adam Tauman Kalai and Santosh S Vempala. 2024. Calibrated language models must hallucinate. In *Proceedings of the 56th Annual ACM Symposium on Theory of Computing*, pages 160–171.

Alexandre Lacoste, Alexandra Luccioni, Victor Schmidt, and Thomas Dandres. 2019. Quantifying the carbon emissions of machine learning. *arXiv preprint arXiv:1910.09700*.

Patrick Lewis, Ludovic Denoyer, and Sebastian Riedel. 2019. Unsupervised question answering by cloze translation. In *Proceedings of the 57th Annual Meeting of the Association for Computational Linguistics*, pages 4896–4910, Florence, Italy. Association for Computational Linguistics.

Njall Skarphedinsson, Breki Gudmundsson, Steinar Smari, Marta Kristin Larusdottir, Hafsteinn Einarsson, Abuzar Khan, Eric Nyberg, and Hrafn Loftsson. 2023. GameQA: Gamified mobile app platform for building multiple-domain question-answering datasets. In *Proceedings of the 17th Conference of the European Chapter of the Association for Computational Linguistics: System Demonstrations*, pages 152–160, Dubrovnik, Croatia. Association for Computational Linguistics.

Vésteinn Snæbjarnarson and Hafsteinn Einarsson. 2022a. Cross-lingual QA as a stepping stone for monolingual open QA in Icelandic. In *Proceedings of the Workshop on Multilingual Information Access (MIA)*, pages 29–36, Seattle, USA. Association for Computational Linguistics.

Vésteinn Snæbjarnarson and Hafsteinn Einarsson. 2022b. Natural questions in Icelandic. In *Proceedings of the Thirteenth Language Resources and Evaluation Conference*, pages 4488–4496, Marseille, France. European Language Resources Association.

Aarohi Srivastava, Abhinav Rastogi, Abhishek Rao, Abu Awal Md Shoeb, Abubakar Abid, Adam Fisch, Adam R Brown, Adam Santoro, Aditya Gupta, Adrià Garriga-Alonso, et al. 2022. Beyond the imitation game: Quantifying and extrapolating the capabilities of language models. *arXiv preprint arXiv:2206.04615*.

Steinþór Steingrímsson, Sigrún Helgadóttir, Eiríkur Rögnvaldsson, Starkaður Barkarson, and Jón Guðnason. 2018. Risamálheild: A very large Icelandic text corpus. In *Proceedings of the Eleventh International Conference on Language Resources and Evaluation (LREC 2018)*, Miyazaki, Japan. European Language Resources Association (ELRA).

Yi Yang, Wen-tau Yih, and Christopher Meek. 2015. WikiQA: A challenge dataset for open-domain question answering. In *Proceedings of the 2015 Conference on Empirical Methods in Natural Language Processing*, pages 2013–2018, Lisbon, Portugal. Association for Computational Linguistics.

DUDU: A Treebank for Ottoman Turkish in UD Style

Enes Yılandiloğlu **Janine Siewert**
University of Helsinki, Finland
{enes.yilandiloglu, janine.siewert}@helsinki.fi

Abstract

This paper introduces a recently released Ottoman Turkish (ota) treebank in Universal Dependencies (UD) style, DUDU. The DUDU Treebank consists of 1,064 automatically annotated and manually corrected sentences. The texts were manually collected from various academic or literary sources available on the Internet. Following preprocessing, the sentences were annotated using a MaCHAMP-based neural network model utilizing the large language model (LLM) architecture and manually corrected. The treebank became publicly available with the 2.14 release, and future steps involve expanding the treebank with more data and refining the annotation scheme. The treebank is the first and only treebank that utilizes the IJMES transliteration alphabet. The treebank not only gives insight on Ottoman Turkish lexically, morphologically, and syntactically, but also provides a small but robust test set for future computational models for Ottoman Turkish.

1 Introduction

Among several treebank projects, the Universal Dependencies treebank project establishing a cross-linguistically consistent treebank annotation scheme for many languages (Nivre et al., 2016, 1659), stands out as the largest collection of treebanks sharing the same annotation scheme (Jøhndal, 2020, 18). Although UD has numerous treebanks for modern languages, historical languages such as Ottoman Turkish remain significantly underrepresented. This paper introduces the DUDU Treebank, one of the first Ottoman Turkish treebanks annotated in the Universal Dependencies (UD) style. The DUDU Treebank consists of 1,064 Latin-transliterated automatically annotated and manually corrected sentences from various genres. The treebank employs the standard Ottoman Turkish transliteration alphabet to handle the alphabet change.

2 Background

Languages from historical periods have always been an engrossing research topic for scholars. The proliferation of computational linguistics methods has accelerated such research in the recent years (e.g., (Harris, 1962)), and UD treebanks project is the manifestation of this process. The UD treebanks aim to provide the sentence's lemma, universal part-of-speech tag (UPOS), XPOS, and mapping for the relationship between arguments (dependency) (see (Nivre et al., 2016) for further explanation). The language analyzed in this paper is Ottoman Turkish, the official and literary language of the Ottoman Empire (Göksel and Kerslake, 2005, 10) and "a variant of the Perso-Arabic script" consisting of 31 letters (Redhouse, 1884, 1). It was used from the 14th century until the 20th century, up until the decision taken by the Republic of Turkey in 1928 to replace with Latin script (Resmî Gazete, 1928). Unlike the BOUN treebank (Özateş et al., 2024), another treebank for Ottoman Turkish in UD, the DUDU treebank utilizes IJMES Transliteration System to prevent information loss caused by alphabet changes and includes the gender feature, which is absent in modern Turkish but crucial in Ottoman Turkish grammar.

3 Data

A total of 1,064 automatically annotated and manually corrected sentences consisting of 10,012 tokens and 10,287 syntactic words which indicates that 273 tokens are fused forms that are split into multiple syntactic words. The longest sentence has 91 words while the shortest has two

Proceedings of the Third Workshop on Resources and Representations for Under-Resourced Languages and Domains (RESOURCEFUL-2025), pages 74–79, March 2, 2025 ©2025 Association for Computational Linguistics

words. The treebank includes 3,133 lemmas and 15 universal POS tags. The morphological annotation covers 67 unique features, including number distinctions (singular: 5,816 instances; plural: 1,001 instances; dual: 3 instances), gender (female: 644 instance; mascular: 110 instances), proper name type (e.g., geography: 173; person: 334), and tense/aspect marking (e.g., past: 1,067 instances; present: 489 instances). Among 38 unique dependency relations, the most common dependency relations are obliques (1,191 instances), noun modifiers (1,291 instances), and objects (657 instances). Various written works from 14th to 20th century were collected as data. Sentences were from various topics including biographical texts, national newspapers, religious texts, fictional works such as stories, instructional texts, popular culture articles, and essays. The main purpose of including data from various registers was to initiate a creation of a representative treebank for the language. The texts were collected from various academic journals, dissertations, and literary sources on the Internet. The texts were transcribed from Perso-Arabic letters to Latin by domain experts; however, with some mistakes. In this research, the Latin transcribed versions were utilized. This initial work focuses on laying the foundation for future research on Ottoman Turkish by leveraging existing modern Turkish treebanks and LLM models instead of focusing on establishing a large treebank.

4 Methodology

In the annotation process, both automatic and manual annotation were leveraged. Initially, we created a seed dataset with only 85 sentences by correcting and manually transforming Ottoman Turkish sentences into their modern equivalents. These sentences were later used to train the annotation model with existing modern Turkish treebanks, as detailed in the following three subsections. Once the initial treebank was created, a model trained on the Ottoman Turkish data was used to annotate unseen sentences without manually transforming phase, which were manually corrected. Following the manual correction phase, these sentences were added into the training dataset and the model retrained. This iterative process significantly improved annotation efficiency.

4.1 Preprocessing

Due to human errors and the lack of standardization in the transcription scheme (e.g., not using a consistent transcription alphabet), a preprocessing step was essential to normalize the data before the annotation phase. This step included comparing the transcribed text with the original Perso-Arabic script manually to correct errors made by the transcriber, if the original script was accessible to the authors. Although the mistakes were minimal, these changes ensured the standardization of the data within the transliteration system for Ottoman Turkish. The primary reason for utilizing the transliteration alphabet instead of modern Turkish alphabet was to more accurately represent Ottoman Turkish with Latin characters. While some transcribers used only the modern Turkish alphabet, some transcribers employed the Ottoman Turkish transliteration alphabet suggested by the IJMES Transliteration System (Cambridge University Press, n.d.), a standardised method for converting the Perso-Arabic script into the Latin alphabet while preventing information loss. In the Ottoman Turkish alphabet, not every letter has a direct equivalent in the modern Turkish Latin alphabet. As a result, multiple Ottoman letters can be represented by the same letter in modern Turkish leading to the loss of information. For instance, the two letters in Perso-Arabic alphabet represented by *k* and *k* in IJMES Transliteration System for Ottoman Turkish are demonstrated by only *k* in modern Turkish alphabet which removes the nuance. This situation, if not addressed with utilizing the IJMES transliteration alphabet, not only leads to morphological ambiguity when words with different meanings are Latinized with the modern Turkish alphabet but also prevents the accurate reflection of Ottoman Turkish orthography. Additionally, it was found that during the transcription phase, punctuation marks were sometimes inserted in the text by the domain expert to make the text clear although there was no punctuation mark in the original sentence in Perso-Arabic script. For such cases, the punctuation marks were removed in preprocessing phase. However, if a word was misspelled in the original text or the punctuation mark was present in the original text, no changes were made. Furthermore, since several books in the data sources were not OCR'd, some sentences were manually transliterated. Following the standardization, the sentences were saved to retrieve

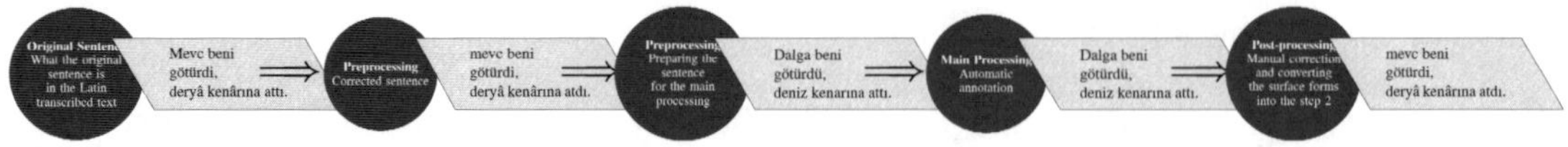

Figure 1: The initial annotation workflow for Ottoman Turkish treebank creation.

later as "corrected Latin-transliterated sentences". Originally, the sentences were quite different from modern Turkish ones, especially lexically. Thus, the words in Ottoman Turkish sentences, which were heavily influenced by Arabic and Persian elements, were manually transformed into their modern Turkish equivalents without altering the morphological structure of the words or the syntactic structure of the sentence since the model was trained via modern Turkish treebanks. This step ensured high accuracy for the model during the automatic annotation process which will be discussed in next subsection. Since the data was in the IJMES transliteration system, LLMs for Arabic and Persian could not be utilized. Moreover, the absence of tools particularly trained on Ottoman Turkish data was another factor to use modern Turkish data to parse Ottoman Turkish sentences.

4.2 Main Processing

After the sentences were manually transformed to resemble modern Turkish, they were ready to be processed by MaCHAMP, "a flexible toolkit for multi-task learning and fine-tuning of NLP problems"(van der Goot et al., 2021). The MaCHAMP architecture was chosen because of the easiness of the implementation and capability for multi-task learning enabling to annotate all necessary fields for the Ottoman Turkish treebank. The annotation model was trained on over one million sentences from the four existing modern Turkish (tr) treebanks in Universal Dependencies (Sulubacak et al., 2016; Kuzgun et al., 2020, 2021; Marşan et al., 2022). The use of multiple treebanks allowed the model to see more data that enhances its performance in rare and complex linguistic structures. For the task of annotation Ottoman Turkish sentences, we utilised two different transformers. Until we have sufficient data, we used bert-base-multilingual-cased transformer, a large language model to handle multilingual data, (Devlin et al., 2018) as the backbone architecture. After having around 500 sentences, we deployed XLM-RoBERTa base (Conneau et al., 2019), another multilingual transformer model. The model performed five tasks: (I) morphological analysis, (II) lemmatization, (III) UPOS annotation, (IV) XPOS annotation, and (V) dependency parsing. To mitigate overfitting, a dropout rate of 0.2 was utilised and early stopping was applied after 19 epochs. Loss and score results for the training and development phase can be seen in Table 1, below.

Table 1: Model's performance results.

Task	Train Loss	Development Loss	Train Score	Development Score
Lemmatization	0.3647	1.6630	0.8467	0.6758
Morphological Analysis	0.1216	0.2654	0.9647	0.9350
UPOS	0.2106	0.8509	0.9423	0.8336
XPOS	0.0698	0.4214	0.9731	0.9040
Dependency LAS	0.0460	1.2093	0.9863	0.7965

The model just served to create a base annotation to make the process time efficient and to ease the workload. Afterwards, the automatically annotated sentences were corrected by hand.

4.3 Post-processing

After automatically annotating the transformed sentences via the model, the intermediate transformed sentences were automatically converted back to their forms in the IJMES system using a script. Subsequently, the results were manually reviewed through "Annotatrix" (Tyers et al., 2018) and corrected. Furthermore, since the model was trained on modern Turkish datasets, it was unable to annotate any feature absent in modern Turkish treebanks such as "gender", a significant feature in Ottoman Turkish especially in the construction of noun phrases since all Arabic and Persian words in the noun phrase should share the same gender. Therefore, the "gender" feature was manually added during the post-processing phase. In addition to the gender feature, the value "dual" for number feature was also added for words such as *ṭarafeyn* (meaning to "two sides"), even though it does not exist in modern Turkish. Figure 1 can be used to explain the whole pipeline to create the initial dataset. In Figure 1, following the transcribed sentence, *mevc beni götürdi, deryâ kenârına attı* (the wave carried me, threw to the sea shore), the manually corrected sentence with the IJMES transliteration system can be seen in the second phase. Subsequently, *â* was automatically replaced with *a* and *mevc* was manually converted into *dalga*, its modern counterpart to obtain better performance from the model trained using modern Turkish, not Ottoman Turkish. Following the fourth phase, where the sentence was automatically annotated, the sentence was automatically converted to the second phase, the predicted lemma, and other fields were manually corrected.

4.4 Iterative Training

After establishing the initial treebank with 85 sentences using the method described above, we trained a model using Ottoman Turkish data with MaCHAMP. Subsequently, we annotated Ottoman Turkish sentences with this model and manually corrected the annotations. Then, we retrained the model with more data and used the improved model for the next annotation phase. This process was iterated until we reached 1,064 sentences. During the iterative training phase, we skipped step 3 shown in Figure 1. Furthermore, we found that the XLM-RoBERTa base yielded the best results among various transformer models when sufficient data were available. With the final dataset, the model was trained with a dropout rate of 0.3 and early stopping applied in the 58th epoch. The performance results for the model can be found in the following.

Table 2: Last Model's Performance Results.

Task	Train Loss	Development Loss	Train Score	Development Score
Lemmatization	0.2509	0.5787	0.9313	0.8534
Morphological Analysis	0.4143	0.9946	0.8898	0.7686
UPOS	0.0389	0.4896	0.9895	0.8976
XPOS	0.0774	0.4927	0.9761	0.8911
Dependency LAS	0.1728	3.5904	0.8933	0.6757

5 Challenges

The main challenge was due to the fact that the Ottoman Turkish language was affected by Arabic and Persian not only lexically, but also grammatically (Göksel and Kerslake, 2005, iii). This meant a comprehensive knowledge of Turkish, as well as Arabic and Persian, was required to address these challenges. The main two challenges related to Arabic elements in Ottoman Turkish were noun phrase structure in Arabic and gender feature. Firstly, dataset contains several Arabic phrases as fixed expressions. Since they function as single units and were mostly idiomatized in Ottoman Turkish, they were treated as single units. A good example of this is *fi'l-vâḳi'*. The phrase, formed with the preposition *fi'* (meaning "in") and the noun *vâḳi'* (meaning "fact"), is in a noun phrase structure and translates to "in fact" or "indeed". Such fixed expressions were shown as single units rather than as separate ones, as shown below:

Table 3: Annotated Arabic fixed noun phrase.

ID	Form	Lemma	POS	Morph	Head	Deprel
-	ve's-selâm	ve's-selâm	INTJ	-	30	discourse

On the other hand, we chose to split non-fixed Arabic noun phrases, since each lexical component contributes to the sentence with its morphological and syntactic features, as seen in the *şeyhü'l-beled* ("the religious leader of the town") example, below:

Table 4: Annotated Arabic non-fixed noun phrase.

<table>
<tr><th>ID</th><th>Form</th><th>Lemma</th><th>POS</th><th>Morph</th><th>Head</th><th>Deprel</th><th>Misc</th></tr>
<tr><td>4-5</td><td>şeyhü'l-beled</td><td>-</td><td>-</td><td>-</td><td>-</td><td>-</td><td>-</td></tr>
<tr><td>4</td><td>şeyh</td><td>şeyh</td><td>NOUN</td><td>Case=Nom|Number=Sing|Person=3</td><td>5</td><td>nmod:poss</td><td>-</td></tr>
<tr><td>5</td><td>ü'l-beled</td><td>beled</td><td>NOUN</td><td>Case=Gen|Number=Sing|Person=3</td><td>6</td><td>nmod:poss</td><td>-</td></tr>
</table>

Another challenge emerged from the gender feature in Arabic and Persian words. Although the gender of words in noun phrases is irrelevant in Turkish, because there is no gender agreement, in Arabic, the words involved in the noun phrase must have the same gender (Göksel and Kerslake, 2005, iii). Gender plays a significant role in Ottoman Turkish noun phrases and the automatic annotation model did not assign the gender feature due to the absence of gender information in the training data. Thus, the gender feature was manually added during the post-processing when necessary. This enrichment aimed to better reflect the linguistic characteristics of Ottoman Turkish in the treebank. Furthermore, Ottoman Turkish, particularly in religious texts, often contains entire sentences in Arabic. To reduce the complexity of the work, such sentences from the treebank were excluded. The challenge related to Persian features in Ottoman Turkish was mainly aroused by *izafet*, "by which the head of a noun phrase was linked to the modifying noun or adjective that followed it" (Göksel and Kerslake, 2005, iii). In Persian noun phrases, the suffix attaches to the modifier rather than the head noun. If the phrase includes a head noun and an adjective, the suffix applies to the adjective, marking the entire phrase. Although not grammatical in modern Turkish, this structure is common in Ottoman Turkish. An example of *izafet* from the dataset can be *ḥuḳûḳ-u meşrû‘* (meaning "legitimite rights"). In such cases, during the post-processing phase, the morphological analysis of the adjective, which functions as the modifier, was manually corrected as shown below.

Table 5: Example for an Annotated Persian noun phrase.

ID	Form	Lemma	POS	Morph	Head	Deprel	Misc
13	tîr-i	tîr	NOUN	-	16	nmod	-
14	tîze	tîz	ADJ	Case=Dat	13	amod	-

In Table 5, while *tîz* ("sharp") is an adjective and cannot take the dative case when it modifies a noun, *tîr* ("sword") in modern Turkish, it is grammatical in Ottoman Turkish. Although challenges listed above both signify the necessity to know, at some degree, the grammar of the languages which were in contact with the target language and demonstrates the requisite of having the post-processing including manual correction to solve the issues.

6 Conclusion and Future Work

To conclude, the DUDU treebank, as the first Ottoman Turkish treebank using the IJMES transliteration alphabet, provides a foundation for further research on different aspects of the Ottoman Turkish language, particularly in lexical, morphological, and syntactic analysis, but also beyond these areas. Furthermore, it also demonstrates that a model trained in the treebanks of a language's present-day form can be utilized for the analysis of its low-resourced historical form, in this case, Ottoman Turkish leveraging LLM. Future work will focus on expanding the treebank with more data to serve a wide spectrum of language use in Ottoman Turkish and adding new features which modern Turkish lacks; however, Ottoman Turkish has. Unfortunately, for this version, the genres cannot be separated by sentence ids. The order of the sentences is chronology-based rather than genre-based, and the earliest written sentence is at the top. In addition, it is planned to add the original form of the sentence in Perso-Arabic letters to the treebank. Lastly, we plan to publicly release the trained model, which is trained on the final dataset, on the Internet to make it available accessible for further research. In the end, the treebank was created by the first author of this paper with the name DUDU and was published in the UD v2.14 release[1]. The work is currently in progress to expand the treebank to at least 20,000 words for the next release.

References

Cambridge University Press. n.d. *IJMES transliteration chart*.

Alexis Conneau, Kartikay Khandelwal, Naman Goyal, Vishrav Chaudhary, Guillaume Wenzek, Francisco Guzmán, Edouard Grave, Myle Ott, Luke Zettlemoyer, and Veselin Stoyanov. 2019. Unsupervised cross-lingual representation learning at scale. *CoRR*, abs/1911.02116.

Jacob Devlin, Ming-Wei Chang, Kenton Lee, and Kristina Toutanova. 2018. BERT: pre-training of deep bidirectional transformers for language understanding. *CoRR*, abs/1810.04805.

Rob van der Goot, Ahmet Üstün, Alan Ramponi, Israa Sharaf, and Barbara Plank. 2021. Massive choice, ample tasks (machamp): A toolkit for multi-task learning in nlp. In *Proceedings of the 16th Conference of the European Chapter of the Association for Computational Linguistics: System Demonstrations*, pages 176–197. Association for Computational Linguistics.

Aslı Göksel and Celia Kerslake. 2005. *Turkish: A Comprehensive Grammar*, taylor & francis e-library edition. Routledge, London, UK.

Zellig S. Harris. 1962. *String Analysis of Sentence Structure*. Mouton, The Hague.

Marius Jøhndal. 2020. Treebanks for historical languages and scalability. In Elliott Lash, Feng Qiu, and David Stifter, editors, *Morphosyntactic Variation in Medieval Celtic Languages: Corpus-Based Approaches*, pages 15–26. De Gruyter Mouton, Berlin, Boston.

Aslı Kuzgun, Neslihan Cesur, Bilge Nas Arıcan, Merve Özçelik, Büşra Marşan, Neslihan Kara, Deniz Baran Aslan, and Olcay Taner Yıldız. 2020. On building the largest and cross-linguistic turkish dependency corpus. In *2020 Innovations in Intelligent Systems and Applications Conference (ASYU)*, pages 1–6. IEEE.

Aslı Kuzgun, Neslihan Cesur, Olcay Taner Yıldız, Oğuzhan Kuyrukçu, Arife Betül Yenice, Bilge Nas Arıcan, and Ezgi Sanıyar. 2021. UD_Turkish-Kenet. `https://github.com/UniversalDependencies/UD_Turkish-Kenet`.

Barış Marşan, Selçuk F. Akkurt, Müge Şen, Melike Gürbüz, Onur Güngör, Şule B. Özateş, Sibel Üsküdarlı, Arzucan Özgür, Tunga Güngör, and Barış

[1]DUDU Treebank is available at (Yılandiloğlu, 2024).

Öztürk. 2022. Enhancements to the boun treebank reflecting the agglutinative nature of turkish. *arXiv preprint*.

Joakim Nivre, Marie-Catherine de Marneffe, Filip Ginter, Yoav Goldberg, Jan Hajič, Christopher D. Manning, Ryan McDonald, Slav Petrov, Sampo Pyysalo, Natalia Silveira, Reut Tsarfaty, and Daniel Zeman. 2016. Universal Dependencies v1: A multilingual treebank collection. In *Proceedings of the Tenth International Conference on Language Resources and Evaluation (LREC'16)*, pages 1659–1666, Portorož, Slovenia. European Language Resources Association (ELRA).

Şaziye Özateş, Tarık Tıraş, Efe Genç, and Esma Bilgin Tasdemir. 2024. Dependency annotation of Ottoman Turkish with multilingual BERT. In *Proceedings of The 18th Linguistic Annotation Workshop (LAW-XVIII)*, pages 188–196, St. Julians, Malta. Association for Computational Linguistics.

James W. Redhouse. 1884. *Ottoman Turkish language: A simplified grammar.* The Swiss Bay.

Resmî Gazete. 1928. Türk harflerinin kabul ve tatbiki hakkında kanun (law on the acceptance and application of turkish letters).

Umut Sulubacak, Memduh Gökırmak, Francis Tyers, Çağrı Çöltekin, Joakim Nivre, and Gülşen Eryiğit. 2016. Universal dependencies for turkish. In *Proceedings of COLING 2016, the 26th International Conference on Computational Linguistics*, Osaka, Japan.

Francis M. Tyers, Mariya Sheyanova, and Jonathan North Washington. 2018. Ud annotatrix: An annotation tool for universal dependencies. In *Proceedings of the 16th International Workshop on Treebanks and Linguistic Theories (TLT16)*, pages 10–17.

Enes Yılandiloğlu. 2024. Universal dependencies dudu treebank v2.14. Universal Dependencies, v2.14.

A Simple Audio and Text Collection-Annotation Tool Targeted to Brazilian Indigenous Language Native Speakers

Gustavo Padilha Polleti
Universidade de São Paulo
gustavo.polleti@gmail.com

Fabio G. Cozman
Universidade de São Paulo

Fabricio Gerardi
Universität Tübingen

Abstract

In this paper we present an audio and text annotation tool for indigenous languages with focus on native speakers, initially developed for Brazilian indigenous languages. Our tool simplifies the process of language resource annotation and employs gamefication techniques typically found in language learning games. Then we describe the annotation tool and present preliminary results for the Bororo language. We discuss the limitations of our tool, highlighting ethical and practical implementation concerns.

1 Introduction

Audio and text annotation tools are key for documenting and building resources for endangered languages (Brugman and Russel, 2004). Existing tools are mostly designed for linguistic professionals and focus on formal description of language resources, such as dependency treebanks and lexical databases. While such tools are fundamental for properly documenting languages, only linguist experts can operate them, and they remain often unknwon outside academia. Hence, despite the pressing need for annotated corpora, language annotation tools remain costly and dependent on scarcely available experts. Annotation tools, in their current form, can hardly scale to address the 2,680 languages at risk of extinction by the end of this century (Wurm, 2001; Lewis, 2009).

Furthermore, ethical and practical concerns arise when we consider that experts who operate language annotation tools are often not members of the indigenous communities themselves (Pinhanez et al., 2023). It is hard to ensure that data annotation procedures are compliant with ethical guidelines (Lewis et al., 2020), such as the Los Pinos Declaration [1], or even that annotations are validated by actual indigenous speakers.

We argue that next-generation tools should be designed for use by lay indigenous speakers to accelerate the data collection and annotation process. While there are few linguist experts, indigenous communities are large. In particular, Brazil is home to a significant number of languages. For example, the Xavante language population alone represents more than 27,000 people. These languages are collectively referred to here as Brazilian Indigenous Languages (BILs). In spite of the high number of languages spoken in Brazil (estimated around 180, see (glo, 2024)), this number is declining fast as populations age and many languages are not learned by younger generations.

In this work, we propose and implement an initial language annotation tool that can be used directly by native speakers in indigenous communities without expert linguistic knowledge. Our proposal simplifies the annotation process so as to only collect words in audio and written text format. Our tool allows indigenous speakers to annotate words with their own speech, perform translations and associate morphemes to word tokens. The main goal is to achieve a source dataset of paired instances, which doe not require further work to develop dependency treebanks, natural language processing tools, and other resources.

We employ a gamification-based design (Sykes, 2018) to maximize engagement among native speakers, encouraging them to produce a high volume of annotations in the shortest possible time. Recognizing the limited availability of indigenous community members, we prioritize a highly user-friendly interface to ensure accessibility and ease of use.

We guide speakers/users through the annotation process by specifying the target word and direct-

[1] https://unesdoc.unesco.org/ark:/48223/pf0000374030

Proceedings of the Third Workshop on Resources and Representations for Under-Resourced Languages and Domains (RESOURCEFUL-2025), pages 80–85, March 2, 2025 ©2025 Association for Computational Linguistics

ing their input to an internal speech recognition component, which transcribes the audio into written text. This transcription includes preliminary annotations, such as morphological information and translations. Speakers can then review, refine, and confirm the prefilled text and annotations before proceeding to the next word.

To enhance usability and minimize friction, we integrate automated annotation components, such as speech recognition. We also address challenges associated with limited computational resources. In our prototype, we employ lightweight models and heuristics that can run offline in a standard web browser or mobile app. Finally, we present preliminary results for the Bororo language as a proof of concept.

The paper is organized as follows. Section 2 describes our annotation tool design and its development, including data sources and methods. Section 3 presents preliminary results for the Bororo language. Section 4 discusses the challenges and limitations of our prototype and offers concluding remarks.

2 Methodology

Our data collection and annotation tool aims to empower native speaker communities to collect and annotate language resources by themselves without requiring expert linguistic knowledge. Our tool takes the form of a game, similar to formats often found in language learning game apps from both industry (e.g. Duolingo) and the literature (Polleti, 2024; von Ahn, 2006; Katinskaia et al., 2017).

The tool follows a linear progression structure, where the user advances by completing units. In order to do so, the user is asked to annotate a series of specific words, similar to language exercises. In the annotation screen, depicted in Figure 1 (top), the user is asked to provide speech audio translation in native language for a given Portuguese word. In the figure, the tool asks for a speech translation of the Portuguese word for jaguar, "Onça Pintada", to the Bororo language. First, the user records their speech in native language. The user should say the given word only once within 10 seconds. After the audio recording finishes, we run a speech recognition model to generate a transcript. In our Bororo language example, we have a Bororo-Portuguese dictionary available (Ferraz Gerardi; Polleti et al., 2024), thus, we know in advance that the target word, or the Bororo translation for "onça ointada", is "adugo". However, there are many alternative ortographies or even regional synonyms that can be absent in our knowledge base. In order to avoid enforcing a specific ortography by presenting the target word beforehand, we allow the user to freely annotate so as to preserve linguistic diversity. Next, we check whether the produced transcript matches the target word from the dictionary entry. If a match is found (Figure 1a), we retrieve an image representing the word concept, the written word in native language and its description from the dictionary entry. Finally, the user can make editions if necessary (such as providing an alternative orthography), confirm changes and move on to the next. On the other hand, if we cannot assert that the transcript matches the target word (Figure 1b), the user is required to fill up the written translation and description manually before moving to the next. The tool may fail to properly identify a match by several reasons; for example, the speech recognition may fail, the dictionary may be incomplete or may not contain all synonyms or simply the user translation may be incorrect. We allow the user to retry recording the speech translation multiple times, so if the speech recognition fails due to background noises, computer glitches or any other intermitent issues, it can succeed in a second attempt. If the matching keeps failing even after multiple retries, users can always fill the written translation and description manually. We provide autocomplete options based on lexical similarity to speed up the manual filling process. Additionally, we also provide an option for the user to skip the current annotation and move to the next. For example, if the user does not know the translation for the given word, we want to save time and avoid incorrect annotations by giving them the option to immediately move on to the next. The whole annotation process is depicted in Figure 2.

Now we focus on the speech recognition model and on the word matching heuristic. We propose to reuse speech recognition models that were trained for other languages to be used for low-resource languages. In our proof of concept for the Bororo language, we employed the Web Speech API's Speech Recognition model for Brazilian Portuguese (pt-BR), which can run offline and is available in most web browsers (e.g. Chrome,

Edge, Safari, except Firefox). Back to our example, note that "Adugo" is a romanized word. Most writing systems for brazilian indigenous languages were romanized with strong Portuguese language influence, Bororo language included. We observed that the speech recognition model often produced transcripts of portuguese words that are phonetically similar the original Bororo word. For example, the transcript for the word "Adugo" results in "Adubo", which is a portuguese word with completely different meaning but phonetically similar to the Bororo word. Since Bororo writing system is romanized, we could perform a lexical similarity search between the portuguese transcript and the known Bororo vocabulary to find good match candidates. Additionally, since we know the target word, we can consider a match if the target word has high lexical similarity to the transcript. In our prototype, we built a similarity score based on levenshtein distance and applied an arbitrary 0.9 threshold as the heuristic criteria to tell whether the speech to text process matches or not the target word. Table 1 presents some examples from our prototype. Despite minor spelling issues, for our few examples, we can observe that the portuguese speech recognition model is able to produce phonetically similar transcripts for Bororo words, which can produce accurate matches when coupled to our heuristic.

We define our similarity score as:

$$1-(distance(a,b)/(length(a)+length(b))+\epsilon),$$

where a and b are the target word and transcript, respectively, $distance$ refers to the weighted Levenshtein distance function, $length$ s returns the total number of characters in a string and ϵ is a hyperparameter that smoothes the similarity score for small words. We observed that our similarity score is often too strict when comparing small sized strings. To avoid missing potential matches, we introduced ϵ to smoothen the distance metric for small strings. In our prototype we arbitrarily used $\epsilon = 3$. To illustrate, consider the words "caro" and "karo": they are both very similar, their Levenshtein distance is only 1, but our similarity score would yield only 0.875 if we did not take ϵ into account. Additionally, we apply NFD unicode normalization form in the transcript string before calculating the similarity score.

3 Results

We still need to evaluate our proposal more broadly with the Bororo indigenous community to measure community adoption and engagement. This will require a more comprehensive evaluation of our processes and methods to measure, for example, how effective the speech recognition model is in speeding up the annotation process. At this point, we ran simulated experiments to get preliminary results on: (1) the speech to text recall, (2) how much time the speech to text saves in the annotation process, i.e. the speed up. First, to measure recall, we sampled 50 words from the Bororo dictionary, generated correct speech audio for them and ran a simulation to evaluate how many instances our speech to text process was able to find a match, the fraction of matches over the total number of instances is what we refer to as recall. We obtained 0.56 recall, 28 matches out of 50 words, as presented in Table 2. Next, we got all the words we were able to find a match and asked a volunteer from our University to use the annotation tool, first with the speech to text support and later without it, filling all the information manually. Given that the volunteer is not a native speaker, he had access to the target words and their descriptions during the experiment. We compared the completion times between the volunteer filling it with and without speech to text support to get preliminary insight into the annotation speed up. The volunteer took 3 minutes and 12 seconds to complete the annotation of 28 words, compared to 4 minutes and 33 seconds without speech to text support. We obtained 29.7% speed up, saving around 1 minute in our experiment setup, as presented in Table 3.

Table 2: Speech to text simulation metrics.

Metric	**Result**
Recall	56% (28 matches out of 50)
No transcript	2% (1 out of 50)

Table 3: Completion time results.

Scenario	**Total Completion time**
without Speech to Text	273 secs (4 min 33 secs)
with Speech to Text	192 secs (3 min 12 secs)
Relative Speed Up	29.7%

Table 1: Bororo speech to text examples. The target word is highlighted in the matching candidates.

Target word (en)	Target word (native)	Transcript (pt)	Match Candidates
jaguar	adugo	adubo	**adugo**, arugo, atugo
rain	bubutu	bubu tu	**bubutu**
scarlet macaw	nabure	naburi	**nabure**
howler monkey	pai	pai	**pai**
woman	aredy	aredo	aredo, taredo, **aredy**, arego, arudo, arudu
wart	akogo	acogo	**akogo**, apogo, arogo, ecogo
fish	karo	caro	**karo**, ocaro, care, caru
eye	joku	jogo	jodo, jomo, joto, jugo, joga
anteater	apogo	apogo	**apogo**, apogoe, apodo, akogo
seed bug	arogo	arrogo	**arogo**
potato	tadari	padari	padaro, **tadari**
nose	eno	(no transcript)	(no match)
dog	arigao	arigato	**arigao**
banana	bako	barco	(no match)
grandmother	marugo	marugo	**marugo**

(a) Successful speech recognition and information retrieval. The transcript identified the word "adugo" and retrieved the associated jaguar image and description.

(b) Failed speech recognition and information retrieval. The transcript failed to indentify a matching word so the user was required to fill manually.

Figure 1: Example of a single session: the user was asked to record the translation in Bororo for the word "jaguar". It depicts autocomplete success and failure scenarios.

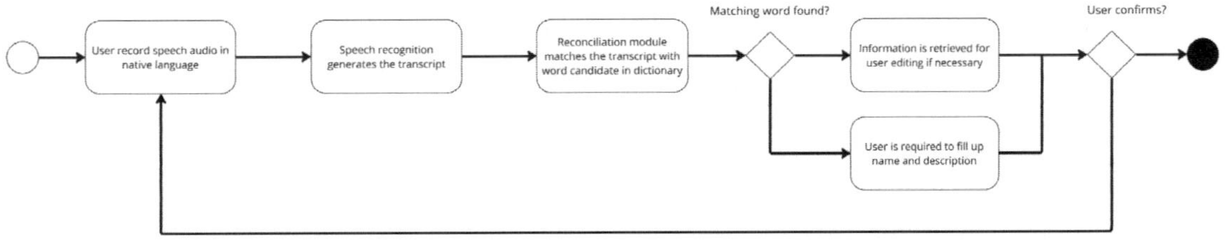

Figure 2: Annotation process diagram.

4 Concluding Remarks & Limitations

The annotation tool introduced in this work represents a significant step forward in the advancement of resources for Brazilian indigenous languages. Our proposed design allows native speakers, who do not necessarily require specific linguistic knowledge, to perform annotations in audio and text resources. Our design avoids biases towards specific ortographies by allowing the user to freely annotate their speech and written forms. At the same time, we incorporate speech to text and autocomplete components to speed up the annotation process.

Despite the promising benefits, our prototype falls short in multiple aspects that we now examine. First, our tool currently only supports word annotation. We consider it to be a natural step to evolve our methods to enable sentence annotation. Before we can support sentences, we must require word annotation to be fully functional, which implies better autocomplete and speech recognition capabilities. Additionally, users annotations can vary significantly and we still do not have a proper process to create consensus around them. The orthography currently used by the Bororo people was developed by Catholic missionaries and is not well-suited to their language (see Colbacchini 1925 and Colbacchini 1942). Recent publications have adopted a different orthography, which occasionally leads to minor discrepancies. For example, we have two ortographies for the word "rain" in Bororo, which are "Bubutu" (old) and "Bybyty" (new). If our tool presents "Bubutu" to users, they may be confused as our tool is incentivizing an outdated ortography. Once the Bororo Corpus (Ferraz Gerardi et al., 2024) is completed, this issue is expected to be resolved, as all sources will be unified under a standardized orthography.

One significant issue stems from the fact that Bororo territories are not contiguous, resulting in variations in pronunciation among different regions. These differences can sometimes lead to mockery of speakers from areas where the language is less commonly spoken, as if their way of speaking were "incorrect." This poses an important ethical concern, as it may cause speakers to feel that a new orthography privileges certain pronunciations over others. This concern becomes even more relevant when we consider that our tool employs automatic speech recognition models, which may incentivize specific accents. Given that the speech recognition models were trained in foreign languages, biases towards pronunciation similar to the Portuguese language may occur.

There is still room for improvement in our speech to text process. We considered applying more sophisticated approaches, such as accoustic models (Li et al., 2022, 2020), for zero shot speech recognition in indigenous languages, but models like those require stable internet connectivity as they are too large to run in offline devices. We are currently limited to work with models that can run in the web browser or mobile app so they can be actually used in the field. Future work should conduct evaluate varied speech to text methods and improve their performance.

At this point, we have only implemented a proof of concept for the Bororo language; thus, it is still necessary to assess how well the methods introduced in this work generalize to other languages. Endangered language revitalization requires the development of annotated resources (Miyagawa et al., 2023). We believe that our proposal can be extended to annotate languages beyond Brazilian ones. Similar strategies around phonetical similarities have already been employed in other contexts (Mæhlum and Ivanova, 2023).

Future work should evaluate the effectiveness of our annotation tool in partnership with native speakers and assert its value. We hope our preliminary research can help scaling up data annotation for endangered languages and produce rich data sources to support revitalization initiatives.

Acknowledgments

The second author was partially supported by CNPq grant 305753/2022-3. We also thank support by CAPES Finance Code 001. The authors of this work would like to thank the Center for Artificial Intelligence (C4AI-USP) and the support from the São Paulo Research Foundation (FAPESP grant 2019/07665-4) and from the IBM Corporation.

The third author is supported by the European Research Council (ERC) under the European Union's Horizon 2020 research and innovation programme (Grant agreement No. 834050).

References

2024. Glottolog 5.1. Accessed: 2024-12-15.

L. von Ahn. 2006. Games with a purpose. *Computer*, 39(6):92–94.

Hennie Brugman and Albert Russel. 2004. Annotating multi-media/multi-modal resources with ELAN. In *Proceedings of the Fourth International Conference on Language Resources and Evaluation (LREC'04)*, Lisbon, Portugal. European Language Resources Association (ELRA).

Antonio Colbacchini. 1925. *I Bororos orientali:" Orarimudoge" del Matto Grosso (Brasile)*. Società editrice internazionale.

Antonio Colbacchini. 1942. *Os Boróros orientais*. Companhia Editora Nacional, São Paulo.

Fabrício Ferraz Gerardi. *Bororo Dictionary*. Forthcoming. Available upon request.

Fabrício Ferraz Gerardi, Daniel Sollberger, and Luis Toribio Serrano. 2024. Corpus bororo (corbo) (v0.2).

Anisia Katinskaia, Javad Nouri, and Roman Yangarber. 2017. Revita: a system for language learning and supporting endangered languages. In *Proceedings of the joint workshop on NLP for Computer Assisted Language Learning and NLP for Language Acquisition*, pages 27–35, Gothenburg, Sweden. LiU Electronic Press.

Jason Edward Lewis, Angie Abdilla, Noelani Arista, Kaipulaumakaniolono Baker, Scott Benesiinaabandan, Michelle Brown, Melanie Cheung, Meredith Coleman, Ashley Cordes, Joel Davison, Kūpono Duncan, Sergio Garzon, D. Fox Harrell, Peter-Lucas Jones, Kekuhi Kealiikanakaoleohaililani, Megan Kelleher, Suzanne Kite, Olin Lagon, Jason Leigh, Maroussia Levesque, Keoni Mahelona, Caleb Moses, Isaac ('Ika'aka) Nahuewai, Kari Noe, Danielle Olson, 'Ōiwi Parker Jones, Caroline Running Wolf, Michael Running Wolf, Marlee Silva, Skawennati Fragnito, and Hēmi Whaanga. 2020. Indigenous protocol and artificial intelligence position paper. Project Report 10.11573/spectrum.library.concordia.ca.00986506, Aboriginal Territories in Cyberspace, Honolulu, HI. Edited by Jason Edward Lewis. English Language Version of "Ka?ina Hana ?Ōiwi a me ka Waihona ?Ike Hakuhia Pepa Kūlana" available at: https://spectrum.library.concordia.ca/id/eprint/990094/.

M. Paul Lewis, editor. 2009. *Ethnologue: Languages of the World*, sixteenth edition. SIL International, Dallas, TX, USA.

Xinjian Li, Siddharth Dalmia, Juncheng Li, Matthew Lee, Patrick Littell, Jiali Yao, Antonios Anastasopoulos, David R. Mortensen, Graham Neubig, Alan W Black, and Florian Metze. 2020. Universal phone recognition with a multilingual allophone system. In *ICASSP 2020 - 2020 IEEE International Conference on Acoustics, Speech and Signal Processing (ICASSP)*, pages 8249–8253.

Xinjian Li, Florian Metze, David Mortensen, Shinji Watanabe, and Alan Black. 2022. Zero-shot learning for grapheme to phoneme conversion with language ensemble. In *Findings of the Association for Computational Linguistics: ACL 2022*, pages 2106–2115, Dublin, Ireland. Association for Computational Linguistics.

Petter Mæhlum and Sardana Ivanova. 2023. Phonotactics as an aid in low resource loan word detection and morphological analysis in sakha. In *Proceedings of the Second Workshop on Resources and Representations for Under-Resourced Languages and Domains (RESOURCEFUL-2023)*, pages 111–120, Tórshavn, the Faroe Islands. Association for Computational Linguistics.

So Miyagawa, Kanji Kato, Miho Zlazli, Salvatore Carlino, and Seira Machida. 2023. Building Okinawan lexicon resource for language reclamation/revitalization and natural language processing tasks such as Universal Dependencies treebanking. In *Proceedings of the Second Workshop on Resources and Representations for Under-Resourced Languages and Domains (RESOURCEFUL-2023)*, pages 86–91, Tórshavn, the Faroe Islands. Association for Computational Linguistics.

Claudio S. Pinhanez, Paulo Cavalin, Marisa Vasconcelos, and Julio Nogima. 2023. Balancing social impact, opportunities, and ethical constraints of using ai in the documentation and vitalization of indigenous languages. In *Proceedings of the Thirty-Second International Joint Conference on Artificial Intelligence, IJCAI-23*, pages 6174–6182. International Joint Conferences on Artificial Intelligence Organization. AI for Good.

Gustavo Polleti. 2024. Building a language-learning game for Brazilian indigenous languages: A case study. Technical report, arXiv:2403.14515.

Gustavo Polleti, Fabio Cozman, and Fabrício Gerardi. 2024. Unified knowledge-graph for brazilian indigenous languages: An educational applications perspective. In *Anais do XV Simpósio Brasileiro de Tecnologia da Informação e da Linguagem Humana*, pages 159–164, Porto Alegre, RS, Brasil. SBC.

Julie M Sykes. 2018. Digital games and language teaching and learning. *Foreign Language Annals*, 51(1):219–224.

S.A. Wurm. 2001. *Atlas of the world's languages in danger of disappearing*. Unesco Pub.

First Steps in Benchmarking Latvian in Large Language Models

Inguna Skadiņa[1, 2, 3], **Bruno Bakanovs**[2, 4], **Roberts Darģis**[1, 3]
[1] Institute of Mathematics and Computer Science, University of Latvia
[2] University of Latvia
[3] {inguna.skadina, roberts.dargis}@lumii.lv
[4] bakanovs26@gmail.com

Abstract

The performance of multilingual large language models (LLMs) in low-resource languages, such as Latvian, has been under-explored. In this paper, we investigate the capabilities of several open and commercial LLMs in the Latvian language understanding tasks. We evaluate these models across several well-known benchmarks, such as the Choice of Plausible Alternatives (COPA) and Measuring Massive Multitask Language Understanding (MMLU), which were adapted into Latvian using machine translation. Our results highlight significant variability in model performance, emphasizing the challenges of extending LLMs to low-resource languages. We also analyze the effect of post-editing on machine-translated datasets, observing notable improvements in model accuracy, particularly with BERT-based architectures. We also assess open-source LLMs using the Belebele dataset, showcasing competitive performance from open-weight models when compared to proprietary systems. This study reveals key insights into the limitations of current LLMs in low-resource settings and provides datasets for future benchmarking efforts.

1 Introduction

The recent progress of large language models (LLMs) has made them very popular and widely used. Being the most widely used natural language processing technique (NLP) today, LLMs differ in their performance depending on several key factors, such as, the quality and size of the training data, the model architecture, the computational resources used for training, and the specific tasks they are evaluated on.

Most of the language data used for training LLMs is in English and few other widely spoken languages, while other languages, especially less- and low-resourced, are represented by very small portions of data. For example, in recently developed EuroLLM Multilingual Language Models for Europe, English language data form 50% of training data, while low-resourced languages, such as Latvian, Lithuanian, Estonian, Finnish, and others are represented by about 1% of data (Martins et al., 2024). As a result, although many language models are multilingual and powerful in language transfer, they have generally demonstrated considerably less reliable results on low-resource languages (Lai et al., 2023; Ahuja et al., 2024).

The fast growth of LLMs in size, language coverage, and overall quality, has made benchmarking critical for assessing LLM performance and capabilities across various tasks. A wide range of benchmarks are available to evaluate different capabilities of large language models. They span multiple categories, including natural language understanding and generation, robustness, ethics, or biases of the models (Chang et al., 2024). LLMs have demonstrated impressive gains on natural language understanding (NLU) benchmarks, starting from GLUE (Wang et al., 2018) and SuperGLUE (Wang et al., 2019) with 10 tasks related to different NLU problems, followed by MMLU (Hendrycks et al., 2020) covering nearly 60 subjects and Bigbench (Srivastava et al., 2023) with more than 200 tasks, as well as many other benchmarks. However, many of these benchmarks focus on the English language, as well as some other widely spoken languages and only some attempts have been made to evaluate LLM performance on low-resource languages.

A recent study of LLMs for European languages (Ali and Pyysalo, 2024) has identified eight EU languages as low-resource (Croatian, Estonian, Irish, Latvian, Lithuanian, Maltese, Slovak, and

Proceedings of the Third Workshop on Resources and Representations for Under-Resourced Languages and Domains (RESOURCEFUL-2025), pages 86–95, March 2, 2025 ©2025 Association for Computational Linguistics

Slovene).

The aim of this paper is to conduct an initial assessment of natural language understanding and reasoning skills of different LLMs for the low-resource Latvian language:

- our first group of experiments aims to evaluate NLU capabilities of different BERT family (Devlin et al., 2019) LLMs using Choice of Plausible Alternatives (COPA) dataset (Section 3);
- as next, we evaluate the performance of two commercial LLMs (ChatGPT-3.5 Turbo and Google Gemini 1.0) on widely used Measuring Massive Multitask Language Understanding (MMLU) dataset (Section 4);
- finally, we use a multilingual Belebele dataset to understand the impact of machine translation on the performance of different open-source LLMs (Section 5).

We provide the datasets used in our experiments to facilitate further benchmarking of Latvian[1], ensuring that researchers have access to the resources necessary to replicate and build upon our work. By making these datasets publicly available, we aim to support the development of robust tools and methodologies for the Latvian language, as well as foster collaboration and facilitate advancements in natural language understanding for low-resourced languages.

2 Related Work

Latvian is an Indo-European language of the Baltic branch with about 1.5 million native speakers. Taking into account its size, it is rather well supported by language technologies (Skadiņa et al., 2022). However, in the context of LLMs the Latvian language is a low-resource language (Ali and Pyysalo, 2024).

Before 2024, only limited research has been conducted on the performance of BERT family language models (e.g., Znotiņš and Bārzdiņš (2020), Vīksna and Skadiņa (2020)). A widely used Latvian dataset to assess LLM performance on different natural language processing tasks (NER, POS-tagging, dependency parsing) is FullStack-LV dataset (Gruzitis et al., 2018). Comparison of several BERT family models that include Latvian (mBERT (Devlin et al., 2019), LVBERT (Znotiņš and Bārzdiņš, 2020), and LitLat BERT (Ulčar and Robnik-Šikonja, 2021)) has been performed by Ulčar and Robnik-Šikonja (2021). The evaluation showed that the LitLat BERT model has the best performance in named entity recognition, part-of-speech tagging, and word analogy tasks, whereas LVBERT demonstrated the best score for the dependency parsing task.

Until 2024, there were no datasets available to assess the natural language understanding and reasoning skills of LLMs in Latvian and compare them across different models or languages. For example, mBERT's performance has been evaluated using the XNLI dataset (Conneau et al., 2018) - an evaluation corpus for language transfer and cross-lingual sentence understanding in 15 languages, but it does not contain any Latvian samples. Similarly, the dataset for the evaluation of multilingual LLMs developed by Okapi (Lai et al., 2023), in which the English part was translated with the help of ChatGPT, covers 26 languages, but does not include any of the the Baltic languages (the "smallest" language is Danish with 6 million speakers, followed by Slovak with 7 million speakers).

Latvian is mentioned as one of the languages on which the GPT-4 model was evaluated with MMLU benchmark (Achiam et al., 2023). The prompts were machine-translated from English into Latvian. When comparing GPT-4's 3-shot accuracy on MMLU across different languages, English reaches 85.5% (only 70.1% for GPT 3.5), while Latvian – 80.9% (Achiam et al., 2023).

Different approach has been chosen by Darģis et al. (2024), who used standardized Latvian high school centralized graduation exams as a benchmark dataset. They showed that several open-source models have reached competitive performance in NLU tasks, narrowing the gap with GPT-4, while keeping notable deficiencies in natural language generation tasks (specifically in generating coherent and contextually appropriate text analyses).

Recently META has released the Belebele benchmark (Bandarkar et al., 2024). This benchmark was used to evaluate three masked language models (XLM-V, INFOXLM and XLM-R) and several LLMs (GPT3.5-TURBO, FALCON, and LLAMA). The accuracy of these models for the Latvian language varies from 37.6% for FALCON

[1] https://github.com/LUMII-AILab/VTI-Data

40B 5-shot In-Context Learning model to 74.1% for Translate-Train-All XLM-V Large model.

Finally, European LLM leader-board that includes Latvian has been recently published on HuggingFace.[2] This leaderboard provides a comparison of more than 15 open-source multilingual LLMs across several machine-translated benchmarks – ARC, GSM8K, HellaSwag, MMLU and TruthFullQA.

3 Evaluation of BERT Family Models

While today LLMs offer broad multilingual capabilities, they may not always be the best solution for low-resourced languages, thus in some cases BERT-based models still remain relevant as a cost-effective, adaptable, and open-source alternative for research and real-world applications in under-represented languages. Although several BERT models include Latvian, their NLU capabilities have not been assessed due to the absence of necessary evaluation datasets.

3.1 COPA Dataset

In our first experiment, conducted in early spring of 2024, we evaluated several BERT models using the machine-translated [3] version of the Choice of Plausible Alternatives (COPA) dataset (Roemmele et al., 2011).

The COPA dataset consists of 1000 commonsense casual reasoning samples. The task is to select the alternative that more plausibly has a causal relation with the premise. The dataset is split equally into two parts, one for development and the other for evaluation.

3.2 Selected Models

The following models that include Latvian have been selected: multilingual BERT model (mBERT, Devlin et al. (2019)), LVBERT (Znotiņš and Bārzdiņš, 2020), and LitLat BERT (Ulčar and Robnik-Šikonja, 2021). mBERT and LVBERT models implement the BERT reference architecture, while the LitLat BERT model is based on RoBERTa-base architecture (Liu et al., 2019). The mBERT model is pre-trained on a corpus that includes text from 104 languages, the LitLat BERT model is trained on Latvian (LV), Lithuanian (LT), and English (EN), and LVBERT is trained solely on Latvian. None of them share training datasets; however, there is some overlap between mBERT and LVBERT models, as they both contain Wikipedia datasets. Table 1 summarizes language models selected for the evaluation, their language coverage and the parameter count.

Model	Languages	Parameters (million)
mBERT	104 lang.	110
LVBERT	LV	110
LitLat BERT	LV, LT, EN	125

Table 1: Selected language models.

	Machine-translated	Post-edited
mBERT	54.62%	55.00%
LVBERT	**60.38%**	61.54%
LitLat BERT	58.46%	**62.69%**

Table 2: Accuracy of BERT models on COPA dataset.

3.3 Experimental Setup

BERT models require fine-tuning of the pre-trained model for COPA task. For this, model weights were acquired from HugginFace website.[4] We added an additional linear layer and a softmax function to the pre-trained models. During the fine-tuning process for the COPA task, we experimented with different learning rates (5e-5, 4e-5, 3e-5, 2e-5) while keeping the batch size fixed at 32 and training for 10 epochs.

We split the development dataset into 400 samples used for training and 100 samples for validation. The highest accuracy on the validation dataset on all models was achieved using 5e-5 learning rate.

3.4 Results

The evaluation dataset consists of 500 machine-translated samples, from which 260 were post-edited by native Latvian speaker. Table 2 compares the evaluation results between 260 machine-translated and post-edited samples.

[2] https://huggingface.co/spaces/openGPT-X/european-llm-leaderboard

[3] In this experiment we used Tilde Translator https://tilde.ai/machine-translation/

[4] https://huggingface.co/google-bert/bert-base-multilingual-cased, https://huggingface.co/AiLab-IMCS-UL/lvbert, https://huggingface.co/EMBEDDIA/litlat-bert

Notably, post-edited machine translation samples bring an improvement of a few percentages. The most significant improvement has been observed for the LitLat BERT model with more than 4 percentage points. Similar gains have been noticed with BERT models in Estonian, where the post-editing lead to an improvement of a few percentages (Kuulmets et al., 2022). When compared to English BERT model (70.6%) the Latvian models perform significantly worse.

4 Evaluation of Commercial LLMs

As next, in spring 2024, we evaluated the performance of several commercial models on the Latvian language to assess their capabilities in handling low-resource languages.

4.1 MMLU Dataset

Measuring Massive Multitask Language Understanding (MMLU) benchmark (Hendrycks et al., 2020) consists of various multiple-choice questions across 57 different subjects, grouped in four categories: human sciences (philosophy, history, jurisprudence, etc.), social sciences (economics, sociology, geography, etc.), STEM (high school mathematics, college computer science, etc.), and miscellaneous (finance, accounting, global facts, etc.). The motivation for selecting MMLU benchmark comes from both its popularity and the fact that the results are available for wide-range of LLMs, including OpenAI's GPT-4 (Achiam et al., 2023), Google's Gemini family of models (GeminiTeam et al., 2024), and the recently announced NVIDIA's NVLM 1.0 (Dai et al., 2024). Similarly to COPA, MMLU was not available in Latvian, and thus was machine-translated for our experiments.

4.2 Selected Language Models

For our experiments, we selected two cost-effective AI models that support Latvian and are available via a public API: GPT-3.5 Turbo[5] and Google Gemini 1.0 Pro.[6] These models were chosen based on their balance of affordability and performance, making them suitable for conducting comprehensive tests without exceeding budget constraints.

[5] https://platform.openai.com/docs/models/gpt-3-5-turbo

[6] https://ai.google.dev/gemini-api/docs/models/gemini

	Machine-translated	Post-edited
ChatGPT-3.5 Turbo	78.79%	81.82%
Gemini 1.0 Pro	81.82%	90.90%

Table 3: MMLU evaluation results (accuracy) in sociology domain with machine-translated and post-edited prompts.

4.3 Experimental Setup

The evaluation of ChatGPT-3.5 Turbo and Gemini Pro 1.0 was performed using the API provided by the developers of the models. During the evaluation of Gemini Pro 1.0, the safety filters were disabled, since with the default configuration for some prompts, no answer was provided. Both models were evaluated using 2-shot prompts, i.e., the first two multiple-choice question-answer pairs serve as examples and the model is expected to provide the correct answer for the third question.

During the evaluation, we observed that sometimes the output of models is inconsistent with the expected format. For example, if the correct answer is **D**, the model could also output variations, e.g., **(D)**, **D. 0,4**, or **(D) 0,4**. These cases were also considered as correct answers. This approach differs from Laskar et al. (2023) where the authors performed additional manual evaluation of prompts.

4.4 Results

Table 4 shows the evaluation results of machine-translated MMLU dataset per subject for both Gemini Pro 1.0 and ChatGPT-3.5 Turbo models. Overall, the accuracy of Gemini 1.0 Pro is 6.09 percentage points higher than ChatGPT-3.5 Turbo. For multiple subjects the difference of accuracy exceeds 20 percentage points. For instance, college biology, econometrics, human sexuality. However, there are also subjects, in which ChatGPT-3.5 Turbo model performed better, like computer security and public relations.

Our choice of few-shot prompts differs from those reported for English. ChatGPT-3.5 Turbo reached 67% accuracy for English using 0-shot prompts. The average accuracy of our results for Latvian across all subjects is 52.58%. The difference is significant, considering that our evaluation provided two additional examples. For English ChatGPT-3.5 Turbo accuracy of 5-shot prompts is around 70% and for Gemini 1.0 Pro accuracy is

Subject	ChatGPT-3.5 Turbo	Gemini Pro 1.0
abstract algebra	**37.500**	32.260
anatomy	**46.600**	44.190
astronomy	54.000	**72.920**
business ethics	**48.480**	40.625
clinical knowledge	**57.950**	55.290
college biology	37.500	**62.500**
college chemistry	34.375	**37.930**
college computer science	39.390	**41.940**
college mathematics	24.240	**40.000**
college medicine	57.890	**58.930**
college physics	**29.410**	28.125
computer security	**78.780**	63.630
conceptual physics	29.410	**52.000**
econometrics	31.580	**52.630**
electrical engineering	41.600	**56.520**
elementary mathematics	**43.200**	41.530
formal logic	31.430	**37.140**
global facts	33.330	**39.390**
high school biology	64.070	**77.450**
high school chemistry	**42.420**	42.370
high school computer science	63.630	**78.790**
high school European history	70.900	**77.780**
high school geography	61.530	**78.460**
high school government and politics	65.625	**79.370**
high school macroeconomics	50.000	**69.230**
high school mathematics	**34.090**	30.120
high school microeconomics	55.700	**69.620**
high school physics	40.810	**45.830**
high school psychology	65.190	**80.190**
high school statistics	40.270	**42.860**
high school US history	63.240	**76.120**
high school world history	64.100	**69.620**
human aging	55.400	**64.380**
human sexuality	58.130	**78.570**
international law	**75.000**	65.000
jurisprudence	69.400	**88.890**
logical fallacies	51.850	**53.700**
machine learning	40.540	**50.000**
management	73.530	**76.470**
marketing	78.200	**89.120**
medical genetics	**66.670**	63.640
miscellaneous	66.530	**71.150**
moral disputes	52.170	**59.650**
moral scenarios	**26.510**	24.480
nutrition	63.730	**64.700**
philosophy	60.109	**67.000**
prehistory	**59.260**	52.880
professional accounting	30.430	**47.190**
professional law	33.140	**51.970**
professional medicine	51.110	**66.670**
professional psychology	50.980	**53.000**
public relations	**72.200**	50.000
security studies	53.090	**56.250**
sociology	78.780	**80.600**
US foreign policy	72.720	**78.790**
virology	43.640	**48.150**
world religions	**75.440**	66.670
Average	52.577	**58.672**

Table 4: Comparison of Gemini Pro 1.0 and ChatGPT-3.5 Turbo on MMLU (accuracy, %).

around 71.8% .

We also verify the impact of post-editing. As the dataset is vast, post-editing was performed only for the prompts of the sociology subject. The results in Table 3 show an increase of accuracy for both models – ChatGPT-3.5 Turbo achieves a 3.03 percentage point increase, while Gemini 1.0 Pro achieves a more substantial gain of 9,08 percentage points.

5 Evaluation of Open LLMs

We continue to explore the impact of machine translation on benchmarking using the recently released multilingual Belebele dataset, which includes Latvian. We compare the performance of several popular open-weight LLM families (Gemma, Llama, Mistral, and Qwen) using both the original and machine-translated versions of the dataset.

5.1 Belebele Dataset

Belebele is a multiple-choice machine reading comprehension dataset (Bandarkar et al., 2024). The dataset was created without the use of machine translation technology, relying solely on experts fluent in English and the target language. For each language the dataset contains 900 questions. Each question is based on a short passage from the FLORES-200 dataset (NLLBTeam et al., 2022) and has four multiple choice answers.

To assess the impact of machine translation we translated English (EN) part of the Belebele dataset into Latvian (LV) and Latvian part into English using two different machine translation strategies – machine translation system DeepL[7] and GPT-4o-mini with system prompting. We used the original English and Latvian parts of this dataset as references to evaluate translations. Results of the automatic evaluation are summarized in Table 5. For both translation directions DeepL demonstrates better translation (BLEU (Papineni et al., 2002) and ChrF (Popović, 2015) scores), when compared to GPT-4o-mini. Since Latvian is a low-resource morphologically rich free-word order language, automatic scores for English->Latvian machine translation direction are lower than for Latvian->English direction.

[7]https://www.deepl.com/en/translator

```
LV: Izlasi tekstu un atbildi uz jautājumu:
EN: Read the text and answer to the question:

{{flores_passage}}
{{question}}
A: {{option1}}
B: {{option2}}
C: {{option3}}
D: {{option4}}

LV: Atbildi formātā 'Pareizā atbilde ir X',
kur X ir pareizās atbildes burts.

EN: Answer in form 'Correct answer is X',
where X is the letter of the correct answer.
```

Figure 1: Prompt structure.

5.2 Selected Language Models

The most popular open LLM families were selected: Gemma2 (GemmaTeam et al., 2024), Llama3 (Dubey et al., 2024), Mistral-large (Jiang et al., 2023) and Qwen (Bai et al., 2023). A 5-bit K-quantized version was used for every model. We also included OpenAI's GPT-4o and GPT-4o-mini models for reference as the most popular closed commercial models.

5.3 Experimental Setup

All tests were run using the Ollama toolkit[8] on a computer with 8x interconnected Nvidia A100 80GB GPUs.

The questions were asked directly in a zero-shot approach with each model's default system prompt (see Figure 1).

Some models answered with just the required phrase, some also added explanation. Therefore we used a case-insensitive regular expression:

(?:Atbilde ir|Answer is)[*\s(]*([A-D])

to find the model's answer in the response.

Each question was asked three times with three different seeds to test the robustness of the models. Robustness was measured as percentage of questions to which the model chose the same answer in all three cases. The top models scored 99% robustness on human translated English data and 98% for human translated Latvian data.

5.4 Results

The evaluation results (accuracy) for different LLMs are summarized in Table 6. Each of 900 questions is considered to be answered correctly only if all three responses were equal and correct.

[8]https://github.com/ollama/ollama

Language pair	Section	BLEU		chrF	
		DeepL	GPT	DeepL	GPT
English->Latvian	passages	0.36	0.28	65.8	60.6
English->Latvian	questions	0.29	0.18	64.7	53.1
English->Latvian	answers	0.32	0.22	64.4	58.2
Latvian->English	passages	0.43	0.38	69.3	67.3
Latvian->English	questions	0.48	0.34	69.7	61.4
Latvian->English	answers	0.34	0.26	63.7	62.0

Table 5: Evaluation of DeepL and GPT-4o-mini translations (BLEU and ChrF scores).

	English			Latvian		
Model	DeepL	GPT	Belebele	DeepL	GPT	Belebele
gemma2:27b	85%	87%	94%	90%	87%	91%
gemma2:9b	82%	85%	94%	87%	85%	88%
gemma2:2b	69%	73%	83%	55%	54%	58%
gpt-4o	**87%**	88%	95%	**93%**	**90%**	**94%**
gpt-4o-mini	83%	86%	94%	88%	85%	88%
llama3.1:405b	**87%**	**89%**	**96%**	91%	**90%**	92%
llama3.1:70b	84%	87%	94%	87%	85%	87%
llama3.1:8b	71%	74%	87%	62%	59%	63%
mistral-large:123b	**87%**	88%	**96%**	86%	80%	85%
qwen2:72b	85%	87%	94%	87%	84%	87%
qwen2:7b	79%	79%	89%	63%	61%	67%
qwen2.5:72b	85%	87%	**96%**	89%	87%	91%
qwen2.5:32b	86%	**89%**	95%	88%	86%	91%
qwen2.5:14b	83%	85%	94%	76%	73%	78%
Average	82%	85%	93%	82%	79%	83%

Table 6: Evaluation results for different LLMs on original (Belebele column) and machine translated (DeepL and GPT columns) datasets (accuracy).

5.4.1 Original Belebele Dataset

The best result of 96% accuracy for English is achieved by several models - Qwen2.5, Mistral-large, Llama3.1, while for Latvian only gpt-4o achieved 94% accuracy, followed by several open LLMs - llama3.1:405b with 92% accuracy and gemma2:27b and qwen2.5:72b and 32b with 91% accuracy. gpt-4o also seems the most balanced model with only one percentage point difference in accuracy between Latvian and English.

In general, the model's accuracy seems to correlate with the parameter size - the smaller the model, the lower is accuracy. Although our results are not directly comparable with the results obtained by the authors of the Belebele dataset, it seems that most recent LLMs demonstrate better "understanding" of low-resource languages and the results of the best open-weight LLMs differ only by 2-3 percentage points when compared to commercial ones.

5.4.2 Machine Translated Datasets

Evaluation results in Table 6 demonstrate a decrease of accuracy in case of machine-translated datasets. For English, the accuracy for the machine-translated dataset is always below 90%, dropping by at least 5 percentage points.

In case of Latvian, most of the models demonstrate comparable performance for both original and machine-translated datasets, with only a 1-3 percentage point decrease when tested on MT-datasets.

Although the automatic evaluation of MT (see Table 5) indicated that DeepL MT outperformed GPT in terms of standard MT quality metrics, the results for English in this natural language understanding task showed a different trend. Specifically, models demonstrated better performance when using the GPT-translated dataset rather than the DeepL-translated version.

6 Conclusion

In this study, we provided an initial assessment of several large language models' performance in Latvian across different natural language understanding tasks.

Results of our evaluation of multilingual commercial and open-source models highlights the disparities in model accuracy when applied to low-resource languages.

Our findings indicate that for the low-resource language Latvian, the top-performing LLMs can achieve similar results on both the original (human-created) and machine-translated datasets. However, machine translation proved less effective for high-resource language benchmarks, such as English, where it significantly impacted model accuracy.

While machine translation offers a feasible route to generate benchmarks for low-resource languages, it is not without its pitfalls. The choice of translation method and the inherent properties of the language models significantly influence the outcomes of benchmarking exercises.

Additionally, the benchmarking of open-source LLMs against proprietary systems reveals a narrowing performance gap. Despite these advances, significant challenges remain, including the lack of comprehensive evaluation datasets tailored to Latvian.

By introducing adapted versions of the COPA[9] and MMLU[10] datasets and evaluating models on the Belebele dataset, this paper lays the groundwork for further research in benchmarking.[11]

Future work should focus on creating robust, high-quality datasets specifically for low-resource languages and exploring novel architectures that can better generalize across linguistic diversity.

Acknowledgments

This work was supported by the "Language Technology Initiative" project (No. 2.3.1.1.i.0/1/22/I/CFLA/002), funded by the European Union Recovery and Resilience Mechanism Investment and the National Development Plan.

[9] Datasets available at https://github.com/LUMII-AILab/VTI-Data/tree/main/copa

[10] Datasets available at https://github.com/LUMII-AILab/VTI-Data/tree/main/mmlu

[11] Datasets from all our experiments are available at https://github.com/LUMII-AILab/VTI-Data

References

Josh Achiam, Steven Adler, Sandhini Agarwal, Lama Ahmad, Ilge Akkaya, Florencia Leoni Aleman, Diogo Almeida, Janko Altenschmidt, Sam Altman, Shyamal Anadkat, et al. 2023. Gpt-4 technical report. *arXiv preprint arXiv:2303.08774*.

Sanchit Ahuja, Divyanshu Aggarwal, Varun Gumma, Ishaan Watts, Ashutosh Sathe, Millicent Ochieng, Rishav Hada, Prachi Jain, Maxamed Axmed, Kalika Bali, and Sunayana Sitaram. 2024. Megaverse: Benchmarking large language models across languages, modalities, models and tasks. *arXiv preprint arXiv:2311.07463*.

Wazir Ali and Sampo Pyysalo. 2024. A survey of large language models for European Languages. *arXiv preprint arXiv:2408.15040*.

Jinze Bai, Shuai Bai, Yunfei Chu, Zeyu Cui, Kai Dang, Xiaodong Deng, Yang Fan, Wenbin Ge, Yu Han, Fei Huang, Binyuan Hui, Luo Ji, Mei Li, Junyang Lin, Runji Lin, Dayiheng Liu, Gao Liu, Chengqiang Lu, Keming Lu, Jianxin Ma, Rui Men, Xingzhang Ren, Xuancheng Ren, Chuanqi Tan, Sinan Tan, Jianhong Tu, Peng Wang, Shijie Wang, Wei Wang, Shengguang Wu, Benfeng Xu, Jin Xu, An Yang, Hao Yang, Jian Yang, Shusheng Yang, Yang Yao, Bowen Yu, Hongyi Yuan, Zheng Yuan, Jianwei Zhang, Xingxuan Zhang, Yichang Zhang, Zhenru Zhang, Chang Zhou, Jingren Zhou, Xiaohuan Zhou, and Tianhang Zhu. 2023. Qwen technical report. *arXiv preprint arXiv:2309.16609*.

Lucas Bandarkar, Davis Liang, Benjamin Muller, Mikel Artetxe, Satya Narayan Shukla, Donald Husa, Naman Goyal, Abhinandan Krishnan, Luke Zettlemoyer, and Madian Khabsa. 2024. The belebele benchmark: a parallel reading comprehension dataset in 122 language variants. In *Proceedings of the 62nd Annual Meeting of the Association for Computational Linguistics (Volume 1: Long Papers)*, pages 749–775, Bangkok, Thailand. Association for Computational Linguistics.

Yupeng Chang, Xu Wang, Jindong Wang, Yuan Wu, Linyi Yang, Kaijie Zhu, Hao Chen, Xiaoyuan Yi, Cunxiang Wang, Yidong Wang, et al. 2024. A survey on evaluation of large language models. *ACM Transactions on Intelligent Systems and Technology*, 15(3):1–45.

Alexis Conneau, Ruty Rinott, Guillaume Lample, Adina Williams, Samuel R. Bowman, Holger Schwenk, and Veselin Stoyanov. 2018. Xnli: Evaluating cross-lingual sentence representations. In *Proceedings of the 2018 Conference on Empirical Methods in Natural Language Processing*. Association for Computational Linguistics.

Wenliang Dai, Nayeon Lee, Boxin Wang, Zhuoling Yang, Zihan Liu, Jon Barker, Tuomas Rintamaki, Mohammad Shoeybi, Bryan Catanzaro, and Wei Ping. 2024. Nvlm: Open frontier-class multimodal llms. *arXiv preprint arXiv:2409.11402*.

Roberts Darģis, Guntis Bārzdiņš, Inguna Skadiņa, Normunds Gruzitis, and Baiba Saulite. 2024. Evaluating open-source LLMs in low-resource languages: Insights from Latvian high school exams. In *Proceedings of the 4th International Conference on Natural Language Processing for Digital Humanities*, pages 289–293, Miami, USA. Association for Computational Linguistics.

Jacob Devlin, Ming-Wei Chang, Kenton Lee, and Kristina Toutanova. 2019. BERT: Pre-training of deep bidirectional transformers for language understanding. In *Proceedings of the 2019 Conference of the North American Chapter of the Association for Computational Linguistics: Human Language Technologies, Volume 1 (Long and Short Papers)*, pages 4171–4186, Minneapolis, Minnesota. Association for Computational Linguistics.

Abhimanyu Dubey, Abhinav Jauhri, Abhinav Pandey, Abhishek Kadian, Ahmad Al-Dahle, Aiesha Letman, Akhil Mathur, Alan Schelten, Amy Yang, Angela Fan, Anirudh Goyal, Anthony Hartshorn, Aobo Yang, Archi Mitra, Archie Sravankumar, Artem Korenev, Arthur Hinsvark, Arun Rao, Aston Zhang, Aurelien Rodriguez, Austen Gregerson, Ava Spataru, Baptiste Roziere, Bethany Biron, Binh Tang, Bobbie Chern, Charlotte Caucheteux, Chaya Nayak, Chloe Bi, Chris Marra, Chris McConnell, Christian Keller, Christophe Touret, Chunyang Wu, Corinne Wong, and et al. 2024. The llama 3 herd of models. *arXiv preprint arXiv:2407.21783*.

GeminiTeam, Rohan Anil, Sebastian Borgeaud, Jean-Baptiste Alayrac, Jiahui Yu, Radu Soricut, Johan Schalkwyk, Andrew M. Dai, Anja Hauth, et al. 2024. Gemini: A family of highly capable multimodal models. *arXiv preprint arXiv:2312.11805*.

GemmaTeam, Morgane Riviere, Shreya Pathak, Pier Giuseppe Sessa, Cassidy Hardin, Surya Bhupatiraju, Léonard Hussenot, Thomas Mesnard, Bobak Shahriari, Alexandre Ramé, Johan Ferret, Peter Liu, Pouya Tafti, Abe Friesen, Michelle Casbon, Sabela Ramos, Ravin Kumar, Charline Le Lan, Sammy Jerome, Anton Tsitsulin, Nino Vieillard, Piotr Stanczyk, Sertan Girgin, Nikola Momchev, Matt Hoffman, Shantanu Thakoor, Jean-Bastien Grill, Behnam Neyshabur, Olivier Bachem, Alanna Walton, Aliaksei Severyn, Alicia Parrish, and et. 2024. Gemma 2: Improving open language models at a practical size. *arXiv preprint arXiv:2408.00118*.

Normunds Gruzitis, Lauma Pretkalnina, Baiba Saulite, Laura Rituma, Gunta Nespore-Berzkalne, Arturs Znotins, and Peteris Paikens. 2018. Creation of a balanced state-of-the-art multilayer corpus for NLU. In *Proceedings of the Eleventh International Conference on Language Resources and Evaluation (LREC 2018)*, Miyazaki, Japan. European Language Resources Association (ELRA).

Dan Hendrycks, Collin Burns, Steven Basart, Andy Zou, Mantas Mazeika, Dawn Song, and Jacob Steinhardt. 2020. Measuring massive multitask language understanding. *arXiv preprint arXiv:2009.03300*.

Albert Q. Jiang, Alexandre Sablayrolles, Arthur Mensch, Chris Bamford, Devendra Singh Chaplot, Diego de las Casas, Florian Bressand, Gianna Lengyel, Guillaume Lample, Lucile Saulnier, Lélio Renard Lavaud, Marie-Anne Lachaux, Pierre Stock, Teven Le Scao, Thibaut Lavril, Thomas Wang, Timothée Lacroix, and William El Sayed. 2023. Mistral 7b. *arXiv preprint arXiv:2310.06825*.

Hele-Andra Kuulmets, Andre Tättar, and Mark Fishel. 2022. Estonian language understanding: a case study on the copa task. *Baltic Journal of Modern Computing*, 10.

Viet Lai, Chien Nguyen, Nghia Ngo, Thuat Nguyen, Franck Dernoncourt, Ryan Rossi, and Thien Nguyen. 2023. Okapi: Instruction-tuned large language models in multiple languages with reinforcement learning from human feedback. In *Proceedings of the 2023 Conference on Empirical Methods in Natural Language Processing: System Demonstrations*, pages 318–327. Association for Computational Linguistics.

Md Tahmid Rahman Laskar, M Saiful Bari, Mizanur Rahman, Md Amran Hossen Bhuiyan, Shafiq Joty, and Jimmy Xiangji Huang. 2023. A systematic study and comprehensive evaluation of chatgpt on benchmark datasets. *arXiv preprint arXiv:2305.18486*.

Yinhan Liu, Myle Ott, Naman Goyal, Jingfei Du, Mandar Joshi, Danqi Chen, Omer Levy, Mike Lewis, Luke Zettlemoyer, and Veselin Stoyanov. 2019. Roberta: A robustly optimized BERT pretraining approach. *CoRR*, abs/1907.11692.

Pedro Henrique Martins, Patrick Fernandes, João Alves, Nuno M. Guerreiro, Ricardo Rei, Duarte M. Alves, José Pombal, Amin Farajian, Manuel Faysse, Mateusz Klimaszewski, Pierre Colombo, Barry Haddow, José G. C. de Souza, Alexandra Birch, and André F. T. Martins. 2024. Eurollm: Multilingual language models for Europe. *arXiv preprint arXiv:2409.16235*.

NLLBTeam, Marta R. Costa-jussà, James Cross, Onur Çelebi, Maha Elbayad, Kenneth Heafield, Kevin Heffernan, Elahe Kalbassi, Janice Lam, Daniel Licht, Jean Maillard, Anna Sun, Skyler Wang, Guillaume Wenzek, Al Youngblood, Bapi Akula, Loic Barrault, Gabriel Mejia Gonzalez, Prangthip Hansanti, John Hoffman, Semarley Jarrett, Kaushik Ram Sadagopan, Dirk Rowe, Shannon Spruit, Chau Tran, Pierre Andrews, Necip Fazil Ayan, Shruti Bhosale, Sergey Edunov, Angela Fan, Cynthia Gao, Vedanuj Goswami, Francisco

Guzmán, Philipp Koehn, Alexandre Mourachko, Christophe Ropers, Safiyyah Saleem, Holger Schwenk, and Jeff Wang. 2022. No language left behind: Scaling human-centered machine translation. *arXiv preprint arXiv:2207.04672*.

Kishore Papineni, Salim Roukos, Todd Ward, and Wei-Jing Zhu. 2002. Bleu: a method for automatic evaluation of machine translation. In *Proceedings of the 40th Annual Meeting on Association for Computational Linguistics*, ACL '02, page 311–318. Association for Computational Linguistics.

Maja Popović. 2015. chrF: character n-gram F-score for automatic MT evaluation. In *Proceedings of the Tenth Workshop on Statistical Machine Translation*, pages 392–395, Lisbon, Portugal. Association for Computational Linguistics.

Melissa Roemmele, Cosmin Adrian Bejan, and Andrew S Gordon. 2011. Choice of plausible alternatives: An evaluation of commonsense causal reasoning. In *2011 AAAI spring symposium series*.

Inguna Skadiņa, Baiba Saulīte, Ilze Auziņa, Normunds Grūzītis, Andrejs Vasiļjevs, Raivis Skadiņš, and Mārcis Pinnis. 2022. Latvian language in the digital age: The main achievements in the last decade. *Baltic Journal of Modern Computing*, 10(3):490–503.

Aarohi Srivastava, Abhinav Rastogi, Abhishek Rao, Abu Awal Md Shoeb, Abubakar Abid, Adam Fisch, Adam R. Brown, Adam Santoro, Aditya Gupta, Adria Garriga-Alonso, Agnieszka Kluska, Aitor Lewkowycz, Akshat Agarwal, Alethea Power, Alex Ray, Alex Warstadt, Alexander W. Kocurek, Ali Safaya, et al. 2023. Beyond the Imitation Game: Quantifying and extrapolating the capabilities of language models. *Transactions on Machine Learning Research*.

Matej Ulčar and Marko Robnik-Šikonja. 2021. Training dataset and dictionary sizes matter in bert models: the case of baltic languages. In *International Conference on Analysis of Images, Social Networks and Texts*, pages 162–172. Springer.

Rinalds Vīksna and Inguna Skadiņa. 2020. Large language models for Latvian named entity recognition. In *Human Language Technologies - The Baltic Perspective*, volume 328, pages 111–115. IOS Press.

Alex Wang, Yada Pruksachatkun, Nikita Nangia, Amanpreet Singh, Julian Michael, Felix Hill, Omer Levy, and Samuel Bowman. 2019. Superglue: A stickier benchmark for general-purpose language understanding systems. *Advances in neural information processing systems*, 32.

Alex Wang, Amanpreet Singh, Julian Michael, Felix Hill, Omer Levy, and Samuel Bowman. 2018. GLUE: A Multi-Task Benchmark and Analysis Platform for Natural Language Understanding. In *Proceedings of the 2018 EMNLP Workshop BlackboxNLP: Analyzing and Interpreting Neural Networks for NLP*, pages 353–355. Association for Computational Linguistics.

Artūrs Znotiņš and Guntis Bārzdiņš. 2020. Lvbert: Transformer-based model for latvian language understanding. In *Human Language Technologies - The Baltic Perspective*, volume 328, pages 111–115. IOS Press.

On the usage of semantics, syntax, and morphology for noun classification in isiZulu

Imaan Sayed, Zola Mahlaza, Alexander van der Leek, Jonathan Mopp, C. Maria Keet
Department of Computer Science
University of Cape Town
South Africa
{zmahlaza,mkeet}@cs.uct.ac.za
{SYDIMA002,VLKALE003,MPPJON002}@myuct.ac.za

Abstract

There is limited work aimed at solving the core task of noun classification for Nguni languages. The task focuses on identifying the semantic categorisation of each noun and plays a crucial role in the ability to form semantically and morphologically valid sentences. The work by Byamugisha (2022) was the first to tackle the problem for a related, but non-Nguni, language. While there have been efforts to replicate it for a Nguni language, there has been no effort focused on comparing the technique used in the original work vs. contemporary neural methods or a number of traditional machine learning classification techniques that do not rely on human-guided knowledge to the same extent. We reproduce Byamugisha (2022)'s work with different configurations to account for differences in access to datasets and resources, compare the approach with a pretrained transformer-based model, and traditional machine learning models that rely on less human-guided knowledge. The newly created data-driven models outperform the knowledge-infused models, with the best performing models achieving an F1 score of 0.97.

1 Introduction

Solid performance when using modern Natural Language Processing (NLP) approaches, especially ones that are popular with languages like English, is dependent on the availability of large text corpora. Unlike English, all Niger-Congo B[1] (NCB) languages do not have large training datasets; hence, contemporary techniques have not been used for tasks such as noun classification. Since the languages are characterized by agglutinative morphology, have an intricate noun class system, and possess little datasets and tools that can be repurposed for various tasks (Moors et al., 2018), most problems have been tackled with knowledge-infused approaches. The discrepancy of resource availability also means that there are limited efforts to contrast contemporary data-driven and knowledge-infused techniques to determine whether there is any difference in performance.

In this paper, we address this lack of comparison for the task of noun class disambiguation for NCB languages. Using isiZulu, the focus of this paper and the largest language in South Africa by L1 speakers, as a case study the task consists of predicting the noun class (e.g., NC2) when one is given a noun (e.g., *abantu* 'people'). We limit our investigation to this task since it is a crucial but unsolved problem for all NCB languages, isiZulu especially. Due to NCB languages' low-resourced state, the only work that tackles the task for a NCB language was done by Byamugisha (2022) focusing on Runyankore and related languages from Guthrie's Zone J (Maho, 1999).

Byamugisha (2022)'s work deals with the lack of a large dataset of noun and class pairs by introducing a number of modules, each solving some crucial function. Some modules use unlabelled or automatically labelled datasets that, when combined are able to predict the noun class of the noun. Byamugisha's work is a promising start, since it obtained accuracies in the range 80%-87% for Runyankore. The work does not resolve the question of technique comparison; hence, the utility of relying on a multi-modular and knowledge-infused approach that combines morphology, syntax, and morphology vs. machine learning techniques and a neural model, especially a large language model (LLM) adapted via the pretrain-

[1] Some authors use the term Bantu languages

Proceedings of the Third Workshop on Resources and Representations for Under-Resourced Languages and Domains (RESOURCEFUL-2025), pages 96–105, March 2, 2025 ©2025 Association for Computational Linguistics

finetune paradigm for classification, is still unclear. All of the aforementioned models have the potential to classify nouns using morphology, syntax, and morphology but differ in the following way:

System complexity and resource requirements: Knowledge-infused approaches tend to increase the number of sub-modules, each with a clear and dedicated responsibility, hence the complexity of the system increases. While the dedicated functionality of the subcomponents makes the entire system more auditable, such techniques tend to rely on stopgap resources (e.g., models that are trained using automatically labelled datasets (e.g., (Mahlaza et al., 2025)) due to a lack of a context-free grammar that can be used to generate a gold standard dataset unlike Byamugisha (2022)) and they are sometimes inferior with respect to advanced pattern recognition vs. modern blackbox models (e.g., LLMs).

Reliance on morphosyntax: Knowledge-infused approaches have not been used to investigate noun classification while relying only on morphosyntax, in the context of NCB languages, due to the difficulty associated with the lack of clarity regarding effective representations, especially ones that separate semantics from syntax, morphology and other features (see (Huang et al., 2021) for similar challenges with English sentences).

Our approach is two-fold. First, we reproduce Byamugisha's knowledge-infused noun classifier for isiZulu, while noting the differences in resource requirements and their availability. The primary goal is to determine how best to build a syntactic-semantic model for isiZulu since there is no Context Free Grammar (CFG) that can be used to generate labelled and unlabelled datasets. This requires that we identify how changes in training corpora characteristics for the data-driven components affect accuracy. In that regard, we consider various options for labels in the labelled data (concord, noun class, or both), training corpus size, annotation quality (manually annotated by an expert or automatically labelled), and data-level (sentential, phrasal, or word-based).

Second, we create various supervised machine learning classifiers (k-Nearest Neighbours (kNN) algorithm, decision trees, Support Vector Machines (SVM)), and deep learning based models (a fully connected feed-forward neural network and a fine-tuned version of the Serengeti language model (Adebara et al., 2023)). We compare all the models using a larger dataset (cf. Byamugisha (2022)) made up of nouns and their classes to ascertain whether one can obtain similar or superior performance by relying on a traditional ML model that makes use of morphosyntax only. We also investigate whether similar, or superior, performance can be achieved via a neural model that relies on morphological, syntax, and semantic knowledge trained from scratch or adapted from a pre-trained multilingual LLM (in this case, Serengeti (Adebara et al., 2023)).

Our results showed that the neural-based and traditional ML models perform the best. The best multi-modular model that relies on human-guided knowledge achieves an F1 score of 0.71 while the best neural model and traditional ML models have scores of 0.97.

The rest of the paper is structured such that Sections 2-3 introduce noun classification and the existing models, Section 4 details the created dataset, Sections 5-7 introduce our models, Section 8 presents the results, Section 9 discusses, and Section 10 concludes.

2 NCB noun classification

NCB languages are found in more than 54 countries, with an estimated 240 million speakers, and they have a lot of diversity (Gowlett, 2014). Nonetheless, they all have a noun class system that categorises each noun to one of 23 classes, as informally summarized in Table 1 for isiZulu. To demonstrate the impact of the noun classes on the formation of sentences, consider the following example English sentence and its translation:

English: The dog is unhealthy
The$_{article}$ dog$_{subj.\ noun}$ is$_{singl.identifier}$ un$_{negation}$-healthy$_{adjective}$

IsiZulu: *Inja ayiphilile*
I$_{NC9}$-nja$_{stem}$ a$_{neg.preprefix}$-yi$_{NC9\ SC}$-philile$_{adjective\ root}$

The formation of the word *ayiphilile* 'is unhealthy' relies on identifying the noun class (here: NC9) of the subject *inja* 'dog'. However, there are no models for automatically classifying nouns into their respective classes for isiZulu.

Table 1: List of NCB, including isiZulu, noun classes and the semantics that govern inclusion for each class (Source: (Byamugisha, 2022))

Noun class	Example semantic categorization
1, 2	People and kinship
3, 4	Plants, nature, and some parts of the body
5, 6	Fruits, liquids, some parts of the body and paired things
7, 8	Inanimate objects
9, 10	Tools and animals
11	Long thin stringy objects, languages,and inanimate objects
12, 13	Diminutives
14	Abstract concepts
15	Infinitives and parts of the body
16, 17, 18	Locative classes
19	Diminutives
20, 21, 22	Augmentatives
23	Locative

3 Existing models for noun classification

The only work that has tackled the task at hand, for NCB languages at least, was conducted by Byamugisha and it took inspiration from the existing linguistic theory on the NCB noun class system by modelling the possible avenues for classifying a noun namely the morphological prefix, semantic categorization and syntactical context (Byamugisha, 2022). They pursue the task via a multimodular knowledge-infused model, whose function will now be described.

The simplest avenue relies on the prefix. Byamugisha's model uses the morphological prefix information to classify a noun if it is unique. For instance, the noun *abantu* 'people' has as prefix *aba-* and stem *-ntu* and the prefix *aba-* is unique to NC2, the noun will be correctly classified. The noun *umuntu* 'person' has as prefix *umu-*, but it is ambiguous, because the prefix associated with both NC1 and NC3 is either *um-* or *umu-* depending on the number of syllables of the stem. This simple model will only output a prediction if a unique prefix is found otherwise it is considered ambiguous and continues to the next step.

When the prefix is insufficient, it draws on the semantic generalizations to determine the noun class. This is done by training a new model to determine similar words, using FastText[2] with a corpus of 1 million sentences, to determine a noun's semantic neighbours. For instance, for the Runyankore noun *omuntu* 'person' from NC1, the model determines that the nearest neighbours are *omugyesi* 'reaper' (NC1), *omutaahi* 'companion' (NC1), *omukoreesa* 'overseer' (NC1), *omushomesa* 'teacher' (NC1), and *omukuru* 'elder' (NC1). The semantic information derived from the nearest neighbours allows discerning between ambiguous classes, since information associated with, e.g., *omuntu* 'person' (NC1) can be used to distinguish it from the noun *omukono* 'arm', based on the noun class frequencies associated with its neighbours. The noun *omukono* shares the same prefix *omu-*, but one retrieves different neighbours, such as *omunwa* 'mouth' (NC3), *omutwe* 'head' (NC3), *eriino* 'tooth' (NC5), and *enkokora* 'elbow' (NC9), i.e., body parts, vs. *omuntu* 'person' and certain roles they play. Fundamentally, the differentiation between the two is done by analysing the noun classes associated with the neighbouring words and ascertaining that NC1 is the most common class among the neighbours for *omuntu* 'person', hence, the input noun is inferred to belong to the same class.

The determination of the most common class among the neighbours requires filtering out some elements. Specifically, when given neighbouring nouns, without any labels, a corpus made up of 1 million sentences is used to train a FastText classifier, where the corpus' is annotated with parts-of-speech, the noun class, and the concord (where possible). The resulting model is used to annotate the input neighbouring words and if these predictions are found to be inconsistent then they are dropped from consideration. The concord annotation is then used for the syntax-based filtering step because it is unique among the classes (Gowlett, 2014; Maho, 1999).

Alternative work involving processing NCB nouns exists, but it does not tackle the problem of noun classification; specifically, the efforts on building morphological analysers (Bosch et al., 2008), morphological generators (Bosch and Pretorius, 2003), part-of-speech taggers (De Pauw et al., 2012), and noun pluralization tools (Byamugisha et al., 2018, 2017) show attempts to

[2]https://radimrehurek.com/gensim/models/fasttext.html

deal with the ambiguity of nouns. Other researchers have created a massively multilingual transformer-based encoder-only language model, named Serengeti, whose training data includes isiZulu (Adebara et al., 2023). However, none of these models have been investigated, despite their potential capability, to classify nouns or to compare them with Byamugisha (2022)'s approach.

4 New dataset for the experiments

The aim of the experiments is to ascertain and compare the performance of multiple methods, detailed in Sections 5-7. In this section, we describe the dataset that is used to compare the techniques.

We created a new isiZulu dataset by extracting nouns and their classes from the Oxford Zulu-English dictionary (de Schryver, Gilles-Maurice, 2015) via optical character recognition and manual cleaning. We created two versions of the dataset where one version is labelled with a single noun class, either singular or plural depending on the modality of the noun, and the second is labelled with the singular and plural classes. For instance, the word *umuntu* 'person' is labelled with the singular noun class 1 in one dataset and labelled with the singular and plural combined classes 1/2 in another. The dataset version that combines noun classes is only used to train some of the traditional machine learning models and the details are provided in Section 6.

The number of nouns per class in the dataset is listed in Table 2. We used an 80-20 train-test split.

Table 2: Distribution of nouns per class in the dataset used for training and testing models.

Class	% of nouns	|nouns|
1	4.80	110
1a	6.37	144
2	4.13	94
2a	2.11	48
3	7.02	160
4	3.82	87
5	12.99	296
6	10.14	231
7	10.05	229
8	7.33	167
9	13.08	299
10	6.80	155
11	4.30	98
14	2.63	60
15	4.43	101
	Total	2279

5 Knowledge-infused models

We created multiple variations of Byamugisha (2022)'s multi-modular classifier to support isiZulu. This is done by creating multiple versions of each module in the architecture, labelled A-G in Figure 1. We now turn to describe the design decisions and resources used.

Component A This module identifies the noun class via the noun's prefix. We use Table 7 to determine if a noun has a unique prefix hence it is possible to uniquely determine its noun class. When the prefix is unique then we resolve the noun class while ensuring that we prioritise values that have the longest length. For instance, when a noun begins with the prefix *aba-* then it can be uniquely identified as belonging to NC2, however, a noun such as *umthandazo* 'prayer' can be classified to NC1 or NC3. When a noun's class is ambiguous then the noun is passed to the following modules.

Component B and C These modules take first responsibility in the pipeline to determine the class when a noun's prefix is not unique. They first embed words in a vector space as a means of identifying similar words. Words are embedded using two possible models; both versions are FastText skipgram models, motivated by our interpretation of the work done for Runyankore. One version is a pre-trained isiZulu model created using 1 million sentences sourced from Dlamini et al. (2021). It was trained with 300 dimensions, and subwords are formed using n-grams in the range of 3-6. The alternative model is trained on 180 000 unlabelled web-crawled sentences, whose sources are listed in Table 3. For each word representation, we identify K similar words using the traditional kNN algorithm, where K was selected from the range 10 to 200.

Component D This module takes each of the predicted neighbouring nouns, produced by modules B and C, and labels them with a noun class and/or a class-specific concord using a classifier. This annotation classifier is trained from scratch. Since we do not have access to a context-free grammar to generate training data à la Byamugisha (2022) for the classifier, we investigated the use of different datasets to determine the impact of certain characteristics (e.g., annotation quality); all features are listed in Table 4. Seven classifier versions were developed, each with FastText's supervised training capability and its hyperparameter autotuning feature (Joulin et al., 2017). Training data was split in the ratio 80/20 for training and validation respectively. As an internal evaluation approach, the performance of each classifier is tested on the Keet dataset listed in Table 3.

Component E and F These modules are responsible for automatically filtering nearest-neighbouring nouns using either a part-of-speech classifier or regular expressions. Since module D did not annotate the words with a part-of-speech, these modules rely on a newly trained POS classifier for the annotations. The classifier was trained on web-crawled data with simplified POS tags and sourced from (du Toit and Puttkammer, 2021). The new classifier is able to identify verbs with 96% accuracy when tested against the combined gold standard datasets listed in Table 4. When the current modules use the trained classifier, they remove all neighbouring words that are identified as verbs. These modules also rely on an alternative filter that removes verbs by matching their subject concord using regular expressions based on the work by Keet and Khumalo (2017), along with additional rules from the Oxford isiZulu Bilingual Dictionary (de Schryver, Gilles-Maurice, 2015).

The second phase of filtering removes words that do not contain a morpheme associated with their predicted noun class. There are two alternative models considered to achieve this. The first version (i.e., subword-level) removes a neighbour if the morpheme associated with predicted label is not contained in the word, by matching all possible versions of it (including phonological conditioned variations) (Keet and Khumalo, 2017). The second model (i.e., word-level) filters neighbours based on their subwords. It fetches the character n-gram range for the word model, computes all substrings for the word that matches that length, labels each subword with a noun class and concord using the previously mentioned classifier and returns True if the neighbour's predicted label is in the set of predictions for its subwords.

Component G This module is responsible for identifying the noun class from the set of annotated words produced by the previous steps in the pipeline. It does so by computing the frequencies for each noun class found in the dataset and identifies the class with the highest count in the final list of nearest neighbours. The most common class is then used as the final prediction.

Table 3: List of datasets used to build the annotation classifiers required for the isiZulu knowledge-infused model.

Dataset	Size	Type	Label
Web-crawled data (Leipzig CC - isiZulu 2016 Mixed Corpus) (Leipzig University, 2024)	180 000	Sent.	✗
NCHLT Morph. Corpus (Gaustad and Puttkammer, 2022)	45 000	Word	✓
Ukwabelana (Spiegler et al., 2010)	21 416	Word	✓
Gaustad & McKellar (Gaustad and McKellar, 2024)	50 000	Word	✓
Keet (sourced from author and (Gilbert and Keet, 2018))	795	Word	✓

We compared the various versions of the knowledge-infused model by determining their accuracies on the Keet dataset, listed in Table 3. The evaluation results will be discussed in Section 8. For the final evaluation, we compute the precision, recall, and F1 scores using the test set detailed in Section 4 for the best performing models.

6 Traditional machine learning models

To create novel supervised ML models that rely on morphosyntax, and possibly syntax and semantics, for noun classification we considered four supervised machine learning algorithms and models. In addition, we also experimented with various ways of preprocessing and representing the nouns. We describe the choices made regarding these elements in the following subsections.

Noun forms We investigate the use of compressed and uncompressed versions of each noun

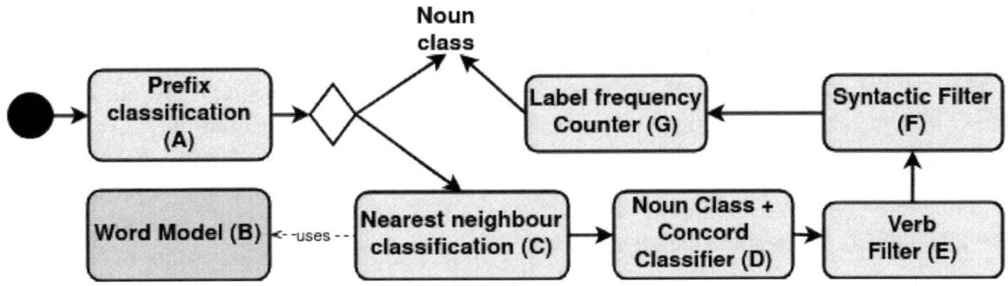

Figure 1: Architecture of the approximated knowledge-infused model for noun classification.

Table 4: Datasets used to train a word embedding model for the replicated classifier. Abbreviations: SN = Sentence, Part = Partial, B = Bronze, G = Gold, W = Word, SC = Subject concord, NC = Noun class, and PC = Possessive concord.

Dataset name	**Label(s)**	**Size**	**Level**
Automatically labelled datasets (Bronze)			
SN-B	SC, NC	103 895	SN
SN-B-PartSN	SC, NC	103 895	Phrase
SN-BW	SC, NC	336 029	Word
N-BW	NC	246 362	Word
Expert labelled datasets (Gold)			
Full-GW	SC, NC, OC, PC, Verb	61 954	Word
SN-GW	SC, NC	50 954	Word
N-GW	NC	36 713	Word

and this is done to address the hypothesis that the compressed form of the morphosyntactic model will outperform the surface-form variant, drawing from the existing literature surrounding the accuracy gains observed when compressing text in the context of topic classification (i.e., (Jiang et al., 2023)). Specifically, nouns are compressed using gzip with all the default parameters found in Jiang et al. (2023) but we use a single time parameter (i.e., 0) instead of relying on the current time.

Noun representations We convert each noun into a vector by relying on term frequencies, obtained via *scikit-learn*'s *TfidfVectorizer* and *TfVectorizer* with the same 'character' and 'lowercase=false' parameters to ensure that we only consider character level n-grams within the nouns and account for capitalization. When creating vector representations, we made use of term frequency (TF) and term frequency inverse document frequency (TF-IDF) to determine the impact of taking into account the rarity of an n-gram in the noun set (Shahmirzadi et al., 2019).

Models We investigated the use of a nearest neighbours classifier, decision tree, and a support vector machine, all created using *scikit-learn*[3]. The main hyper-parameter adjusted and tested for in the case of kNN was the number of neighbours considered, otherwise all defaults for the *scikit-learn*'s *KNNClassifier* class were used. For the decision tree, we adjusted the tree depth, in addition to assigning an integer to the random state parameter to achieve deterministic behaviour. We also combatted overfitting via cost complexity pruning; otherwise, all defaults for the *scikit-learn*'s *DecisionTreeClassifier* class were used. For the SVM, we used a linear kernel since it leads to faster training speed and tends to be less prone to overfitting (Rochim et al., 2021).

We also created an ensemble variation of the kNN, SVM, and DT models. Specifically, we created models that first predict dual noun classes hence they predict the plural and singular noun classes first. For instance, when given the noun *abantu* 'people' each model would predict the noun class pair '1/2'. The final noun class prediction is then determined based on the two predicted classes (i.e., 1 and 2) based on the probability associated with each of the two classes via the *predictProb* function from the *scikit-learn* library.

We computed the precision, recall, and F1 scores for all models using the test set.

7 Deep learning-based models

We created two types of deep learning models. One is a simple neural network that is trained from

[3]https://scikit-learn.org/

scratch while the second is a pre-trained large language model that supports isiZulu and fine-tuned for the task at hand. We describe each of the models in the following subsections.

Simple feed-forward neural network We created a fully connected feed-forward neural (FNN) network that consists of an input layer, two hidden layers, and an output layer. The FNN was trained using isiZulu embeddings sourced from Adelani (2022), therefore, it may capture not only morphosyntax but other linguistic features. We relied on *FastTextKeyedVectors* for loading the embeddings so that out-of-vocabulary words can be inferred. The hidden layers make use of a ReLU activation function and they are followed by dropout layers to prevent over-fitting. The neural network's hyper-parameters are listed in Table 6. This was created to act a simple baseline for the pre-trained model.

Pre-trained LLM We also fine-tuned Serengeti (Adebara et al., 2023), a model based on the XLM-R (Conneau et al., 2020) architecture, by updating all parameters through the *transformers* library[4] and the *trainer* application programming interface[5] using a training batch size of 16, with 100 training warm-up steps, and a weight decay of 0.01. Serengeti was originally pre-trained and tested on a variety of tasks which include named entity recognition, part of speech tagging, and phrase chunking but not noun classification hence there is no additional baseline to compare against, other than the newly created FNN.

We computed the precision, recall, and F1 scores for both models using the test set.

8 Results

The results of the internal evaluation of the reproduced knowledge-infused technique are presented in Figure 2. The best performing model relies on a expert labelled dataset, with syntax and verb information, for component D (*N-GW* in Table 4), which achieves an accuracy of 85%. The best performing model that was created from the largest automatically labelled dataset, at the word-level, has an accuracy that is lower by 16.99%. The prefix-only models that only rely on the prefix to classify nouns perform the worst with an accuracy of 36.6%.

The results from comparing all the developed models are provided in Table 5. The traditional machine learning-based approaches that rely only on morphosyntax, make use of compressed data, and used in an ensemble approach, perform the best. Specifically, the best support vector machine model has an F1 score of 0.9736. The model performs comparably to the best model that relies on morphology, syntax, and semantics with 0.965 and performs slightly better than the best performing morphosyntax-based model that makes use of uncompressed data (3% difference).

9 Discussion

We now revisit the problem of inferring a noun's noun class by the various techniques and determining whether the use of semantics, syntax, and morphology, in a human-guided setting, yields the best results. The results obtained show that the neural-based models that make use of semantics, syntax, and morphology without human-guidance (the FNN and pre-trained LLM) and the traditional machine learning models that rely only on morphology, with less human-guided knowledge, perform better.

For NC detection, is better to rely on data-driven models that use human-guided knowledge in a less labour intensive approach where there are fewer modules so that errors are not propagated and have less negative impact on performance. This is evidenced by the observation that all the models that achieve an F1 score above 0.9, as listed in Table 5, do not rely on significant human guidance that ensures that the task is solved via only the prefix or a semantic approach that mandates the identification of semantically similar words and infers the noun class based on related words. Even if the 'good performance' threshold is lowered to an F1 score of 0.8, we see that none of the knowledge-infused models obtained by replicating the work by (Byamugisha, 2022) can be considered as having good performance. In fact, all 14 models that meet that standard are either neural-based or make use of traditional machine learning models.

The performance difference between the FNN and LLM is small (4%), in particular considering the simplicity of the FNN. This suggests that pre-training offers limited benefit for the current task. When comparing the traditional machine learning

[4]https://huggingface.co/docs/transformers/index

[5]https://huggingface.co/docs/transformers/main_classes/trainer

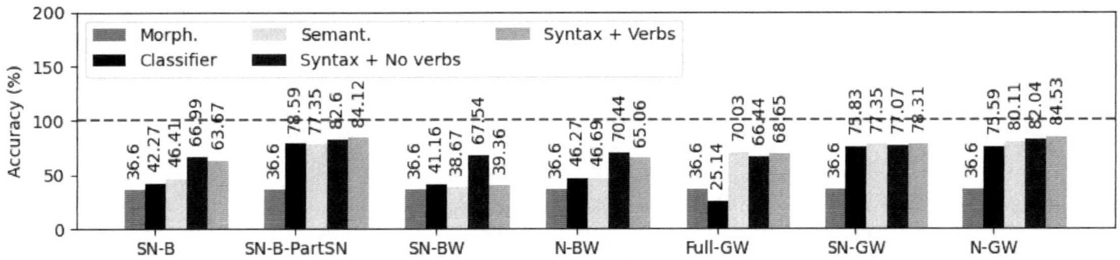

Figure 2: Accuracies in replicated models, across the models that differ based on the datatset used for the NC-Concord classifier module. The abbreviates used correspond to those detailed in Table 4.

Table 5: Precision, recall, and F1 scores of the best performing models. Abbreviations: FT = Fine-tuned, Ens = Ensemble, Prec = Precision, Rec = Recall, TF = Term frequency, and IDF = Inverse document frequency

Model	Prec.	Rec.	F1
Morphology, syntax, and semantics			
SN-B	0.714	0.591	0.604
SN-BP-PartSN	0.768	0.736	0.714
SN-BW	0.795	0.675	0.686
N-BW	0.743	0.641	0.655
Full-GW	0.625	0.565	0.576
SN-GW	0.789	0.771	0.762
N-GW	0.725	0.729	0.713
FNN	0.9213	0.9273	0.9209
Serengeti-FT	0.9642	0.9666	0.9650
Morphosyntax-based (uncompressed)			
kNN-TFIDF	0.7094	0.7149	0.6979
kNN-TF	0.6968	0.7281	0.6928
kNN-Ens.	0.7269	0.7302	0.7060
SVM-TFIDF	0.8222	0.8421	0.8273
SVM-TF	0.8424	0.8509	0.8439
SVM-Ens.	0.9367	0.9429	0.9385
DT-TFIDF	0.7300	0.7478	0.7133
DT-TF	0.7961	0.7917	0.7902
DT-Ens.	0.7916	0.8052	0.7691
Morphosyntax-based (compressed)			
kNN-TFIDF	0.8640	0.8770	0.8585
kNN-TF	0.8349	0.8070	0.7970
kNN-Ens.	0.8693	0.8662	0.8632
SVM-TFIDF	0.8608	0.8487	0.8419
SVM-TF+	0.8947	0.8904	0.8883
SVM-Ens.	**0.9742**	**0.9736**	**0.9736**
DT-TFIDF	0.8824	0.8706	0.8642
DT-TF	0.9038	0.8904	0.8859
DT-Ens.	0.9094	0.8991	0.8918

models, we see that most of the models that use compressed data perform better than their counterparts that use uncompressed data. In fact, the ensemble SVM model also outperforms deep learning models. This suggests Jiang et al. (2023)'s findings on the utility of compression also apply in the context of a Nguni language. Since not all the compression-based models outperform the neural models, this might demonstrate that there is utility in using minimal knowledge in traditional machine learning models. This is because the best performing model is an ensemble that exploits the fact that it is easier to identify the plural and singular noun classes of a noun vs. predicting the singular or plural in isolation. Then it disambiguates between just the plural vs. singular classes instead of 15, unlike the single class prediction problem. As such, this may indicate that there is value in using insights about a language in less labour intensive ways.

10 Conclusions

In reproducing the work by (Byamugisha, 2022) with different configurations and techniques, the results showed that the neural and ML models perform best, with an F1 score of 0.97, while the replicated models achieve a score of 0.71 despite their reliance on human-guided knowledge.

In future work, we plan to consider also other NCB languages and determine whether the number of 'ambiguous' prefixes among the number of prefixes might influence a technique's performance. We also plan to investigate the use of transformer-based and decoder-focused models.

Acknowledgments

This work was financially supported in part by the National Research Foundation (NRF) of South Africa (Grant Number and CPRR23040389063).

References

Ife Adebara, AbdelRahim Elmadany, Muhammad Abdul-Mageed, and Alcides Alcoba Inciarte. 2023. Serengeti: Massively multilingual language models for Africa.

David Ifeoluwa Adelani. 2022. *Natural language processing for African languages*. Phd thesis, Faculty of Mathematics and Computer Science of Saarland University.

Sonja Bosch, Laurette Pretorius, and Axel Fleisch. 2008. Experimental bootstrapping of morphological analysers for Nguni languages. *Nordic Journal of African Studies*, 17(2):23.

Sonja E Bosch and Laurette Pretorius. 2003. Building a computational morphological analyser/generator for Zulu using the Xerox finite-state tools. In *Proceedings of the Workshop on Finite-State Methods in Natural Language Processing, 10th Conference of the European Chapter of the Association for Computational Linguistics*, pages 27–34.

Joan Byamugisha. 2022. Noun class disambiguation in Runyankore and related languages. In *Proceedings of the 29th International Conference on Computational Linguistics*, pages 4350–4359, Gyeongju, Republic of Korea. International Committee on Computational Linguistics.

Joan Byamugisha, C. Maria Keet, and Brian DeRenzi. 2017. Toward an NLG system for Bantu languages: first steps with Runyankore (demo). In *Proceedings of the 10th International Conference on Natural Language Generation, INLG 2017, Santiago de Compostela, Spain, September 4-7, 2017*, pages 154–155. Association for Computational Linguistics.

Joan Byamugisha, C. Maria Keet, and Langa Khumalo. 2018. Pluralising nouns in isiZulu and related languages. In *Computational Linguistics and Intelligent Text Processing*, pages 271–283, Cham. Springer International Publishing.

Alexis Conneau, Kartikay Khandelwal, Naman Goyal, Vishrav Chaudhary, Guillaume Wenzek, Francisco Guzmán, Edouard Grave, Myle Ott, Luke Zettlemoyer, and Veselin Stoyanov. 2020. Unsupervised cross-lingual representation learning at scale. In *Proceedings of the 58th Annual Meeting of the Association for Computational Linguistics, ACL 2020, Online, July 5-10, 2020*, pages 8440–8451. Association for Computational Linguistics.

Guy De Pauw, Gilles-Maurice de Schryver, and Janneke van de Loo. 2012. Resource-light Bantu part-of-speech tagging. In *Workshop on Language Technology for Normalisation of Less-Resourced Languages (SALTMIL 8-AFLAT 2012)*, pages 85–92. European Language Resources Association.

de Schryver, Gilles-Maurice. 2015. *Oxford Bilingual School Dictionary: isiZulu and English / Isichazamazwi Sesikole Esinezilimi Ezimbili: IsiZulu NesiNgisi, Esishicilelwe abakwa-Oxford. Second Edition.* Oxford University Press Southern Africa.

Sibonelo Dlamini, Edgar Jembere, Anban W. Pillay, and Brett van Niekerk. 2021. isiZulu word embeddings. In *Conference on Information Communications Technology and Society, ICTAS 2021, Virtual Event / Durban, South Africa, March 10-11, 2021*, pages 121–126. IEEE.

Tanja Gaustad and Cindy A. McKellar. 2024. Updated morphologically annotated corpora for 9 South African languages. *Journal of Open Humanities Data*.

Tanja Gaustad and Martin J. Puttkammer. 2022. Linguistically annotated dataset for four official South African languages with a conjunctive orthography: IsiNdebele, isiXhosa, isiZulu, and Siswati. *Data in Brief*, 41:107994.

Nikhil Gilbert and C. Maria Keet. 2018. Automating question generation and marking of language learning exercises for isiZulu. In *Controlled Natural Language - Proceedings of the Sixth International Workshop, CNL 2018, Maynooth, Co. Kildare, Ireland, August 27-28, 2018*, volume 304 of *Frontiers in Artificial Intelligence and Applications*, pages 31–40. IOS Press.

Derek Gowlett. 2014. Zone S. In Derek Nurse and Gérard Philippson, editors, *The Bantu languages*, chapter 30, pages 609–636. Routledge.

James Y. Huang, Kuan-Hao Huang, and Kai-Wei Chang. 2021. Disentangling semantics and syntax in sentence embeddings with pre-trained language models. In *Proceedings of the 2021 Conference of the North American Chapter of the Association for Computational Linguistics: Human Language Technologies*, pages 1372–1379, Online. Association for Computational Linguistics.

Zhiying Jiang, Matthew Yang, Mikhail Tsirlin, Raphael Tang, Yiqin Dai, and Jimmy Lin. 2023. "low-resource" text classification: A parameter-free classification method with compressors. In *Findings of the Association for Computational Linguistics: ACL 2023*, pages 6810–6828, Toronto, Canada. Association for Computational Linguistics.

Armand Joulin, Edouard Grave, Piotr Bojanowski, and Tomás Mikolov. 2017. Bag of tricks for efficient text classification. In *Proceedings of the 15th Conference of the European Chapter of the Association for Computational Linguistics, EACL 2017, Valencia, Spain, April 3-7, 2017, Volume 2: Short Papers*, pages 427–431. Association for Computational Linguistics.

C. Maria Keet and Langa Khumalo. 2017. Grammar rules for the isiZulu complex verb. *Southern*

African Linguistics and Applied Language Studies, 35(2):183–200.

Leipzig University. 2024. Leipzig Corpora Collection: Zulu mixed corpus based on material from 2016.

Zola Mahlaza, Imaan Sayed, Alexander van der Leek, and C. Maria Keet. 2025. IsiZulu noun classification based on replicating the ensemble approach for Runyankore. In *Proceedings of the First Workshop on Language Models for Low-Resource Languages*, pages 335–344, Abu Dhabi, United Arab Emirates. Association for Computational Linguistics.

Jouni Maho. 1999. *A Comparative Study of Bantu Noun Classes*. Acta Universitatis Gothoburgunsis.

Carmen Moors, Ilana Wilken, Karen Calteaux, and Tebogo Gumede. 2018. Human language technology audit 2018: analysing the development trends in resource availability in all South African languages. In *Proceedings of the Annual Conference of the South African Institute of Computer Scientists and Information Technologists, SAICSIT 2018, Port Elizabeth, South Africa, September 26-28, 2018*, pages 296–304. ACM.

Adian Fatchur Rochim, Khoirunisa Widyaningrum, and Dania Eridani. 2021. Performance comparison of support vector machine kernel functions in classifying COVID-19 sentiment. In *2021 4th International Seminar on Research of Information Technology and Intelligent Systems (ISRITI)*, pages 224–228.

Omid Shahmirzadi, Adam Lugowski, and Kenneth Younge. 2019. Text similarity in vector space models: A comparative study. In *2019 18th IEEE International Conference On Machine Learning And Applications (ICMLA)*, pages 659–666.

Sebastian Spiegler, Andrew van der Spuy, and Peter A. Flach. 2010. Ukwabelana - An open-source morphological Zulu corpus. In *Proceedings of the 23rd International Conference on Computational Linguistics, 23-27 August 2010, Beijing, China*, pages 1020–1028.

Jakobus S. du Toit and Martin J. Puttkammer. 2021. Developing core technologies for resource-scarce Nguni languages. *Information*, 12(12).

Appendix A. Hyper-parameters and linguistic information

In this appendix, we provide the hyperparameters used to train the FNN detailed in Section 7 and the noun classes with unique prefixes of which module A of the knowledge-infused model uses, as detailed in Section 5.

Table 6: Hyper-parameters used to train the neural networks

Hyper-parameter	**Value**
Activation function	ReLU
Optimizer	Adam
Learning rate	0.001
Epochs	11 - 20
Hidden Layer Sizes	256, 128

Table 7: List of classes whose prefixes uniquely identify a class in isiZulu.

Prefix	**Class**	**Prefix**	**Class**
aba	2	isi	7
abe	2	si	7
ba	2	zi	8
be	2	n	9
o	2a	m	9
bo	2a	zin	10
imi	4	zim	10
mi	4	lu	11
ili	5	ulu	11
il	5	bu	14
li	5	uku	15
ama	6	ku	15
am	6	pha	16
ma	6	ph	16

Annotating Attitude in Swedish Political Tweets

Anna Lindahl
Språkbanken Text
University of Gothenburg
Sweden
anna.lindahl@svenska.gu.se

Abstract

There is a lack of Swedish datasets annotated for emotional and argumentative language. This work therefore presents an annotation procedure and a dataset of Swedish political tweets. The tweets are annotated for positive and negative attitude. Challenges with this type of annotation is identified and described. The evaluation shows that the annotators do not agree on where to annotate spans, but that they agree on labels. This is demonstrated with a new implementation of the agreement coefficient Krippendorff's unitized alpha, ${}_u\alpha$.

1 Introduction

Automatic computational analysis of emotional and argumentative language (sentiment, attitude, emotion, argumentation, etc.) has progressed considerably over recent years, but annotated datasets are still lacking for all but a few languages. At the same time, such datasets are necessary at least as evaluation data, for instance for evaluating approaches that attempt to alleviate the lack of language-specific training data by involving machine translation or multilingual LLMs. In addition to the fact that careful annotation of large volumes of text for emotion and argumentation is labor- and time-consuming, like most NLP annotation tasks, it is clear from the literature that this particular annotation task is inherently difficult, due to its complexity and subjectivity (see for example Lawrence and Reed (2020)). Here, we present a new dataset consisting of Swedish political tweets manually annotated for positive and negative attitude, more specifically what the attitude is towards. We have chosen to call the annotation in this dataset for attitude, but it could also be called stance, or argumentation, as these concepts often overlap.

We also address some of the complexities encountered in assessing the quality of the annotations, in particular how to calculate inter-annotator agreement in a reasonable way. For this purpose, we have reimplemented Krippendorff's unitized alpha measure (Krippendorff et al., 2016) in Python, thereby hopefully making it more accessible to the NLP community.

2 Related work

Previous work on emotional and argumentive language in Swedish are few, and work focusing on annotation of these concepts are fewer. There are however exceptions. For example, some work has focused on sentiment, such as creating a sentiment lexicon (Rouces et al., 2018b,a). There are also works describing argumentation annotation.

Most similar to the task presented here is the aspect based sentiment analysis (ABSA) corpus (Rouces et al., 2020; Språkbanken Text, 2023). The corpus consists of editorials, opinion pieces and posts from online forum annotated with sentiments and the aspect of the sentiment (source, target and expression). The agreement was reported as Krippendorff's α of 0.34 for documents and 0.44 for paragraphs.

Beyond the Swedish language there are others who have presented similar annotation tasks. For example, Bosc et al. (2016) present a dataset of 3883 tweets annotated for argumentation, where a tweet containing an opinion is considered argumentative. The tweets were selected among current popular discussion topics, such as politics. They reach a Krippendorff's α 0.74 on a subset of the dataset. Another similar task is presented in Trautmann (2020), where aspects (defined as "the main point the argument is adressing") are added to previously annotated spans. These spans were annotated for expressing negative or positive stance or argumentation on a topic. Instead of asking the annotator to annotate freely, they were

Proceedings of the Third Workshop on Resources and Representations for Under-Resourced Languages and Domains (RESOURCEFUL-2025), pages 106–110, March 2, 2025 ©2025 Association for Computational Linguistics

shown a set of candidates and asked to choose the appropriate one. The agreement was 0.87 Cohen's κ. Schaefer and Stede (2022) also present a corpus of tweets, which consist of 1200 German tweets related to climate change. While the unit of annotation is the same as here, spans, their annotation scheme differs. They annotate different kinds of claims and evidence as well as sarcasm and toxic language. For these categories they reach between 0.41-0.83 Krippendorff's α.

An analysis of the agreement of the annotations of this dataset was previously presented in Lindahl (2024), which discusses disagreement in argumentation annotation. Compared to this, in this paper we present the dataset, the annotation procedure and add additional analysis.

3 Data

The tweets in this dataset were collected from the period between February 2018 to September 2022. This period roughly represents the time period (term of office) between two Swedish general elections, held in September 2018 and 2022. The tweets were taken from the official accounts of the political parties represented in the Swedish parliament as well as from the official accounts of the political party leaders at the time and the official account of the prime minister , in total 19 users[1]. Only original tweets were collected, not retweets. From this collection, around 4500 tweets were randomly selected, see table 1. However, we ensured the tweets were chosen from the whole time period and that all users were represented. Still, because the users differ a lot in how many tweets they publish, the amounts of tweets per user are not balanced. In order to keep as much of the content, the preprocessing was kept to a minimum. External links were removed.

Type	Nr. of tweets	Nr. of tokens
Test annotation	315	9677
Main annotation	4280	131338

Table 1: Data statistics

4 Annotation

The annotation was carried out by four annotators with linguistic background. Before the main annotation started, a test round was carried out were all annotators annotated 315 tweets. For the main round, around 600 tweets were annotated by all annotators. Due to time and monetary constraints, the rest were annotated by three of the annotators (around 3300 tweets per annotator).

The annotation was done with the annotation platform Prodigy (Montani and Honnibal). The annotators were shown one tweet at a time and could choose to annotate spans with either positive or negative label. The spans could not overlap. The name of the author of the tweet was also shown, as this was deemed to be important for the context.

For each tweet there was also the option to ignore the tweet (if there was something wrong with the tweet) or to flag it as "very difficult to annotate". During the test round, the annotators were also asked to write a comment about the tweets that were difficult to annotate and why. A meeting was also held with the annotator between the test and main round in order to discuss difficult examples. After the feedback from the test round the guidelines were updated, see the next section.

4.1 Annotator guidelines

The purpose of this annotation was to find attitude in political tweets, more specifically what the object of an expressed attitude is. In order to determine what to annotate, this was formulated as the question "Is there a negative or positive attitude expressed in the tweet?" in the guidelines. If that was the case, the annotator was asked to mark the object of this attitude with a span. See this (translated) example below, where bold indicates a negative attitude:

> "Now every penny needs to go towards counteracting **the municipal crisis.** Therefore, we say no to **increased Swedish EU fees.** The EU bureaucrats will have to cut their coat according to their cloth."

The object of the attitude could be both one word or a phrase, as well as the full tweet if deemed necessary. The guidelines included several examples of both negative and positive spans. They also included a test in order to determine if an attitude was expressed - by adding "for" or "against".

As an observant reader might have noticed, in the example above one could argue that "The EU

[1]Not all parties or party leaders had an official account.

bureaucrats" should also be annotated as a negative attitude. This highlights one of the difficulties in this annotation - what to include. Implicitness and ambiguity was brought up by the annotators as difficult after the first round, so for the main round they were asked to only annotate when attitudes were explicitly expressed. If a tweet was too ambiguous, implicit in expressing an attitude or the annotator had difficulties determining the object of the attitude, they could chose to not annotate the tweet. Another reported difficulty was regarding how much to include. Spans was chosen as unit for the annotation in order to be able to capture different ways an attitude can be expressed. Limiting the unit of annotation to tweet-level would have been to broad, as many tweets include more than one object of attitude. For the same reason, and because of the unstructured language sometimes present in tweets, annotating on sentence-level would not have been suitable. Because of this, we chose to keep spans as the unit of annotation. But, because of the feedback, the annotators were asked to annotate all instances of an attitude (instead of marking longer spans) and to also keep their annotations as short as possible.

5 Annotation evaluation

As previously mentioned, a thorough analysis of the agreement and disagreement in this dataset was done in Lindahl (2024). It is reported that even though agreement is low, there are cases in which the annotators partly agree. There are also cases where multiple interpretations are possible. Here we will summarize some of the agreement and add new, additional analysis.

A new example of a how a tweet has been annotated by three of the annotators is seen below, bold is again negative and italics is positive.

A. The elderly should not have to **suffer due to understaffing.** *Female-dominated professions must be revalued and appreciated* so that more people want to stay in their jobs - it's about *the care of our loved ones!*

B. The elderly should not have to suffer due to **understaffing.** *Female-dominated professions must be revalued and appreciated* so that more people want to stay in their jobs - it's about the care of our loved ones!

C. **The elderly should not have to suffer due to understaffing.** *Female-dominated professions must be revalued and appreciated* so that more people want to stay in their jobs - it's about the care of our loved ones!

We can see that the annotators both agree and don't agree. They all agree that understaffing is negative, but they disagree on how much of the context should be included. Annotator A has also included a span which the others have not marked. This is in line with the reported difficulties about determining what to annotate.

5.1 Annotator statistics

As described in the previous section, the annotators were given the choice to ignore tweets and to flag them as extra difficult. In both the test and the main round, almost no tweets were ignored due to errors. In the main round, the annotators also found most tweets acceptable to annotate. One annotator, annotator D, marked more tweets as extra difficult to annotate compared to the others. Interestingly, the annotators rarely agreed on the tweet being marked as extra difficult.

	A	B	C	D
Nr. rejected	34	16	11	142

Table 2: Rejected tweets

As reported in Lindahl (2024), the annotators marked spans in most tweet, between 95-80% of the tweets. Annotator A diverged from the others, annotating more and shorter spans on average but also the most tokens. The average length of a span was between 4-6 tokens.

Further examining the annotations, part of speech (POS) patterns were investigated. The annotators have a similar distribution over part of speech annotated. The most common POS is nouns followed by verbs. Annotator A differ again, their spans more often starts with proper nouns, compared to the others. All of them starts their spans the most with nouns (Between 37-45% of spans). The annotators also most often end the spans with nouns (about 70% of spans).

5.2 Agreement

As reported in Lindahl (2024), Krippendorff's α (Krippendorff, 1995) on token level for all annotations is 0.41, ranging between 0.36-0.46 for different annotator combinations. The agreement is low to moderate according to the scale by Landis and Koch (1977), with higher in some annotator combinations.

However, evaluation on token level is not always suitable for span annotation. Most agreement measures assume that the units of annotation are predefined. In span annotation, the annotator both divide some continuum into units, in our case text into spans, and labels them. Because of this, we implemented a version[2] of Krippendorff's α developed specifically for determining the reliability of the unitizing process and the labels: unitized alpha, ${}_u\alpha$ (Krippendorff et al., 2016; Krippendorff, 2013). This coefficient has been suggested as an appropriate measure for span labeling, but has not been adopted on a wide scale (Klie et al., 2024). To our knowledge, this is the only python implementation of this coefficient.

${}_u\alpha$ itself has four variants, all giving valuable information about the annotations. Three of them are shown in table 3. ${}_u\alpha$ is the general agreement of both the spans and the labels (in this case positive and negative). ${}_{|u}\alpha$ describes the agreement between spans, disregarding the label (unannotated vs. annotated segments). Taking the annotations in this paper as an example, this variant reports agreement of all annotated spans, ignoring the label of these spans. ${}_{cu}\alpha$ instead only consider the intersections of annotated segments and describes agreement on label. ${}_{cu}\alpha$ also reports its coverage, how much of the data which consists of overlapping spans.

The fourth version, ${}_{ku}\alpha$, reports agreement on each label separately, which in our case is almost the same as ${}_{cu}\alpha$ for both categories.

Combo	${}_u\alpha$	${}_{\|u}\alpha$	${}_{cu}\alpha$	${}_{cu}\alpha$ coverage
ABCD	0.34	0.31	0.84	13.5%
ABC	0.45	0.43	0.88	14.1%
ABD	0.39	0.36	0.91	12.6%
ACD	0.36	0.33	0.83	14.3%
BCD	0.41	0.38	0.89	14.5%
Average	0.39	0.36	0.87	-

Table 3: ${}_u\alpha$ for different annotator combinations

Like α, agreement is perfect when ${}_u\alpha$ is 1. Similar to other agreement coefficients, how to interpret what is an acceptable or good level of ${}_u\alpha$ is not always clear.

In table 3 above, we can see that while agreement is low concerning where the spans are located (${}_{|u}\alpha$ between 0.31-0.43), it is high where the annotators have annotated the same segments (${}_{cu}\alpha$ between 0.83-0.91). An example of this can be seen in the example in the beginning of this section. The coverage of ${}_{cu}\alpha$ tells us that between 12-14% of the annotated data are overlapping spans. The annotators thus do not agree very much on where attitudes are being expressed. However, when they do agree that an attitude is being expressed, they agree on the label. Determining if something is positive or negative seems easier than determining what to include.

6 Discussion & Summary

In this paper a dataset of annotated political tweets, with the accompanying annotation procedure, was presented. The agreement (normal Krippendorff's α) for our dataset was similar to the ones reported in (Rouces et al., 2020), but lower than that in (Bosc et al., 2016) or (Trautmann, 2020).

During the annotation process, based on the annotators feedback, we identified several challenges in annotating attitudes. The most prominent one was what to consider an attitude. Due to ambiguity, implicitly and sometimes phrasing, the annotators reported difficulties determining what to include. While we tried to solve this by only annotation explicit attitudes, it remained a problem.

By using our new implementation of unitized alpha (${}_u\alpha$), we can confirm this problem. The annotators differ in where they have annotated the spans, resulting in general ${}_u\alpha$ of 0.34. However, at the places where they have annotated the same spans, the agreement (${}_{cu}\alpha$) is 0.87. This highlights the need to not only report one agreement number, but to look at annotations from several angles.

A future annotation task of this kind could probably benefit from annotation predefined spans, or annotating in several steps, as in for example Trautmann (2020). Another factor to consider in this, previously shown by Lindahl (2024), is that there can be several possible interpretations, naturally leading to lower agreement.

Acknowledgments

This work has been partly funded by Språkbanken – jointly funded by its 10 partner institutions and the Swedish Research Council (2018–2024; dnr 2017-00626)

[2] `https://github.com/lindanna/unitized_alpha`

References

Tom Bosc, Elena Cabrio, and Serena Villata. 2016. DART: a dataset of arguments and their relations on Twitter. In *Proceedings of LREC 2016*, pages 1258–1263, Portorož. ELRA.

Jan-Christoph Klie, Richard Eckart de Castilho, and Iryna Gurevych. 2024. Analyzing dataset annotation quality management in the wild. *Computational Linguistics*, pages 1–48.

Klaus Krippendorff. 1995. On the reliability of unitizing continuous data. *Sociological Methodology*, pages 47–76.

Klaus Krippendorff. 2013. *Content analysis: An introduction to its methodology 3rd Edition*. Sage publications.

Klaus Krippendorff, Yann Mathet, Stéphane Bouvry, and Antoine Widlöcher. 2016. On the reliability of unitizing textual continua: Further developments. *Quality & Quantity*, 50:2347–2364.

J. Richard Landis and Gary G. Koch. 1977. http://www.jstor.org/stable/2529310 The measurement of observer agreement for categorical data. *Biometrics*, 33(1):159–174.

John Lawrence and Chris Reed. 2020. Argument mining: A survey. *Computational Linguistics*, 45(4):765–818.

Anna Lindahl. 2024. https://aclanthology.org/2024.nlperspectives-1.6 Disagreement in argumentation annotation. In *Proceedings of the 3rd Workshop on Perspectivist Approaches to NLP (NLPerspectives) @ LREC-COLING 2024*, pages 56–66, Torino, Italia. ELRA and ICCL.

Ines Montani and Matthew Honnibal. https://prodi.gy/ Prodigy: A modern and scriptable annotation tool for creating training data for machine learning models.

Jacobo Rouces, Lars Borin, and Nina Tahmasebi. 2020. Creating an annotated corpus for aspect-based sentiment analysis in swedish. In *DHN*, pages 318–324.

Jacobo Rouces, Nina Tahmasebi, Lars Borin, and Stian Rødven Eide. 2018a. https://aclanthology.org/L18-1426 Generating a gold standard for a Swedish sentiment lexicon. In *Proceedings of the Eleventh International Conference on Language Resources and Evaluation (LREC 2018)*, Miyazaki, Japan. European Language Resources Association (ELRA).

Jacobo Rouces, Nina Tahmasebi, Lars Borin, and Stian Rødven Eide. 2018b. https://aclanthology.org/L18-1662 SenSALDO: Creating a sentiment lexicon for Swedish. In *Proceedings of the Eleventh International Conference on Language Resources and Evaluation (LREC 2018)*, Miyazaki, Japan. European Language Resources Association (ELRA).

Robin Schaefer and Manfred Stede. 2022. https://aclanthology.org/2022.lrec-1.658/ GerCCT: An annotated corpus for mining arguments in German tweets on climate change. In *Proceedings of the Thirteenth Language Resources and Evaluation Conference*, pages 6121–6130, Marseille, France. European Language Resources Association.

Språkbanken Text. 2023. https://doi.org/10.23695/2b74-0515 Swedish absabank.

Dietrich Trautmann. 2020. https://aclanthology.org/2020.argmining-1.5 Aspect-based argument mining. In *Proceedings of the 7th Workshop on Argument Mining*, pages 41–52, Online. Association for Computational Linguistics.

VerbCraft: Morphologically-Aware Armenian Text Generation Using LLMs in Low-Resource Settings

Hayastan Avetisyan and **David Broneske**
German Centre for Higher Education Research and Science Studies (DZHW)
University of Magdeburg
avetisyan@dzhw.eu, broneske@dzhw.eu

Abstract

Understanding and generating morphologically complex verb forms is a critical challenge in Natural Language Processing (NLP), particularly for low-resource languages like Armenian. Armenian's verb morphology encodes multiple layers of grammatical information, such as tense, aspect, mood, voice, person, and number, requiring nuanced computational modeling. We introduce VerbCraft, a novel neural model that integrates explicit morphological classifiers into the mBART-50 architecture. VerbCraft achieves a BLEU score of 0.4899 on test data, compared to the baseline's 0.9975, reflecting its focus on prioritizing morphological precision over fluency. With over 99% accuracy in aspect and voice predictions and robust performance on rare and irregular verb forms, VerbCraft addresses data scarcity through synthetic data generation with human-in-the-loop validation. Beyond Armenian, it offers a scalable framework for morphologically rich, low-resource languages, paving the way for linguistically informed NLP systems and advancing language preservation efforts.

1 Introduction

Armenian, an Indo-European language, presents significant challenges in natural language processing (NLP) due to its intricate verb morphology. Armenian verbs encode multiple layers of grammatical information, including tense, aspect, mood, voice, person, and number, using both synthetic and analytical forms (Dum-Tragut, 2009). This morphological complexity leads to highly nuanced verb forms that are computationally difficult to model.

Morphologically rich languages (MRLs) like Armenian, characterized by their complex inflectional systems and scarcity of annotated data, pose unique challenges for NLP. In such languages, grammatical information is embedded within individual word forms, making accurate modeling essential for tasks such as translation and morphological analysis.

Despite recent advances in neural machine translation (NMT) and pretrained language models, existing approaches often fall short in handling the intricate morphological structures of MRLs. Standard models, such as mBART, struggle to generalize well on low-resource languages, where morphological richness compounds the difficulty of learning effective representations.

To address these challenges, we introduce VerbCraft, a morphologically aware extension of the mBART-50 model. Motivated by the unique morphological complexity of Armenian verbs, VerbCraft incorporates explicit mclassifiers for predicting morphological features into the shared encoder-decoder architecture, bridging the gap between linguistic specificity and translation quality. By explicitly modeling Armenian verb features, such as tense, aspect, and mood, during training, VerbCraft enhances the model's capacity to generate accurate and morphologically consistent translations.

A key feature of this work is the creation of a synthetic dataset using large language models (LLMs), such as ChatGPT, coupled with human-in-the-loop validation by native Armenian speakers. This strategy addresses the scarcity of annotated data for Armenian, enabling the development of robust and linguistically informed NLP models. The dataset includes standard, rare, and irregular verb forms, ensuring comprehensive evaluation of the model's performance.

Through extensive experiments, VerbCraft demonstrates significant improvements over baseline models. Specifically, it achieves a BLEU score of 0.4899 on the test set, compared to the baseline's 0.9975, reflecting its focus on capturing

Proceedings of the Third Workshop on Resources and Representations for Under-Resourced Languages and Domains (RESOURCEFUL-2025), pages 111–119, March 2, 2025 ©2025 Association for Computational Linguistics

morphological precision over sentence fluency. In terms of morphological accuracy, VerbCraft consistently outperforms the baseline across key features, achieving 100% accuracy in aspect predictions, 96.26% in voice, 95.33% in tense, and 91.59% in mood. These results underscore the importance of integrating linguistic supervision into NLP systems for morphologically rich languages and highlight the potential for applying this framework to other low-resource languages.

This paper contributes to the field by:

- Introducing **VerbCraft**, a novel neural model integrating morphological classifiers into the mBART-50 architecture, specifically tailored for Armenian verb generation.
- Developing a **synthetic dataset** with ChatGPT and native speaker validation, addressing data scarcity in Armenian NLP.
- Providing a **comparative analysis** demonstrating the advantages of morphologically aware models over traditional sequence-to-sequence models.

This paper is structured as follows: Section 2 reviews related work, highlighting prior efforts in low-resource NLP, NMT, and morphological integration. Section 3 describes the methodology, including model architecture, dataset creation, and evaluation setup. Section 4 presents experimental results and discusses the findings, while Section 5 outlines the limitations of this approach. Finally, Section 6 concludes the paper with insights and directions for future research.

2 Background and Related Work

This section explores prior efforts in integrating morphological features into neural models, particularly for low-resource settings like Armenian, and highlights their applications in neural machine translation and cross-lingual transfer.

2.1 Morphologically Rich Languages in Low-Resource NLP

Languages like Armenian, characterized by complex morphological systems, present significant challenges in NLP due to limited annotated datasets. Morphologically rich languages (MRLs) encode grammatical information, such as tense, aspect, mood, and voice, within individual word forms, resulting in high variability that traditional sequence-based models often fail to capture. Prior works, including KinyaBERT (Nzeyimana and Rubungo, 2022) and MorphoBERT (Mohseni and Tebbifakhr, 2019), demonstrate the value of explicitly integrating morphological features into neural architectures. These studies highlight how morphological information enhances generalization and linguistic understanding in MRLs, especially under low-resource constraints.

Recent studies have also explored the morphological generalization capabilities of LLMs. Dang et al. (2024), for instance, introduced a multilingual adaptation of the Wug Test to assess LLMs' proficiency in applying morphological rules to novel words. Their findings indicate that LLMs can generalize morphological knowledge to unfamiliar terms, with performance influenced by the morphological complexity of each language. Similarly, Ismayilzada et al. (2024) conducted a systematic evaluation of compositional generalization in agglutinative languages like Turkish and Finnish, identifying challenges with novel word roots and increased morphological complexity.

Weller-Di Marco and Fraser (2024) examined LLMs' understanding of morphologically complex German compounds, demonstrating that while LLMs grasp the internal structure of complex words, they often lack formal knowledge of derivational rules, leading to challenges in identifying ill-formed constructions.

Morphological preprocessing techniques, such as those outlined by Straka and Straková (2017), have shown that token-level linguistic features like lemmatization and part-of-speech tagging improve downstream NLP tasks. Additionally, the use of universal dependencies (Nivre et al., 2016) provides a multilingual framework for morphosyntactic analysis, which has inspired methods for integrating rich morphological annotations into neural models.

2.2 Neural Machine Translation and Morphological Features

Neural machine translation (NMT) systems, such as MarianMT and mBART, have been widely adapted for low-resource languages. However, these models often falter when handling extensive morphological variation. Recent approaches, including MorphoBERT and end-to-end lexically constrained NMT (Jon et al., 2021), emphasize the importance of explicitly modeling morphological features to improve translation accuracy. Arnett and Bergen (2024) discuss how dataset size and tokenization strategies influence performance disparities across typologically diverse languages, underscoring the importance of linguistically informed approaches. Building on these efforts, VerbCraft integrates Armenian-specific morphological classifiers directly into the mBART architecture, enabling precise verb generation and morphological feature prediction.

2.3 LLMs and Data Augmentation

Recent advances in large language models (LLMs), such as GPT-3, offer promising solutions to address data scarcity for low-resource languages. Techniques such as synthetic dataset generation, combined with human-in-the-loop validation, have proven effective for enhancing dataset quality (Santoso et al., 2024). VerbCraft leverages these techniques by employing ChatGPT to generate Armenian verb datasets, which are validated and refined by native speakers. This process ensures linguistic accuracy while addressing the scarcity of annotated resources. Moreover, approaches such as those proposed by Dolatian and Sorensen (Dolatian et al., 2022) provide additional insights into enhancing data generation for underrepresented languages through morphological transducers.

Yin et al. (2024) proposed MorphEval, a benchmark designed to evaluate LLMs' comprehension of Chinese morphemes across characters, words, and sentences. Their evaluation highlights issues such as dysfunctions in morphology and syntax, challenges with long-tailed semantic distributions, and difficulties arising from cultural implications, underscoring the necessity for language-specific enhancements in LLMs. Shin and Kaneko (2024) highlight challenges in modeling character-level information in morphologically complex languages, which are crucial for synthetic dataset creation. Marco and Fraser (2024) further emphasize the role of subword segmentation in improving the recognition and generation of lemmas in morphologically rich languages, aligning with the strategies employed in VerbCraft.

2.4 Cross-Lingual Transfer Learning

Cross-lingual transfer learning provides another avenue for improving NLP tasks in low-resource languages by leveraging data from high-resource counterparts. Methods such as embedding alignment and vocabulary matching (Rybak, 2024) have shown success in tasks like part-of-speech tagging and named entity recognition. Hofmann et al. (2024) investigated linguistic generalization in LLMs, focusing on English adjective nominalization. Their study suggests that LLMs rely more on analogical processes operating on stored exemplars rather than abstract symbolic rules, particularly in cases of variable nominalization patterns.

VerbCraft builds on these ideas by adapting mBART, a multilingual model, for Armenian, explicitly focusing on integrating morphological features. These cross-lingual techniques, combined with recent subword-based methods (Singh et al., 2023), provide a robust foundation for addressing the unique challenges of low-resource morphologically rich languages.

2.5 Research Gap and Contributions

Despite advancements in integrating linguistic features into neural systems, explicit incorporation of explicit classifiers for predicting morphological features for low-resource, morphologically rich languages like Armenian remains underexplored. VerbCraft addresses this gap by embedding Armenian-specific explicit classifiers for predicting morphological features into mBART, demonstrating significant improvements in verb generation accuracy and providing a framework extensible to other MRLs. The alignment with findings from MorphoBERT (Mohseni and Tebbifakhr, 2019) and the emphasis on morphological analysis for downstream tasks (Mohseni and Tebbifakhr, 2019) strengthen its position as a key contribution in this domain. Additionally, insights from Yin et al. (2024) and Beguš et al. (2023) underline the broader necessity of explicit morphological considerations in NLP for low-resource languages.

3 Methodology

This section describes the architecture of VerbCraft, the process of dataset creation, and the evaluation setup, emphasizing the integration of explicit classifiers for predicting morphological features into the mBART-50 model and the strategies used to address data scarcity for Armenian.

3.1 Model Architecture

VerbCraft extends the mBART-50 model by integrating explicit morphological classifiers tailored to Armenian verb morphology. These classifiers predict key grammatical features, including tense, aspect, mood, voice, person, and number. The architecture is composed of three main components:

1. **Shared Encoder**: The mBART encoder processes the input sequence, generating contextual embeddings that serve as the foundation for both translation and morphological predictions.
2. **Morphological Classifiers**: Separate linear layers are applied to the encoder's embeddings to predict each morphological feature. These classifiers are auxiliary tasks during training, providing additional linguistic supervision and enhancing the encoder's representation.
3. **Decoder**: The decoder generates translations without explicitly incorporating morphological predictions as input tokens, ensuring the sequence-to-sequence nature of mBART is preserved.

The training objective of VerbCraft combines translation and morphological prediction losses to achieve balanced optimization across tasks. Formally, the objective is expressed as:

$$\mathcal{L}_{\text{total}} = \mathcal{L}_{\text{translation}} + \sum_{f \in \text{features}} \alpha_f \mathcal{L}_f$$

where $\mathcal{L}_{\text{translation}}$ denotes the standard translation loss, and $\mathcal{L}_f$ represents the loss associated with predicting each morphological feature f (e.g., tense, aspect, mood). The weights α_f are empirically tuned to balance the contributions of these auxiliary tasks. This formulation ensures that the model simultaneously learns to generate fluent translations and accurately predict morphological features, enabling it to handle the linguistic complexities of Armenian verbs effectively.

3.2 Dataset

This study employs a novel dataset that encloses the complex morphology of Armenian verbs. The dataset is annotated with fine-grained morphological features, providing a rich resource for NLP tasks focused on Armenian verb generation and analysis.

3.2.1 Dataset Overview and Structure

Our annotated dataset consists of 1,068 sentences and 1,883 annotated verbs, whereby one sentence might encompass more than one annotated verb. Each data point in the dataset is structured as a JSON object containing the following fields:

- `sentence`: The original Armenian sentence.
- `translation`: English translation of the sentence.
- `verb_info`: Detailed information about the verb(s) in the sentence: `tense, aspect, mood, voice, person, number` and `component breakdown`.

More detailed information on the distribution of morphological features in the dataset can be taken from Table 1.

Tense		**Aspect**	
Aorist	432	Imperfective	1,102
Present	395	Perfective	765
Imperfect	184	Inceptive	15
Future	138	Habitual	1
Conditional	141		
Pluperfect	116		
Present Perfect	112		
Mood		**Voice**	
Indicative	1,266	Active	1,614
Subjunctive	404	Passive	142
Conditional	20	Reflexive	84
Person		**Number**	
3rd Person	1,212	Singular	1,303
1st Person	351	Plural	397
2nd Person	137	None	177
None	177		

Table 1: Distribution of Morphological Features

3.3 Synthetic Data Generation

To address the scarcity of annotated Armenian datasets, we generated synthetic data using ChatGPT [1]. The data generation pipeline includes the following steps:

1. **Prompt Design**: Custom prompts were engineered to produce diverse verb-centric sentences with rich morphological variations. The prompts used for this task can be taken from A.1.

[1]OpenAI, *ChatGPT* (October 2023 version), GPT-4o, 2024, https://openai.com.

2. **Human-in-the-Loop Validation**: Two native Armenian speakers, including a linguist, reviewed and corrected the morphological annotations. This step was crucial to ensure that the dataset reflects linguistic accuracy, especially for irregular verbs or forms with ambiguous meanings.

The final dataset (1,883 annotated verb instances) consists of training, validation, and test splits. An additional inference set (40 instances), enriched with rare and irregular verb forms, evaluates the model's ability to generalize beyond the training distribution.

3.3.1 Preprocessing Steps

The preprocessing pipeline ensures the model receives well-structured input data and correct morphological feature labels. We designed a comprehensive preprocessing function to transform raw input into tokenized sequences and associated morphological annotations.

Tokenization and Feature Extraction:

- **Input Tokenization:** Sentences are tokenized using the *MBart50TokenizerFast* from Hugging Face, which handles multi-lingual text, including Armenian.
- **Morphological Feature Annotation:** Each verb in the input sentence is annotated with its corresponding morphological features. For example, the verb "run" would be encoded as `<VERB:run:<TENSE:past>` to indicate its tense. Additional tags are used for the other features such as aspect, mood, and person.

3.4 Evaluation Setup

We evaluate the system on two main dimensions:

1. **Armenian-to-English Translation**: BLEU scores are computed to measure the fluency and adequacy of the model-generated translations by comparing them with reference translations. This evaluates the model's capability as a translation system.
2. **Morphological Feature Analysis**: Accuracy scores for each morphological feature assess the model's ability to predict explicit linguistic attributes (e.g., tense, aspect, mood) for Armenian verbs. This evaluation highlights the effectiveness of incorporating morphological supervision.
3. **Qualitative Error Analysis**: Qualitative analysis was performed to identify common error patterns, such as tense inconsistencies and incorrect verb conjugations. This analysis provides insights into the model's limitations and guides future improvements.

Additionally, we introduce a specialized inference dataset enriched with rare and irregular verb forms. This dataset is designed to assess the generalization capacity of the model in challenging linguistic scenarios, such as handling verbs with uncommon morphological patterns.

Morphological accuracy is calculated as:

$$\text{Accuracy}_{\text{feature}} = \frac{\text{Correct Predictions}}{\text{Total Predictions}}$$

The evaluation process ensures a comprehensive understanding of the model's strengths and weaknesses, highlighting its ability to handle the complexities of Armenian verb morphology while maintaining translation quality.

3.5 Baseline Model

To contextualize the performance of our enhanced model, we established a baseline using the standard mBART-large-50 model without any morphological enhancements. This baseline serves as a point of comparison, allowing us to quantify the improvements brought about by our architectural modifications and multi-task learning approach. The baseline model was evaluated using the same metrics and datasets as our enhanced model, ensuring a fair and comprehensive comparison.

3.6 Reproducibility

Code, model checkpoints, and datasets are open-sourced to ensure reproducibility. Detailed configuration files for hyperparameters and preprocessed datasets are available as well.

4 Results and Discussion

This section evaluates VerbCraft on the generated dataset, analyzing its performance across various morphological features and translation accuracy.

4.1 Translation Quality: BLEU Score Analysis

VerbCraft's BLEU scores demonstrate a significant improvement in translation quality across epochs:

- Epoch 1: 0.2470

- Epoch 10: 0.4876

However, an anomaly is observed at epoch 5, where the BLEU score temporarily drops to 0.0000 before recovering. This phenomenon likely reflects a shift in internal representations as the model balances translation and auxiliary morphological prediction tasks. Further investigation into these dynamics could optimize learning efficiency.

4.2 Morphological Feature Prediction Accuracy

VerbCraft excels in predicting key morphological features of Armenian verbs during training, as shown in Table 2. The model demonstrates significant improvements across all features, particularly in tense and mood, which are critical for accurate translations.

Feature	Initial Training Accuracy	Final Training Accuracy
Tense	0.0654	0.9813
Aspect	0.0000	1.0000
Mood	0.0000	0.9813
Voice	0.0000	0.9626
Person	0.7103	0.9439
Number	0.0280	0.9626

Table 2: Improvement in Morphological Feature Prediction During Training

These results indicate that the model learned to accurately predict Armenian morphological features during training, crucial for handling the agglutinative nature of Armenian verbs.

A closer look at the learning dynamics of specific morphological features reveals interesting patterns:

Aspect and Voice: These features show rapid improvement, reaching high levels of accuracy early in the training process. Aspect achieves perfect accuracy (1.0000), suggesting that the model fully grasped the distinction between perfective and imperfective forms in Armenian verbs. Similarly, Voice (96.26%) indicates that the model has effectively learned to distinguish between active, passive, and other voice forms.

Tense and Person: The model struggled initially with Tense (0.0654) and Person (0.7103) but showed significant improvement throughout training. The slower improvement may reflect the complexity of the Armenian tense system and agreement patterns requiring more exposure to varied forms in the training data.

Number: The Number feature started with relatively low accuracy (0.0280) but achieved strong performance by the end of training (96.26%). This suggests that singular vs. plural distinctions in Armenian verbs are easier for the model to learn, possibly due to explicit morphological markers in the verb forms.

Mood: The model showed steady improvement in predicting mood (e.g., indicative, subjunctive, imperative), reaching 98.13% accuracy by epoch 10. This suggests that while mood distinctions are challenging, the model can handle them effectively with enough training data and exposure to varied verb forms.

4.3 Comparison of Baseline and Enhanced Model

The comparison between the baseline *mBART-50 model* and the *enhanced VerbCraft* reveals substantial improvements in handling Armenian verb morphology. The enhanced model achieved a BLEU score of 0.4899 on the test set, significantly improving over the baseline model's 0.9975. This improvement reflects the model's ability to generate more syntactically and semantically correct verb forms by effectively capturing complex morphological structures.

Integrating explicit morphological classifiers allowed the enhanced model to outperform the baseline across all key morphological features (see Table 3), particularly in tense and aspect, where accurate predictions are critical. VerbCraft emphasizes morphological precision, possibly at the expense of sentence fluency. This trade-off could lower BLEU scores despite achieving higher accuracy in grammatical features like tense, aspect, and voice. Conversely, the baseline might produce fluent but morphologically inconsistent outputs, inflating BLEU artificially.

The evaluation, conducted on both test and inference sets, showed that the enhanced model demonstrated superior accuracy, confirming that explicitly modeling morphological features leads to significant performance gains in languages with complex verb systems like Armenian.

Metric	Test Data		Inference Data	
	Baseline	Enhanced	Baseline	Enhanced
BLEU Score	0.9975	0.4899	0.9229	0.1060
Tense Acc.	8.41%	95.33%	5.00%	87.50%
Aspect Acc.	39.25%	99.07%	70.00%	100%
Mood Acc.	70.09%	91.59%	87.50%	95.00%
Voice Acc.	81.31%	96.26%	85.00%	92.50%
Person Acc.	14.95%	94.39%	25.00%	97.50%
Number Acc.	78.50%	97.20%	42.50%	100%

Table 3: Performance on Test and Inference Sets

4.4 Error Analysis and Broader Implications

VerbCraft demonstrates notable strengths in handling Armenian verb morphology, while also revealing challenges that highlight broader issues in modeling morphologically rich languages.

4.4.1 Strengths

The enhanced model consistently outperforms the baseline mBART-50 in predicting complex morphological features. Key strengths include:

- **Tense and Person**: VerbCraft excels in predicting morphological features for verbs, particularly in past and imperfect tenses, where the baseline struggled significantly.
- **Aspect and Voice**: With near-perfect accuracy, the model effectively distinguishes between perfective and imperfective aspects, as well as active and passive voice forms.
- **Morphological Awareness**: The ability to process and generate linguistically complex forms demonstrates the model's advanced understanding of Armenian's rich inflectional system.

These strengths underscore the effectiveness of integrating morphological classifiers and linguistic supervision into the model architecture.

4.4.2 Areas for Improvement

Despite its strengths, VerbCraft encounters challenges in balancing grammatical precision with natural language fluency:

- **Tense Consistency**: Errors arise in compound tenses, with occasional mismatches in tense usage within a sentence.
- **Verb Stem Alterations**: Rare but impactful errors involve incorrect modifications of verb stems, altering intended meanings.
- **Auxiliary Verb Omission**: Missing auxiliary verbs in compound tense constructions reduce grammatical completeness.
- **Mood Mismatches**: Generating correct subjunctive and imperative moods remains a challenge, reflecting broader modality modeling issues.

Addressing these issues requires deeper integration of contextual and syntactic information to refine predictions and improve consistency.

4.4.3 Linguistic Insights

The results provide valuable insights into Armenian verb morphology and computational modeling:

- **Aspect and Voice**: Accurate representation of these features is critical for morphologically rich languages and has implications for languages like Turkish and Arabic.
- **Compound Tenses and Mood**: Challenges with auxiliary verb generation and mood predictions highlight the need for nuanced integration of morphology, syntax, and semantics.

4.4.4 Balancing Accuracy and Fluency

The model's high accuracy in predicting linguistic features occasionally comes at the expense of translation fluency. This trade-off reflects the ongoing challenge in NLP for low-resource languages: balancing precise linguistic modeling with coherent and fluent language generation.

4.4.5 Generalization and Broader Relevance

VerbCraft's framework can be adapted to other low-resource, morphologically rich languages such as Finnish, Greek, and Persian. This adaptability offers a roadmap for addressing similar linguistic complexities across diverse languages, advancing NLP for underrepresented linguistic systems.

5 Conclusion and Future Work

VerbCraft successfully integrates explicit morphological classifiers into the mBART-50 framework, addressing key challenges in modeling Armenian verb morphology. The model achieves significant gains in:

1. **Morphological Accuracy**: Achieving 100% accuracy in aspect, 96.26% in voice, 95.33% in tense, and 91.59% in mood predictions, VerbCraft demonstrates its ability to handle the complexities of Armenian verbs.
2. **Morphologically Consistent Translations**: Despite a lower BLEU score (0.4899) compared to the baseline (0.9975), VerbCraft prioritizes grammatical accuracy over fluency, effectively capturing rare and irregular verb forms.

This study establishes a foundation for advancing NLP systems tailored to morphologically rich, low-resource languages. By integrating linguistic supervision into neural architectures, VerbCraft demonstrates the potential for improving both linguistic precision and translation quality.

Building on these findings, future work will focus on several key areas of improvement and expansion. Firstly, **enhanced contextual modeling** will be explored to address challenges such as tense consistency, auxiliary verb generation, and mood prediction. This will involve incorporating advanced mechanisms to refine the model's contextual understanding.

Secondly, the approach will be extended to include **broader linguistic features**, such as noun morphology and additional dialectal variations. This expansion aims to increase the model's generality and applicability across diverse linguistic contexts.

Thirdly, the methodology will be adapted for **scalability to other languages**, including Greek, Persian, and Turkish. This adaptation will test the framework's potential effectiveness and flexibility in handling diverse linguistic systems.

Additionally, **dataset enrichment** will be prioritized by expanding the current dataset with natural text and multimodal data. This step aims to improve the model's robustness and ability to understand and process richer contextual information.

Finally, future efforts will focus on **integrating syntax and semantics** into the model. By unifying these linguistic layers, the model can achieve holistic linguistic representation, addressing complex phenomena like compound tenses and modal constructions.

Future efforts will address the trade-off between grammatical precision and fluency, optimizing VerbCraft for broader NLP applications while maintaining its focus on linguistic accuracy.

6 Limitations

While VerbCraft represents a significant advancement in morphologically aware NLP for low-resource languages, several limitations warrant attention. VerbCraft faces challenges in balancing accuracy and fluency, with occasional inconsistencies in tense, mood, and auxiliary verb generation. Its reliance on synthetic data and limited dialectal coverage highlight areas for dataset enrichment. Scalability to unrelated languages remains untested, and resource constraints pose practical challenges for widespread adoption. Addressing these issues will refine and generalize the framework further.

A Appendix

A.1 ChatGPT Prompts

Prompt for Dataset Generation: "Generate a diverse set of Armenian sentences with verbs annotated for their morphological features. For each sentence, ensure the verb is annotated with the following features: tense, aspect, mood, voice, person, and number. Include both regular and irregular verbs, as well as a mix of common and rare forms. The output should be formatted in JSON. For each verb, provide: 1) The Armenian sentence. 2) The English translation of the sentence. 3) A detailed breakdown of the verb's morphological features (tense, aspect, mood, voice, person, and number). Generate at least 50 examples featuring verbs across various tenses, aspects, moods, and voices. Ensure the inclusion of sentences containing irregular verbs and complex verb forms, such as the future subjunctive and compound tenses, to capture the full range of Armenian verb morphology." The data was generated between 05.08.2024 and 18.08.2024.


```
{
    "sentence": "Նա գնում էր խանութ:",
    "translation": "He was going to the store."
    "verb_info": {
        "word": "գնում էր",
        "lemma": "գնալ",
        "tense": "imperfect",
        "aspect": "imperfective",
        "mood": "indicative",
        "voice": "active",
        "person": "3",
        "number": "singular",
        "components": [
            {"form": "գնում", "type": "participle"},
            {"form": "էր", "type": "auxiliary", "lemma": "լինել"}
        ]
    }
}
```


Figure 1: Example output (in JSON format).

A.2 Data Split

Number of training samples: 854 Number of validation samples: 107 Number of test samples: 107

References

Catherine Arnett and Benjamin K Bergen. 2024. Why do language models perform worse for morphologically complex languages? *arXiv preprint arXiv:2411.14198*.

Gašper Beguš, Maksymilian Dabkowski, and Ryan Rhodes. 2023. Large linguistic models: Analyzing theoretical linguistic abilities of llms. *arXiv preprint arXiv:2305.00948*.

Anh Dang, Limor Raviv, and Lukas Galke. 2024. Morphology matters: Probing the cross-linguistic morphological generalization abilities of large language models through a wug test. In *13th edition of the Workshop on Cognitive Modeling and Computational Linguistics (CMCL 2024)*, pages 177–188. Association for Computational Linguistics (ACL).

Hossep Dolatian, Daniel Swanson, and Jonathan Washington. 2022. A free/open-source morphological transducer for western armenian. In *Proceedings of the workshop on processing language variation: Digital armenian (DigitAm) within the 13th language resources and evaluation conference*, pages 1–7.

J Dum-Tragut. 2009. Armenian: Modern eastern armenian. amsterdam. *Netherlands, Benjamins*.

Valentin Hofmann, Leonie Weissweiler, David Mortensen, Hinrich Schütze, and Janet Pierrehumbert. 2024. Derivational morphology reveals analogical generalization in large language models. *arXiv e-prints*, pages arXiv–2411.

Mete Ismayilzada, Defne Circi, Jonne Sälevä, Hale Sirin, Abdullatif Köksal, Bhuwan Dhingra, Antoine Bosselut, Lonneke van der Plas, and Duygu Ataman. 2024. Evaluating morphological compositional generalization in large language models. *arXiv preprint arXiv:2410.12656*.

Josef Jon, João Paulo Aires, Dusan Varis, and Ondřej Bojar. 2021. End-to-end lexically constrained machine translation for morphologically rich languages. In *Proceedings of the 59th Annual Meeting of the Association for Computational Linguistics and the 11th International Joint Conference on Natural Language Processing (Volume 1: Long Papers)*, pages 4019–4033.

Marion Marco and Alexander Fraser. 2024. Subword segmentation in llms: Looking at inflection and consistency. In *Proceedings of the 2024 Conference on Empirical Methods in Natural Language Processing*, pages 12050–12060.

Mahdi Mohseni and Amirhossein Tebbifakhr. 2019. Morphobert: A persian ner system with bert and morphological analysis. In *Proceedings of The First International Workshop on NLP Solutions for Under Resourced Languages (NSURL 2019) co-located with ICNLSP 2019-Short Papers*, pages 23–30.

Joakim Nivre, Marie-Catherine De Marneffe, Filip Ginter, Yoav Goldberg, Jan Hajic, Christopher D Manning, Ryan McDonald, Slav Petrov, Sampo Pyysalo, Natalia Silveira, et al. 2016. Universal dependencies v1: A multilingual treebank collection. In *Proceedings of the Tenth International Conference on Language Resources and Evaluation (LREC'16)*, pages 1659–1666.

Antoine Nzeyimana and Andre Niyongabo Rubungo. 2022. Kinyabert: a morphology-aware kinyarwanda language model. In *Proceedings of the 60th Annual Meeting of the Association for Computational Linguistics (Volume 1: Long Papers)*, pages 5347–5363.

Piotr Rybak. 2024. Transferring bert capabilities from high-resource to low-resource languages using vocabulary matching. In *Proceedings of the 2024 Joint International Conference on Computational Linguistics, Language Resources and Evaluation (LREC-COLING 2024)*, pages 16745–16750.

Joan Santoso, Patrick Sutanto, Billy Cahyadi, and Esther Setiawan. 2024. Pushing the limits of low-resource ner using llm artificial data generation. In *Findings of the Association for Computational Linguistics ACL 2024*, pages 9652–9667.

Andrew Shin and Kunitake Kaneko. 2024. Large language models lack understanding of character composition of words. *arXiv preprint arXiv:2405.11357*.

Telem Joyson Singh, Sanasam Ranbir Singh, and Priyankoo Sarmah. 2023. Subwords to word back composition for morphologically rich languages in neural machine translation. In *Proceedings of the 37th Pacific Asia Conference on Language, Information and Computation*, pages 691–700.

Milan Straka and Jana Straková. 2017. Tokenizing, pos tagging, lemmatizing and parsing ud 2.0 with udpipe. In *Proceedings of the CoNLL 2017 shared task: Multilingual parsing from raw text to universal dependencies*, pages 88–99.

Marion Weller-Di Marco and Alexander Fraser. 2024. Analyzing the understanding of morphologically complex words in large language models. In *Proceedings of the 2024 Joint International Conference on Computational Linguistics, Language Resources and Evaluation (LREC-COLING 2024)*, pages 1009–1020.

Yaqi Yin, Yue Wang, and Yang Liu. 2024. Chinese morpheme-informed evaluation of large language models. In *Proceedings of the 2024 Joint International Conference on Computational Linguistics, Language Resources and Evaluation (LREC-COLING 2024)*, pages 3165–3178.

Post-OCR Correction of Historical German Periodicals using LLMs

Vera Danilova and **Gijs Aangenendt**
Uppsala University
Dept. of History of Science and Ideas
Thunbergsvägen 3P, 752 38, Uppsala, Sweden
first_name.last_name@idehist.uu.se

Abstract

Optical Character Recognition (OCR) is critical for accurate access to historical corpora, providing a foundation for processing pipelines and reliable interpretation of historical texts. Despite advances, the quality of OCR in historical documents remains limited, often requiring post-OCR correction to address residual errors. Building on recent progress with instruction-tuned Llama 2 models applied to English historical newspapers, we examine the potential of German Llama 2 and Mistral models for post-OCR correction of German medical historical periodicals. We perform instruction tuning using two configurations of training data, augmenting our small annotated dataset with two German datasets from the same time period. The results demonstrate that German Mistral enhances the raw OCR output, achieving a lower average word error rate (WER). However, the average character error rate (CER) either decreases or remains unchanged across all models considered. We perform an analysis of performance within the error groups and provide an interpretation of the results. The code and resources are publicly available.[1]

1 Introduction

The effectiveness of transcription methods, such as optical character recognition (OCR), in processing historical documents critically influences the accuracy of search and analysis in text processing pipelines (Lyu et al., 2021). Despite advances in OCR technology, library and archive collection transcriptions often contain significant errors and noise due to factors such as scan quality, language, layout complexity, and character similarity. Inaccuracies in OCR transcriptions can propagate through multistep historical text processing pipelines, hinder performance on downstream Natural Language Processing (NLP) tasks, and create a risk of distorted interpretations (Lopresti, 2008; van Strien et al., 2020). Post-OCR correction plays an important role in mitigating these errors and improving transcription quality.

We focus on the post-correction of a dataset from an ongoing project[2] on the modern history of medicine, which explores ten European patient organizations. In this paper, we consider the periodical of the German Diabetes Association "Der Diabetiker", issued between 1951 and 1990. The materials predate the German spelling and punctuation reform of 1996, when new rules were implemented regarding the double s (ß), consonants, capitalization, hyphenation, and loanwords, making the dataset different from modern texts. The quality of raw OCR output varies significantly, with simpler layouts achieving higher accuracy, while complex multicolumn layouts containing advertisements and rare fonts often result in numerous errors.

In this paper, we address the following research questions:

1. Can the previously successful approach for post-OCR correction of an English-language historical newspaper dataset (Thomas et al., 2024) be effectively adapted using German-specific models? Additionally, will generative models outperform BART (Lewis et al., 2020) in reducing key metrics like the average Character Error Rate (CER) and Word Error Rate (WER)?

2. How does augmentation with a different source (National Library dataset including re-

[1] https://github.com/veraDanilova/ocr_post-correction_RESOURCEFUL-2025

[2] http://actdisease.org

Proceedings of the Third Workshop on Resources and Representations for Under-Resourced Languages and Domains (RESOURCEFUL-2025), pages 120–129, March 2, 2025 ©2025 Association for Computational Linguistics

ligious and cultural articles) contribute to the quality of post-OCR correction?

3. Given that our dataset includes both challenging pages with high initial CER and easier pages with near-perfect recognition, can post-correction improve difficult errors without compromising the quality of already well-recognized pages?

This paper unfolds as follows. Section 2 describes prior research. In Section 3, we present our annotated dataset alongside the augmentation datasets. Section 4 lays out the experimental setup. Finally, Section 5 discusses our findings and Section 6 concludes the paper.

2 Related Work

Post-OCR correction of historical documents has become a central theme at the International Conference on Document Analysis and Recognition (ICDAR). The conference hosted two competitions in 2017 and 2019 dedicated to post-OCR correction, introducing two key tasks: error detection and error correction. Sequence-to-sequence neural machine translation emerged as the dominant methodology among the most successful approaches showcased at this conference (Chiron et al., 2017; Rigaud et al., 2019). The authors of the competition emphasize that historical newspapers and periodicals continue to pose a substantial challenge to OCR systems, mainly due to their intricate layouts and typographic diversity (Rigaud et al., 2019). Following the conclusion of these competitions, the benchmarks were further utilized to advance the state of the art in post-OCR correction of newspapers with pre-trained models, specifically by finetuning BART (Soper et al., 2021).

Thomas et al. (2024) are the first to explore the instruction tuning of generative models for post-OCR correction of an English dataset of 19th century newspapers. Llama 2 models (Touvron et al., 2023) are reported to considerably outperform BART. The authors emphasize the adaptability of models like Llama 2 to downstream tasks with limited instruction-tuning data (Zhou et al., 2024) in contrast to machine translation models like BART that typically depend on large volumes of parallel data for optimal performance (Xu et al., 2024).

This paper addresses a real-world scenario involving a very limited annotated dataset of German historical medical periodicals, characterized by varying quality in the initial OCR. The dataset includes layouts and fonts that are easily recognized by models, as well as more complex layouts with distorted reading order, images, and advertisements featuring rare fonts and skewed text. Given the small size of this dataset, which precludes instruction tuning, we augment it with a German dataset from the ICDAR 2019 competition, which includes a similar time period and source - newspapers. Additionally, we explore augmentation using another ICDAR 2019 dataset, which represents a different source - cultural and religious materials from the German National Library.

This study does not explore augmentation with synthetic data. While artificially inserted errors can enhance model performance, they may fail to capture the complexity and diversity of real-world OCR errors, limiting the models' generalization ability (Jasonarson et al., 2023). This is particularly relevant for our dataset, where typical error insertion is insufficient due to the intricate challenges posed by complex layouts, such as those with advertisements. We leave the exploration of error generation approaches for our specific context to future work.

Our experiments contribute to post-OCR correction for German historical documents by comparing the performance of a finetuned German BART model with instruction-tuned German generative models, such as Llama 2 13b and Mistral 7b(Jiang et al., 2023). Beyond evaluating average performance metrics, we focus on error categories to better understand how the models handle specific types of errors and whether they degrade the quality in areas where OCR is already accurate.

3 Data

3.1 Der Diabetiker

The dataset contains pages from the patient organization periodical, Der Diabetiker (1951-1990), published by the German Diabetes Association[3]. The journal was digitized using ABBYY FineReader 14[4]. Deskew and straighten lines were

[3]The periodical changed name in 1971 to Diabetes-Journal

[4]https://www.abbyy.com/company/news/abbyy-finereader-14-pdf-solution/

selected as image processing steps in the workflow.

To create the ground truth, we manually corrected a sample consisting of 35 pages selected to represent layout complexity and time period. The quality of simple layouts is generally high, while most issues are concentrated in the more complex layouts. Pages considered as simple layout have only one or two columns, text in a common font (Times New Roman or Arial), and no advertisements or titles breaking the columns. Pages considered as complex layout contain full page advertisements, multi-text columns interspersed with advertisements and images, and rare fonts.

Overall, we collected 20 pages with complex layouts (12 pages from the period 1951-1970 and 8 pages from the period 1970-1990), and 15 pages with simple layouts (7 pages from the period 1951-1970 and 8 pages from the period 1970-1990).

3.2 Augmentation Datasets

To augment the training dataset, we utilize two ICDAR-19 competition datasets with ground truth for OCR post-correction: the Neue Zürcher Zeitung (NZZ) and the IMPACT German National Library dataset (GNL) [5].

The NZZ dataset includes 96 front pages of the Swiss newspaper Neue Zürcher Zeitung, covering the period from 1780 to 1947. Front pages were chosen because they typically contain highly relevant material. They include but not exclusively consist of advertisements.

The GNL dataset is a subset of the IMPACT dataset (Papadopoulos et al., 2013) that consists of 150 pages from various time periods. According to our manual analysis, it is mostly written in contemporary German, spanning different domains such as art, literature, and religion, with some excerpts in Latin. Neither the ICDAR-2019 competition nor the official description of the full version in Papadopoulos et al. (2013) provide detailed information on the distribution of time periods and domains within the German segment. However, the latter reports that the full version of the IMPACT dataset is predominantly composed of 19th-century data, accounting for 316k of the total 602k pages, followed by 20th-century data with 160k pages. More than half of the dataset consists of book pages (335k pages).

[5] `https://zenodo.org/records/3515403`

For NZZ and GNL datasets, special alignment files are provided to match OCR-ed text with ground-truth spans. Manual review of the aligned spans showed that in four NZZ pages and eleven GNL pages, the reading order was restored in the ground truth. Therefore, the OCR and ground truth spans are either partially or completely misaligned. Additionally, multiple pages exhibit partial mismatches due to missing text in the OCR output. The next section outlines the dataset types used to evaluate the impact of these misalignments.

4 Experimental Setup

In this study, we evaluate German BART and generative models, Llama 2 13b and Mistral 7b, comparing their WER and CER metrics[6] against raw OCR outputs.

At the core of the training process lies a base dataset consisting of Der Diabetiker pages, a small annotated collection, combined with NZZ, a comparable newspaper source. To evaluate the impact of dataset composition, we train the models with and without augmentation using GNL, which adds greater diversity to the data.

The training data is structured in two configurations: one that retains misaligned spans and another that excludes them.

To deepen our understanding of models' performance, we analyze their handling of diverse OCR errors across three distinct error categories.

Our primary focus is the correction of errors in the Der Diabetiker test data. The approach identified as successful will be further refined and expanded for application in post-OCR correction of the entire German segment of our project's dataset of patient organizations' periodicals.

4.1 Data Pre-processing

Pre-processing for all datasets includes removing extra spaces and duplicates. Additionally, we control for input context length based on the insights from previous work. For Der Diabetiker, we use the segmentation into paragraphs provided by the raw OCR output. For NZZ and GNL, the splitting strategy is detailed below.

[6] WER is the ratio of the minimum number of word substitutions, deletions, and insertions (word edit distance) required to transform the recognized text into the ground truth, divided by the total number of words in the ground truth. Similarly, CER is the character edit distance divided by the total number of characters in the ground truth.

Context length. We divided the NZZ and GNL pages into spans at newline characters, resulting in an average span length of 168 characters with a standard deviation of 32. This decision was motivated by prior work, which discussed the impact of text length on OCR post-correction (Veninga, 2024). Models like finetuned ByT5 (Xue et al., 2022) and Llama-2 7b, in zero-shot and few-shot settings, were found to be sensitive to context length. Long or very short spans make it challenging for these models to learn effectively.

To further investigate this, we analyzed results from prior work (Thomas et al., 2024) regarding OCR text length and CER reduction for the Llama 2 13b model. The table summarizing the results is provided by the authors in the associated GitHub repository[7]. It revealed that OCR texts exceeding 400 characters, though constituting a small fraction of the test set (38 out of 2792 texts), suffered a significant increase in errors (CER reduction = -190). At the same time, shorter spans showed notable improvement (CER reduction = 60). Given that the corresponding training set had an average text length of 124 characters, we decided to finetune on spans between 100 and 200 characters.

Training dataset configurations. To evaluate the impact of misalignments discussed in the previous Section on models' performance, we use two configurations of training sets for each of the datasets. ALL-DATA includes the full dataset without filtering, while FILTERED excludes any mismatched entries. Furthermore, we apply whitespace correction (Bast et al., 2023) to the NZZ ground truth, addressing issues such as merged words and unseparated punctuation marks that we identified in this dataset. In the FILTERED dataset, all Latin texts identified in the GNL dataset are removed.

4.2 Training and Test Data Description

Training data. The resulting training dataset is composed of three distinct parts. Der Diabetiker makes up 6% of the training data, the NZZ dataset contributes 56%, and the GNL dataset accounts for the remaining 38%. We vary the inclusion of the GNL portion in our experiments, as this dataset is more distant from the target data source (medical periodicals) and time period, whereas NZZ is more closely aligned with the target source and time frame.

[7]https://github.com/Shef-AIRE/llms_post-ocr_correction

	ALL-DATA	FILTERED
No. text spans	6371	4985
No. tokens	150k	118k
μ CER	0.85	0.24
σ CER	6.45	2.19

Table 1: General description of the training dataset configurations. CER statistics reflect the initial raw OCR quality

	ALL-DATA		FILTERED	
	μ CER	σ CER	μ CER	σ CER
NZZ	0.7	6.34	0.23	2.8
GNL	1.21	7.05	0.31	0.34
DD	0.03	0.09	0.03	0.09

Table 2: CER statistics for raw OCR grouped by data source and dataset configuration. DD stands for Der Diabetiker

The general description of the resulting training dataset configurations including the three datasets is provided in Table 1.

The CER statistics for raw OCR, grouped by data source and training set configuration, are presented in Table 2. It presents the average and standard deviation of the CER for each section of the training dataset, providing insight into the OCR quality across the dataset-specific training samples before and after filtering.

The initial OCR quality for Der Diabetiker is generally high, as reflected in the CER statistics for the training data shown in Table 2. To ensure a balanced representation of different error magnitudes in both the training and test sets, we examined the error categories within the Der Diabetiker data. Through this analysis, we found that approximately 7% of the data (54 out of 760 paragraphs) has a CER of 0.1 or higher, where the OCR output resulted in text spans that were significantly altered, making it nearly impossible to understand the meaning without the surrounding context. These errors occurred in pages with complex layouts and rare fonts. In contrast, 31% of the paragraphs (242 out of 760) had a CER between 0 and 0.1, with minor errors like missing umlauts, lowercase letters instead of capitals, and spacing issues. While these errors occasionally altered the meaning of some words, the overall meaning of

OCR Text	Ground Truth	CER	CER_interval
für das Arzt-Patient-Uerhältnis eher schädlich als nütz- lich sind? Hat schließlich, um auch diese Frage noch Dr. Josef Issels begrüßt vor Prozeßbeginn Staatsanwalt	für das Arzt-Patient-Verhältnis eher schädlich als nütz¬ lich sind? Hat schließlich, um auch diese Frage noch Dr. Josef Issels begrüßt vor Prozeßbeginn Staatsanwalt	0.0121951219 512195	<0.1&!=0
Abb. 33 Offnen einer Sprudelflasche Durch Änderung der Lage der Sprudelflasche strömt der Druck der senkrecht aufsteigenden Kohlensäure: a b. c. a) voll gegen die Öffnung	Abb. 33 Öffnen einer Sprudelflasche Durch Änderung der Lage der Sprudelflasche strömt der Druck der senkrecht aufsteigenden Kohlensäure: a. b. c. a) voll gegen die Öffnung	0.0117647058 823529	<0.1&!=0
'^ÄX"^ • Komplikationen und deren Vor¬ sorge beim juvenilen Diabetes • Immunsuppression	sche Aspekte. • Komplikationen und deren Vor¬ sorge beim juvenilen Diabetes • Immunsuppression	0.1494252873 563218	>=0.1

Table 3: Examples of raw OCR CER error categories - minor (<0.1&!=0) and major (>=0.1)

the text remained largely recoverable. The remaining 464 paragraphs had perfect OCR (CER = 0).

Based on these observations, we decided to use the identified error categories to balance the Der Diabetiker data in both the training and testing sets. This approach allows us to better assess model performance, particularly in terms of how well the models handle perfect OCR text (ensuring they do not degrade its quality) and how they perform with varying levels of error. The following error categories were introduced for both data balancing and further analysis:

- [NONE]: CER = 0 – perfectly recognized text
- [MINOR]: 0 < CER < 0.1 – minor errors that do not significantly alter the text. These include issues such as missing umlauts, lowercase letters instead of capitals, and spacing errors, where the text remains recognizable and the meaning is generally preserved.
- [MAJOR]: CER >= 0.1 – substantial errors that significantly alter the text, where the meaning of the text is changed or obscured. Examples can include missing half-lines or sequences of characters that are unrecognizable due to page damage, where context is essential for comprehension. Furthermore, problems arise when the scan inadvertently includes partial text from adjacent pages.

An example of this categorization is shown in Figure 3

Test data. The test set consists of 376 paragraphs from Der Diabetiker, selected through shuffling and stratified sampling according to the CER error category. It includes 23 paragraphs with major errors, 146 with minor errors, and 207 with perfect OCR.

4.3 Finetuning Setup

As a baseline, we finetune German BART base[8] on our sequence pairs. This model is a finetuned version of *facebook/bart-base* on the German MultiLingual Summarization dataset, MLSUM (Scialom et al., 2020).

For instruction tuning of generative models, we train LoRA adapters (Hu et al., 2021) with PEFT (Mangrulkar et al., 2022) following the methodology from (Thomas et al., 2024). We use Llama 2 13b models specifically optimized to process German text[9].

Additionally, we experiment with the German Mistral 7B, which is recommended by the developers for offering a good trade-off between performance and computational efficiency. The prompt is the translation into German of the prompt from (Thomas et al., 2024). The exact prompt formulation is as follows:

```
    f"""### Anweisung:
Korrigieren Sie die OCR-Fehler
im bereitgestellten Text.

### Eingabe:
{example['OCR Text']}

### Antwort:
{example['Ground Truth']}
"""
```

We conduct finetuning using two combined scenarios:

1. A comparison between ALL-DATA, which includes mismatching spans, and manually filtered data (FILTERED).

[8] https://huggingface.co/Shahm/bart-german

[9] https://github.com/jphme/EM_German

OCR Text	Ground Truth	old_CER	CER_interval	Model Correction	new_CER	CER_reduction
von Diabetikern besonders geschätzt. Schulte-Maure! Kornbrennerei seit 1848, Castrop-Rauxel ...zpoaäfes Ce Zhre diätetischen Vabriegsmitlel 2	von Diabetikern besonders geschätzt. Schulte-Rauxel Kornbrennerei seit 1848, Castrop-Rauxel ...wo kaufen Sie Ihre diätetischen Nahrungsmittel?	0.13	>=0.1	von Diabetikern besonders geschätzt. Schulte-Rauxel Kornbrennerei seit 1848, Castrop-Rauxel ...zur Herstellung diätetischen Vollkornmittel 2	0.18	-36.8

Table 4: Post-OCR correction of an advertisement by Mistral 7b (ALL-DATA, not augmented with GNL)

2. In addition to the first setup, we compare the base training set, which includes Der Diabetiker and NZZ, with the same set augmented by GNL, denoted as [+GNL].

4.4 Evaluation Metrics

We measure average CER and WER, as well as CER and WER within error categories for the proposed training data configurations. WER is particularly critical for our data, as accurate word counts are essential for further comparisons across time periods and are also used for temporal topic modeling.

To investigate improvements in relation to the defined error categories, we assess the percentage of text spans with improved OCR quality compared to those with deteriorated or unchanged quality. This percentage is calculated as the ratio of texts with a positive CER reduction and WER reduction to the total number of texts in each error category. The CER reduction, as defined in previous work (Thomas et al., 2024), is determined using the following formula:

$$\text{CER}_{\text{reduction}} = \left(\frac{\text{CER}(gt, ocr) - \text{CER}(gt, pr)}{\text{CER}(gt, ocr)} \right) \times 100 \quad (1)$$

where *gt* denotes the ground truth, *ocr* represents the OCR output, and *pr* indicates the generative model prediction. WER reduction is calculated similarly using the corresponding WER values. To calculate WER and CER we use JiWER[10], a package for the evaluation of automatic speech recognition systems, which supports CER and WER measures. These measures are computed using the minimum edit distance between one or more reference sentences and their corresponding hypothesis sentences.

[10]https://pypi.org/project/jiwer/

	ALL-DATA		FILTERED	
	CER	WER	CER	WER
raw OCR	0.02	0.09	**0.02**	0.09
BART 140M	0.03	0.1	0.03	0.11
BART 140M [+GNL]	0.03	0.11	0.03	0.11
Mistral 7b	**0.02**	**0.07**	0.07	0.27
Mistral 7b [+GNL]	0.07	0.26	0.1	0.45
Llama-2 13b	0.25	0.28	0.03	**0.08**
Llama-2 13b [+GNL]	0.08	0.28	0.13	0.63

Table 5: Average error rate before (light-gray row) and after post-OCR correction

5 Results

5.1 Average Performance

Table 5 presents the average CER and WER across various models and dataset configurations. On average, none of the models achieves a reduction in CER. BART demonstrates stable performance across all configurations; however, it slightly increases both CER and WER, thereby deteriorating the initial OCR quality. Among the generative models, Mistral 7b stands out by maintaining CER levels and achieving a 22% reduction in WER when trained on the complete dataset without filtering (ALL-DATA).

In Table 4, we present an example of successful word correction by Mistral 7b trained on ALL-DATA and not augmented with GNL. The paragraph is categorized as a major error, as its initial raw OCR score is 0.13. The red frame highlights the OCR error that was subsequently corrected by the model, as shown in the green frame within the model correction column. The context includes the name of the location, Castrop-Rauxel, associated with the company Schulte-Rauxel. We have highlighted in blue the contextual information that could potentially assist the model in making the correction.

We identified several instances where the Mistral 7b model successfully recovered words from context. In contrast, other models, including

	ALL-DATA						FILTERED					
	[MINOR]		[MAJOR]		[ALL]		[MINOR]		[MAJOR]		[ALL]	
	CER	WER	CER	WER	CER	WER	CER	WER	CER	WER	CER	WER
BART 140M	26	25	26	17	26	24	29	26	35	30	29	26
BART 140M [+GNL]	25	24	30	22	25	24	25	24	39	35	27	25
Mistral 7b	**61**	**64**	39	35	**58**	**60**	51	48	30	39	48	47
Mistral 7b [+GNL]	53	56	43	43	52	55	**54**	**57**	43	**57**	**53**	**57**
Llama-2 13b	54	58	**52**	43	54	56	51	50	**48**	43	51	49
Llama-2 13b [+GNL]	53	55	43	**52**	52	55	49	50	**48**	35	48	48

Table 6: Percentage of corrected paragraphs in terms of WER and CER in each error category (%)

BART, were unable to perform similar corrections for the same paragraphs. Further investigation is required to understand the factors contributing to this difference.

We conducted a manual analysis of a subset of model outputs where a decrease in CER was observed. In several instances, the models exhibited repetition of punctuation marks and words after partially correcting the input sequence. Additionally, LLaMA 2 occasionally reproduced parts of the prompt in its output. These repetitions were not filtered out prior to metric evaluation. Further investigation is needed to better understand and mitigate these issues.

When trained on the manually filtered dataset (FILTERED), all models exhibit an increase in the average CER (Table 5). This outcome may be attributed to the reduced dataset size following the filtering process. However, Llama-2 13b demonstrates an 11% improvement in WER despite the reduction in dataset size.

On average, we observe that the inclusion of GNL data does not lead to improvements in the reduction of either CER or WER. Nevertheless, it is worth noting that GNL data might prove beneficial in addressing specific types of errors within error categories - minor or major. To explore this possibility further, we conduct a detailed analysis of models' performance within categories in the following.

5.2 Performance in Error Groups

To investigate how models perform across the error categories outlined in Section 4.2, we calculate the percentage of texts in the test set where error rates improved following post-OCR correction.

As detailed in Section 4.2, the test set comprises 23 paragraphs classified as having major errors and 146 paragraphs categorized as having minor errors. The percentage of corrected paragraphs is determined by computing the ratio of paragraphs within a given error category that exhibited a positive CER or WER reduction after post-correction (CER or WER reduction > 0) to the total number of paragraphs in that category.

We analyze this performance across three distinct categories: minor errors, major errors, and the combined category (all errors), which aggregates all instances where the initial raw OCR CER was greater than 0. Table 6 summarizes the percentage of corrected paragraphs for each model and dataset configuration, offering a comprehensive view of how effectively these models address errors across categories.

Among the models evaluated, BART demonstrated the least success in correcting paragraphs across both minor and major error categories.

Mistral 7b corrected over 60% of paragraphs with minor errors in terms of both WER and CER when trained on the ALL-DATA configuration. However, its performance dropped when dealing with more challenging errors, with the model correcting less than half of the paragraphs containing such difficult issues.

In contrast, Llama-2 demonstrated a more balanced performance across error categories. It corrected more than half of the paragraphs in terms of CER without augmentation, and over half in terms of WER when GNL augmentation was applied.

Through our manual analysis, we observed that Mistral, in particular, exhibited a certain level of creativity when handling major errors, when using the same configuration settings as the other models. This creativity was apparent in its ability to address complex error patterns, but it sometimes led to substitutions that, while contextually relevant, deviated from the exact ground truth. In these instances, Mistral was able to replace nonsensical or garbled character sequences with text that, although thematically similar, did not align perfectly with the original source.

For example, as shown in Table 4, Mistral

	ALL-DATA		FILTERED	
	ERR %	GT %	ERR %	GT %
BART 140M	**24**	72	20	60
BART 140M [+GNL]	**24**	70	**22**	62
Mistral 7b	11	90	14	84
Mistral 7b [+GNL]	12	**91**	14	**87**
Llama-2 13b	12	87	17	80
Llama-2 13b [+GNL]	13	86	17	83

Table 7: Percentage of paragraphs with unchanged error (ERR) and those with preserved perfect OCR quality (GT). The highest percentages in both columns are highlighted

corrected the misrecognized part of the paragraph, which in the ground truth should have read "...wo kaufen Sie ihre diätetischen Nahrungsmittel?" (translating to "...where do you buy your dietary foods?") by replacing it with "...zur Herstellung diätetischen Vollkornsmittel" ("...for the production of dietary whole grain products"). While both sequences are related in topic (dietary foods), the produced variations decrease the accuracy.

When we remove misaligned text spans from the dataset (in the FILTERED dataset configuration), the addition of GNL augmentation begins to show a positive impact on error correction for Mistral across both error categories. Specifically, Mistral corrects 10% more paragraphs in terms of WER and 5% more in terms of CER when GNL is included, compared to the configuration without it.

This could be attributed, in part, to the larger size of the ALL-DATA dataset, which is 27.8% larger than the FILTERED dataset. Additionally, the inclusion of misaligned passages may be enhancing Mistral 7b's ability to recover words from context. These misaligned spans could provide valuable contextual clues, aiding the model in making more accurate corrections. This potential relationship between misalignment and model performance warrants further exploration to fully understand how these factors interact and contribute to the model's effectiveness.

Interestingly, when we examine the results in the major error category for both dataset configurations, both BART and Mistral show improvements with the inclusion of GNL, demonstrating better performance in terms of both CER and WER. This suggests that the addition of GNL augmentation may help both models address more challenging errors.

We further investigate the cases with the perfect initial OCR (error-free cases) to determine which models preserve a higher proportion of accurately OCR-ed spans. In addition, we analyze spans with zero CER reduction to identify which models leave a higher percentage of errors unchanged compared to others. The results are summarized in Table 7, where GT indicates the percentage of OCR spans that perfectly match the ground truth, and ERR reflects the percentage of spans with unchanged errors. BART exhibits a higher percentage of unchanged errors compared to the generative models and preserves fewer perfectly OCR-ed spans than both Llama 2 and Mistral. In contrast, Mistral models, retain the highest proportion of accurately OCR-ed spans.

6 Conclusion

This paper compares the performance of large language models, specifically BART as an encoder-decoder, and Llama 2 13b and Mistral as generative models, for post-OCR correction of the German historical periodical Der Diabetiker, published by the German Diabetes Association. We examine the impact of different dataset configurations and the effect of dataset augmentation with data from a distant source.

The results suggest that BART detects fewer errors compared to the generative models. However, since BART does not correct these errors, it also avoids introducing larger changes — an issue that we observe in the generative models. Also, BART tends to correct more spans that were already accurate in the first place, leading to unnecessary modifications. This behavior aligns with the average CER and WER scores in Table 5, where BART shows a decline in OCR quality, but the degradation is not as severe as observed with some generative models. This could imply that BART's stability comes at the cost of detecting fewer errors overall.

Among the evaluated models, Mistral 7b stands out as the most promising in terms of performance on historical data from patient organization periodicals. It achieves a significant 22% improvement in average WER and retains the highest proportion of correctly OCR-ed paragraphs compared to other models. Despite these strengths, Mistral maintains the average CER without improvement, and further investigation is needed to understand how it handles major errors. Specifically, more research is required to manage the model's creativity in generating corrections, ensuring that it produces more accurate and contextually relevant outputs without deviating from the ground truth.

6.1 Acknowledgements

This research is funded by the European Union (ERC, ActDisease, ERC-2021-STG 10104099). Views and opinions expressed are however those of the author(s) only and do not necessarily reflect those of the European Union or the European Research Council. Neither the European Union nor the granting authority can be held responsible for them.

The authors would like to thank the **Centre for Digital Humanities and Social Sciences** at Uppsala University for providing us with the computational resources for training and evaluating our models.

References

Hannah Bast, Matthias Hertel, and Sebastian Walter. 2023. Fast whitespace correction with encoder-only transformers. In *Proceedings of the 61st Annual Meeting of the Association for Computational Linguistics (Volume 3: System Demonstrations)*, pages 389–399, Toronto, Canada. Association for Computational Linguistics.

Guillaume Chiron, Antoine Doucet, Mickaël Coustaty, and Jean-Philippe Moreux. 2017. Icdar2017 competition on post-ocr text correction. In *2017 14th IAPR International Conference on Document Analysis and Recognition (ICDAR)*, volume 01, pages 1423–1428.

Edward J. Hu, Yelong Shen, Phillip Wallis, Zeyuan Allen-Zhu, Yuanzhi Li, Shean Wang, Lu Wang, and Weizhu Chen. 2021. Lora: Low-rank adaptation of large language models.

Atli Jasonarson, Steinór Steingrímsson, Einar Sigursson, Árni Magnússon, and Finnur Ingimundarson. 2023. Generating errors: OCR post-processing for Icelandic. In *Proceedings of the 24th Nordic Conference on Computational Linguistics (NoDaLiDa)*, pages 286–291, Tórshavn, Faroe Islands. University of Tartu Library.

Albert Q. Jiang, Alexandre Sablayrolles, Arthur Mensch, Chris Bamford, Devendra Singh Chaplot, Diego de las Casas, Florian Bressand, Gianna Lengyel, Guillaume Lample, Lucile Saulnier, Lélio Renard Lavaud, Marie-Anne Lachaux, Pierre Stock, Teven Le Scao, Thibaut Lavril, Thomas Wang, Timothée Lacroix, and William El Sayed. 2023. Mistral 7b.

Mike Lewis, Yinhan Liu, Naman Goyal, Marjan Ghazvininejad, Abdelrahman Mohamed, Omer Levy, Veselin Stoyanov, and Luke Zettlemoyer. 2020. BART: Denoising sequence-to-sequence pre-training for natural language generation, translation, and comprehension. In *Proceedings of the 58th Annual Meeting of the Association for Computational Linguistics*, pages 7871–7880, Online. Association for Computational Linguistics.

Daniel Lopresti. 2008. Optical character recognition errors and their effects on natural language processing. In *Proceedings of the Second Workshop on Analytics for Noisy Unstructured Text Data*, AND '08, page 9–16, New York, NY, USA. Association for Computing Machinery.

Lijun Lyu, Maria Koutraki, Martin Krickl, and Besnik Fetahu. 2021. Neural ocr post-hoc correction of historical corpora. *Transactions of the Association for Computational Linguistics*, 9:479–493.

Sourab Mangrulkar, Sylvain Gugger, Lysandre Debut, Younes Belkada, Sayak Paul, and Benjamin Bossan. 2022. Peft: State-of-the-art parameter-efficient fine-tuning methods. `https://github.com/huggingface/peft`.

Christos Papadopoulos, Stefan Pletschacher, Christian Clausner, and Apostolos Antonacopoulos. 2013. The impact dataset of historical document images. In *Proceedings of the 2nd International Workshop on Historical Document Imaging and Processing*, HIP '13, page 123–130, New York, NY, USA. Association for Computing Machinery.

Christophe Rigaud, Antoine Doucet, Mickaël Coustaty, and Jean-Philippe Moreux. 2019. Icdar 2019 competition on post-ocr text correction. In *2019 International Conference on Document Analysis and Recognition (ICDAR)*, pages 1588–1593.

Thomas Scialom, Paul-Alexis Dray, Sylvain Lamprier, Benjamin Piwowarski, and Jacopo Staiano. 2020. MLSUM: The multilingual summarization corpus. In *Proceedings of the 2020 Conference on Empirical Methods in Natural Language Processing (EMNLP)*, pages 8051–8067, Online. Association for Computational Linguistics.

Elizabeth Soper, Stanley Fujimoto, and Yen-Yun Yu. 2021. BART for post-correction of OCR newspaper text. In *Proceedings of the Seventh Workshop on Noisy User-generated Text (W-NUT 2021)*, pages 284–290, Online. Association for Computational Linguistics.

Daniel van Strien, Kaspar Beelen, Mariona Ardanuy, Kasra Hosseini, Barbara McGillivray, and Giovanni Colavizza. 2020. Assessing the impact of ocr quality on downstream nlp tasks. In *Proceedings of the 12th International Conference on Agents and Artificial Intelligence*, pages 484–496, Valletta, Malta. SCITEPRESS - Science and Technology Publications.

Alan Thomas, Robert Gaizauskas, and Haiping Lu. 2024. Leveraging LLMs for post-OCR correction of historical newspapers. In *Proceedings of the Third Workshop on Language Technologies for Historical and Ancient Languages (LT4HALA) @ LREC-COLING-2024*, pages 116–121, Torino, Italia. ELRA and ICCL.

Hugo Touvron, Louis Martin, Kevin Stone, Peter Albert, Amjad Almahairi, Yasmine Babaei, Nikolay Bashlykov, Soumya Batra, Prajjwal Bhargava, Shruti Bhosale, Dan Bikel, Lukas Blecher, Cristian Canton Ferrer, Moya Chen, Guillem Cucurull, David Esiobu, Jude Fernandes, Jeremy Fu, Wenyin Fu, Brian Fuller, Cynthia Gao, Vedanuj Goswami, Naman Goyal, Anthony Hartshorn, Saghar Hosseini, Rui Hou, Hakan Inan, Marcin Kardas, Viktor Kerkez, Madian Khabsa, Isabel Kloumann, Artem Korenev, Punit Singh Koura, Marie-Anne Lachaux, Thibaut Lavril, Jenya Lee, Diana Liskovich, Yinghai Lu, Yuning Mao, Xavier Martinet, Todor Mihaylov, Pushkar Mishra, Igor Molybog, Yixin Nie, Andrew Poulton, Jeremy Reizenstein, Rashi Rungta, Kalyan Saladi, Alan Schelten, Ruan Silva, Eric Michael Smith, Ranjan Subramanian, Xiaoqing Ellen Tan, Binh Tang, Ross Taylor, Adina Williams, Jian Xiang Kuan, Puxin Xu, Zheng Yan, Iliyan Zarov, Yuchen Zhang, Angela Fan, Melanie Kambadur, Sharan Narang, Aurelien Rodriguez, Robert Stojnic, Sergey Edunov, and Thomas Scialom. 2023. Llama 2: Open foundation and fine-tuned chat models.

Martijn Veninga. 2024. LLMs for OCR Post-Correction. Master Thesis in Computer Science.

Haoran Xu, Young Jin Kim, Amr Sharaf, and Hany Hassan Awadalla. 2024. A paradigm shift in machine translation: Boosting translation performance of large language models. In *The Twelfth International Conference on Learning Representations*.

Linting Xue, Aditya Barua, Noah Constant, Rami Al-Rfou, Sharan Narang, Mihir Kale, Adam Roberts, and Colin Raffel. 2022. Byt5: Towards a token-free future with pre-trained byte-to-byte models. *Transactions of the Association for Computational Linguistics*, 10:291–306.

Chunting Zhou, Pengfei Liu, Puxin Xu, Srini Iyer, Jiao Sun, Yuning Mao, Xuezhe Ma, Avia Efrat, Ping Yu, Lili Yu, Susan Zhang, Gargi Ghosh, Mike Lewis, Luke Zettlemoyer, and Omer Levy. 2024. Lima: less is more for alignment. In *Proceedings of the 37th International Conference on Neural Information Processing Systems*, NIPS '23, Red Hook, NY, USA. Curran Associates Inc.

From Words to Action: A National Initiative to Overcome Data Scarcity for the Slovene LLM

Špela Arhar Holdt
University of Ljubljana
arharhs@ff.uni-lj.si

Špela Antloga
University of Ljubljana; University of Maribor
spela.antloga@fri.uni-lj.si

Tina Munda
University of Ljubljana
tina.munda@gmail.com

Eva Pori
University of Ljubljana
eva.pori@ff.uni-lj.si

Simon Krek
University of Ljubljana; IJS
simon.krek@ijs.si

Abstract

Large Language Models (LLMs) have demonstrated significant potential in natural language processing, but they depend on vast, diverse datasets, creating challenges for languages with limited resources. The paper presents a national initiative that addresses these challenges for Slovene. We outline strategies for large-scale text collection, including the creation of an online platform to engage the broader public in contributing texts and a communication campaign promoting openly accessible and transparently developed LLMs.

1 Introduction

Extremely large language models, such as GPT-4, have demonstrated remarkable advancements across various natural language processing tasks, sparking widespread interest in their applications. However, their reliance on vast and diverse datasets makes them inherently biased toward well-resourced languages. For languages like Slovene, with a smaller speaker base and limited data availability, this disparity poses a significant challenge, hindering the development of robust language-specific LLMs.

Recent studies have highlighted similar challenges faced by other low-resource languages, underscoring the need for comprehensive multilingual evaluation and language-specific model development. (Lai et al., 2023) provide an in-depth assessment of ChatGPT's performance across multiple languages, revealing its uneven effectiveness in low-resource contexts. Their evaluation, covering seven tasks and 37 languages, exposes significant performance gaps in both low- and extremely low-resource languages. Likewise, (Alam et al., 2024) explore the broader landscape of LLMs for low-resource languages, addressing their multilingual, multimodal, and dialectal complexities. Their findings emphasize the necessity of language-specific initiatives and reveal the persistent limitations of LLMs for medium- to low-resource languages, largely due to the lack of representative datasets.

While these studies highlight the performance-related limitations of current LLMs for low-resource languages, an equally pressing concern is their accessibility. The proprietary nature and high computational demands of existing models restrict access for many research organizations and smaller companies, underscoring the need for open-access alternatives. Addressing this issue requires not only the development of computationally efficient models, but also the creation of large, diverse, and high-quality datasets tailored to specific languages.

For smaller language communities, such as Slovene, the search for texts to be included in LLMs must extend well beyond readily available online sources, as these alone are insufficient to support the development. In this paper, we introduce a national initiative aimed at overcoming these obstacles for Slovene, detailing our strategies for large-scale text collection and community engagement for the development of openly available Slovene LLMs.

2 Project framework and previous work

LLMs have introduced a major shift in the field of Natural Language Processing (NLP), offering more efficient fine-tuning for common NLP tasks while simplifying their implementation (Brown et al., 2020). The datasets serve as the foundational infrastructure analogous to a root system that sustains and nurtures the development of LLMs (Liu et al., 2024). Therefore, preparing language data for LLMs is a crucial step that directly impacts their performance across various tasks.

Proceedings of the Third Workshop on Resources and Representations for Under-Resourced Languages and Domains (RESOURCEFUL-2025), pages 130–136, March 2, 2025

The effectiveness of NLP tasks relies heavily on the scale of the language model's training, which is directly influenced by access to large, diverse datasets spanning various domains (Kaplan et al., 2020). Moreover, diversity in training data plays a crucial role in enhancing the generalization capabilities of large models, enabling downstream tasks, as outlined in (Ali et al., 2019), to effectively leverage knowledge even with limited training data (Brown et al., 2020).

In the ongoing *PoVeJMo—Adaptive Natural Language Processing with Large Language Models* project,[1] we aim to develop several computationally efficient and open-access large language models trained on Slovene language data. These models will also be adapted and evaluated for selected industry use cases, such as enhancing Slovene speech recognition and synthesis for industrial systems, preparing museum materials and interactive systems, as well as for medical applications and infrastructure code generation.

We have first gathered 9.2 billion tokens from freely available sources, including existing language corpora and other openly accessible Slovene-language data, providing a solid foundation for the project. The initial dataset includes different types of text, such as news articles up to and including September 2023 (Kosem et al., 2023), academic works (Žagar et al., 2022), web crawls (mC4 (Raffel et al., 2020), MaCoCu (Bañón et al., 2023), CC100 (Wenzek et al., 2019)), and various Slovene reference and specialized corpora included in the Metafida database (Erjavec, 2023)). The GaMS-1B-Chat language model, with one billion parameters, has been trained on this language material (Vreš et al., 2024).

While this initial model provides valuable insights into the effects of training on Slovene data, it is roughly a thousand times smaller than the largest models (e.g., used for the latest version of ChatGPT), makes errors frequently, and highlights the need for further text collection to improve performance.[2]

[1]The project is funded between 2023 and 2026 by the Slovenian Research and Innovation Agency ARIS and the EU Recovery and Resilience Facility. More information on `https://www.cjvt.si/povejmo/en/project/`.

[2]GaMS-1B-Chat can be tested at `https://povejmo.si/klepet/` (at the moment, the interface is only available in Slovene).

3 National text-collection campaign

We have estimated that the development of a sufficiently large model requires approximately 40 billion additional words. The estimation of the required amount of training data is heuristic and approximate, derived from two approaches. The first approach is based on the findings of the LLama model study (Touvron et al., 2023). The study illustrates the decline in the loss function as the number of training tokens increases, where, on average, two tokens correspond to one word. For most models, including LLaMa 7B, which is the closest equivalent to GaMS, the most significant decrease in the loss function occurs up to approximately 100 billion tokens (that is, around 50 billion words). We expect to collect around 10 billion words from freely available online resources (currently 9.2 billion; see Section 2), while an additional 40 billion will need to be gathered using alternative approaches.[3] The second approach relies on LLM scaling laws, which suggest that a model of size x requires at least $5x$ to $10x$ words for effective training, though in practice the requirement is often even greater. Given that the larger GaMS model is expected to have approximately 10 billion parameters, it would require a minimum of 50 billion words to achieve optimal performance.

This ambitious undertaking necessitated the development of a comprehensive communication and operational strategy. The key components of this strategy include: (1) identifying and engaging potential contributors of textual materials; (2) developing efficient mechanisms for text submission; (3) implementing secure and scalable storage systems; (4) establishing effective and reliable processes for tracking and documenting all text acquisition activities; and (5) defining the metadata framework to ensure systematic organization and accessibility of collected texts. Beyond these operational aspects, strategy (6) addresses legal and ethical considerations associated with data collection and usage, while also prioritizing (7) promotional and dissemination activities to build public awareness and support. A key objective of these efforts is to emphasize the importance of developing a large-scale language model for Slovene, highlighting its far-reaching implications for tech-

[3]The observed trend indicates that the loss function continues to decrease even to 1,500 billion tokens, and in the case of LLaMa 3, where 3,000 billion tokens were used, the loss function still exhibited a downward trajectory, although more pronounced for larger models.

nological innovation and cultural preservation.

Our text collection campaign operates through two main strategies. On the one hand, we engage with large-scale text providers such as national libraries, publishing houses, media organizations, government ministries, and other significant contributors, strongly advocating for the value and potential impact of creating a Slovene LLM and encouraging them to contribute their textual resources. On the other hand, we reach out to individuals, inviting them to donate their own texts to both actively support and directly contribute to the co-creation of the Slovene language model.

Each of these two groups presents unique requirements and demands distinct approaches to communication and engagement. Beyond the technical challenges of acquiring and processing the material, the primary obstacles lie in legal constraints. Current Slovene legislation permits the use of copyrighted material for data mining. However, this does not apply to material available on the web unless it is provided under an appropriate license. However, this does not include the material available on the web. This legal framework imposes significant limitations on the ability to gather and utilize existing Slovene texts for model training.

Addressing this issue involves two potential approaches. The first option is to advocate for legislative reform, urging lawmakers to amend the copyright laws to accommodate the specific needs of language technology development. Such a legal adjustment could facilitate broader access to textual resources while ensuring that intellectual property rights are respected in a manner compatible with technological advancements. However, this approach is inherently time-intensive and comes with no guarantee of success. It places the outcome largely outside of our control, as it depends on the willingness of policymakers to adopt the proposed changes and the eventual implementation of new legal frameworks.

Given these uncertainties, we have determined that a more pragmatic and immediate approach is to actively seek permission from copyright holders to use their texts for the purpose of building a Slovene LLM. This strategy, while more labour-intensive, allows us to make direct progress without waiting for external factors to align. This approach requires substantial effort on our part, as it involves identifying relevant stakeholders, initiating discussions, addressing potential concerns, and negotiating agreements. A significant challenge in this process arises from the hesitation of some stakeholders, particularly media outlets and publishers, who are concerned about the uncertain societal implications of artificial intelligence and its potential impact on their work.

3.1 Engaging with large-scale providers

Our experiences with addressing large-scale text providers so far suggest that stakeholders often prefer to maintain the status quo, choosing to wait and observe who among them will take the first step. This creates a paradoxical situation: while applications such as ChatGPT, which rely on data from other languages, are already widely used also in the Slovene language, there is hesitation about building a Slovene-specific model or, more precisely, about allowing access to copyrighted text to build the model. The primary concern seems to be uncertainty about what will happen with the texts, specifically how and why the data will be used, whether there is potential for misuse, and what safeguards are in place to ensure that the texts are handled responsibly and ethically. A general conclusion could be drawn that stakeholders are willing to use an English-based model, which requires no contribution of their own texts, but they might be hesitant about contributing when it comes to developing a Slovene model.

In response, our communication strategy emphasizes the importance of preserving Slovene as a digital language. We argue that a Slovene language model is essential to ensure that the language remains comparable and competitive with other similar languages in the digital age. This initiative is framed as a collective effort, where every contribution helps to achieve a shared benefit—enhancing and improving resources for everyone. Additionally, we highlight the advantage of building this model independently, rather than solely relying on foreign corporations. By taking control of the process, we can ensure transparency in the types of texts included and maintain the ability to use the model for our specific needs.

In the meantime, the European Union has also recognized the importance of this issue and is actively working toward creating a publicly available large language model for all European languages. This initiative aims to provide equal opportunities for both commercial and non-commercial use

Figure 1: The section of the web portal where the interested participants can provide their texts (https://zbiranje.povejmo.si/).

across European languages. In this context, the amount of Slovene text collected directly impacts the positioning of the Slovene language within this broader European framework. Thus, one of our messages to the public is that building a Slovene language model is a matter of national interest. It ensures that Slovene can be effectively integrated into products and services developed by companies, benefiting both businesses and the wider community.

3.2 Engaging with individuals

To address individuals or groups that do not fall into the category of large-scale text providers and to encourage their contribution of textual resources for the development of the Slovene language model, we designed a targeted promotional strategy. As part of this effort, we participated in radio and television programs focused on language or technology-related topics, where we explained the concept of LLMs, the processes involved in their development, their potential applications, and the importance of individual engagement. In addition, we organized or participated in roundtable discussions and expert panels that facilitated debates on the advantages and concerns surrounding the creation of such a model.

To facilitate the widest possible text collection, we developed a web portal (https://povejmo.si/) where participants can submit their texts (Figure 1) while accessing essential information about the phases of developing a large generative language model, details of the text collection campaign, and answers to frequently

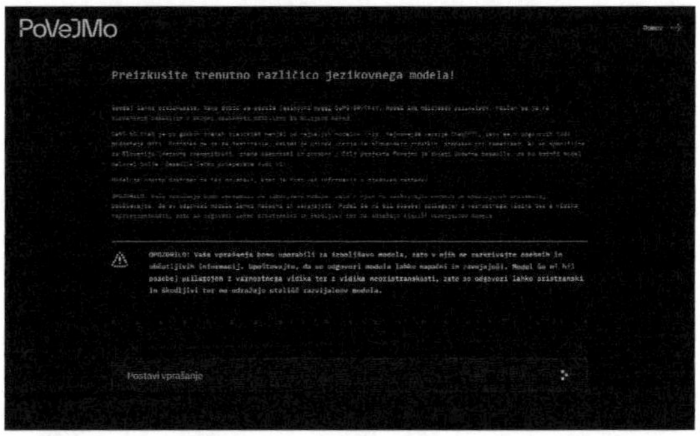

Figure 2: The section of the web portal where the interested participants can test the existing model (https://povejmo.si/klepet/).

asked questions. To ensure trust and encourage participation, we highlighted both the purpose and values of the text-collection project. The project's goals include supporting developmental independence by creating a Slovene-specific language model, ensuring a controlled and secure process for data handling, promoting open accessibility of the model, improving the machine understanding and generation of Slovene, overcoming language barriers, and capturing Slovenia's national specifics. The project is guided by three key values: openness, ensuring transparency, clear methodologies, and secure data handling; ethics, with a commitment to privacy, anonymity, and proper consent; and inclusiveness, fostering the participation of diverse groups to reflect the richness of the Slovene language.

In Appendix A, we include the translated *Agreement for the use of copyrighted works in connection with text collection in the PoVeJMo project* to demonstrate the implemented legal solution.

The web portal also features an interactive section where users can try GaMS-1B-Chat, developed on the current version of the language model (Figure 2). As mentioned in Section 2, the current version still underperforms, however, this limitation also serves as a call for action: if we aim to develop a more accurate and robust model, a significantly larger dataset of Slovene texts is essential.

4 Data Storage and processing protocol

We have implemented a comprehensive protocol for securely managing the storage, encryption, transmission, and processing of data throughout all stages of its lifecycle. Data is received through network connections or on portable storage devices, which may contain unencrypted or optionally encrypted data using a temporary key set by the data owner. Once received, data undergoes decryption (if necessary) on a secure system, is re-encrypted with a new encryption key, and then securely uploaded to the primary storage system. Backup copies of the encrypted data are created and stored on a secondary system to ensure disaster resilience. During processing, unencrypted data is used exclusively for the duration of the analysis or transformation. Owners define specific rules for further sharing of their data, such as limiting its use to the project or permitting broader access to other researchers within Slovenia, the EU, or beyond.

Data is transferred between systems using encrypted channels (e.g., SSL/TLS, SSH). Data minimization principles are applied, providing only the necessary subsets of data for specific use cases, packaged as encrypted "data bundles". All data transfers are tracked to ensure accountability, with detailed records of which data was shared and with whom. Processing on high-performance computing systems (e.g., Vega supercomputer) or specialized research infrastructures (e.g., FRIDA at the Faculty of Computer and Information Science) adheres to strict security protocols. Data is stored in encrypted form and decrypted only temporarily during processing. After processing, unencrypted data is securely deleted. Future improvements may include leveraging Confidential Computing technologies for enhanced security.

Access management prioritizes security and simplicity, given the initial small group of users. Encryption keys are manually tracked and managed by the project lead, with backups maintained securely. Data bundles for specific use cases are encrypted with unique keys assigned to each user, employing AES symmetric encryption for efficiency and security. As the number of users or datasets grows, more advanced access management systems will be introduced.

5 Conclusion and Future Work

This paper has outlined the national initiative to overcome data scarcity and support the development of a Slovene large language model. By implementing diverse text-gathering scenarios, including a user participation portal and an extensive communication strategy, the project has actively addressed the unique challenges faced by languages with a small speaker base.

At the time of this paper's submission, the foundational infrastructure for collecting Slovene-language texts has been fully established, including a user-friendly portal for contributions and robust protocols for data storage and processing. A nationwide promotional campaign was launched, aiming to mobilize broad participation from both institutions and individuals. By the time of the workshop, we anticipate being able to report on the first campaign's outcomes, including the volume and diversity of collected texts and their suitability for training the Slovene large language model. These results will provide valuable insights into the scalability and replicability of such initiatives for other less-resourced languages.

Acknowledgments

The research program *Language Resources and Technologies for Slovene* (P6-0411) and the projects Adaptive Natural Language Processing with Large Language Models and Large Language Models for Digital Humanities (GC-0002) are funded by the Slovenian Research and Innovation Agency.

References

Firoj Alam, Shammur Absar Chowdhury, Sabri Boughorbel, and Maram Hasanain. 2024. Llms for low resource languages in multilingual, multimodal and dialectal settings. In *Proceedings of the 18th Conference of the European Chapter of the Association for Computational Linguistics: Tutorial Abstracts*, pages 27–33.

Abbas Raza Ali, Marcin Budka, and Bogdan Gabrys. 2019. Towards meta-learning of deep architectures for efficient domain adaptation. In *PRICAI 2019: Trends in Artificial Intelligence: 16th Pacific Rim International Conference on Artificial Intelligence, Cuvu, Yanuca Island, Fiji, August 26–30, 2019, Proceedings, Part II 16*, pages 66–79. Springer.

Marta Bañón, Malina Chichirau, Miquel Esplà-Gomis, Mikel L. Forcada, Aarón Galiano-Jiménez, Cristian García-Romero, Taja Kuzman, Nikola Ljubešić, Rik van Noord, Leopoldo Pla Sempere, Gema Ramírez-Sánchez, Peter Rupnik, Vít Suchomel, Antonio Toral, and Jaume Zaragoza-Bernabeu. 2023. http://hdl.handle.net/11356/1795 Slovene web corpus MaCoCu-sl 2.0. Slovenian language resource repository CLARIN.SI.

Tom Brown, Benjamin Mann, Nick Ryder, Melanie Subbiah, Jared D Kaplan, Prafulla Dhariwal, Arvind

Neelakantan, Pranav Shyam, Girish Sastry, Amanda Askell, et al. 2020. Language models are few-shot learners. *Advances in neural information processing systems*, 33:1877–1901.

Tomaž Erjavec. 2023. http://hdl.handle.net/11356/1775 Corpus of combined slovenian corpora metaFida 1.0. Slovenian language resource repository CLARIN.SI.

Jared Kaplan, Sam McCandlish, Tom Henighan, Tom B Brown, Benjamin Chess, Rewon Child, Scott Gray, Alec Radford, Jeffrey Wu, and Dario Amodei. 2020. Scaling laws for neural language models. *arXiv preprint arXiv:2001.08361*.

Iztok Kosem, Jaka Čibej, Kaja Dobrovoljc, Tomaž Erjavec, Nikola Ljubešić, Primož Ponikvar, Mihael Šinkec, and Simon Krek. 2023. http://hdl.handle.net/11356/1879 Monitor corpus of slovene trendi 2023-09. Slovenian language resource repository CLARIN.SI.

Viet Dac Lai, Nghia Trung Ngo, Amir Pouran Ben Veyseh, Hieu Man, Franck Dernoncourt, Trung Bui, and Thien Huu Nguyen. 2023. Chatgpt beyond english: Towards a comprehensive evaluation of large language models in multilingual learning. *arXiv preprint arXiv:2304.05613*.

Andy Liu, Mona Diab, and Daniel Fried. 2024. Evaluating large language model biases in persona-steered generation. *arXiv preprint arXiv:2405.20253*.

Colin Raffel, Noam Shazeer, Adam Roberts, Katherine Lee, Sharan Narang, Michael Matena, Yanqi Zhou, Wei Li, and Peter J Liu. 2020. Exploring the limits of transfer learning with a unified text-to-text transformer. *Journal of machine learning research*, 21(140):1–67.

Hugo Touvron, Thibaut Lavril, Gautier Izacard, Xavier Martinet, Marie-Anne Lachaux, Timothée Lacroix, Baptiste Rozière, Naman Goyal, Eric Hambro, Faisal Azhar, et al. 2023. Llama: Open and efficient foundation language models. *arXiv preprint arXiv:2302.13971*.

Domen Vreš, Martin Božič, Aljaž Potočnik, Tomaž Martinčič, and Marko Robnik Šikonja. 2024. Generative model for less-resourced language with 1 billion parameters. pages 485–511.

Guillaume Wenzek, Marie-Anne Lachaux, Alexis Conneau, Vishrav Chaudhary, Francisco Guzmán, Armand Joulin, and Edouard Grave. 2019. Ccnet: Extracting high quality monolingual datasets from web crawl data. *arXiv preprint arXiv:1911.00359*.

Aleš Žagar, Matic Kavaš, Marko Robnik-Šikonja, Tomaž Erjavec, Darja Fišer, Nikola Ljubešić, Marko Ferme, Mladen Borovič, Borko Bošković, Milan Ojsteršek, and Goran Hrovat. 2022. http://hdl.handle.net/11356/1449 Abstracts from the KAS corpus KAS-abs 2.0. Slovenian language resource repository CLARIN.SI.

Appendix A

Copy of the Agreement for the use of copyrighted works in connection with text collection in the PoVeJMo project

Article 1 (Introductory Provisions)

1.1. The Contractor is a scientific research organization engaged in building open-access large language models for the Slovenian language, among other activities, within the framework of the program Adaptive Natural Language Processing with Large Language Models (PoVeJMo) (hereinafter: PoVeJMo program), which is implemented under the Public Call for Co-financing of Long-term Large Research and Innovation Collaborative Programs at TRL 3-6 within the Recovery and Resilience Plan (RRP).

1.2. With the aim of developing open-access large language models for the Slovenian language, the Contractor collects various types of texts. [NAME SURNAME] manages this process on behalf of and for the Contractor's account.

Article 2 (Subject of the License)

2.1. By this license, the Copyright Holder transfers to the Contractor all economic copyrights, related rights, and other rights of the author as defined by the Slovenian Copyright and Related Rights Act (hereinafter: ZASP), necessary for the development of open-access large language models for the Slovenian language, particularly the right of reproduction, the right to make available to the public, and the right of adaptation.

2.2. The transfer of rights to the Contractor is non-exclusive, royalty-free, indefinite in duration, and unlimited in territorial scope, allowing the Contractor to build open-access large language models for the Slovenian language, including the execution of the long-term PoVeJMo program.

2.3. The Copyright Holder agrees that the Contractor may freely transfer the granted rights to third parties for the purpose of developing open-access large language models for the Slovenian language.

2.4. The subject of this agreement pertains to the rights of the following copyrighted works:

- Copyrighted Work 1
- Copyrighted Work 2
- ...

Article 3 (Obligations of the Copyright Holder)

3.1. The obligations of the Copyright Holder include:

- Enabling the Contractor access to the copyrighted works in digital form via the online portal (https://povejmo.si/) or by another method agreed upon in an annex to this agreement.
- Collaborating with the Contractor to ensure the successful development of open-access large language models for the Slovenian language, particularly in the implementation of the PoVeJMo program.

3.2. The Copyright Holder guarantees that they hold all rights to the copyrighted works specified in Article 2.4, thereby enabling the Contractor to obtain all necessary permissions for their use in developing open-access large language models for the Slovenian language.

Article 4 (Obligations of the Contractor)

4.1. The obligations of the Contractor include:

- Using the copyrighted works specified in Article 2.4 of this agreement and any copies thereof created during the development of open-access large language models for the Slovenian language solely for that purpose and storing them in a secure environment that ensures an appropriate level of security, proportionate and limited to what is necessary for safe storage and prevention of unauthorized use.
- The works from Article 2.4 are exclusively used for the development of open-access large language models for the Slovenian language.

Article 5 (Data Protection)

5.1. The Contractor and the Copyright Holder agree to protect and process any personal data in accordance with the provisions of the Slovenian Personal Data Protection Act (Official Gazette of the Republic of Slovenia, No. 163/22, hereinafter: ZVOP-2) and Regulation (EU) 2016/679 of the European Parliament and of the Council of 27 April 2016 on the protection of natural persons with regard to the processing of personal data and on the free movement of such data, repealing Directive 95/46/EC (OJ L 119, 4.5.2016, hereinafter: General Data Protection Regulation).

Article 6 (Final Provisions)

6.1. The Contractor and the Copyright Holder agree that this agreement shall be governed by Slovenian law, and any matters not regulated by this agreement shall be governed by the provisions of ZASP and the Slovene Obligations Code (hereinafter: OZ).

6.2. This license is drawn up in two (2) identical copies, one (1) for each party. Any modifications or amendments to this agreement are possible only with mutual consent and in writing.

6.3. The Contractor and the Copyright Holder commit to resolving any disputes amicably. If a dispute cannot be resolved, the competent court at the Contractor's registered office shall have jurisdiction over dispute resolution.

Assessing the Similarity of Cross-Lingual Seq2Seq Sentence Embeddings Using Low-Resource Spectral Clustering

Nelson Moll
University of Maryland
nmoll@umd.edu

Tahseen Rabbani
Yale University
tahseen.rabbani@yale.edu

Abstract

In this work, we study the cross-lingual distance of machine translations through alignment of seq2seq representations over small corpora. First, we use the M2M100 model to collect sentence-level representations of The Book of Revelation in several languages. We then perform unsupervised manifold alignment (spectral clustering) between these collections of embeddings. As verses between translations are not necessarily aligned, our procedure falls under the challenging, but more realistic non-correspondence regime. The cost function associated with each alignment is used to rank the relative (machine) similarity of one language to another. We then perform correspondent alignment over another cluster of languages, this time using FLORES+ parallel NLLB model embeddings. Our experiments demonstrate that the representations of closely-related languages group closely, and are cheap to align (requiring <1000 sentences) via our strategy.

1 Introduction

Assessing the similarities and differences between languages, that is, comparative linguistics, requires the consideration of historical factors, vocabulary, phonology, and written script Georgi et al. (2010); Starostin (2000); Anttila (1989). Computational linguists adopting lexicostatistical techniques can study language distances by measuring the evolution of cognates Gudschinsky (1956). Comparative analysis which operates purely at the word level, such as ranking Levensthein distances (a string-edit metric) Sturrock (2000), has been both widely used and disputed Greenhill (2011). In parallel, the machine learning community recognized the need for sentence-level processing to produce high-quality translations. The attention mechanism, common to transformer-based language models Vaswani (2017), considers the semantic contribution of all tokens (word/sub-word units) in an input to develop an output.

The quality of machine translation has drastically improved in recent years due to the advent of attention-based sequence-to-sequence (seq2seq) models which intake sentences in a source language and output a corresponding translation in a target language Sutskever (2014); Cho (2014). Sharp improvements in multilingual training strategies have resulted in so-called many-to-many translation models that can accept many source-target language pairs. Many-to-many translation models, such as the M2M100 Fan et al. (2021) and NLLB Costa-jussà et al. (2022), can accept pairs from 100 and 200 widely-spoken languages, respectively.

Given a specified source language, the M2M100 and NLLB models tokenize an input and pass it along several attention layers which encode the specified sentence(s) to real-valued embeddings Phuong and Hutter (2022). Such representations produced by deeper encoder layers are thought to embody abstract semantic meaning critical to developing coherent, high-quality output in the decoding phase Vaswani (2017); Clark (2019); Voita et al. (2019). Intuitively, we would expect that closely related languages produce similar representations. If we regard sentences as concepts, language generation benefits from the alignment of closely-related concepts (The et al., 2024). We expect the syntactical and figurative structure of sentences to align more closely among related languages, thus we want to investigate whether many-to-many transformer representations are capturing this dynamic.

In this work, we propose a low-resource strategy for assessing how a many-to-many machine translation model encoder groups languages. First, we collect the sentence representations over a common corpus across a cluster of Slavic, Indo-

Proceedings of the Third Workshop on Resources and Representations for Under-Resourced Languages and Domains (RESOURCEFUL-2025), pages 137–142, March 2, 2025 ©2025 Association for Computational Linguistics

Aryan/Dravidian, Romance languages, Scandinavian, Turkic/Mongolic, and Bantu languages. For this paper, we use the mean pooling of hidden states over the entire sequence to get a sentence-level representation, in line with other works Xu et al. (2020); Kudugunta et al. (2019). For one group of language families, the common corpus is the Book of Revelation (BoR). For the other group, the common text is a collection of parallel (i.e., correspondent) sentences from the FLORES-200 dataset Costa-jussà et al. (2022). We validate our method over this correspondent dataset to verify alignment is working as expected in a naive setting. In comparison to the work of Kudugunta et al. (2019) which uses an irreproducible web crawl to generate hundreds of thousands to tens of millions of parallel sentence pairs Uszkoreit et al. (2010), our resource is low-resource: *we only require* < 1000 *sentences per language pair to perform our clustering.*

We treat each language's set of embeddings as a discrete manifold. Then, we perform a pairwise manifold alignment via spectral clustering Wang and Mahadevan (2009) and use the associated cost to produce an ordering of machine-lingual similarities. For the BoR corpus, since translations are not necessarily verse-aligned, we are performing alignment without correspondence – a much more challenging regime, and realistic scenario for ultra low-resource languages. Our similarity rankings over both BoR and FLORES+ closely correspond to established analyses in comparative linguistics Bella et al. (2021) along with a few sharp deviations that may indicate the preference of M2M100 and NLLB to occasionally place representations of less related languages close to one another.

2 Comparison Algorithm

The semantics of a language, referring to its meaning and how words and phrases convey ideas, often follow distinct patterns based on the relationships between words, contexts, and usage. These patterns can be observed in how words group together, how similar meanings emerge in different contexts, or how words with similar meanings are often used in comparable syntactic structures.

Spectral clustering Von Luxburg (2007); Law et al. (2017) can be applied to identify these semantic patterns by analyzing the structure of a similarity matrix constructed from the relationships between words or phrases. We follow the method of Wang and Mahadevan (2009), referred to as manifold alignment without correspondence, and describe this process explicitly in Section 2.1. We must use a "without-correspondence" strategy as variations in translations (in our case, of the Christian Bible), can produce different verse-orderings and shuffled semantics which prevents a verse-to-verse (1-1) correspondence between two languages.

In our case, we used the heat kernel similarity on a suggestion by Wang and Mahadevan (2009) for language comparison. By representing sentences as real-valued vectors in high-dimensional space using encoder embeddings (e.g., M2M100/NLLB representations), we can calculate pairwise similarities, which are then used to create a graph where nodes represent vectors in these representations, and the edges are given quantitatively by their similarity matrix. The spectral clustering algorithm then partitions this graph into clusters by projecting these vector representations onto a set of vectors given by solutions to a generalized eigenvector solution (see Section 2.2). This method hopes to potentially reveal similarities between machine representations of languages by comparing these projections, which are closely related to the clusters. In particular, we examine the square sum of the first d eigenvalues as defined by the general eigenvector equation as given in Section 2.1.

Chowdhury et al. (2021) also used a graph-based approach to study the similarities between languages. They created graph Laplacians between given languages at the word level. Our method considers language at the sentence level and, instead creates a joint graph based on their combined information. Motivated by Wang and Mahadevan (2009), we opt for the combined graph approach due to a belief that we can measure the distance between two languages by considering spectral data associated to a submanifold derived from a combination of data from the graphs of both languages.

2.1 Algorithm Sketch

Let $X = [x_1, x_2, \ldots, x_n]$ and $Y = [y_1, y_2, \ldots, y_n]$ be $p \times m$ and $q \times n$ matrices, respectively. For our application, X and Y are the mean poolings of hidden sentences states. The rows are the representations and the columns are the features. Let $|| \; x_2 \; ||$ denote the Euclidean distance. Define the $(k+1) \times (k+1)$ matrix R_{x_l} by $R_{x_l}^{i,j} = \frac{\|z_j - z_i\|_2}{\delta_X}$, where $z_1 = x_l$ and $z_2, \ldots, z_{k+1}$ are x_l's k-closest neighbors and δ_X is the standard deviation for the pairwise distances between the x_j. We now define the similarity matrix W_x by $W_x = \exp\left(-\|R_{x_i} - R_{x_j}\|_F\right)$, where $\|A\|_F = \sqrt{\text{trace}(A^T A)}$ is the Frobenius norm of the matrix A. The matrix W_x is sometimes called the similarity matrix.

Let the diagonal matrix D_x be defined by $D_x^{i,i} = \sum_j W_x^{i,j}$, and let $L_x = D_x - W_x$. We similarly define a family of matrices in terms of Y. Let

$$Z = \begin{bmatrix} X & 0 \\ 0 & Y \end{bmatrix} \text{ and } D = \begin{bmatrix} D_x & 0 \\ 0 & D_y \end{bmatrix}.$$

Define W by $W^{i,j} = \exp\left(-\text{dist}(R_x, R_y)/\delta_{X,Y}\right)$, where $\text{dist}(R_x, R_y)$ and $\delta_{X,Y}$ are defined in Wang and Mahadevan (2009) or in the Appendix. Let B_x be the diagonal matrix with $B_x^{i,i} = \sum_j W^{i,j}$ and $B_y^{j,j} = \sum_i W^{i,j}$. We define the distance function $d(\cdot)$ as

$$\begin{aligned}
d(R_{x_i}, R_{y_j}) &= \min_{1 \le h \le k!} \min\{d_1(h), d_2(h)\}, \text{where} \\
d_1(h) &= \|\{R_{y_j}\}_h - k_1 R_{x_i}\|_F, \\
d_2(h) &= \|k_2\{R_{y_j}\}_h - R_{x_i}\|_F, \\
k_1 &= trace(R_{x_i}^T \{R_{y_j}\}_h)/trace(R_{x_i}^T R_{x_i}) \\
k_2 &= trace(\{R_{y_j}\}_h^T R_{x_i}^T)/trace(\{R_{y_j}\}_h^T \{R_{y_j}\}_h).
\end{aligned}$$

Here, h is a permutation of the k possible choices for R_{y_i}. The quantity $\delta_{X,Y}$ is the standard deviation of the set $\{dist(R_{x_i}, R_{y_j}) : x_i \in X, y_j \in Y\}$.

Further, define

$$L = \begin{bmatrix} L_x + \mu B_x & -\mu W \\ -\mu W^T & L_y + \mu B_y \end{bmatrix}.$$

Consider the solutions for λ in the equation

$$Z^T L Z \gamma = \lambda Z^T D Z \gamma. \tag{1}$$

Next, index the generalized eigenvalues from least to greatest and consider the first d eigenvalues $\{\lambda_i : 1 \le i \le d\}$ and calculate $K(d) = \sum_{i=1}^{d} |\lambda_i|^2$. This $K(d)$ will be used to measure the alignment quality between two languages.

2.2 Cost Function

The cost function from Wang and Mahadevan (2009) is given as

$$\begin{aligned}
C(\gamma) = C(\alpha, \beta) &= \sum_{i,j} \mu(\alpha^T x_i - \beta^T y_j)^2 W^{i,j} \\
&+ \frac{1}{2} \sum_{i,j} \mu(\alpha^T x_i - \alpha^T y_j)^2 W_x^{i,j} \\
&+ \frac{1}{2} \sum_{i,j} \mu(\beta^T y_i - \beta^T y_j)^2 = \gamma^T Z^T L Z \gamma,
\end{aligned}$$

where $\gamma^T = [\alpha^T, \beta^T]^T$ is a solution to the generalized eigenvalue problem Eqn. 1. Note that if we normalize γ by dividing the constant $\sqrt{|\gamma^T Z^T D Z \gamma|}$ then $C(\gamma) = |\lambda|^2$. The cost function $C(\alpha, \beta)$ from Wang and Mahadevan (2009) is minimized by the generalized eigenvectors for the above equation. Hence we define the new cost function $K(d) = \sum_{i=1}^{d} |\lambda_i|^2$, where the λ_i are the eigenvalues for the above equation. The minimum possible value of $K(d)$ is 0 (manifolds are identical) while the maximum is unbounded, though in practice we do not observe it to exceed 1000.

3 Experiments

In this section, we produce a ranking of (machine) language distances. We review our distances against prevailing comparative linguistics theory.

Dataset. Our corpora to compare encoder manifolds are the Book of Revelation (BoR) of the Christian Bible and the FLORES+ dataset (dev split). We choose the BoR due to (1) its widely available translations and (2) since it contains a diverse set of vocabulary and vivid imagery this can help further probe for concept alignment. For the BoR, we source these translations from the digital eBible corpus Akerman et al. (2023). Revelations has a diverse set of words describing abstract visions. We thought this diversity would help separate out some of the differences in the languages we consider. For each family, we attempt to choose translations of the BoR descending from a common pivot or consistent translator, though this is not always possible. FLORES+ sentences are 1-1 aligned between all languages and professionally translated.

Languages. For the non-correspondent BoR clustering task, we consider three clusters of languages: (French, Italian, Spanish, Portuguese), (German, Russian, Ukrainian, Polish), (Kannada, Hindi, Bengali, Gujarati). For the correspondent FLORES+ task, we consider three new clusters of languages: (Icelandic, Swedish, Danish, Norwegian Bokmål), (Swahili, Kirundi, Kinyarwanda, Luganda), (Khalkha Mongolian, Kyrgyz, Tatar, Kazakh). In each quadruplet, we include a challenge (grey) language which is widely accepted to be the most dissimilar of its group despite close geographic proximity.

	Italian	Portuguese	French
Portuguese	239		
French	313	153	
Spanish	101	174	296

Table 1: **Romance Language Distances.** Our method generally places Italian, Spanish, and Portuguese close together, but controversially ranks French closer to Portuguese than the other Romance languages.

	Bengali	Hindi	Kannada
Hindi	21		
Kannada	98	304	
Gujarati	231	360	365

Table 2: **Indo-Aryan/Dravidian Language Distances.** Our ranking overall tends to cluster the Indo-Aryan languages Bengali, Hindi, and Gujarati together. It erroneously places Kannada, a Dravidian language, not as far away for several orderings.

	German	Russian	Polish
Russian	325		
Polish	397	252	
Ukrainian	228	220	155

Table 3: **Slavic/Germanic Language Distances.** Our ranking overall tends to cluster the Slavic languages together.

	Swedish	Danish	Nor. Bok.
Danish	299		
Nor. Bok.	76	228	
Icelandic	577	600	619

Table 4: **East/West Scandinavian Language Distances.** Our ranking clusters members of the East Scandinavian family closer together than with Icelandic, which is closer to Old Norse.

	Kh. Mong.	Tatar	Kazakh
Tatar	744		
Kazakh	226	413	
Kyrgyz	600	436	461

Table 5: **Turkic/Mongolic Language Distances.** Kazakh, Tatar, and Kyrgyz (all members of the Turkic Kipchak branch), and generally clustered together. The method commits an error by viewing Khalka Mongolian and Kazakh as closest.

	Swahili	Luganda	Swahili
Luganda	497		
Kirundi	317	298	
Kinyarw.	254	299	282

Table 6: **Great Lakes/Sabaki Bantu Language Distances.** The alignment generally views the Great Lakes Bantu languages as close. Our method commits a single error by viewing Swahili (a Sabaki Bantu language) as the closest language to Kirundi.

Model. For each translation of the BoR, we push every verse through the M2M100 (418M model) and extract the mean pooling of hidden states over the entire sequence to get a sentence-level representation. For each language, this results in roughly 403 points in $\mathbb{R}^{1024}$. For translations of FLORES+, we use NLLB (600M model) mean pooling embeddings of 997 sentences also in $\mathbb{R}^{1024}$. We choose $d = 400$ eigenvalues to construct our cost $K(d)$ (as described in Section 2.2 as this explained roughly 90% of covariance across all individual language graph Laplacians. We ran all experiments using only a CPU.

4 Experimental Analysis

4.1 Non-Correspondent Alignment

Tables 1, 2, and 3 depict our seq2seq spectral clustering rankings via manifold alignment without correspondence over the BoR. A higher spectral clustering score indicates a higher cost for manifold alignment.

Our spectral rank successfully tends to group close languages together. This indicates that the manifold alignment is easier for the core similar languages, thus their representations may occupy similar regions in the ambient space. Our ranking, though generally accurate is not immune to errors – for example, placing Kannada, a Dravidian language, very close to some Indo-Aryan languages.

4.2 Correspondent Alignment

Tables 4, 5, and 6 depict rankings via manifold alignment with correspondence over FLORES+. To perform parallel alignment, we set $W = I$ in Section 2.1. Our results generally fall in line with what is found in Bella et al. (2021).

Swedish, Danish, and Norwegian Bokmål are closely related members of the East Scandinavian group within the Northern Germanic family and our clustered closely by our method. Kahlkha Mongolian, a member of the Mongolic languages, shares typological features but is less related to the Turkic group. Our approach does commit an error by judging Khalkha Mongolian as closer to Kazakh than the other Kipchak languages. Swahili, although a Bantu language, is part of the Sabaki group, differs in vocabulary from the other three. Our methodology erroneously views Swahili as the closest language to Kirundi (which is, in fact, Kinyarwanda).

5 Conclusion

In this work, we study how seq2seq translation models group languages together. We conduct this assessment by extracting M2M100 and NLLB hidden representations of sentences of various languages over small, common corpora. We observe that the embedding manifolds of closely related languages likely contain similar structures as they, on average, do not incur high spectral clustering costs. In contrast to Kudugunta et al. (2019), we require < 1000 sentences and can perform clustering without parallel alignment, thus framing our method as a low-resource strategy.

References

Vesa Akerman, David Baines, Damien Daspit, Ulf Hermjakob, Taeho Jang, Colin Leong, Michael Martin, Joel Mathew, Jonathan Robie, and Marcus Schwarting. 2023. The ebible corpus: Data and model benchmarks for bible translation for low-resource languages. *arXiv preprint arXiv:2304.09919*.

Ramio Anttila. 1989. Historical and comparative linguistics. *John Ben Jamins Publishing Companym*.

Gábor Bella, Khuyagbaatar Batsuren, and Fausto Giunchiglia. 2021. A database and visualization of the similarity of contemporary lexicons. In *International Conference on Text, Speech, and Dialogue*, pages 95–104. Springer.

Kyunghyun Cho. 2014. Learning phrase representations using rnn encoder-decoder for statistical machine translation. *arXiv preprint arXiv:1406.1078*.

Koel Dutta Chowdhury, Cristina España-Bonet, and Josef van Genabith. 2021. Tracing source language interference in translation with graph-isomorphism measures. In *Proceedings of the International Conference on Recent Advances in Natural Language Processing (RANLP 2021)*, pages 375–385.

Kevin Clark. 2019. What does bert look at? an analysis of bert's attention. *arXiv preprint arXiv:1906.04341*.

Marta R Costa-jussà, James Cross, Onur Çelebi, Maha Elbayad, Kenneth Heafield, Kevin Heffernan, Elahe Kalbassi, Janice Lam, Daniel Licht, Jean Maillard, et al. 2022. No language left behind: Scaling human-centered machine translation. *arXiv preprint arXiv:2207.04672*.

Angela Fan, Shruti Bhosale, Holger Schwenk, Zhiyi Ma, Ahmed El-Kishky, Siddharth Goyal, Mandeep Baines, Onur Celebi, Guillaume Wenzek, Vishrav Chaudhary, et al. 2021. Beyond english-centric multilingual machine translation. *Journal of Machine Learning Research*, 22(107):1–48.

Ryan Georgi, Fei Xia, and William Lewis. 2010. Comparing language similarity across genetic and typologically-based groupings. In *Proceedings of the 23rd international conference on computational linguistics (Coling 2010)*, pages 385–393.

Simon J Greenhill. 2011. Levenshtein distances fail to identify language relationships accurately. *Computational Linguistics*, 37(4):689–698.

Sarah C Gudschinsky. 1956. The abc's of lexicostatistics (glottochronology). *Word*, 12(2):175–210.

Sneha Reddy Kudugunta, Ankur Bapna, Isaac Caswell, Naveen Arivazhagan, and Orhan Firat. 2019. Investigating multilingual nmt representations at scale. *arXiv preprint arXiv:1909.02197*.

Marc T Law, Raquel Urtasun, and Richard S Zemel. 2017. Deep spectral clustering learning. In *International conference on machine learning*, pages 1985–1994. PMLR.

Mary Phuong and Marcus Hutter. 2022. Formal algorithms for transformers. *arXiv preprint arXiv:2207.09238*.

Sergei Starostin. 2000. Comparative-historical linguistics and lexicostatistics. *Time depth in historical linguistics*, 1:223–265.

Shane Sturrock. 2000. Time warps, string edits, and macromolecules–the theory and practice of sequence comparison. david sankoff and joseph kruskal. *Genetics Research*, 76(3):327–329.

I Sutskever. 2014. Sequence to sequence learning with neural networks. *arXiv preprint arXiv:1409.3215*.

LCM The, Loïc Barrault, Paul-Ambroise Duquenne, Maha Elbayad, Artyom Kozhevnikov, Belen Alastruey, Pierre Andrews, Mariano Coria, Guillaume Couairon, Marta R Costa-jussà, et al. 2024. Large concept models: Language modeling in a sentence representation space. *arXiv preprint arXiv:2412.08821*.

Jakob Uszkoreit, Jay Ponte, Ashok Popat, and Moshe Dubiner. 2010. Large scale parallel document mining for machine translation. In *Proceedings of the 23rd International Conference on Computational Linguistics (Coling 2010)*, pages 1101–1109.

A Vaswani. 2017. Attention is all you need. *Advances in Neural Information Processing Systems*.

Elena Voita, David Talbot, Fedor Moiseev, Rico Sennrich, and Ivan Titov. 2019. Analyzing multi-head self-attention: Specialized heads do the heavy lifting, the rest can be pruned. *arXiv preprint arXiv:1905.09418*.

Ulrike Von Luxburg. 2007. A tutorial on spectral clustering. *Statistics and computing*, 17:395–416.

Chang Wang and Sridhar Mahadevan. 2009. Manifold alignment without correspondence. In *IJCAI*, volume 2, page 3.

Hongfei Xu, Josef van Genabith, Qiuhui Liu, and Deyi Xiong. 2020. Probing word translations in the transformer and trading decoder for encoder layers. *arXiv preprint arXiv:2003.09586*.

Voices of Luxembourg: Tackling Dialect Diversity in a Low-Resource Setting

Nina Hosseini-Kivanani, Christoph Schommer, Peter Gilles
University of Luxembourg
Esch-Belval, Esch-sur-Alzette, Luxembourg
{nina.hosseinikivanani, christoph.schommer, peter.gilles}@uni.lu

Abstract

Dialect classification is essential for preserving linguistic diversity, particularly in low-resource languages such as Luxembourgish. This study introduces one of the first systematic approaches to classifying Luxembourgish dialects, addressing phonetic, prosodic, and lexical variations across four major regions. We benchmarked multiple models, including state-of-the-art pre-trained speech models like Wav2Vec2, XLSR-Wav2Vec2, and Whisper, alongside traditional approaches such as Random Forest and CNN-LSTM. To overcome data limitations, we applied targeted data augmentation strategies and analyzed their impact on model performance. Our findings highlight the superior performance of CNN-Spectrogram and CNN-LSTM models while identifying the strengths and limitations of data augmentation. This work establishes foundational benchmarks and provides actionable insights for advancing dialectal NLP in Luxembourgish and other low-resource languages.

1 Introduction

Dialectal research plays a critical role in understanding linguistic diversity and cultural identity. Luxembourgish, a West Germanic language spoken by over 600,000 people, presents unique challenges due to its regional phonetic, prosodic, and lexical variations. Limited annotated resources and influences from German and French complicate automated dialect classification (Hovy, 2015; Adda-Decker et al., 2014).

Luxembourgish dialects are categorized into four regions: North, East, South, and Center. Each region exhibits distinct linguistic traits, with the northern dialect displaying the most divergence and the central region aligning closely with the standard variety (Gilles, 2023).

Automatic dialect classification has practical importance in improving automatic speech recognition (ASR) and machine translation systems and in enabling more inclusive digital archiving of dialectal data. Previous work has underscored the importance of dialect identification in preserving linguistic diversity and supporting sociolinguistic research (Kantharuban et al., 2023). However, Luxembourgish, like other low-resource languages, lacks substantial annotated datasets for automated processing, which hinders the development of robust models for dialect classification. Moreover, Luxembourgish's multilingual setting presents additional challenges, as shown by existing research in Luxembourgish ASR and related linguistic tasks (Gilles et al., 2023; Nguyen et al., 2023; Song et al., 2023).

1.1 Linguistic Variability Across Luxembourgish Dialects

Luxembourgish dialects display considerable variation in lexical, phonetic, and prosodic structures influenced by geographic factors (Gilles, 1998). To illustrate, we present a sample sentence rendered in the four main dialects—North, East, South, and Center—along with phonetic transcriptions. This example highlights the differences in pronunciation and vocabulary that complicate automated dialect classification due to regional speech patterns.

These examples underscore the challenges in distinguishing Luxembourgish dialects due to lexical differences (e.g., "Fregdig" vs. "Freiden") and phonetic variations (e.g., vowel lengthening and consonant shifts). Automatic dialect classification models must account for these subtleties to handle distinct regional forms accurately.

In this study, we address these challenges by

Proceedings of the Third Workshop on Resources and Representations for Under-Resourced Languages and Domains (RESOURCEFUL-2025), pages 143–152, March 2, 2025 ©2025 Association for Computational Linguistics

Region	Dialectal Sentence	Phonetic Transcription
North	Eng Frau hott e Fregdig di schwarz Kléider gebikst.	[æŋ fʀɑʊ hot ə fʀægdiç diː ʃwɑʀts klɜidɐ gəbɪkst]
East	En Fra hott e Freddig di schwarz Klääder gebéit.	[eːn fʀaː hot ə fʀædɪç diː ʃwɑts klɛːdɐ gəbɜit]
South	Eng Fra huet e Freiden di schwoarz Kleeder gebitzt.	[æŋ fʀaː huet ə fʀɑɪdən diː ʃwɔːɐts kleːdə gəbitst]
Center	Eng Fra huet e Freideg déi schwaarz Kleeder gebitzt.	[æŋ fʀaː huet ə fʀɑɪdeç dɜi ʃwaːʀts kleːdə gəbitst]

Table 1: Example Sentence in Luxembourgish Dialects with Phonetic Transcriptions

employing data augmentation techniques to increase sample diversity and improve model robustness, particularly for underrepresented dialects. Our methodology explores phonetic, prosodic, and lexical features across various classifiers, including both traditional machine learning algorithms and neural network models.

This paper contributes to computational linguistics by:

1. Introducing one of the first comprehensive studies on Luxembourgish dialect classification, investigating the impact of data augmentation on model performance in a low-resource setting.

2. Establishing performance benchmarks across multiple model architectures, including Random Forest, CNN-Spectrogram, CNN-LSTM, Wav2Vec2, Whisper, and XLSR-Wav2Vec2 to create a foundation for future research in Luxembourgish and other low-resource languages.

These contributions establish Luxembourgish as a compelling case study in low-resource language processing and illustrate the broader applications of dialectal NLP research. Our results underscore the importance of linguistic equity and highlight directions for future research in multilingual and dialectal NLP.

2 Related Work

Automatic dialect classification has advanced significantly in high-resource languages, where annotated datasets and sophisticated processing tools facilitate robust model performance. For instance, substantial work has been conducted in Arabic (Harfash and Abdul-kareem, 2017), Chinese (Ng and Lee, 2008), German (Dobbriner and Jokisch, 2019), and English (Etman and Louis, 2015). In these languages, the availability of extensive data resources enables classification approaches to take advantage of phonetic, prosodic, and lexical features, supporting higher accuracy and model robustness. For example, Harfash and Abdul-kareem (2017) improved dialect classification in Arabic by incorporating phonetic and prosodic cues, while Ng and Lee (2008) applied entropy-based measures to enhance Chinese dialect classification, highlighting the versatility of feature-based methods in these contexts. In high-resource settings, models often use a combination of rule-based linguistic knowledge (Biadsy and Hirschberg, 2009) and data-driven machine learning techniques that benefit from large training corpora, allowing them to learn complex patterns effectively (Ali et al., 2016).

In contrast, low-resource languages like Luxembourgish lack the annotated datasets and processing infrastructure needed for accurate dialect classification, presenting unique challenges for computational linguistics. For low-resource languages, researchers have explored strategies such as synthetic data generation and unsupervised learning to mitigate data scarcity. Transfer learning, for example, can leverage pre-trained models in related languages, using phonetic similarities to improve dialect classification in under-resourced contexts (Shah et al., 2023; Khosravani et al., 2021). Data augmentation has also emerged as a critical strategy for low-resource languages, allowing researchers to expand datasets and introduce variability, as demonstrated in tasks involving accent and dialect variation (Ullah et al., 2023; Xu et al., 2021).

For Luxembourgish, however, computational research remains relatively limited. Existing studies have focused mainly on its phonetic and syntactic characteristics (Gilles and Trouvain, 2013), as well as distinctive phonological features (Gilles, 2014), with limited exploration of automated dialect classification. Research on regional phonetic variation in Luxembourgish indicates that its dialects are influenced by neighboring German and French, with generational shifts contributing further to its linguistic diversity (Conrad, 2023). This complexity requires tailor-made classifiers and careful feature engineering to capture subtle distinctions in phonetics and prosody that are integral to Luxembourgish dialectal variation (Snoeren et al., 2011). Computational studies have suggested that cross-lingual models that utilize resources from German and French could improve Luxembourgish speech recognition (Nguyen et al., 2023), highlighting both the potential and the computational challenges that the classification of the Luxembourgish dialect entails (Adda-Decker et al., 2014).

Future progress in Luxembourgish dialect classification may benefit from techniques like data augmentation, which has proven successful in other low-resource contexts. For instance, Xu et al. (2021) demonstrated that targeted data augmentation techniques, such as pitch and speed modifications, significantly improved the accuracy of dialect classification for Chinese dialects, underscoring the value of these methods to improve model performance in low-resource settings. Such approaches could potentially be adapted for Luxembourgish, where similar variability in phonetic and prosodic features across dialects could benefit from targeted augmentation.

Building on this foundation, our study introduces a model for the classification of Luxembourgish dialects that integrates linguistic insights with computational techniques specifically designed for low-resource settings. By applying data augmentation strategies, we address the constraints imposed by limited annotated data, contributing to the broader field of dialect classification for underrepresented languages. This work aims to lay the groundwork for Luxembourgish NLP, underscoring the importance of dialectal research in multilingual NLP and advancing methodologies for low-resource language processing.

3 Methodology

3.1 Dataset and Preprocessing

The dataset used in this study was crowd-sourced through a smartphone application developed as part of a prior project [redacted]. Participants were asked to translate sentences spontaneously from German or French into their Luxembourgish dialect.

Attribute	**Category**	**Count**
Total Audio Files		1720
	Unique Entries	1720
Gender	Female	1210
	Male	510
Age Group	25–34	567
	35–44	377
	45–54	352
	55–64	277
	65+	132
Dialect Region	Center	762
	South	482
	East	293
	North	168

Table 2: Demographic Distribution of the Luxembourgish Dialect Dataset.

The dataset (Table 2) includes 1720 unique audio samples annotated with gender, age group, and dialect region. The samples reflect Luxembourgish's four main dialect regions: Center, South, East, and North, with the Center being the most represented. To evaluate whether age groups were evenly distributed across dialect regions, we conducted a chi-square test. The results indicated that age distribution did not differ significantly by dialect region ($\chi^2(6) = 5.73$, $p = 0.45$), suggesting the four regions are relatively balanced with respect to participants' ages.

For feature extraction, Mel-Frequency Cepstral Coefficients (MFCCs) were computed using the *torchaudio* and *librosa* libraries, capturing phonetic features essential for dialectal differentiation. Additionally, the mean and standard deviation of each waveform were calculated to provide statistical descriptors of each audio signal. Together, these features allow the model to learn from both phonetic characteristics and statistical patterns across dialects, supporting accurate dialect classification.

3.2 Model Architecture and Training

In this study, we explore multiple approaches to dialect classification, leveraging both traditional machine learning techniques and advanced deep learning models. Our methodology includes six key approaches, each with unique strengths in handling different aspects of speech data. All classifiers were implemented in Python 3.9. For the Random Forest classifier, we used *scikit-learn* to handle training and evaluation, and *Optuna* for hyperparameter tuning. For the DL models (CNN-Spectrogram, CNN-LSTM, Wav2Vec2, XLSR-Wav2Vec2, and Whisper), we used *PyTorch* along with the *torchaudio* library for audio processing; hyperparameter tuning was also managed via *Optuna*. This integrated setup allowed us to maintain a consistent development pipeline across both traditional and DL methods.

1. Random Forest with AutoML Tuning: We use Random Forest as a baseline classifier and employ AutoML (Optuna (Akiba et al., 2019)) for hyperparameter optimization. Random Forest is a robust ensemble model noted for its interpretability and effectiveness in handling tabular, low-dimensional features. AutoML tuning identifies optimal configurations, establishing a strong benchmark for comparison with deeper architectures (Ramadhan et al., 2017).

2. Wav2Vec Model: Wav2Vec 2.0 is a pre-trained model for speech representation learning, capturing nuanced phonetic and acoustic features. By fine-tuning Wav2Vec2 on our dialectal data, we leverage its ability to detect subtle variations in pronunciation, tone, and rhythm—key elements in dialect classification. Its extensive pre-training makes it highly effective, even with limited labeled data (Das et al., 2023).

3. Whisper Model: Whisper (Radford et al., 2023) is a sequence-to-sequence model designed for automatic speech recognition (ASR) and robust transcription across various languages. In our approach, we leverage Whisper for dialect classification by fine-tuning it on Luxembourgish dialect data. Specifically, we modify its final classification layer to predict dialect labels rather than transcriptions. We extract Whisper's intermediate acoustic embeddings from its final transformer layers and pass them through a fully connected classifier, which outputs softmax probabilities over the dialect classes. This method enables Whisper to capture subtle phonetic and prosodic differences among Luxembourgish dialects while benefiting from its inherent robustness to noise and diverse acoustic conditions. Compared to other models such as Wav2Vec2 and CNN-based approaches, Whisper's sequence-to-sequence architecture allows it to use broader context across speech segments, making it particularly effective in capturing dialectal shifts that span longer temporal patterns.

4. XLSR-Wav2Vec2 Model: The Cross-Lingual Speech Representation (XLSR) variant of Wav2Vec2 extends the model's capabilities to multiple languages by learning universal speech representations. Fine-tuning XLSR-Wav2Vec2 (Conneau et al., 2021) on our dialectal data leverages these cross-lingual features, facilitating more accurate detection of subtle acoustic patterns that may overlap across dialects or language families. This approach is especially useful when the available labeled data for each dialect is limited.

5. CNN on Spectrograms: We apply Convolutional Neural Networks (CNNs) to Mel spectrograms, treating them as 2D images. CNNs excel in identifying spatial patterns—such as phonetic markers, intonation shifts, and accent variations—by leveraging their proven effectiveness in image processing. This approach highlights visual representations of acoustic features for clearer insight into dialect differences (Alrehaili et al., 2023).

6. CNN-LSTM Hybrid Model: To capture both spatial and temporal patterns, we integrate CNN and Long Short-Term Memory (LSTM) layers. The CNN layers learn spatial features from each spectrogram frame, while the LSTM layers model temporal dependencies such as rhythm and sequential patterns across frames. This combined architecture offers a more holistic understanding of dialectal characteristics (China et al., 2018).

Through these six approaches, we explore how different models capture dialectal differences in speech, analyzing which features—ranging from the phonetic details learned by Wav2Vec2, XLSR-Wav2Vec2, and Whisper to the spatial and temporal patterns identified by CNN-Spectrogram and CNN-LSTM—are most effective for dialect classification.

The CNN model for dialect classification was designed to process spectrogram data as a 2D image-like input, beginning with a 2D convolutional layer with 32 filters (kernel size of 3×3), followed by additional convolutional and max-pooling layers to capture spatial features from the spectrograms. For the CNN-LSTM model, this convolutional stack was followed by an LSTM layer to capture temporal dependencies across spectrogram frames. Both models used padding to ensure consistent input dimensions. The architecture was optimized using categorical cross-entropy loss and an Adam optimizer with a learning rate of 0.001. Each model was trained over 15 epochs with five cross-validation folds to evaluate robustness. To handle class imbalance, we incorporated a weighted sampler in the DataLoader, using class weights calculated per fold to emphasize learning on underrepresented dialect classes, improving model generalizability across dialects.

3.3 Data Augmentation

To address data imbalance within the Luxembourgish dialect dataset, we implemented data augmentation techniques using controlled variations in speed and pitch to enhance sample diversity and model robustness. Specifically, we targeted underrepresented dialect classes (Northern and Eastern) to generate additional samples. In total, we created 820 new audio samples, increasing the dataset size from 1720 to 2540 recordings.

We applied time stretching with a 1.2x speed factor to generate faster-paced versions of each sample, creating tempo variations that reflect natural speaking speed differences without altering phonetic content. Pitch shifting was also used to create tonal variations by adjusting playback at a 50ms chunk level with crossfade transitions. This replicates natural differences in vocal tone, helping to distinguish differences between dialects and individual speakers.

We implemented these augmentations using the *pydub* library (Robertson, 2010), which enabled systematic file augmentation while preserving originals. Augmented files were prioritized for dialects below the median frequency (i.e., Northern and Eastern), addressing class imbalance effectively. Furthermore, to maintain demographic consistency, we mirrored the gender and age distributions for each new sample, ensuring that both male and female speakers across various age ranges were also augmented when needed. The final dataset became more balanced, reducing the disparity between the best- and worst-represented dialects from 594 recordings to 147 recordings difference. Parallel processing was employed to manage the computational load, ensuring efficient augmentation of underrepresented dialects.

After augmentation, the dataset included 2540 audio clips, with each dialect represented by at least 500 samples. The mean clip length was 3.2 seconds (SD = 0.8), with a similar distribution of lengths across dialects, genders, and age groups. On average, each audio sample contained approximately 6.3 tokens of spoken text (SD = 1.1), with a total vocabulary of 1,550 unique Luxembourgish tokens (up from 1,100 prior to augmentation). This increase in unique tokens reflects the added lexical variability introduced by augmentation and ensures that minority dialects are not underrepresented in the linguistic feature space.

Baseline (Without Augmentation)				
Model	**Northern**	**Central**	**Southern**	**Eastern**
Random Forest	63/61/62	58/60/60	56/57/57	55/55/55
Wav2Vec2	**70/72/72**	69/70/70	70/71/71	69/69/70
Whisper	67/69/68	66/67/66	68/69/69	64/65/65
XLSR-Wav2Vec2	68/70/69	66/68/67	69/70/69	63/64/64
CNN-Spectrogram	72/71/73	71/71/71	**72/74/73**	**70/69/71**
CNN-LSTM	72/70/72	**73/72/71**	69/72/70	68/71/72
Optimized (With Augmentation)				
Model	**Northern**	**Central**	**Southern**	**Eastern**
Random Forest	71/69/71	65/63/65	63/61/63	59/58/59
Wav2Vec2	**75/74/75**	72/71/72	73/72/73	70/71/71
Whisper	72/72/73	70/70/70	72/72/72	67/69/68
XLSR-Wav2Vec2	72/73/72	69/70/70	71/72/71	66/66/66
CNN-Spectrogram	76/74/76	74/73/74	**79/76/78**	**78/75/76**
CNN-LSTM	76/73/74	**75/74/73**	77/75/77	72/70/71

Table 3: Performance Comparison Between Baseline (Without Augmentation) and Optimized (With Augmentation) Results for Luxembourgish Dialect Classification. Each cell shows Accuracy/Precision/Recall (%). **Bold** indicates the highest performance metric.

3.4 Evaluation and Metrics

To evaluate model performance in dialect classification, we used four key metrics: accuracy (overall correctness), precision (minimizing false positives), and recall (capturing true instances) to evaluate each model. Each table reports per-class accuracy, precision, and recall, giving insight into how models handle each dialect.

We applied stratified sampling during training to ensure balanced dialect representation in the dataset, helping to address class imbalance and maintain model performance across all dialects. Early stopping was implemented to halt training when the validation loss did not improve over five consecutive epochs, thereby preventing overfitting. A batch size of 16 was chosen to balance computational efficiency and convergence speed, while the Adam optimizer was used to adjust the learning rate adaptively, ensuring stable and effective convergence during training.

4 Results

Table 3 presents a comparison of model performance on Luxembourgish dialect classification under two conditions: baseline (without data augmentation) and optimized (with data augmentation). Six primary models were evaluated: Random Forest, Wav2Vec2, Whisper, XLSR-Wav2Vec2, CNN-Spectrogram, and CNN-LSTM. Performance, evaluated through accuracy, precision, and recall metrics, was measured across Northern, Central, Southern, and Eastern dialects for each model.

4.1 Baseline Performance (Without Augmentation)

In the *baseline* setting (see Table 3), all models exhibit moderate accuracy (55%–73%), reflecting the challenges posed by a relatively small and imbalanced dataset:

CNN-Spectrogram attains the highest accuracy in the Northern (72%) and Southern (72%) dialects, underscoring CNNs' effectiveness in extracting spatial patterns (e.g., phonetic cues) from spectrograms. CNN-LSTM excels in classifying the Central dialect (73% accuracy), possibly due to its capacity to capture temporal dependencies along with spatial cues. Wav2Vec2 also performs strongly, particularly for Northern and Southern dialects (70% accuracy), benefiting from its robust self-supervised speech representations. Random Forest consistently lags behind the neural models, particularly for the Southern and Eastern dialects, reflecting its limited ability to model complex acoustic cues. Whisper and XLSR-Wav2Vec2 provide competitive results but do not surpass the CNN-based or standard Wav2Vec2 models in most dialects. Eastern dialect classification remains the most challenging for all approaches. This is consistent with its underrepresentation in the dataset and with prior observations that Eastern exhibits phonetic overlaps with adjacent dialects, compounding classification difficulties.

4.2 Optimized Performance (With Augmentation)

Applying speed and pitch augmentation yields performance gains across all models, particularly for underrepresented Northern and Eastern dialects (see Table 3):

Random Forest sees an overall accuracy increase of 4–5%, indicating that extra variability in the training set helps even simpler classifiers. Wav2Vec2 improves to 75% accuracy for Northern and 70% for Eastern, confirming that its self-supervised features benefit from augmented data. Whisper and XLSR-Wav2Vec2 also enjoy small but consistent boosts across all dialects, reinforcing the notion that multilingual or sequence-to-sequence approaches capitalize on the broader acoustic variability introduced by augmentation. CNN-Spectrogram emerges as the top performer in most dialects post-augmentation: 76% accuracy in Northern, 79% in Southern, and 78% in Eastern, highlighting CNNs' capacity to adapt to new spectrogram variations (e.g., pitch-shifted or speed-stretched speech). CNN-LSTM remains highly competitive, matching CNN-Spectrogram in Northern dialect classification (76%) and excelling in the Central dialect (75% accuracy). Its ability to capture both spatial and temporal cues remains beneficial. These findings confirm that data augmentation helps mitigate class imbalance, particularly for Northern and Eastern dialects, which see some of the largest proportional gains. However, the overall improvements—while meaningful—remain limited by the modest size of the dataset. Gathering more recordings and exploring advanced or multi-parameter augmentation techniques (e.g., multiple speed factors, SpecAugment) could further boost performance.

5 Discussion

The results demonstrate that data augmentation can contribute to modest but consistent improvements in dialect classification for Luxembourgish, a low-resource language. These findings align with prior studies highlighting the effectiveness of CNNs and end-to-end ASR models, such as Wav2Vec, in handling spectrogram data for dialect and language classification tasks.

CNNs have proven effective in extracting meaningful features from spectrograms, which are crucial for distinguishing subtle phonetic and prosodic differences across dialects. For example, Alrehaili et al. (2023) reported that CNNs achieved 83% accuracy in Arabic dialect classification, capitalizing on their capacity to process spatial information within spectrograms. Similarly, Revay and Teschke (2019) demonstrated CNNs' suitability for language identification across multiple languages, achieving up to 89% accuracy by focusing on acoustic cues encoded in spectrograms (Revay and Teschke, 2019). Prior studies support our findings, showing that CNN-based models, such as CNN-Spectrogram and CNN-LSTM, achieved competitive accuracy (68-73%) on Luxembourgish dialects, with further improvements post-augmentation.

Research supports the effectiveness of CNN-LSTM architectures in dialect classification, especially for capturing both spatial and temporal linguistic patterns. For instance, CNN-LSTM models have shown high accuracy in dialect classification tasks for Arabic, where they effectively captured dialectal sentiment variations across regional Arabic texts (Abu Kwaik et al., 2019). Similar success has been observed in distinguishing tonal versus non-tonal Indian languages using acoustic data, where the model's ability to capture temporal dependencies significantly improved classification outcomes (China et al., 2018). Studies on dialectal sentiment analysis for Roman Urdu and English have further highlighted CNN-LSTM's adaptability, demonstrating the model's capacity to capture linguistic nuances in dialects within social media contexts (Khan et al., 2022). In general, CNN-LSTM hybrids improve dialect classification accuracy by effectively capturing both localized phonetic features and sequential temporal dynamics (She and Zhang, 2018).

Additionally, research on self-supervised models like Wav2Vec has demonstrated the model's ability to capture detailed phonetic and acoustic features, enabling it to perform well even in low-resource dialect classification tasks. Wav2Vec embeddings have proven effective in detecting dialect-specific nuances and handling out-of-distribution dialect data (Das et al., 2023). Studies also show that fine-tuning Wav2Vec on dialectal datasets enables it to capture phonetic variations in pronunciation, tone, and rhythm, essential for effective dialect classification (Baevski et al., 2019). Furthermore, Wav2Vec has demonstrated robustness across low-resource languages, achieving notable improvements in speech recognition for underrepresented dialects (Yi et al., 2020).

These findings align with our results, where the CNN-LSTM model showed consistent performance gains after augmentation, underscoring the utility of combining convolutional and sequential layers to handle the complex linguistic structures present in Luxembourgish dialects. Our findings also resonate with prior work in low-resource dialect classification. For instance, in the study by Wang et al. (2021), a multilingual ASR model improved classification accuracy for Chinese dialects, significantly reducing classification errors. Although we did not directly utilize this approach, Wav2Vec's pretraining on multilingual datasets may have contributed to its relative robustness in Luxembourgish dialect classification. This ability to handle a range of dialectal inputs, even with limited training data, illustrates the model's value in low-resource language contexts.

The improvements observed with data augmentation, while modest, highlight its potential to enhance model robustness, particularly for dialects with lower representation. Kethireddy et al. (2020) explored similar strategies by introducing augmented spectrogram features, leading to gains in dialect classification accuracy. In our study, augmenting the dataset by adjusting pitch and tempo introduced additional variability, helping the models to generalize better. This approach was especially beneficial for the Random Forest model, which lacks the feature extraction capabilities of CNNs and ASR models. Despite the limited scale of the improvements, these findings underscore the utility of data augmentation as a practical approach to mitigate the effects of data scarcity in dialect classification tasks.

Our CNN-LSTM model, designed to capture both spatial and temporal dependencies, also showed consistent gains with augmentation. Chemudupati et al. (2023) demonstrated that Wav2Vec could maintain robust performance across diverse conditions, including real-world "in-the-wild" settings with noisy and reverberant audio. Although the Luxembourgish dataset does not include such variability, the slight improvements in recall and precision seen in our CNN-LSTM model after augmentation suggest that temporal architectures may add value in dialectal classification tasks, especially in capturing sequential acoustic features.

Overall, the updated performance metrics reported in Table 3 confirm that CNN-Spectrogram achieved top accuracy in Southern (79%) and Eastern (78%) dialects following augmentation, while CNN-LSTM matched or surpassed other approaches in Central (75%) and Northern (76%). Wav2Vec2 also registered stable improvements (e.g., 70% accuracy for Eastern) after incorporating time-stretch and pitch-shift strategies. Notably, the Random Forest benefited substantially from augmentation, gaining about 4–5% in accuracy—particularly in Northern and Eastern dialects—underscoring the value of enriched data variability even for non-neural classifiers.

5.1 Limitations of the work

One key limitation is the lack of sufficiently diverse data, which poses a risk of overfitting and makes it difficult to capture subtle phonetic or lexical nuances in border regions. Additionally, our augmentation experiments are limited to a single set of parameters, leaving open the possibility that other augmentation methods or intensities might yield higher improvements. Finally, while Whisper and XLSR-Wav2Vec2 adapt well to multilingual contexts, further tuning (e.g., multiple epochs, domain adaptation) could potentially boost their performance.

6 Conclusions

We introduced a comprehensive methodology for Luxembourgish dialect classification, pairing data augmentation (speed/pitch shifts) with a spectrum of models from *Random Forest* to *CNN-LSTM* and pretrained *Whisper* / *Wav2Vec2* variants. Our results highlight:

CNN-Spectrogram achieves top accuracies in Northern, Southern, and Eastern dialects after augmentation, showcasing its spatial feature-extraction strengths. CNN-LSTM outperforms other models in Central Luxembourgish, suggesting the value of modeling temporal dependencies in dialect classification. Wav2Vec2 remains consistently strong across all dialects, affirming the resilience of self-supervised speech representations. Data augmentation partially mitigates imbalance, boosting performance the most in underrepresented dialects (Northern and Eastern). Though the improvements are modest, they demonstrate the potential of augmentation in low-resource dialect classification. Future work should explore more advanced augmentation pipelines (e.g., SpecAugment, multiple pitch/speed factors) and target larger-scale data collection, possibly leveraging multilingual transfer from related Germanic varieties. These steps will be instrumental in achieving broader robustness and higher accuracy for Luxembourgish and other low-resource dialects.

References

Kathrein Abu Kwaik, Motaz Saad, Stergios Chatzikyriakidis, and Simon Dobnik. 2019. Lstm-cnn deep learning model for sentiment analysis of dialectal arabic. In *Arabic Language Processing: From Theory to Practice: 7th International Conference, ICALP 2019, Nancy, France, October 16–17, 2019, Proceedings 7*, pages 108–121. Springer.

Martine Adda-Decker, Lori Lamel, Gilles Adda, and Thomas Lavergne. 2014. A first lvcsr system for luxembourgish, a low-resourced european language. In *Human Language Technology Challenges for Computer Science and Linguistics: 5th Language and Technology Conference, LTC 2011, Poznań, Poland, November 25–27, 2011, Revised Selected Papers 5*, pages 479–490. Springer.

Takuya Akiba, Shotaro Sano, Toshihiko Yanase, Takeru Ohta, and Masanori Koyama. 2019. Optuna: A next-generation hyperparameter optimization framework. In *Proceedings of the 25th ACM SIGKDD international conference on knowledge discovery & data mining*, pages 2623–2631.

Ahmed Ali, Najim Dehak, Pierre Cardinal, Sameer Khurana, Sree Harsha Yella, Jim Glass, Peter Bell, and Steve Renals. 2016. Automatic dialect detection in arabic broadcast speech. In *Proceedings of Interspeech*, pages 2934–2938, San Francisco, CA, USA.

Meaad Alrehaili, Tahani Alasmari, and Areej Aoalshutayri. 2023. Arabic speech dialect classification using deep learning. In *2023 1st International Conference on Advanced Innovations in Smart Cities (ICAISC)*, pages 1–5. IEEE.

Alexei Baevski, Steffen Schneider, and Michael Auli. 2019. vq-wav2vec: Self-supervised learning of discrete speech representations. *arXiv preprint arXiv:1910.05453*.

Fadi Biadsy and Julia Hirschberg. 2009. Using prosody and phonotactics in arabic dialect identification. In *Interspeech*, volume 9, pages 208–211.

Vamsikrishna Chemudupati, Marzieh Tahaei, Heitor Guimaraes, Arthur Pimentel, Anderson Avila, Mehdi Rezagholizadeh, Boxing Chen, and Tiago Falk. 2023. On the transferability of whisper-based representations for" in-the-wild" cross-task downstream speech applications. *arXiv e-prints*, pages arXiv–2305.

Chuya China, Dipjyoti Bisharad, and Rabul Hussain Laskar. 2018. Automatic classification of indian languages into tonal and non-tonal categories using cascade convolutional neural network (cnn)-long short-term memory (lstm) recurrent neural networks. In *2018 International Conference on Signal Processing and Communications (SPCOM)*, pages 492–496. IEEE.

Alexis Conneau, Alexei Baevski, Ronan Collobert, Abdelrahman Mohamed, and Michael Auli. 2021. Unsupervised cross-lingual representation learning for speech recognition. *Interspeech 2021*.

François Conrad. 2023. Regional differences in the evolution of the merger of /ʃ/ and ç in luxembourgish. *Journal of the International Phonetic Association*, 53(1):29–46.

Sourya Dipta Das, Yash Vadi, Abhishek Unnam, and Kuldeep Yadav. 2023. Unsupervised out-of-distribution dialect detection with mahalanobis distance. In *Proceedings of the 24th Annual Conference of the International Speech Communication Association (INTERSPEECH 2023)*, Dublin, Ireland. International Speech Communication Association.

Johanna Dobbriner and Oliver Jokisch. 2019. Towards a dialect classification in german speech samples. In *Speech and Computer: 21st International Conference, SPECOM 2019, Istanbul, Turkey, August 20–25, 2019, Proceedings 21*, pages 64–74. Springer.

A Etman and AA Louis. 2015. American dialect identification using phonotactic and prosodic features. In *2015 SAI Intelligent Systems Conference (IntelliSys)*, pages 963–970. IEEE.

Peter Gilles. 1998. Virtual convergence and dialect levelling in luxembourgish. *Folia lingüística: Acta Societatis Linguisticae Europaeae*, 32(1):69–82.

Peter Gilles. 2014. Phonological domains in luxembourgish and their relevance for the phonological system. *Syllable and word languages*, pages 279–304.

Peter Gilles. 2023. Regional variation, internal change and language contact in luxembourgish_ results from an app-based language survey. *Taal en Tongval*, 75(1).

Peter Gilles, Léopold Edem Ayité Hillah, and Nina Hosseini Kivanani. 2023. Asrlux: Automatic speech recognition for the low-resource language luxembourgish. In *Proceedings of the 20th International Congress of Phonetic Sciences*, pages 3091–3095. Guarant International.

Peter Gilles and J. Trouvain. 2013. Illustrations of the ipa: Luxembourgish. *Journal of the International Phonetic Association*, 43.

Esra J Harfash and A Hassan Abdul-kareem. 2017. Automatic arabic dialect classification. *International Journal of Computer Application*, 8887.

Dirk Hovy. 2015. Demographic factors improve classification performance. In *Proceedings of the 53rd annual meeting of the association for computational linguistics and the 7th international joint conference on natural language processing (Volume 1: Long papers)*, pages 752–762.

Anjali Kantharuban, Ivan Vulić, and Anna Korhonen. 2023. Quantifying the dialect gap and its correlates across languages. *arXiv preprint arXiv:2310.15135*.

Rashmi Kethireddy, Sudarsana Reddy Kadiri, Paavo Alku, and Suryakanth V Gangashetty. 2020. Mel-weighted single frequency filtering spectrogram for dialect identification. *IEEE Access*, 8:174871–174879.

Lal Khan, Ammar Amjad, Kanwar Muhammad Afaq, and Hsien-Tsung Chang. 2022. Deep sentiment analysis using cnn-lstm architecture of english and roman urdu text shared in social media. *Applied Sciences*, 12(5):2694.

Abbas Khosravani, Philip N Garner, and Alexandros Lazaridis. 2021. Learning to translate low-resourced swiss german dialectal speech into standard german text. In *2021 IEEE Automatic Speech Recognition and Understanding Workshop (ASRU)*, pages 817–823. IEEE.

Raymond WM Ng and Tan Lee. 2008. Entropy-based analysis of the prosodic features of chinese dialects. In *2008 6th International Symposium on Chinese Spoken Language Processing*, pages 1–4. IEEE.

Le Minh Nguyen, Shekhar Nayak, and Matt Coler. 2023. Improving luxembourgish speech recognition with cross-lingual speech representations. In *2022 IEEE Spoken Language Technology Workshop (SLT)*, pages 792–797.

Alec Radford, Jong Wook Kim, Tao Xu, Greg Brockman, Christine McLeavey, and Ilya Sutskever. 2023. Robust speech recognition via large-scale weak supervision. In *International conference on machine learning*, pages 28492–28518. PMLR.

Muhammad Murtadha Ramadhan, Imas Sukaesih Sitanggang, Fahrendi Rizky Nasution, and Abdullah Ghifari. 2017. Parameter tuning in random forest based on grid search method for gender classification based on voice frequency. *DEStech transactions on computer science and engineering*, 10(2017).

Shauna Revay and Matthew Teschke. 2019. Multiclass language identification using deep learning on spectral images of audio signals. *arXiv preprint arXiv:1905.04348*.

Jiaaro Robertson. 2010. pydub: Audio processing library for python. Version 0.25.1, accessed October 31, 2024.

Riya Shah, Milin Patel, Barkha M Joshi, Jayna Shah, and Ronak Roy. 2023. Recognizing indian languages speech sound using transfer learning approach. In *2023 4th International Conference on Electronics and Sustainable Communication Systems (ICESC)*, pages 853–859. IEEE.

Xiangyang She and Di Zhang. 2018. Text classification based on hybrid cnn-lstm hybrid model. In *2018 11th International symposium on computational intelligence and design (ISCID)*, volume 2, pages 185–189. IEEE.

Natalie D Snoeren, Martine Adda-Decker, and Gilles Adda. 2011. Pronunciation and writing variants in an under-resourced language: the case of luxembourgish mobile n-deletion. In *Human Language Technology. Challenges for Computer Science and Linguistics: 4th Language and Technology Conference, LTC 2009, Poznan, Poland, November 6-8, 2009, Revised Selected Papers 4*, pages 70–81. Springer.

Yewei Song, Saad Ezzini, Jacques Klein, Tegawende Bissyande, Clément Lefebvre, and Anne Goujon. 2023. Letz translate: Low-resource machine translation for luxembourgish. In *2023 5th International Conference on Natural Language Processing (ICNLP)*, pages 165–170. IEEE.

Asad Ullah, Alessandro Ragano, and Andrew Hines. 2023. Reduce, reuse, recycle: Is perturbed data better than other language augmentation for low resource self-supervised speech models. *arXiv e-prints*, pages arXiv–2309.

Ding Wang, Shuaishuai Ye, Xinhui Hu, Sheng Li, and Xinkang Xu. 2021. An end-to-end dialect identification system with transfer learning from a multilingual automatic speech recognition model. In *Interspeech*, pages 3266–3270.

Fan Xu, Yangjie Dan, Keyu Yan, Yong Ma, and Mingwen Wang. 2021. Low-resource language discrimination toward chinese dialects with transfer learning and data augmentation. *Transactions on Asian and Low-Resource Language Information Processing*, 21(2):1–21.

Cheng Yi, Jianzhong Wang, Ning Cheng, Shiyu Zhou, and Bo Xu. 2020. Applying wav2vec2. 0 to speech recognition in various low-resource languages. *arXiv e-prints*, pages arXiv–2012.

The Application of Corpus-Based Language Distance Measurement to the Diatopic Variation Study (on the Material of the Old Novgorodian Birchbark Letters)

Ilia Afanasev
MTS AI LLC
ilia.afanasev.1997@gmail.com

Olga Lyashevskaya
HSE University
Vinogradov Russian Language Institute RAS
olesar@gmail.com

Abstract

The paper presents a computer-assisted exploration of a set of texts, where qualitative analysis complements the linguistically aware vector-based language distance measurements, interpreting them through close reading and thus proving or disproving their conclusions. It proposes using a method designed for small raw corpora to explore the individual, chronological, and gender-based differences within an extinct single territorial lect, known only by a scarce collection of documents.

The material under consideration is the Novgorodian birchbark letters, a set of rather small manuscripts (not a single one is more than 1000 tokens) that are witnesses of the Old Novgorodian lect, spoken on the territories of modern Novgorod and Staraya Russa at the first half of the first millennium CE.

The study shows the existence of chronological variation, a mild degree of individual variation, and almost absent gender-based differences. Possible prospects of the study include its application to the newly discovered birchbark letters and using an outgroup for more precise measurements.

1 Introduction

This article discusses the complexities of studying the variation with the low-resourced data on the material of the corpus of the East Slavic birchbark letters, dated from 1020 to 1500 CE, found in the territories of modern Russia (among others, Staraya Russa, Pskov, Moscow, Smolensk) and Belarus (Viciebsk[1], Mscislaŭ[2]); the most well-known site with the most manuscripts, where they were originally discovered, is Novgorod (Zaliznjak, 2004).

The research investigates three distinct types of variation: variation within a collection of doculects from the same place and time, time variation, and gender variation. The latter two are impossible to study without the first one (with a high level of individual variety, it is not possible to produce more effective research with more approximation) and are crucial for the study of Old Novgorodian, allowing one to understand the social dynamics within the society and the reflection of its development on its language. They are also irreplaceable for the building of the Old Novgorodian lect resources as they help to capture its ever-changing state until its extermination in the XV - XVI centuries CE.

Birchbark letters are usually small fragmented texts, so there is no way to use a more traditional lectometry (Shim and Nerbonne, 2022) or a corpus-based (Gamallo et al., 2020) methodology. The study requires a method designed for small raw corpora. The method relies on the combination of frequency-based metrics, string similarity measures, and a set similarity coefficient and their application to the subtoken-level units.

The research is based on three hypotheses:

H1. The differences detected by the proposed method among the individual documents are insignificant.

H2. The differences among the chronological periods of Old Novgorodian are significant.

H3. Genderlects are present in Old Novgorodian, there were significant differences between

[1]Most commonly called Vitebsk after the Russian variant; this article gives the official Belarusian transliteration for it and the other mentioned Belarusian cities.

[2]Most commonly called Mstsislaw after the Russian variant.

Proceedings of the Third Workshop on Resources and Representations for Under-Resourced Languages and Domains (RESOURCEFUL-2025), pages 153–164, March 2, 2025 ©2025 Association for Computational Linguistics

the style of writing between men and women.

To test the hypotheses, the article uses a combination of quantitative and qualitative analysis, aimed at differentiating between random distributional skewings and regular significant differences. The important constraint is that the proposed method is intended to be preliminary, its results are not set in stone and require subsequent exploration by a human scholar, which this article is going to perform. However, it is necessary to state that a thorough qualitative analysis will require a detailed close reading of hundreds of texts (Zaliznjak, 2004), so the study concentrates on the method application and the exploration of its results.

The structure of the study is as follows. Section 2 expounds on the history of the Old Novgorodian studies and defines the present research gap. Section 3 provides detailed information on the utilised data. Section 4 explains the method and the means of analysis. Section 5 reports on the results of the experiments. Section 6 is a conclusion that outlines the future research prospects.

2 Related Work

The East Slavic birchbark letters have been known in the field of Slavic studies since the second half of the XX century (Zhukovskaja, 1959), however, for a long time they failed to gain recognition, as scholars perceived them as erroneous and illiterate, thus having little to contribute to the language study (Isačenko et al., 1980), which is a common misconception in traditional and generative studies (Otheguy and Stern, 2011). Only during the last two decades have the linguistic features of birchbark letters received acceptance as a full-fledged resource of information on lects spoken at the corresponding territory (Krys'ko, 1998; Zaliznjak, 2004). Since then, a significant body of work has been produced, with topics ranging from the language of these manuscripts(Andersen, 2006; Kwon, 2016; Gippius and Schaeken, 2011; Dekker, 2018), including the genderlect variation (Zaliznjak, 1993) and sociolinguistics (Lebedeva, 2003), to the creation of a network of linguistic databases that includes Birchbark Letter Database[3] (BLD), and Russian National Corpus [4] (RNC).

Old Novgorodian is part of a large group of historical and contemporary lects, generally called fragmented languages, which are attested only partially and by rather low-resourced corpora (in the best-case scenario, less than 100 000 tokens, in the worst-case scenario, less than 100 tokens) (Baglioni and Rigobianco, 2024). These lects present a significant challenge to the NLP methods due to their low-resourcedness and heterogeneity (Swaelens et al., 2023; Doyle and McCrae, 2024; Lyashevskaya and Afanasev, 2021). Old Novgorodian and the cases akin to it (Verhelst, 2020–2021) add a new layer to the complexity of the task, as the texts themselves frequently lack significant parts due to the damage to the original manuscript.

Despite the relative well-studiedness of the Old Novgorodian (Zaliznjak, 2004) and a high awareness of the low-resourcedness problem in NLP (Dione, 2019), there are crucial lacunae in the current research. Some types of language variation in the birchbark letters gained attention (Zaliznjak, 1993), but not all of them: for example, the chronological division remains understudied (Zaliznjak, 2004). The 2010s advancements in computational methodology (Nerbonne et al., 2013) were not applied to the language variation within Old Novgorodian. At the same time, low-resourced NLP rarely problematises the features of the analysed lects from the linguistic perspective (de Graaf et al., 2022), but rather declares these features as obstacles to be overcome via strictly mathematical algorithm enhancement (Nehrdich and Hellwig, 2022) and only rarely with language-aware methods (Prokić and Moran, 2013). The current study aims to become the first step in the direction of a language-aware computer-assisted study.

3 Data

The research corpus consists of 1249 documents available in the BLD as of February 2025. The distribution is heavily skewed in favour of the Novgorod letters which comprise most of the dataset. It complicates the comparison between different regions. At the same time, some of the non-Novgorod charters are still going to influence the results of comparison by any other criterion (gender or time frame), especially given the number of tokens in some of them. For instance, *Mosk_3*, the third of the charters found in Moscow, has 470 tokens. As one of the biggest manuscripts

[3]http://gramoty.ru/birchbark

[4]https://ruscorpora.ru/en/corpus/birchbark

in the dataset, it may quantitatively outweigh a hundred other charters. To eliminate this noise in measurements that use other criteria, the study data is restricted to charters from Staraya Russa and Novgorod that represent Old Novgorodian in the strict sense (Zaliznjak, 2004).

For the study, these letters undergo several stages of preprocessing [5].

The birchbark letters suffer from being very fragmented, and it is barely possible to use them either in their raw form preserving only the fully visible characters (there is not enough information), or in the processed form containing all the reconstructed characters (which may lead to the researcher bias interfering with the existing variation). Thus, preprocessing starts with creating the middle ground.

The initial step is to exclude all completely non-reconstructible tokens, marked with .... The next stage is the deletion of string breaks, marked with ±±. Following this, each of the charters is joined into a single string. After this, the non-reconstructible parts of the existing tokens (... joined to the tokens in the existing forms) undergo replacement with ♮ signs. The same applies to the parts of the tokens that may be inferred from the context but are not present in the charter in any shape or form, originally surrounded by *()*. If such reconstruction spans between two or more tokens, both the end of the first token before the reconstruction and the beginning of the second token after the reconstruction receive the ♮ sign. The present misspellings, originally designated by {}, are excluded from the texts. The parts of the tokens that are not fully visible but reconstructible with a high degree of certainty, surrounded by *[]*, are taken as is; only the designating signs *[]* are excluded from the resulting text. The final step is to merge the consequent break signs ♮ that appear before the token in cases when the break and/or unrecognisable symbols go before the token that contains a non-reconstructible part. Table 1 shows examples of the transformations that the texts undergo.

The further modifications to the dataset have the purpose of adjusting it for the clusterisation: the letters from Novgorod and Staraya Russa still suffer from an imbalance between the size of different charters: some are too small, consisting only of one token, and some are too big, containing hundreds of tokens. Figure 1 shows the distribution.

For a more straightforward comparison, the next preprocessing step excludes each letter that consists of less than two tokens and five symbols. The letters that consist of more than 60 tokens (an approximate value of *Q3*[6] + *1.5 * (Q3 - Q1)*, with *Q3 = 27.00* and *Q1 = 6.00*) are shortened to the first 45 largest and the first 15 smallest tokens to preserve their features in the set while partially eliminating imbalance. Figure

Original text	**Transformed text**
рж(и)	рж♮
[с]	с
·к· {блъ} блъ	·к· блъ
–ружиного шло с... ... по	♮ружиного шло с♮ по
дар(у с о)[с]ипова	дар♮ ♮сипова
сел=<lb/>а	села

Table 1: The preprocessed parts of the Novgorod birchbark letter 1, compared to the fully preprocessed version, are present in the BLD database.

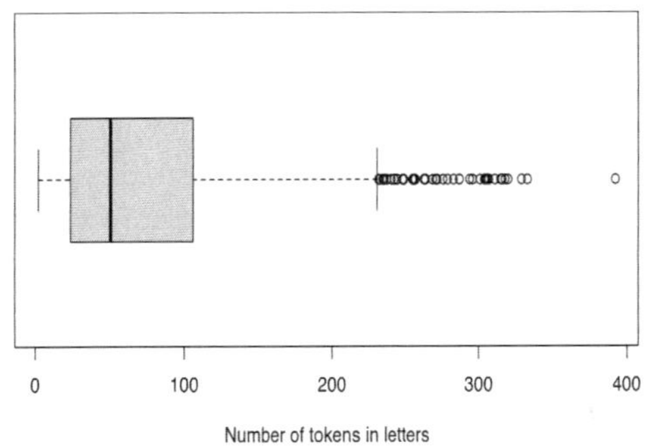

Figure 1: Boxplot for the distribution of the number of tokens in Novgorod and Staraya Russa birchbark letters.

[5] https://zenodo.org/records/14808682

[6] Q denotes quartiles, the cut-off points for the range of numbers that split this range into four more or less equal parts. Q1 is the first quartile, below which lie the first 25% of the range values, for example, 25% of the least frequent words in the language. Q3 is the second quartile, below which lie the final 25% of the range values, such as 25% of the most frequent words in the language.

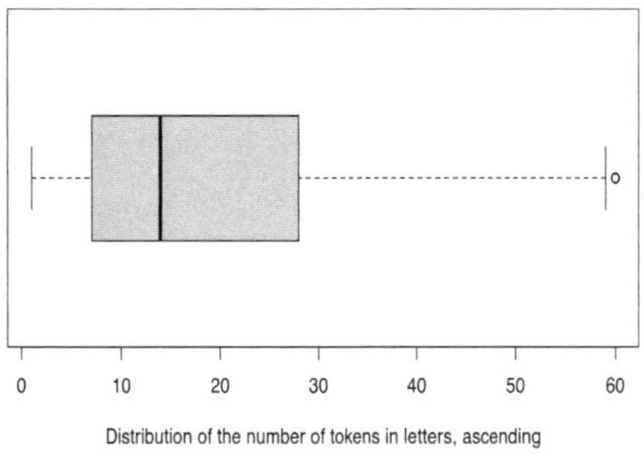

Figure 2: Boxplot for the distribution of the number of tokens in the letters after normalisation.

Experiment	Number of letters	Number of compared lects
1020 - 1140 CE period, internal clusterisation	118	118
1180 - 1240 CE period, internal clusterisation	231	231
1300 - 1360 CE period, internal clusterisation	140	140
Chronological clusterisation	489	3
Gender-based clusterisation	397	2

Table 2: The quantity of the letters, used in the experiments, and their internal grouping.

2 shows the final distribution: here, the only remaining letters are the ones that are more than two tokens or five symbols and less than 60 tokens in length. This contrasts the original distribution, where there was a significant number of letters containing one short token, which are not very useful for comparison purposes, and a dozen of letters that contain several hundred tokens, which significantly overweight the other letters, rendering comparison meaningless.

During the following step, each remaining letter receives two metadata tags, based on the existing analysis: time period and author gender.

Three periods are in the focus of the research: 1020 - 1140 (the early stage (Zaliznjak, 2004)), 1180 - 1240 (marked by the intensive contacts within the Circumbaltic region (Wiemer and Seržant, 2014; Podtergera, 2021)), and 1300 - 1360 (one of the latter stages of the Old Novgorodian development, also marked by the dissolution of the East Slavic area (Stankievič et al., 2007)). The texts assigned to these periods in RNC acquire the corresponding tag, the others get tag *X*.

For most of the texts, there is no possibility to deduce the gender of the author. In such cases, they receive the tag *UNK*. Otherwise, *m* (for authors referred to with masculine gender), and *f* (for authors referred to with feminine gender).

The resulting data frame containing 1158 letters consists of 7 columns, excluding index: *text* (the processed text of the charter), *charter_number* (the index of the letter in the database), *num_token* (number of tokens, excluding punctuation marks), *text_len* (length in symbols, excluding punctuation marks and breaks symbols ♮), *author_gender* - the gender of the author, *date* - the estimated period of text creation, *place* - the estimated place of text creation. Further preprocessing, required for specific language distance measurement methods, will be discussed in the corresponding section.

4 Method

This section consists of three parts that elaborate on the preprocessing of the data for the experiments, applied quantitative methodology, and qualitative analysis. The implementation is available via GitHub[7].

4.1 Preprocessing

The first step of the preprocessing stage is to select the required combination of the letters and their grouping for each of the experiments. The latter includes a document-to-document comparison within the three selected periods, a comparison of the three time periods between themselves, and a comparison of the letters by authors of different genders. Table 2 shows the final numbers for each of the experiments.

The first three experiments in Table 2 elaborate on the internal variation within the given period, so the unit of the analysis is a doculect (a lect of the individual letter). The fourth experiment takes a

[7]https://zenodo.org/records/14808716

more distant look at the differences between periods and groups letters from each period together in a single list. The fifth experiment deals with gender-based classification, so the split is between two genderlects.

After the split, the letters are prepared for distance measurement. Tokens within each lect are split into overlapping character 3-grams, further called *3-shingles* (Zelenkov and Segalovich, 2007), as the extremely fragmentary texts make it impossible to use whole tokens as the main unit of comparison. This way of analysing the texts is akin to byte-pair encoding (BPE) (Gage, 1994), which also utilises subtoken units. 3-shingles are a fixed unit, which, in contrast to BPE, complicates semantic comparison but enables a formal one, especially on the phonetical and morphological levels (Lyashevskaya and Afanasev, 2021), better suited for onomaseological lectometry purposes (Shim and Nerbonne, 2022).

The beginning and end of each token receive special marks, ^ and *$* respectively. Then algorithm removes each 3-shingle containing the ♮ sign as there is no way to deduce the symbols that lie behind it, and, subsequently, it may generate a lot of noise and skew the distributions in a way that does not accurately reflect the linguistic behaviour of the speakers. Thus, the token ♮остер♮ becomes a collection of 3-shingles ост, сте, тер, while token дару becomes a collection of 3-shingles ^да, дар, ару, ру$. If the letter consists only of fragments of the size of two or fewer symbols, it gets completely removed from the dataset. Note, however, that the intact short tokens remain in place (for instance, ^a$), as their deletion would significantly skew the distribution, deleting crucial linguistic information (Kestemont, 2014).

The next step is adding symbol embeddings: as the main unit of the analysis is a 3-shingle, its only possible subtoken is a single symbol, so the vector-space representation should be built for it. For embedding producing, the study employs the FastText (Bojanowski et al., 2017) model, which does not possess the inherent bias of large transformers (Devlin et al., 2019), namely, the information on the other languages, used for pre-training, which can add noise. The hyperparameters for the FastText model are in Appendix A.

The following step is to score the alphabet entropy (Shannon, 1948) for each of the analysed lect groupings, which can be approximated as the average value of the probability of the symbols appearing in their respective positions.

The last part of the preprocessing includes merging 3-shingles for each of the lect groupings and scoring their frequency ranks (the most frequent gets 0, the least frequent - N - 1, where N is the total number of 3-shingles). Frequency ranks are then normalised into the interval of [0;1], as the method requires.

4.2 Distance measurement and clusterisation

As the preliminary experiments have shown, the study employs the most efficient possible setup of the method utilised, which includes multiplying mean DistRank (Gamallo et al., 2017) between the coinciding 3-shingles by a hybrid string similarity measure for the non-coinciding 3-shingles, and dividing by Sørensen-Dice (Sørensen, 1948) coefficient[8] between two lects.

The employed string similarity measure for hybridisation is vector-weighted Jaro distance normalised (VWJDN), a product of Euclidean distance of the sums of symbol embeddings between two 3-shingles, and the Jaro distance between them (Jaro, 1989). The main idea is to emulate the phonetic differences between the sounds that the symbols represent and the distributional differences between the symbols themselves. Jaro distance accounts for transpositions, and thus, for the symbol order. The result of VWJDN undergoes multiplication by alphabet entropy differences between the given lects to account for potential distributional skewings, caused by dissimilarities in the utilisation of the graphic system (Zaliznjak, 2004).

The Sørensen-Dice coefficient between sets (in this case, sets of 3-shingles within the particular lects) A and B is:

$$\frac{2 * |X \cap Y|}{|X| + |Y|}$$

.

The algorithm is provided below.

The results of the combined metric form the distance matrix between all of the present lects. There are two ways to utilise this metric afterwards.

The first one is to use it for creating a clusterisation as is. Here, the unit of analysis is a

[8] In natural language processing evaluation more frequently referred to as F-score(Derczynski, 2016)

Algorithm 1

```
Separate 3-shingles that coincide between lects A and B (A ∩ B) from 3-shingles that do not coincide between A and B (A XOR B)
Calculate mean DistRank(A ∩ B) (Gamallo et al., 2017) between coinciding 3-shingles of A and B
for each 3-shingle a of A that is in (A XOR B) do
    for each 3-shingle b of B that is in (A XOR B) do
        VWJDN(a, b)
    end for
    Select the pair with minimal VWJDN(a, b)
    Calculate VWJDN(a, b) * DistRank(a, b)
end for
for each 3-shingle b of A that is in (A XOR B) do
    for each 3-shingle a of B that is in (A XOR B) do
        VWJDN(b, a)
    end for
    Select the pair with minimal VWJDN(b, a)
    Calculate VWJDN(b, a) * DistRank(b, a)
end for
Score mean between all acquired values for non-coinciding 3-shingles (VWJDND(A, B))
VWJDND(A, B) * DistRank(A∩B)/Sørensen-Dice(A, B)
```

single lect and the values with which the clusterisation algorithm runs are the distances between this lect and all other lects in the dataset. There are two possible ways to do it: perform a hierarchical bootstrap clusterisation with *pvclust* (Suzuki and Shimodaira, 2006) or perform HDBSCAN (Hahsler et al., 2019) over t-distributed Stochastic Neighbour Embedding (t-SNE) (van der Maaten and Hinton, 2008) over Principal Component Analysis (PCA) results (Jolliffe and Cadima, 2016). These are going to be used for inner clusterisation within the chronological periods.

The second one is to transform it into a lower triangular matrix and build a tree-like clusterisation with UPGMA (Sokal and Michener, 1958). This clusterisation algorithm is more effective for the lesser number of closely related lects and the study applies it to group chronological periods.

4.3 Qualitative analysis

The qualitative analysis is the most crucial research step. It takes the resulting clusterisations and attempts to explain the linguistic reasoning (or lack thereof) behind the decisions of the similarity metrics (whether they are correct or not). It uses the information that the utilised software provides, namely, the tables of comparison between all the 3-shingles, to discover the linguistic patterns in the data. As 3-shingles appear across the different tokens, the detection of a pattern goes through two steps. The first includes going through the generated table of correspondences between lects to check for possibly meaningful, based on the preexisting body of work, similarities and dissimilarities, the second – going through the texts of the letters to prove the meaningfulness of the discovered distributional skewings. Table 3 provides the example of the generated table of correspondences.

The aim of qualitative analysis is to either state that the dissimilarities between the groups detected by method are not significant, or to explain them on three key levels: individual (on the level of doculects), chronological (on the level of chronolects), and gender-based (on the level of genderlects).

5 Experiments and Analysis

This part provides the summary of the experiments and the subsequent discussion of the linguistic differences detected by the method.

5.1 Inner variation within the time periods

The experiments that investigate the linguistic variation of the individual letters within chronological periods show significant homogeneity in each one (see Figure 3). However, on the individual level, PCA does not demonstrate significant explanatory power, the differences are initially too small and too scattered across the analysed letters.

The next step includes an attempt to dense the data and provide more power to the final analysis on the first period sample, 1020 - 1140 CE. This stage starts with performing bootstrap clusterisation (hyperparameters are in Appendix B), the results of which become the new 13 groups of lects. These new groupings consist of 2 (an outgroup, letters 431 and 557 from Novgorod) to 30 items, and represent higher-level, more reliable, according to the bootstrap clusterisation (*AU > 85%*),

1180–1240	1020–1140	Metric	Distance
^по	^по	Novgorod birchbark leters by period-1-False-DistRank-True-True-False-weighted_jaro_winkler_wrapper-True - DistRank	0.0012717253073336043
рвн	рва	Novgorod birchbark leters by period-1-False-DistRank-True-True-False-weighted_jaro_winkler_wrapper-True - hybrid	0.4689305328575265

Table 3: A sample of correspondences established by VWJDN.

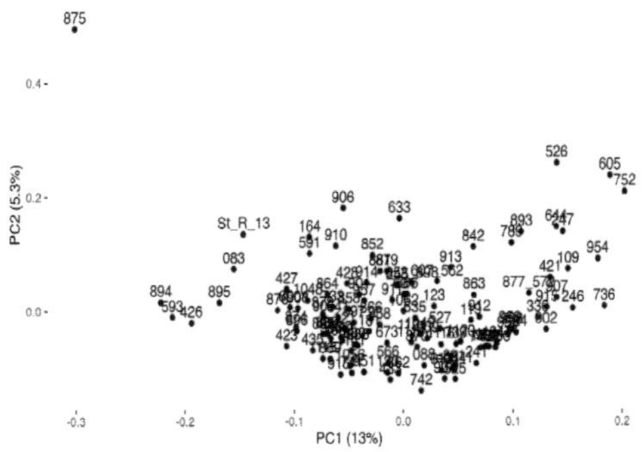

Figure 3: PCA of the distance matrix between the letters, written in the 1020 - 1140 CE.

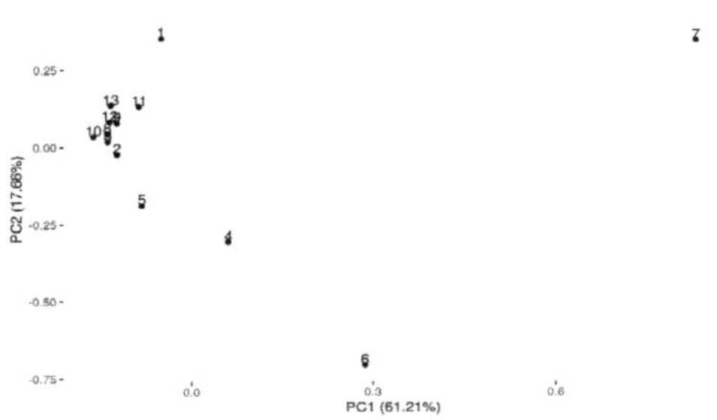

Figure 4: PCA of the distance matrix between the letters, written in the 1020 - 1140 CE, clustered into the higher-level groupings.

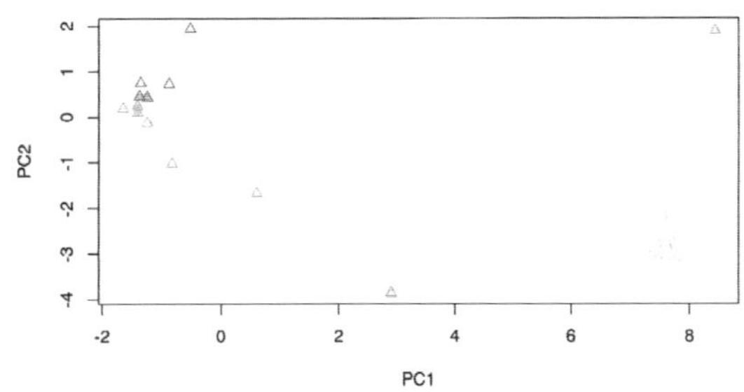

Figure 5: HDBSCAN, run over t-SNE results on PCA of the distance matrix between the letters, written in the 1020 - 1140 CE, clustered into the higher-level groupings.

groupings. This time, it is easier for PCA to represent the key differences (Figure 4).

It is possible to run t-SNE with HDBSCAN over this result (Figure 5), showing the degree of certainty in cluster grouping. These figures include the same data points, with the first providing the information on the exact data point, and the second - on the reliability of clusterisation.

This shows two distinct bigger clusters, with groups 8 and 6 opposed to 12 and 9 as the centres of the clusters, and other groups joining them with a lesser degree of certainty. Group 7, a small higher-level outgroup, is an outlier here as well; PC1 is likely to represent the dissimilarities in the size of the cluster, detected by the Sørencen-Dice coefficient.

Interestingly, the consequences of the phonetic processes, such as the reduced vowel fall, help in joining some higher-level groupings together and not in splitting them. Thus, group 12 contains 3-shingle ьло, while group 9 contains 3-shingle ьлъ, with о and ъ known to become interchangeable symbols (Zaliznjak, 2004), as the first had denoted full vowel and the second - its reduced counterpart, before the reduced vowel fall occured. The distance between these 3-shingles is 0.42. At the same time, group 8 contains completely different 3-shingles, which, together with the 3-shingles of group 12, forms such pairs as еть – окь with a distance of 0.47. These dissimilarities in differences are the main cause of the split between two bigger clusters. Yet, overall the letters of a given time period are homogeneous, and it is safe to treat them further as a uniform entity.

Figure 6: UPGMA (Sokal and Michener, 1958) clusterisation of chronolects, present in the dataset.

5.2 Analysis of chronological clusters

Figure 6 shows the grouping of three chronolects, representing three stages of Old Novgorodian evolution: 1020 - 1140 CE, 1180 - 1240 CE, and 1300 - 1360 CE.

The picture clearly demonstrates the differences between the chronolects, especially between two earlier groups and the later one. It seems that the Old Novgorodian changed between 1240 and 1300 more significantly than between 1140 and 1180, which is likely due to the inner processes as well as to the intensive language contact (Wiemer and Seržant, 2014).

Mostly, however, this is the same lect: the branch length is not exactly large (compare the differences between modern East Slavic territorial lects in (Afanasev and Lyashevskaya, 2024), acquired with the similar methodology, where the branch length is 0.175, and ingroup splits at 0.03). The found pairs of non-coinciding 3-shingles are mostly random (тев of 1300 - 1360 and тет of 1020 - 1140).

Still, some pairs can provide a scholar with a closer look into the ongoing phonetic processes. In the earlier periods, the 3-shingle въх is present in such tokens as въхъ 'entire'. In the later period, the other form for the meaning 'entire' prevailed: вьсь. At the same time, there are graphical differences: the later letters use 3-shingle оду, while the earlier prefer одоу.

Distributions of the coinciding 3-shingles also give a hint into the nature of differences between the stages of the Old Novgorodian development. While sequences with ъ$ and ь that earlier denoted reduced vowels, almost do not change their rank (лъ$ has a value of 0.002), the ones that denoted their full-fledged counterparts changed the distributions significantly (ло$ has a value of 0.15), becoming more frequent.

From the material given, it is possible to conclude the following: the utilised method allows insight into language variation and change which would not be possible on the token level. This becomes crucial in the case of DistRank-based analysis, which uniquely illustrates the dynamics of the reduced vowel fall process, highlighting the complexity of its written dimension.

5.3 Gender-based differences

The genderlects present a significantly more difficult challenge. The distance itself is not big, only 0.12 (for reference, the metric returns the same value between two letter clusters within the same time period). The non-coinciding 3-shingles here demonstrate the absence of any kind of meaningful correspondence, mostly consisting of pairs, akin to саю/ьса.

However, the DistRank behaviour for the symbols that denoted reduced and full vowels is once again suspicious. ло$ has a value of 0.002, while лъ$ has the value of 0.17. Similar occurs with мо$ (0.01) and мъ$ (0.05), то$ (0.07) and тъ$ (0.03), ^въ (0.01) and ^во (0.03). It seems that there were certain dissimilarities in preferences of female and male writers in relation to the ъ$ and о, but even these were restricted (cf. 0.02 for both но$ and нъ$).

The genderlect differences (or, rather, their lack thereof) show the limit of the method utilised. It can pick on the distribution differences, providing a distant reading, based on fixed-size subtoken units, but it inevitably fails when differences are either completely absent (and it seems that Old Novgorodian indeed did not have genderlect differences) or too subtle to pick without the close reading of documents.

6 Conclusion

The paper employed a new method to study individual, chronological, and gender variation within Old Novgorodian. It supported the hypothesis **H2** of chronological variation, showing the similarity between earlier and later periods of the Old Novgorodian development. At the same time, no signs of gender-based variation are present (hypothesis **H3** is thus rejected): from the existing material only it is impossible to claim that Old

Novgorodian had genderlects, which supports the primary qualitative work on the topic, Zaliznjak (1993). Yet the amount of the available material may be misleading: it is possible that there is not enough data. The method statement on the variation within the different time periods highly depends on the letter size, supporting the idea of balancing the corpus before the method application (Afanasev and Lyashevskaya, 2024); hypothesis **H1** is thus supported only partially.

One of the key elements that helped the method to distinguish between different chronological periods and played an important role in other tasks is the contrast between the symbols that denote reduced and full vowels. This is not the only found contrast, as the method was able to find other factors, such as lexical differences. It is also paramount to note that all the components of the combined metric were analysed, and partly proved, during the final qualitative analysis. This affirms the necessity of using lectometry methods for computer-assisted and not computer-driven research.

The acquired classification and the method itself, especially 3-shingle-based representation, will aid the analysis of the newly discovered documents and the exploration of how they fit the existing picture. It will facilitate expert judgment about the period of their creation, aiding theoretical paleographic analysis (Janin and Zaliznjak, 2000). The found similarities and dissimilarities may be included as linguistic features in the existing network of Old Novgorodian databases. The results require further attention and exploration, especially the ones that did not provide any satisfactory conclusions, such as the ъ$ and o distribution differences between the letters authored by men and women. The study shows that the quality of the resources is of the utmost importance for computational methods, especially for language distance measurement. One possible further research direction is using an outgroup (for example, Old East Slavic legal charters) to provide additional linguistic context to the clusterisation trees (Kassian et al., 2021).

Limitations

The research is based on the corpus of fragmented documents that contains all the known data about the Old Novgorodian lect, but definitely not all the data about the lect, which means that the comparison is corpus-driven and may not cover all the spectre of similarities and differences between the sublects (chronolects and genderlects) of Old Novgorodian (Davis, 2017). Furthermore, the dates of the letters creation are approximate, which may have influenced the chronolect comparison results. It is not possible to establish the author's gender for all the letters, therefore the material for the gender-based similarities and differences study is even less than it could have been, which too may have influenced the final comparison.

The applied method uses 3-shingles, the units of sub-token level (Afanasev and Lyashevskaya, 2024), as the main objective of its application is to find the differences between small raw corpora. This means that it captures the variation on the phonological, morphonological, and morphological levels, occasionally being able to account for the lexical differences, thus mostly resembling the character-based comparisons of morphological features and basic vocabulary lists (Kassian et al., 2021; Auderset et al., 2023). The syntactic and pragmatic differences are generally out of scope of this class of methods in general, due to the complications of diachronic syntax studies (Campbell, 2013). And, given the quantity of the material, any kind of the automatic quantitative analysis that does not utilise rigorous manual preprocessing, will not be suitable here as well. These features of Old Novgorodian require further study with other methods.

Acknowledgements

The authors are grateful to the anonymous reviewers for their insightful comments. The remaining errata are ours.

References

Ilia Afanasev and Olga Lyashevskaya. 2024. Measuring language distance based on small raw corpora. In N. Saramandu, M. Nevaci, I. Floarea, I.-M. Farcaș, A. Bojoga, F. R. Constantin, A. Loizo, M. Manta, M. Morcov, and O. Niculescu, editors, *Proceedings of the Xth Congress of the International Society for Dialectology and Geolinguistics*, pages 11–18. Edizioni dell'Orso, Alessandria, Italia.

Henning Andersen. 2006. Future and Future Perfect in the Old Novgorod Dialect. *Russian Linguistics*, 30(1):71–88.

Sandra Auderset, Simon J Greenhill, Christian T DiCanio, and Eric W Campbell. 2023. Subgrouping in a 'dialect continuum': A bayesian phylogenetic analysis of the mixtecan language family. *Journal of Language Evolution*, 8(1):33–63.

Daniele Baglioni and Luca Rigobianco. 2024. *Fragments of Languages: From 'Restsprachen' to Contemporary Endangered Languages*. Brill, Leiden, The Netherlands.

Piotr Bojanowski, Edouard Grave, Armand Joulin, and Tomas Mikolov. 2017. Enriching word vectors with subword information. *Transactions of the Association for Computational Linguistics*, 5:135–146.

Lyle Campbell. 2013. *Historical Linguistics, third edition: An Introduction*. MIT Press.

Joseph Davis. 2017. The semantic difference between italian vi and ci. *Lingua*, 200:107–121.

Simeon Dekker. 2018. *Old Russian Birchbark Letters: A Pragmatic Approach*. Brill, Leiden, The Netherlands.

Leon Derczynski. 2016. Complementarity, F-score, and NLP evaluation. In *Proceedings of the Tenth International Conference on Language Resources and Evaluation (LREC'16)*, pages 261–266, Portorož, Slovenia. European Language Resources Association (ELRA).

Jacob Devlin, Ming-Wei Chang, Kenton Lee, and Kristina Toutanova. 2019. BERT: Pre-training of deep bidirectional transformers for language understanding. In *Proceedings of the 2019 Conference of the North American Chapter of the Association for Computational Linguistics: Human Language Technologies, Volume 1 (Long and Short Papers)*, pages 4171–4186. Association for Computational Linguistics.

Cheikh Bamba Dione. 2019. Developing Universal Dependencies for Wolof. In *Proceedings of the Third Workshop on Universal Dependencies (UDW, SyntaxFest 2019)*, pages 12–23, Paris, France. Association for Computational Linguistics.

Adrian Doyle and John P. McCrae. 2024. Developing a part-of-speech tagger for diplomatically edited Old Irish text. In *Proceedings of the Third Workshop on Language Technologies for Historical and Ancient Languages (LT4HALA) @ LREC-COLING-2024*, pages 11–21, Torino, Italia. ELRA and ICCL.

Philip Gage. 1994. A new algorithm for data compression. *C Users Journal*, 12(2):23–38.

Pablo Gamallo, Jose Ramom Pichel Campos, and Iñaki Alegria. 2017. From language identification to language distance. *Physica A: Statistical Mechanics and its Applications*, 484:152–162.

Pablo Gamallo, Jose Ramom Pichel Campos, and Iñaki Alegria. 2020. Measuring Language Distance of Isolated European Languages. *Information*, 11(4):181–193.

Alexey A. Gippius and Jos Schaeken. 2011. On direct speech and referential perspective in birchbark letters no. 5 from Tver' and no. 286 from Novgorod. *Russian Linguistics*, 35(1):13–32.

Evelien de Graaf, Silvia Stopponi, Jasper K. Bos, Saskia Peels-Matthey, and Malvina Nissim. 2022. AGILe: The first lemmatizer for Ancient Greek inscriptions. In *Proceedings of the Thirteenth Language Resources and Evaluation Conference*, pages 5334–5344, Marseille, France. European Language Resources Association.

Michael Hahsler, Matthew Piekenbrock, and Derek Doran. 2019. dbscan: Fast density-based clustering with r. *Journal of Statistical Software*, 91(1):1–30.

Alexander V. Isačenko, Henrik Birnbaum, L'ubomír Ďurovič, and Eva Salnikow-Ritter. 1980. *Geschichte der russischen Sprache: Bd. Von den Anfängen bis zum Ende des 17. Jahrhunderts [History of the Russian language: the volume from the beginning to the end of the 17th century]*. Geschichte der russischen Sprache [History of the Russian language]. Winter.

Valentin L. Janin and Andrej A. Zaliznjak. 2000. *Novgorodskie gramoty na bereste (iz raskopok 1990–1996 gg.). Paleografija berestjanyh gramot i ih vnestratigraficheskoe datirovanie. [Novgorod birchbark letters (found in 1990-1996). Birchbark letter paleography ad non-stratigraphic dating]*. Russkije slovari [Russian dictionaries].

Matthew A. Jaro. 1989. Advances in record-linkage methodology as applied to matching the 1985 census of tampa, florida. *Journal of the American Statistical Association*, 84(406):414–420. Publisher: [American Statistical Association, Taylor & Francis, Ltd.].

Ian T. Jolliffe and Jorge Cadima. 2016. Principal component analysis: a review and recent developments. *Philosophical Transactions of the Royal Society A: Mathematical, Physical and Engineering Sciences*, 374(2065):20150202. Publisher: Royal Society.

Alexei S. Kassian, Mikhail Zhivlov, George Starostin, A. A. Trofimov, Petr A. Kocharov, Anna Kuritsyna, and Mikhail N. Sayenko. 2021. Rapid radiation of the inner indo-european languages: an advanced approach to indo-european lexicostatistics. *Linguistics*, 59(4):949–979.

Mike Kestemont. 2014. Function words in authorship attribution. from black magic to theory? In *Proceedings of the 3rd Workshop on Computational Linguistics for Literature (CLFL)*, pages 59–66, Gothenburg, Sweden. Association for Computational Linguistics.

Vadim B. Krys'ko. 1998. Drevnij novgorodsko-pskovskij dialekt na obshheslavjanskom fone [old novgorodian/pskovian dialect among the slavic languages]. *Voprosy jazykoznanija [Topics in the study of language]*, 3:74–93.

Kyongjoon Kwon. 2016. Reanimating voices from the past: an alternative reading of Novgorod Birch Bark Letter N370. *Russian Linguistics*, 40(1):79–102.

Elena Je. Lebedeva. 2003. Jelement nasilija v bytovom povedenii novgorodcev XI-XV vv. (po materialam novgorodskih berestjanyh gramot) [element of violence in the everyday behaviour of Novgorodians XI-XV centuries (on the material of the birchbark letters)]. *Novgorod i Novgorodskaja zemlja. Istorija i arheologija [Novgorod and Novgorod land. History and archaeology]*, 17:240–253.

Olga Lyashevskaya and Ilia Afanasev. 2021. An HMM-based PoS Tagger for Old Church Slavonic. *Journal of Linguistics/Jazykovedný casopis*, 72(2):556–567.

Laurens van der Maaten and Geoffrey Hinton. 2008. Visualizing data using t-SNE. *Journal of Machine Learning Research*, 9:2579–2605.

Sebastian Nehrdich and Oliver Hellwig. 2022. Accurate dependency parsing and tagging of Latin. In *Proceedings of the Second Workshop on Language Technologies for Historical and Ancient Languages*, pages 20–25, Marseille, France. European Language Resources Association.

John Nerbonne, Sandrien van Ommen, Charlotte Gooskens, and Martijn Wieling. 2013. Measuring socially motivated pronunciation differences. In Borin, Lars and Anju Saxena, editors, *Approaches to Measuring Linguistic Differences*, number 265 in Trends in Linguistics. Studies and Monographs, pages 107–140. Walter De Gruyter GmbH.

Ricardo Otheguy and Nancy Stern. 2011. On so-called Spanglish. *International Journal of Bilingualism*, 15(1):85–100.

Irina Podtergera. 2021. German, Latin, and Church Slavonic in the language and text of the Smolensk trade treaty of 1229 [in Russian]. *Russkij jazyk v nauchnom osveshhenii*, 1(41):226–276.

Jelena Prokić and Stephan Moran. 2013. Black box approaches to genealogical classification and their shortcomings. In Lars Borin and Anju Saxena, editors, *Approaches to Measuring Linguistic Differences*, number 265 in Trends in Linguistics. Studies and Monographs, pages 429–446. Walter De Gruyter GmbH.

Claude E. Shannon. 1948. A mathematical theory of communication. *Bell System Technical Journal*, 27(3):379–423. _eprint: https://onlinelibrary.wiley.com/doi/pdf/10.1002/j.1538-7305.1948.tb01338.x.

Ryan S.-E. Shim and John Nerbonne. 2022. dialectR: Doing Dialectometry in R. In *Proceedings of the Ninth Workshop on NLP for Similar Languages, Varieties and Dialects*, pages 20–27.

Robert Sokal and Charles Michener. 1958. A statistical method for evaluating systematic relationships. *University of Kansas science bulletin*.

Jan Stankievič, Valer Bulhakaŭ (ed.), and Juraś Paciupa (ed.). 2007. *Jazyk i jazykavieda [Language and Language Science]*, 2 edition. Instytut bielarusistyki [Institute of Belarusian Studies], Vil̗nia [Vil̗nius].

Ryota Suzuki and Hidetoshi Shimodaira. 2006. Pvclust: an R package for assessing the uncertainty in hierarchical clustering. *Bioinformatics*, 22(12):1540–1542.

Colin Swaelens, Ilse De Vos, and Els Lefever. 2023. Evaluating existing lemmatisers on unedited byzantine Greek poetry. In *Proceedings of the Ancient Language Processing Workshop*, pages 111–116, Varna, Bulgaria. INCOMA Ltd., Shoumen, Bulgaria.

Thomas Sørensen. 1948. A method of establishing group of equal amplitude in plant sociobiology based on similarity of species content and its application to analyses of the vegetation on danish commons. In *Biologiske Skrifter/Kongelige Danske Videnskabernes Selskab*.

Nicholaas Verhelst. 2020–2021. The Carthaginian *SUFETES*: (re-)assessing the literary, epigraphical, and archaeological sources. *Carthage Studies*, 12:31–80.

Björn Wiemer and Ilja Seržant. 2014. Introduction. In Ilja Seržant, Björn Wiemer, Benedikt Szmrecsanyi, Natalia Levshina, Sofija Pozharickaja, Aksana Erker, Nina Markova, James Lavine, Hakyung Jung, Margje Post, Elena Galinskaja, Mirosław Jankowiak, and Anna Żebrowska, editors, *Contemporary Approaches to Dialectology: the Area of North, Northwest Russian and Belarusian Dialects*, number 12 in Slavica Bergensia, pages 11–80. Department of Foreign Languages, University of Bergen.

Andrej A. Zaliznjak. 1993. Uchastie zhenshhin v drevnerusskoj perepiske na bereste [participation of women in the old russian birchbark correspondence]. In *Russkaja duhovnaja kul'tura [Russian spiritual culture]*, Trento. University of Trento.

Andrej A. Zaliznjak. 2004. *Drevnenovgorodskij dialekt [Old Novgorodian dialect]*. Jazyki slavjanskoj kul'tury [Languages of the Slavic culture], Moscow.

Yuri G. Zelenkov and Ilya V. Segalovich. 2007. Comparative analysis of near-duplicate detection methods of web documents. In *Digital Libraries: Advanced Methods and Technologies, Digital Collections, 9th All-Russian Scientific Conference RCDL'2007 Proceedings*, Pereslavl'-Zalessky.

Lidija P. Zhukovskaja. 1959. *Novgorodskie berestjanye gramoty [Novgorod birchbark letters]*. Gos. uchebno-pedagog. izd-vo [Scientific-pegagogical state publishing house].

Appendix A

Parameter	Value
vector_size	128
window	15
min_count	1
workers	4
epochs	300
seed	1590
sg	1

Table 4: The parameters for FastText training.

Appendix B

Parameter	Value
nboot	1000
method.dist	euclidean
method.hclust	ward.D2

Table 5: The parameters for bootstrap clusterisation.

“I Need More Context and an English Translation”: Analysing How LLMs identify Personal Information in Komi, Polish, and English

Nikolai Ilinykh
CLASP, FLoV
University of Gothenburg, Sweden
nikolai.ilinykh@gu.se

Maria Irena Szawerna
Språkbanken Text, SFS
University of Gothenburg, Sweden
maria.szawerna@gu.se

Abstract

In this paper we present a pilot study and a qualitative analysis of the errors made by three large language models (LLMs) prompted to identify personal information (PI) in texts written in languages with varying resource availability: Komi (extremely low), Polish (medium), and English (high). Our analysis shows that LLMs perform better in detection of PI when provided with JSON-eliciting prompts. We also conjecture that the rich morphology and inflectionality of languages like Komi and Polish might affect the models' performance. The small-scale parallel dataset of text that we introduce here can be used as a starting point in developing benchmarks for evaluation of PI detection with longer textual contexts and LLMs.

1 Introduction

The lack of data for *low-resourced* languages is a known problem in computational linguistics. This problem can result in biases “within and across societies” (Søgaard, 2022), since the speakers of such languages can effectively be excluded from using language technology tools. Building infrastructure that uses such technology as LLMs to study and preserve low-resourced languages is important.

A key concern in the development of NLP infrastructure is the privacy of the data subjects and other individuals mentioned.[1] Linguistic data typically includes names, family relationships, health status, or other sensitive details, especially when collected texts are personal conversations, narratives, or interviews (Szawerna et al., 2024), and even seemingly scarce or incomplete PI may be used to reidentify the data subject (Salehi et al., 2017) and result in discrimination based on, for example, medical conditions or faith. Methods to obfuscate identities of data subjects have long been employed in linguistics (Thomas, 2010; Wang et al., 2024), but only a few of them have used computational approaches for identification of PI in low-resourced languages like Komi (Hämäläinen et al., 2023). Since personal information has been found in data used to train LLMs for many high-resourced languages – raising concerns about potential leaks in their outputs (Subramani et al., 2023) – it is crucial to protect privacy of data in these languages. However, protecting personal information in low-resourced languages is especially important as these languages already struggle with limited datasets, funding, and institutional support, making them particularly vulnerable to privacy risks.

In this pilot study we take a step towards better PI detection in low-resourced languages and prompt currently available LLMs. Such models, trained on multilingual corpora, can be prompted to perform a range of tasks, from text classification to text generation, even in languages where limited training data is available (A Pirinen, 2024; Purason et al., 2024b). LLMs have been studied in the context of low-resourced Uralic languages for the task of POS tagging (Alnajjar et al., 2024). They have also been used to support the creation of online dictionary tools (Alnajjar et al., 2020). The role of LLMs in PI detection in high-resourced language like English and Chinese has started being explored only recently (Yang et al., 2023), while their role in the context of low-resourced languages for PI detection remains unexplored.

To facilitate research in that direction, here we analyze the differences in the behavior of three LLMs in PI detection in languages with varied resource availability and linguistic structure. We use text data from two Uralic languages, Komi-Permyak and Komi-Zyrian. We construct a paral-

[1] For more on legal requirements regarding privacy in EU, see Official Journal of the European Union (2016).

Proceedings of the Third Workshop on Resources and Representations for Under-Resourced Languages and Domains (RESOURCEFUL-2025), pages 165–178, March 2, 2025 ©2025 Association for Computational Linguistics

lel corpus containing Komi sentences[2] with their Polish and English translations. We prompt Llama 3.1 with 8B parameters (Grattafiori et al., 2024), Mistral 7B (Jiang et al., 2023), and Gemma 2 with 9B parameters (Gemma Team et al., 2024) for PI detection and test six different prompt configurations. Our contributions, therefore, consist of 1) **a small, native speaker-curated parallel corpus of sentences** containing potential personal information in Komi, English, and Polish[3], and 2) **an initial analysis** of how three LLMs perform on the aforementioned dataset with respect to language's resource availability and inflectionality.

2 Materials and Methods

Data We looked at the Universal Dependencies treebanks for Komi-Permyak and Komi-Zyrian (Rueter et al., 2020; Partanen et al., 2018; Zeman et al., 2024) and found that there are 366 sentences in which there is at least one word that is labeled with one of the semantic tags for proper nouns as used in the GiellaLT infrastructure (Pirinen et al., 2023). These semantic tags classify names and nouns into categories such as animal (Sem/Ani), female (Sem/Fem) and male names (Sem/Mal), objects (Sem/Obj), organisations (Sem/Org), places (Sem/Plc), surnames (Sem/Sur), and web addresses (Sem/Web). Blokland et al. (2020) have previously used these semantic tags to identify nouns which are possible instances of PI in a rule-based PI detection system.

Among the sentences with semantic tags for proper nouns, 170 were translated to English and Polish by authors of this study. The sentences were first translated by the first author of this study (a native Komi-Permyak speaker and a proficient English speaker) from Komi-Permyak and Komi-Zyrian to English with the help of Neurotõlge[4] (Yankovskaya et al., 2023; Purason et al., 2024a), Google Translate[5] and Majbyr Translate[6]. Polish translations were created by the second author (a native Polish speaker and a proficient English speaker) based off of the English translations, and with the help of Google Translate in some cases. The original names of people and places were preserved during translation into English and the final form of the translated sentence was always overseen by a human. In the end, our data included 35 sentences with female names, 47 sentences with male names, 49 sentences with place names, and 39 sentences with surnames in them. Some sentences contain more than one name, possibly of different types. Importantly, more information that could be considered personal and which does not necessarily belong to the aforementioned types may be found in sentences, and was impossible to account for during the sentence extraction process. Our resulting dataset can be accessed on Zenodo via `https://zenodo.org/records/14845329`.

PI categories	Text	JSON
PI only	Prompt 1	Prompt 2
Megyesi et al. (2018)	Prompt 3	Prompt 4
Subramani et al. (2023)	Prompt 5	Prompt 6

Table 1: Prompts by tag and output type.

Models and prompts We tested three multilingual pre-trained large language models: Llama 3.1 with 8B parameters (Grattafiori et al., 2024), Mistral 7B (Jiang et al., 2023), and Gemma 2 with 9B parameters (Gemma Team et al., 2024)[7]. The models and their weights were accessed via Ollama[8]. Uploading data containing PI to third-party services is not optimal, which is why we chose models that we were able to run locally. Note that we chose recent LLMs which are similar in size and comparable.

We used six different one-shot prompts, passed to the models together with the sentences, following the official guide on prompting Llama models[9], with a similar structure to the one used by Yang et al. (2023) for PI detection. The prompts varied in terms of (i) the output format (produce a sentence with PI instances replaced with appropriate tags or a JSON structure) and (ii) the PI classification.

[2]Originating from Komi corpora (Rueter et al., 2020; Partanen et al., 2018; Zeman et al., 2024); we feature 143 sentences in Komi-Zyrian and 27 sentences in Komi-Permyak.

[3]It is important to highlight that there exists no comprehensive definition of what it means to be a *low-resourced* language (Nigatu et al., 2024); traditionally, due to small amounts of available data among other things, Komi and many other Uralic languages have been considered low-resourced. Polish boasts a significantly larger collection of corpora, tools and models than Komi (Dadas, 2019), and has been positioned as the higher-resourced counterpart of West Slavic minority languages such as Kashubian, Silesian, or Sorbian (Torge et al., 2023; Rybak, 2024), but in comparison with English, its resources are still very limited.

[4]`https://translate.ut.ee`

[5]`https://translate.google.com`

[6]`https://translate.majbyr.com`

[7]In the paper we refer to these models as **Llama**, **Mistral**, and **Gemma** respectively.

[8]`http://ollama.com`

[9]`https://www.llama.com/docs/how-to-guides/prompting/`

System: You are a multilingual personal information detection tool. Personal information is information that can lead to someone in the text being reidentified, like their name, surname, middle name, patronymic, nickname, where they live, address, city, country, zip code, where they work, study, or spend a lot of their time, what unique lines or modes of transport they travel with, their age, any dates mentioned in the text, phone numbers, personal identity numbers, bank account numbers, other number sequences, e-mail addresses, urls, their work titles, education, types of family relations, information about faith, political beliefs, sexuality, ethnicity, unique achievements, etc.

User: For each token in the given text, determine whether it is a piece of personal information. Return the text with "PI" replacing every instance of personal information.

Example:
Text: I'm from Slovakia , but one of my best friends , Marie , is from Norway .
Result: I'm from PI , but one of my best friends , PI , is from PI.

Text: [PLACEHOLDER]
Result:

Figure 1: One of the prompt templates used in this study. When fed to a model, [PLACEHOLDER] is replaced with an actual text.

For PI classification we used different category formulations: (1) a "PI" category encompassing all personal information, (2) detailed name- and geographical location-related categories inspired by Megyesi et al. (2018), and (3) a slightly re-phrased PI categorization from Subramani et al. (2023). See Table 1 for a summary of the combinations. All of the prompts included the description of the task, tags, output format, and a single example of an input-output pair followed by the input that the model should generate output for. Examples can be found in Figure 1 and Appendix A.

3 General error analysis

After feeding the models the prompt–sentence combinations, we collected their outputs, which we subsequently manually analyzed. We begin with an analysis of the errors encountered and then proceed to examine two specific examples. In this pilot study we did not run any quantitative analysis, as the data we have lacks token-level annotation of PI in two of the three languages. Moreover, the annotation that we do have for Komi is using the GiellaLT tags, and not the aforementioned categories (1-3); thus, our analysis is preliminary.

Komi **Gemma** ignores case markers in words identified as PI. For example, in the Komi-Zyrian sentence *Сійӧ быдмис Парижын, Францияса юркарын* 'He grew up in Paris.INE[10], the capital.INE of France.LOC', the model marks only part of the word *Францияса* 'France.LOC', ignoring the marker *-са*. In contrast, it marks the entire word when it appears in the genitive case in Komi-Permyak, e.g. *Франциялӧн* 'of France.GEN'. When asked to tag PI, **Gemma** often misidentifies the language as Russian or Urdmut and translates the text into English. It also frequently asks for more context to identify PI, refusing to produce an output. **Llama** rarely provides output, referring to concerns about revealing information that could lead to reidentification. Models are good at identifying first names and surnames (albeit worse with culture-specific names), but they struggle with names of places. For example, **Gemma** mistakenly tags *Парижын* 'in Paris.INE' in both Komi varieties as `situation` and *Франция* 'France.NOM' as `society`. **Llama** detects spans correctly, but often assigns the wrong tag: labelling *быдмис* 'grew up' in both Komi varieties as `birth`, *Парижын* 'in Paris.INE' as `records`, *Франция* 'France.NOM' as `birth` and *юркарын* 'the capital.INE' as `society`. While **Mistral** provides output in the requested format, it struggles with tagging, changes spelling and produces many hallucinations. For example, it marks the personal pronoun *Сійӧ* 'he/she.NOM' in Komi-Zyrian as `PI` and completely alters the initial sentence from *Сійӧ быдмис Парижын, Францияса юркарын* 'He grew up in Paris.INE, the capital.INE of France.LOC' to *PI абыдмис Пирижин, PI юркарын*, where only *юркарын* 'the capital.INE' is a correct word.

English **Gemma** can not only mark a name as PI but also sometimes identify and tag related pronouns when asked to provide output in JSON format, e.g. *[...] replied **Galina**, with a dry smile from the corner of **her** mouth [...]*. However, it does not always follow the instructions and sometimes invents tags that are not part of the tagset, such as `<other>` for ambiguous PI categories. In one instance it is also able to assign the `<social>` tag to *Comrade* and `<character>` to *Voroshilov*, where the latter is a surname and the former is a noun referring to *Voroshilov*. **Llama** generates extensive explanations and often refuses

[10]Morphological analysis for Komi words was conducted with the help of uralicNLP: `https://github.com/mikahama/uralicNLP?tab=readme-ov-file`

to perform the task, mirroring its behavior on Komi. It also hallucinates tags and fails to mask multi-token PI spans accurately such as tagging only *Voroshilov* as <firstname_male> in *Comrade Voroshilov*. While deciding whether *Comrade* is a part of a PI span can be problematic, it is not unprecedented to find such titles included in the span: Pilán et al. (2022) include elements like *Mr.* or *Dr.* into the same span as the name and surname. Therefore, it is possible that inclusion of *Comrade* in reference to *Voroshilov* can lead to reidentifcation of this person in a different situation. **Mistral**, while hallucinating and omitting many PI instances, performs better at masking anglophone names. For example, it correctly masks names like *Mary*, *Peter*, and *Jane* using appropriate tags. However, it fails to mask names such as *Svezhov* (ko.: *Свежов)*, *Petya* (ko.: *Петя)*, or *Sasha* (ko.: *Саша)*. Additionally, it masks *Masha* (ko.: *Маша)* as <firstname_unknown>, indicating a lack of understanding of the name's gender (typically female). All models demonstrate (i) a tendency to over-generate and provide unrequested explanations that are difficult to evaluate and (ii) struggle with maintaining consistency in tag assignment.

Polish **Gemma** appears to misclassify inflectional cases of the words thus assigning it to the wrong gender. For example, in the sentence *[...] tuż obok domu Epimowa Punegowa* '[...] in the immediate vicinity of the Epimov.GEN Punegov.GEN house' the model mistakenly assigns *Epimowa* and *Punegowa* to <surname_female> and <surname_male> respectively, while both these are male names. **Llama** refuses to perform the task stating that it cannot give away information that could lead to someone being re-identified. It also incorrectly identifies same words in same sentences across multiple prompts: under two different prompts it tags *cerata* 'oilcloth' as either a street name or a type of a document. **Mistral**'s output is not supplemented by extensive explanations, but the model tends to hallucinate and produce incorrect tags. For example, when asked to mark personal information as PI in *Dorósł w Paryżu, stolicy Francji* 'He grew up in Paris.INS, the capital of France.GEN', while the model assigns PI_City to *Paryżu* and PI_Country to *Francji*, it also incorrectly assigns PI_Name to *Dorósł* which is a verb. Note that these tags are hallucinated - they are not like the ones we have prompted the model to produce. **Mistral** also often translates Polish sentences into English in its output.

3.1 Case analysis

We analyze outputs produced by **Gemma** for the prompt 4 as specified in Table 1, because **Gemma** has shown to be the most consistent in the quality of its outputs. Each example has output for English (top) and tokenized output for Komi-Permyak (middle) and Polish (bottom). We will focus on the two characters mentioned in each sentence: *Petya* and *Masha*. The main reason for choosing these sentences in particular for comparison is that at a first glance, they only differ in terms of what verb they feature. However, in Komi and Polish, these two verbs have a different influence, eliciting specific case endings in the object of the sentence (*Masha*). By comparing these two sentences we can therefore investigate how the model handles this grammatical and morphological diversity.

(1)	*F-M*		*F-F*	
	Petya	*befriends*	*Masha*	.
	F-U		S-U	
	Петя	ёртасьӧ	Машакӧт	.
	F-U		F-F	
	Petja	zaprzyjaźnia się z	Maszą	.

(2)	*F-M*		*F-F*			
	Petya	*loves*	*Masha*			.
	F-U		S-U			
	Петя	любит	Маша	о	с	.
	F-M		S-F			
	Petja	kocha	Maszę			.

In both of the examples in English the model correctly assigned <firstname_male> to *Petya* and <firstname_female> to *Masha*, suggesting that the semantic difference in the verbs has no effect between these two sentences, at least in English. In example 1, in Komi-Permyak, the model marked Петя 'Petya.NOM' as <firstname_unknown> and Машакӧт 'Masha.COM' as <surname_unknown>. For Polish, it identified *Petja* 'Petya.NOM' as <firstname_unknown> and *Maszą* 'Masha.INS' as <firstname_female>. While *Petya* is marked correctly as <firstname_male> when given English text, the model cannot identify the gender in Komi-Permyak and Polish. The model also thinks that Машакӧт 'Masha.COM' is a surname without gender indicator. Mistakes like this (the model thinks there is e.g. no gender indicator) might result in leakage of situational and societal context, because the affix *-кӧт* in *Машакӧт* indicates comitative case that is used to express companionship, and this type of information can be considered personal. In example 2, the model seems to now identify *Petja* 'Petya.NOM' in Polish as <firstname_male>, while thinking that *Maszę* 'Masha.ACC' is an instance of <surname_female>. For Komi-Permyak, the model translates the example into Russian (the original text is *Петя любитӧ Машаӧс* 'Petya.NOM loves Masha.ACC') and tokenizes the affix. This example demonstrates a fragile behavior of **Gemma** and combined with our general error analysis, suggests that models often try to translate input in less familiar language to a language that is more known to them (English, Russian). While Russian and Komi-Permyak share the cyrillic alphabet, the similarities and grammatical differences between two languages cannot be exploited by LLMs, because intricacies in less-resourced languages are then reduced to phenomena in a language with more resources.

4 Discussion and conclusions

Our small qualitative examination suggests that across the languages, models, and prompts that we tested, **Gemma** with JSON-eliciting prompts performs best. Overall, the models exhibited the best performance on the English sentences, followed by Polish, with Komi being the most difficult. One problem for the models is the rich morphology of Komi variants and Polish. The models also denote that they lack context to make a judgment, which highlights the difficulty in disambiguating whether a piece of information is personal or not. They are often trying to default to English or ask for an English translation when asked to perform the task on a low-resourced language that they cannot recognize. The models also learn differently from various tagsets: the one from Subramani et al. (2023) is hard to generalize from, while tags based on Megyesi et al. (2018) appear to be assigned correctly more often. Non-anglophone names, especially Komi ones, are hard for models to tag, especially in terms of the gender.

While Yang et al. (2023) consider their findings for high-resourced languages to be promising, we consider it better to err on the side of caution regarding any conclusions on the performance of LLMs on PI identification task for low-resourced languages. Our impression is that even though the models' perform well on other NLP tasks, in this case, their outputs require manual post-processing and are not immune to hallucinations. This makes them highly unreliable for the incredibly high-stakes task of PI detection on their own with the prompts used, even for high-resourced languages, but especially for the low-resourced ones, where the error rate appears to be higher. Future work should focus on evaluating models on longer texts with more context and further refinement of the best-performing prompts.

This is — to the best of our knowledge — the first study investigating the performance of LLMs on PI detection in more than just high-resourced languages (specifically, in such low-resourced language as Komi), and the first one examining how LLMs handle inflectionality in this task. We are also contributing a novel parallel dataset translated by native speakers. We hope that our work will inspire more research on the topics within the intersection of LLMs, PI detection, and low-resourced languages.

Limitations and Ethical Concerns

This is a preliminary and qualitative analysis. Our experiment featured six different prompts, three different models and three different languages, leading to $6 \times 3 \times 3$ sets of outputs. In order to fully support our claims based on the analysis of these outputs, we require evaluation and statistical analysis. This entails the manual annotation of the outputs and annotation guideline development, which was beyond the scope of this pilot study.

Another limitation of this experiment is the small number of samples, which may not reflect in style and content the types of utterances that are of interest for people wishing to use LLMs to detect personal information. Additionally, the translations into Polish were not done directly from the original, but via intermediate languages. It is also possible that more extensive tweaking of the prompt texts could lead to better performance, at least on the high-resourced language.

We also note that we aggregated the Komi-Zyrian and Komi-Permyak data without considering the differences in the models' performance between them, largely due to the fact that there are so few samples available for Komi-Permyak.

While the data that we used was sourced from openly available corpora and, therefore, likely does not pose any privacy concerns, we want to highlight that we do not encourage the use of LLMs for PI detection without manual post-processing to ensure that no personal information is leaked, as the results are not consistent enough even for English. It is also important to keep in mind that LLMs are computationally rather heavy, and processing larger batches of text will have a noticeable carbon footprint, meaning that more lightweight solutions with similar performance may be a better choice. It is also essential to remember that LLM services hosted online may collect the users' data, so the only way to use them for PI detection without triggering privacy risks is to run them locally, which can impose high hardware requirements.

Acknowledgments

This work has been possible thanks to the funding of numerous grants from the Swedish Research Council. The first author is supported by a grant from the Swedish Research Council (VR project 2014-39) for the establishment of the *Centre for Linguistic Theory and Studies in Probability (CLASP)* at the University of Gothenburg. The second author's work is funded by the project *Grandma Karl is 27 years old: Automatic pseudonymization of research data* with the funding number 2022-02311 for the years 2023-2029. That author is also supported by the Swedish national research infrastructure Nationella Språkbanken, funded jointly by contract number 2017-00626 for the years 2018-2024, as well 10 participating partner institutions.

References

Flammie A Pirinen. 2024. Keeping up appearances—or how to get all Uralic languages included into bleeding edge research and software: generate, convert, and LLM your way into multilingual datasets. In *Proceedings of the 9th International Workshop on Computational Linguistics for Uralic Languages*, pages 123–131, Helsinki, Finland. Association for Computational Linguistics.

Khalid Alnajjar, Mika Hämäläinen, and Jack Rueter. 2024. Leveraging transformer-based models for predicting inflection classes of words in an endangered Sami language. In *Proceedings of the 9th International Workshop on Computational Linguistics for Uralic Languages*, pages 41–48, Helsinki, Finland. Association for Computational Linguistics.

Khalid Alnajjar, Mika Hämäläinen, Jack Rueter, and Niko Partanen. 2020. Ve'rdd. narrowing the gap between paper dictionaries, low-resource NLP and community involvement. In *Proceedings of the 28th International Conference on Computational Linguistics: System Demonstrations*, pages 1–6, Barcelona, Spain (Online). International Committee on Computational Linguistics (ICCL).

Rogier Blokland, Niko Partanen, and Michael Rießler. 2020. A pseudonymisation method for language documentation corpora: An experiment with spoken Komi. In *Proceedings of the Sixth International Workshop on Computational Linguistics of Uralic Languages*, pages 1–8, Wien, Austria. Association for Computational Linguistics.

Sławomir Dadas. 2019. A repository of polish NLP resources. Github.

Gemma Team, Morgane Riviere, Shreya Pathak, Pier Giuseppe Sessa, Cassidy Hardin, Surya Bhupatiraju, Léonard Hussenot, Thomas Mesnard, Bobak Shahriari, Alexandre Ramé, Johan Ferret, Peter Liu, Pouya Tafti, Abe Friesen, Michelle Casbon, Sabela Ramos, Ravin Kumar, Charline Le Lan, Sammy Jerome, Anton Tsitsulin, Nino Vieillard, Piotr Stanczyk, Sertan Girgin, Nikola Momchev, Matt Hoffman, Shantanu Thakoor, Jean-Bastien Grill, Behnam Neyshabur, Olivier Bachem, Alanna Walton, Aliaksei Severyn, Alicia Parrish, Aliya Ahmad, Allen Hutchison, Alvin Abdagic, Amanda Carl, Amy Shen, Andy Brock, Andy Coenen, Anthony Laforge, Antonia Paterson, Ben Bastian, Bilal Piot, Bo Wu, Brandon Royal, Charlie Chen, Chintu Kumar, Chris Perry, Chris Welty, Christopher A. Choquette-Choo, Danila Sinopalnikov, David Weinberger, Dimple Vijaykumar, Dominika Rogozińska, Dustin Herbison, Elisa Bandy, Emma Wang, Eric Noland, Erica Moreira, Evan Senter, Evgenii Eltyshev, Francesco Visin, Gabriel Rasskin, Gary Wei, Glenn Cameron, Gus Martins, Hadi Hashemi, Hanna Klimczak-Plucińska, Harleen Batra, Harsh Dhand, Ivan Nardini, Jacinda Mein, Jack Zhou, James Svensson, Jeff Stanway, Jetha Chan, Jin Peng Zhou, Joana Carrasqueira, Joana Iljazi, Jocelyn Becker, Joe Fernandez, Joost van Amersfoort, Josh Gordon, Josh Lipschultz, Josh Newlan, Ju yeong Ji, Kareem Mohamed, Kartikeya Badola, Kat Black, Katie Millican, Keelin McDonell, Kelvin Nguyen, Kiranbir Sodhia, Kish Greene, Lars Lowe Sjoesund, Lauren Usui, Laurent Sifre, Lena Heuermann, Leticia Lago, Lilly McNealus, Livio Baldini Soares, Logan Kilpatrick, Lucas Dixon, Luciano Martins, Machel Reid, Manvinder Singh, Mark Iverson, Martin Görner, Mat Velloso, Mateo Wirth, Matt Davidow, Matt Miller, Matthew Rahtz, Matthew Watson, Meg Risdal, Mehran Kazemi, Michael Moynihan, Ming Zhang, Minsuk Kahng, Minwoo Park, Mofi Rahman, Mohit Khatwani, Natalie Dao, Nenshad Bardoliwalla, Nesh Devanathan, Neta Dumai, Nilay Chauhan, Oscar Wahltinez, Pankil Botarda, Parker Barnes, Paul Barham, Paul Michel, Pengchong Jin, Petko Georgiev, Phil Culliton, Pradeep Kuppala, Ramona Comanescu, Ramona Merhej, Reena Jana, Reza Ardeshir Rokni, Rishabh Agarwal,

Ryan Mullins, Samaneh Saadat, Sara Mc Carthy, Sarah Cogan, Sarah Perrin, Sébastien M. R. Arnold, Sebastian Krause, Shengyang Dai, Shruti Garg, Shruti Sheth, Sue Ronstrom, Susan Chan, Timothy Jordan, Ting Yu, Tom Eccles, Tom Hennigan, Tomas Kocisky, Tulsee Doshi, Vihan Jain, Vikas Yadav, Vilobh Meshram, Vishal Dharmadhikari, Warren Barkley, Wei Wei, Wenming Ye, Woohyun Han, Woosuk Kwon, Xiang Xu, Zhe Shen, Zhitao Gong, Zichuan Wei, Victor Cotruta, Phoebe Kirk, Anand Rao, Minh Giang, Ludovic Peran, Tris Warkentin, Eli Collins, Joelle Barral, Zoubin Ghahramani, Raia Hadsell, D. Sculley, Jeanine Banks, Anca Dragan, Slav Petrov, Oriol Vinyals, Jeff Dean, Demis Hassabis, Koray Kavukcuoglu, Clement Farabet, Elena Buchatskaya, Sebastian Borgeaud, Noah Fiedel, Armand Joulin, Kathleen Kenealy, Robert Dadashi, and Alek Andreev. 2024. Gemma 2: Improving open language models at a practical size.

Aaron Grattafiori, Abhimanyu Dubey, Abhinav Jauhri, Abhinav Pandey, Abhishek Kadian, Ahmad Al-Dahle, Aiesha Letman, Akhil Mathur, Alan Schelten, Alex Vaughan, Amy Yang, Angela Fan, Anirudh Goyal, Anthony Hartshorn, Aobo Yang, Archi Mitra, Archie Sravankumar, Artem Korenev, Arthur Hinsvark, Arun Rao, Aston Zhang, Aurelien Rodriguez, Austen Gregerson, Ava Spataru, Baptiste Roziere, Bethany Biron, Binh Tang, Bobbie Chern, Charlotte Caucheteux, Chaya Nayak, Chloe Bi, Chris Marra, Chris McConnell, Christian Keller, Christophe Touret, Chunyang Wu, Corinne Wong, Cristian Canton Ferrer, Cyrus Nikolaidis, Damien Allonsius, Daniel Song, Danielle Pintz, Danny Livshits, Danny Wyatt, David Esiobu, Dhruv Choudhary, Dhruv Mahajan, Diego Garcia-Olano, Diego Perino, Dieuwke Hupkes, Egor Lakomkin, Ehab Al-Badawy, Elina Lobanova, Emily Dinan, Eric Michael Smith, Filip Radenovic, Francisco Guzmán, Frank Zhang, Gabriel Synnaeve, Gabrielle Lee, Georgia Lewis Anderson, Govind Thattai, Graeme Nail, Gregoire Mialon, Guan Pang, Guillem Cucurell, Hailey Nguyen, Hannah Korevaar, Hu Xu, Hugo Touvron, Iliyan Zarov, Imanol Arrieta Ibarra, Isabel Kloumann, Ishan Misra, Ivan Evtimov, Jack Zhang, Jade Copet, Jaewon Lee, Jan Geffert, Jana Vranes, Jason Park, Jay Mahadeokar, Jeet Shah, Jelmer van der Linde, Jennifer Billock, Jenny Hong, Jenya Lee, Jeremy Fu, Jianfeng Chi, Jianyu Huang, Jiawen Liu, Jie Wang, Jiecao Yu, Joanna Bitton, Joe Spisak, Jongsoo Park, Joseph Rocca, Joshua Johnstun, Joshua Saxe, Junteng Jia, Kalyan Vasuden Alwala, Karthik Prasad, Kartikeya Upasani, Kate Plawiak, Ke Li, Kenneth Heafield, Kevin Stone, Khalid El-Arini, Krithika Iyer, Kshitiz Malik, Kuenley Chiu, Kunal Bhalla, Kushal Lakhotia, Lauren Rantala-Yeary, Laurens van der Maaten, Lawrence Chen, Liang Tan, Liz Jenkins, Louis Martin, Lovish Madaan, Lubo Malo, Lukas Blecher, Lukas Landzaat, Luke de Oliveira, Madeline Muzzi, Mahesh Pasupuleti, Mannat Singh, Manohar Paluri, Marcin Kardas, Maria Tsimpoukelli, Mathew Oldham, Mathieu Rita, Maya Pavlova, Melanie Kambadur, Mike Lewis, Min Si, Mitesh Kumar Singh, Mona Hassan, Naman Goyal, Narjes Torabi, Nikolay Bashlykov, Nikolay Bogoychev, Niladri Chatterji, Ning Zhang, Olivier Duchenne, Onur Çelebi, Patrick Alrassy, Pengchuan Zhang, Pengwei Li, Petar Vasic, Peter Weng, Prajjwal Bhargava, Pratik Dubal, Praveen Krishnan, Punit Singh Koura, Puxin Xu, Qing He, Qingxiao Dong, Ragavan Srinivasan, Raj Ganapathy, Ramon Calderer, Ricardo Silveira Cabral, Robert Stojnic, Roberta Raileanu, Rohan Maheswari, Rohit Girdhar, Rohit Patel, Romain Sauvestre, Ronnie Polidoro, Roshan Sumbaly, Ross Taylor, Ruan Silva, Rui Hou, Rui Wang, Saghar Hosseini, Sahana Chennabasappa, Sanjay Singh, Sean Bell, Seohyun Sonia Kim, Sergey Edunov, Shaoliang Nie, Sharan Narang, Sharath Raparthy, Sheng Shen, Shengye Wan, Shruti Bhosale, Shun Zhang, Simon Vandenhende, Soumya Batra, Spencer Whitman, Sten Sootla, Stephane Collot, Suchin Gururangan, Sydney Borodinsky, Tamar Herman, Tara Fowler, Tarek Sheasha, Thomas Georgiou, Thomas Scialom, Tobias Speckbacher, Todor Mihaylov, Tong Xiao, Ujjwal Karn, Vedanuj Goswami, Vibhor Gupta, Vignesh Ramanathan, Viktor Kerkez, Vincent Gonguet, Virginie Do, Vish Vogeti, Vítor Albiero, Vladan Petrovic, Weiwei Chu, Wenhan Xiong, Wenyin Fu, Whitney Meers, Xavier Martinet, Xiaodong Wang, Xiaofang Wang, Xiaoqing Ellen Tan, Xide Xia, Xinfeng Xie, Xuchao Jia, Xuewei Wang, Yaelle Goldschlag, Yashesh Gaur, Yasmine Babaei, Yi Wen, Yiwen Song, Yuchen Zhang, Yue Li, Yuning Mao, Zacharie Delpierre Coudert, Zheng Yan, Zhengxing Chen, Zoe Papakipos, Aaditya Singh, Aayushi Srivastava, Abha Jain, Adam Kelsey, Adam Shajnfeld, Adithya Gangidi, Adolfo Victoria, Ahuva Goldstand, Ajay Menon, Ajay Sharma, Alex Boesenberg, Alexei Baevski, Allie Feinstein, Amanda Kallet, Amit Sangani, Amos Teo, Anam Yunus, Andrei Lupu, Andres Alvarado, Andrew Caples, Andrew Gu, Andrew Ho, Andrew Poulton, Andrew Ryan, Ankit Ramchandani, Annie Dong, Annie Franco, Anuj Goyal, Aparajita Saraf, Arkabandhu Chowdhury, Ashley Gabriel, Ashwin Bharambe, Assaf Eisenman, Azadeh Yazdan, Beau James, Ben Maurer, Benjamin Leonhardi, Bernie Huang, Beth Loyd, Beto De Paola, Bhargavi Paranjape, Bing Liu, Bo Wu, Boyu Ni, Braden Hancock, Bram Wasti, Brandon Spence, Brani Stojkovic, Brian Gamido, Britt Montalvo, Carl Parker, Carly Burton, Catalina Mejia, Ce Liu, Changhan Wang, Changkyu Kim, Chao Zhou, Chester Hu, Ching-Hsiang Chu, Chris Cai, Chris Tindal, Christoph Feichtenhofer, Cynthia Gao, Damon Civin, Dana Beaty, Daniel Kreymer, Daniel Li, David Adkins, David Xu, Davide Testuggine, Delia David, Devi Parikh, Diana Liskovich, Didem Foss, Dingkang Wang, Duc Le, Dustin Holland, Edward Dowling, Eissa Jamil, Elaine Montgomery, Eleonora Presani, Emily Hahn, Emily Wood, Eric-Tuan Le, Erik Brinkman, Esteban Arcaute, Evan Dunbar, Evan Smothers, Fei Sun, Felix Kreuk, Feng Tian, Filippos Kokkinos, Firat Ozgenel, Francesco Caggioni, Frank Kanayet, Frank Seide, Gabriela Medina Florez, Gabriella Schwarz, Gada Badeer, Georgia Swee, Gil Halpern, Grant

Herman, Grigory Sizov, Guangyi, Zhang, Guna Lakshminarayanan, Hakan Inan, Hamid Shojanazeri, Han Zou, Hannah Wang, Hanwen Zha, Haroun Habeeb, Harrison Rudolph, Helen Suk, Henry Aspegren, Hunter Goldman, Hongyuan Zhan, Ibrahim Damlaj, Igor Molybog, Igor Tufanov, Ilias Leontiadis, Irina-Elena Veliche, Itai Gat, Jake Weissman, James Geboski, James Kohli, Janice Lam, Japhet Asher, Jean-Baptiste Gaya, Jeff Marcus, Jeff Tang, Jennifer Chan, Jenny Zhen, Jeremy Reizenstein, Jeremy Teboul, Jessica Zhong, Jian Jin, Jingyi Yang, Joe Cummings, Jon Carvill, Jon Shepard, Jonathan McPhie, Jonathan Torres, Josh Ginsburg, Junjie Wang, Kai Wu, Kam Hou U, Karan Saxena, Kartikay Khandelwal, Katayoun Zand, Kathy Matosich, Kaushik Veeraraghavan, Kelly Michelena, Keqian Li, Kiran Jagadeesh, Kun Huang, Kunal Chawla, Kyle Huang, Lailin Chen, Lakshya Garg, Lavender A, Leandro Silva, Lee Bell, Lei Zhang, Liangpeng Guo, Licheng Yu, Liron Moshkovich, Luca Wehrstedt, Madian Khabsa, Manav Avalani, Manish Bhatt, Martynas Mankus, Matan Hasson, Matthew Lennie, Matthias Reso, Maxim Groshev, Maxim Naumov, Maya Lathi, Meghan Keneally, Miao Liu, Michael L. Seltzer, Michal Valko, Michelle Restrepo, Mihir Patel, Mik Vyatskov, Mikayel Samvelyan, Mike Clark, Mike Macey, Mike Wang, Miquel Jubert Hermoso, Mo Metanat, Mohammad Rastegari, Munish Bansal, Nandhini Santhanam, Natascha Parks, Natasha White, Navyata Bawa, Nayan Singhal, Nick Egebo, Nicolas Usunier, Nikhil Mehta, Nikolay Pavlovich Laptev, Ning Dong, Norman Cheng, Oleg Chernoguz, Olivia Hart, Omkar Salpekar, Ozlem Kalinli, Parkin Kent, Parth Parekh, Paul Saab, Pavan Balaji, Pedro Rittner, Philip Bontrager, Pierre Roux, Piotr Dollar, Polina Zvyagina, Prashant Ratanchandani, Pritish Yuvraj, Qian Liang, Rachad Alao, Rachel Rodriguez, Rafi Ayub, Raghotham Murthy, Raghu Nayani, Rahul Mitra, Rangaprabhu Parthasarathy, Raymond Li, Rebekkah Hogan, Robin Battey, Rocky Wang, Russ Howes, Ruty Rinott, Sachin Mehta, Sachin Siby, Sai Jayesh Bondu, Samyak Datta, Sara Chugh, Sara Hunt, Sargun Dhillon, Sasha Sidorov, Satadru Pan, Saurabh Mahajan, Saurabh Verma, Seiji Yamamoto, Sharadh Ramaswamy, Shaun Lindsay, Shaun Lindsay, Sheng Feng, Shenghao Lin, Shengxin Cindy Zha, Shishir Patil, Shiva Shankar, Shuqiang Zhang, Shuqiang Zhang, Sinong Wang, Sneha Agarwal, Soji Sajuyigbe, Soumith Chintala, Stephanie Max, Stephen Chen, Steve Kehoe, Steve Satterfield, Sudarshan Govindaprasad, Sumit Gupta, Summer Deng, Sungmin Cho, Sunny Virk, Suraj Subramanian, Sy Choudhury, Sydney Goldman, Tal Remez, Tamar Glaser, Tamara Best, Thilo Koehler, Thomas Robinson, Tianhe Li, Tianjun Zhang, Tim Matthews, Timothy Chou, Tzook Shaked, Varun Vontimitta, Victoria Ajayi, Victoria Montanez, Vijai Mohan, Vinay Satish Kumar, Vishal Mangla, Vlad Ionescu, Vlad Poenaru, Vlad Tiberiu Mihailescu, Vladimir Ivanov, Wei Li, Wenchen Wang, Wenwen Jiang, Wes Bouaziz, Will Constable, Xiaocheng Tang, Xiaojian Wu, Xiaolan Wang, Xilun Wu, Xinbo Gao, Yaniv Kleinman, Yanjun Chen, Ye Hu, Ye Jia, Ye Qi, Yenda Li, Yilin Zhang, Ying Zhang, Yossi Adi, Youngjin Nam, Yu, Wang, Yu Zhao, Yuchen Hao, Yundi Qian, Yunlu Li, Yuzi He, Zach Rait, Zachary DeVito, Zef Rosnbrick, Zhaoduo Wen, Zhenyu Yang, Zhiwei Zhao, and Zhiyu Ma. 2024. The llama 3 herd of models.

Mika Hämäläinen, Jack Rueter, Khalid Alnajjar, and Niko Partanen. 2023. Working towards digital documentation of Uralic languages with open-source tools and Modern NLP methods. In *Proceedings of the Big Picture Workshop*, pages 18–27, Singapore. Association for Computational Linguistics.

Albert Q. Jiang, Alexandre Sablayrolles, Arthur Mensch, Chris Bamford, Devendra Singh Chaplot, Diego de las Casas, Florian Bressand, Gianna Lengyel, Guillaume Lample, Lucile Saulnier, Lélio Renard Lavaud, Marie-Anne Lachaux, Pierre Stock, Teven Le Scao, Thibaut Lavril, Thomas Wang, Timothée Lacroix, and William El Sayed. 2023. Mistral 7b.

Beáta Megyesi, Lena Granstedt, Sofia Johansson, Julia Prentice, Dan Rosén, Carl-Johan Schenström, Gunlög Sundberg, Mats Wirén, and Elena Volodina. 2018. Learner corpus anonymization in the age of GDPR: Insights from the creation of a learner corpus of Swedish. In *Proceedings of the 7th workshop on NLP for Computer Assisted Language Learning*, pages 47–56, Stockholm, Sweden. LiU Electronic Press.

Hellina Hailu Nigatu, Atnafu Lambebo Tonja, Benjamin Rosman, Thamar Solorio, and Monojit Choudhury. 2024. The zeno's paradox of 'low-resource' languages. In *Proceedings of the 2024 Conference on Empirical Methods in Natural Language Processing*, pages 17753–17774, Miami, Florida, USA. Association for Computational Linguistics.

Official Journal of the European Union. 2016. Consolidated text: Regulation (EU) 2016/679 of the european parliament and of the council of 27 april 2016 on the protection of natural persons with regard to the processing of personal data and on the free movement of such data, and repealing directive 95/46/EC (general data protection regulation) (text with EEA relevance). *Official Journal*, (Document 02016R0679-20160504).

Niko Partanen, Rogier Blokland, KyungTae Lim, Thierry Poibeau, and Michael Rießler. 2018. The first Komi-Zyrian Universal Dependencies treebanks. In *Proceedings of the Second Workshop on Universal Dependencies (UDW 2018)*, pages 126–132, Brussels, Belgium. Association for Computational Linguistics.

Ildikó Pilán, Pierre Lison, Lilja Øvrelid, Anthi Papadopoulou, David Sánchez, and Montserrat Batet. 2022. The text anonymization benchmark (TAB): A dedicated corpus and evaluation framework for text anonymization. *Computational Linguistics*, 48(4):1053–1101.

Flammie Pirinen, Sjur Moshagen, and Katri Hiovain-Asikainen. 2023. GiellaLT — a stable infrastructure for Nordic minority languages and beyond. In *Proceedings of the 24th Nordic Conference on Computational Linguistics (NoDaLiDa)*, pages 643–649, Tórshavn, Faroe Islands. University of Tartu Library.

Taido Purason, Aleksei Ivanov, Lisa Yankovskaya, and Mark Fishel. 2024a. SMUGRI-MT - machine translation system for low-resource Finno-Ugric languages. In *Proceedings of the 25th Annual Conference of the European Association for Machine Translation (Volume 2)*, pages 31–32, Sheffield, UK. European Association for Machine Translation (EAMT).

Taido Purason, Hele-Andra Kuulmets, and Mark Fishel. 2024b. Llms for extremely low-resource finno-ugric languages.

Jack Rueter, Niko Partanen, and Larisa Ponomareva. 2020. On the questions in developing computational infrastructure for Komi-permyak. In *Proceedings of the Sixth International Workshop on Computational Linguistics of Uralic Languages*, pages 15–25, Wien, Austria. Association for Computational Linguistics.

Piotr Rybak. 2024. Transferring BERT capabilities from high-resource to low-resource languages using vocabulary matching. In *Proceedings of the 2024 Joint International Conference on Computational Linguistics, Language Resources and Evaluation (LREC-COLING 2024)*, pages 16745–16750, Torino, Italia. ELRA and ICCL.

Bahar Salehi, Dirk Hovy, Eduard Hovy, and Anders Søgaard. 2017. Huntsville, hospitals, and hockey teams: Names can reveal your location. In *Proceedings of the 3rd Workshop on Noisy User-generated Text*, pages 116–121, Copenhagen, Denmark. Association for Computational Linguistics.

Anders Søgaard. 2022. Should we ban English NLP for a year? In *Proceedings of the 2022 Conference on Empirical Methods in Natural Language Processing*, pages 5254–5260, Abu Dhabi, United Arab Emirates. Association for Computational Linguistics.

Nishant Subramani, Sasha Luccioni, Jesse Dodge, and Margaret Mitchell. 2023. Detecting personal information in training corpora: an analysis. In *Proceedings of the 3rd Workshop on Trustworthy Natural Language Processing (TrustNLP 2023)*, pages 208–220, Toronto, Canada. Association for Computational Linguistics.

Maria Irena Szawerna, Simon Dobnik, Therese Lindström Tiedemann, Ricardo Muñoz Sánchez, Xuan-Son Vu, and Elena Volodina. 2024. Pseudonymization categories across domain boundaries. In *Proceedings of the 2024 Joint International Conference on Computational Linguistics, Language Resources and Evaluation (LREC-COLING 2024)*, pages 13303–13314, Torino, Italia. ELRA and ICCL.

Margaret Thomas. 2010. Names, epithets, and pseudonyms in linguistic case studies: A historical overview. *Names: A Journal of Onomastics*, 58(1):13–23.

Sunna Torge, Andrei Politov, Christoph Lehmann, Bochra Saffar, and Ziyan Tao. 2023. Named entity recognition for low-resource languages - profiting from language families. In *Proceedings of the 9th Workshop on Slavic Natural Language Processing 2023 (SlavicNLP 2023)*, pages 1–10, Dubrovnik, Croatia. Association for Computational Linguistics.

Sixuan Wang, Junjun Muhamad Ramdani, Shuting (Alice) Sun, Priyanka Bose, and Xuesong (Andy) Gao. 2024. Naming research participants in qualitative language learning research: Numbers, pseudonyms, or real names? *Journal of Language, Identity & Education*, pages 1–14.

Jianliang Yang, Xiya Zhang, Kai Liang, and Yuenan Liu. 2023. Exploring the application of large language models in detecting and protecting personally identifiable information in archival data: A comprehensive study*. In *2023 IEEE International Conference on Big Data (BigData)*, pages 2116–2123.

Lisa Yankovskaya, Maali Tars, Andre Tättar, and Mark Fishel. 2023. Machine translation for low-resource Finno-Ugric languages. In *Proceedings of the 24th Nordic Conference on Computational Linguistics (NoDaLiDa)*, pages 762–771, Tórshavn, Faroe Islands. University of Tartu Library.

Daniel Zeman, Joakim Nivre, Mitchell Abrams, Elia Ackermann, Noëmi Aepli, Hamid Aghaei, Željko Agić, Amir Ahmadi, Lars Ahrenberg, Chika Kennedy Ajede, Arofat Akhundjanova, Furkan Akkurt, Gabrielė Aleksandravičiūtė, Ika Alfina, Avner Algom, Khalid Alnajjar, Chiara Alzetta, Erik Andersen, Matthew Andrews, Lene Antonsen, Tatsuya Aoyama, Katya Aplonova, Angelina Aquino, Carolina Aragon, Glyd Aranes, Maria Jesus Aranzabe, Bilge Nas Arıcan, Hórunn Arnardóttir, Gashaw Arutie, Jessica Naraiswari Arwidarasti, Masayuki Asahara, Katla Ásgeirsdóttir, Deniz Baran Aslan, Cengiz Asmazoğlu, Luma Ateyah, Furkan Atmaca, Mohammed Attia, Aitziber Atutxa, Liesbeth Augustinus, Mariana Avelãs, Elena Badmaeva, Keerthana Balasubramani, Miguel Ballesteros, Esha Banerjee, Sebastian Bank, Bryan Khelven da Silva Barbosa, Verginica Barbu Mititelu, Starkaður Barkarson, Rodolfo Basile, Victoria Basmov, Colin Batchelor, John Bauer, Seyyit Talha Bedir, Shabnam Behzad, Juan Belieni, Kepa Bengoetxea, İbrahim Benli, Yifat Ben Moshe, Ansu Berg, Gözde Berk, Riyaz Ahmad Bhat, Erica Biagetti, Eckhard Bick, Agnė Bielinskienė, Esma Fatıma Bilgin Taşdemir, Kristín Bjarnadóttir, Verena Blaschke, Rogier Blokland, Nina Böbel, Victoria Bobicev, Loïc Boizou, Johnatan Bonilla, Emanuel Borges Völker, Carl Börstell, Cristina Bosco, Gosse Bouma, Sam Bowman, Adriane Boyd, Anouck Braggaar, António Branco, Kristina Brokaitė, Aljoscha Burchardt,

Carmen Cabeza, Natalia Cáceres Arandia, Marisa Campos, Marie Candito, Bernard Caron, Gauthier Caron, Catarina Carvalheiro, Rita Carvalho, Lauren Cassidy, Maria Clara Castro, Sérgio Castro, Tatiana Cavalcanti, Gülşen Cebiroğlu Eryiğit, Flavio Massimiliano Cecchini, Giuseppe G. A. Celano, Anila Çepani, Slavomír Čéplö, Neslihan Cesur, Savas Cetin, Özlem Çetinoğlu, Fabricio Chalub, Liyanage Chamila, Claudine Chamoreau, Shweta Chauhan, Yifei Chen, Ethan Chi, Taishi Chika, Yongseok Cho, Jinho Choi, Bermet Chontaeva, Jayeol Chun, Juyeon Chung, Alessandra T. Cignarella, Silvie Cinková, Aurélie Collomb, Çağrı Çöltekin, Miriam Connor, Claudia Corbetta, Daniela Corbetta, Francisco Costa, Marine Courtin, Benoît Crabbé, Mihaela Cristescu, Vladimir Cvetkoski, Netanel Dahan, Ingerid Løyning Dale, Philemon Daniel, Elizabeth Davidson, Leonel Figueiredo de Alencar, Mathieu Dehouck, Martina de Laurentiis, Marie-Catherine de Marneffe, Valeria de Paiva, Mehmet Oguz Derin, Elvis de Souza, Arantza Diaz de Ilarraza, Roberto Antonio Díaz Hernández, Carly Dickerson, Ariani Di Felippo, Arawinda Dinakaramani, Elisa Di Nuovo, Bamba Dione, Peter Dirix, Hoa Do, Kaja Dobrovoljc, Caroline Döhmer, Adrian Doyle, Timothy Dozat, Kira Droganova, Magali Sanches Duran, Puneet Dwivedi, Christian Ebert, Hanne Eckhoff, Masaki Eguchi, Sandra Eiche, Roald Eiselen, Marhaba Eli, Ali Elkahky, Binyam Ephrem, Olga Erina, Tomaž Erjavec, Soudabeh Eslami, Farah Essaidi, Aline Etienne, Wograine Evelyn, Sidney Facundes, Richárd Farkas, Ján Faryad, Federica Favero, Jannatul Ferdaousi, Marília Fernanda, Hector Fernandez Alcalde, Amal Fethi, Jennifer Foster, Theodorus Fransen, Cláudia Freitas, Kazunori Fujita, Katarína Gajdošová, Daniel Galbraith, Edith Galy, Federica Gamba, Marcos Garcia, José María García-Miguel, Moa Gärdenfors, Tanja Gaustad, Efe Eren Genç, Fabrício Ferraz Gerardi, Kim Gerdes, Luke Gessler, Filip Ginter, Gustavo Godoy, Iakes Goenaga, Koldo Gojenola, Memduh Gökırmak, Yoav Goldberg, Gili Goldin, Xavier Gómez Guinovart, Berta González Saavedra, Bernadeta Griciūtė, Matias Grioni, Loïc Grobol, Normunds Grūzītis, Bruno Guillaume, Kirian Guiller, Céline Guillot-Barbance, Tunga Güngör, Vladimir Gurevich, Nizar Habash, Hinrik Hafsteinsson, Jan Hajič, Jan Hajič jr., Mika Hämäläinen, Linh Hà Mỹ, Na-Rae Han, Muhammad Yudistira Hanifmuti, Takahiro Harada, Sam Hardwick, Kim Harris, Naïma Hassert, Dag Haug, Johannes Heinecke, Oliver Hellwig, Felix Hennig, Barbora Hladká, Jaroslava Hlaváčová, Florinel Hociung, Diana Hoefels, Petter Hohle, Nick Howell, Yidi Huang, Marivel Huerta Mendez, Jena Hwang, Takumi Ikeda, Inessa Iliadou, Anton Karl Ingason, Radu Ion, Elena Irimia, Ọlájídé Ishola, Artan Islamaj, Kaoru Ito, Federica Iurescia, Sandra Jagodzińska, Siratun Jannat, Tomáš Jelínek, Apoorva Jha, Katharine Jiang, Mayank Jobanputra, Anders Johannsen, Hildur Jónsdóttir, Fredrik Jørgensen, Markus Juutinen, Hüner Kaşıkara, Nadezhda Kabaeva, Sylvain Kahane, Hiroshi Kanayama, Jenna Kanerva, Neslihan Kara, Ritván Karahóǧa, Andre Kåsen, Tolga Kayadelen, Sarveswaran Kengatharaiyer, Václava Kettnerová, Lilit Kharatyan, Jesse Kirchner, Elena Klementieva, Elena Klyachko, Petr Kocharov, Arne Köhn, Abdullatif Köksal, Kamil Kopacewicz, Timo Korkiakangas, Mehmet Köse, Alexey Koshevoy, Nelda Kote, Natalia Kotsyba, Barbara Kovačić, Jolanta Kovalevskaitė, Emmanuelle Kowner, Simon Krek, Parameswari Krishnamurthy, Sandra Kübler, Adrian Kuqi, Oğuzhan Kuyrukçu, Aslı Kuzgun, Sookyoung Kwak, Kris Kyle, Käbi Laan, Veronika Laippala, Lorenzo Lambertino, Israel Landau, Tatiana Lando, Septina Dian Larasati, Alexei Lavrentiev, John Lee, Phûông Lê Hồng, Alessandro Lenci, Saran Lertpradit, Herman Leung, Maria Levina, Lauren Levine, Cheuk Ying Li, Josie Li, Keying Li, Yixuan Li, Yuan Li, KyungTae Lim, Bruna Lima Padovani, Yi-Ju Jessica Lin, Krister Lindén, Yang Janet Liu, Nikola Ljubešić, Irina Lobzhanidze, Olga Loginova, Lucelene Lopes, Edita Luftiu, Arsenii Lukashevskyi, Stefano Lusito, Anne-Marie Lutgen, Andry Luthfi, Mikko Luukko, Olga Lyashevskaya, Teresa Lynn, Vivien Macketanz, Menel Mahamdi, Jean Maillard, Ilya Makarchuk, Aibek Makazhanov, Francesco Mambrini, Michael Mandl, Christopher Manning, Ruli Manurung, Büşra Marşan, Cătălina Mărănduc, David Mareček, Katrin Marheinecke, Stella Markantonatou, Héctor Martínez Alonso, Lorena Martín Rodríguez, André Martins, Cláudia Martins, Jan Mašek, Hiroshi Matsuda, Yuji Matsumoto, Alessandro Mazzei, Ryan McDonald, Sarah McGuinness, Maitrey Mehta, Pierre André Ménard, Gustavo Mendonça, Hilla Merhav, Tatiana Merzhevich, Paul Meurer, Niko Miekka, Emilia Milano, Aaron Miller, Yael Minerbi, Karina Mischenkova, Anna Missilä, Cătălin Mititelu, Maria Mitrofan, Yusuke Miyao, AmirHossein Mojiri Foroushani, Judit Molnár, Amirsaeid Moloodi, Simonetta Montemagni, Amir More, Laura Moreno Romero, Giovanni Moretti, Shinsuke Mori, Tomohiko Morioka, Shigeki Moro, Bjartur Mortensen, Bohdan Moskalevskyi, Kadri Muischnek, Robert Munro, Yugo Murawaki, Kaili Müürisep, Pinkey Nainwani, Mariam Nakhlé, Juan Ignacio Navarro Horñiacek, Anna Nedoluzhko, Gunta Nešpore-Bērzkalne, Manuela Nevaci, Lûông Nguyễn Thị, Huyền Nguyễn Thị Minh, Yoshihiro Nikaido, Vitaly Nikolaev, Rattima Nitisaroj, Victor Norrman, Alireza Nourian, Maria das Graças Volpe Nunes, Hanna Nurmi, Stina Ojala, Atul Kr. Ojha, Hulda Óladóttir, Adédayọ̀ Olúòkun, Mai Omura, Emeka Onwuegbuzia, Noam Ordan, Petya Osenova, Robert Östling, Annika Ott, Lilja Øvrelid, Şaziye Betül Özateş, Merve Özçelik, Arzucan Özgür, Balkız Öztürk Başaran, Teresa Paccosi, Alessio Palmero Aprosio, Anastasia Panova, Thiago Alexandre Salgueiro Pardo, Hyunji Hayley Park, Niko Partanen, Elena Pascual, Marco Passarotti, Agnieszka Patejuk, Guilherme Paulino-Passos, Giulia Pedonese, Oggi Peeters, Angelika Peljak-Łapińska, Siyao Peng, Siyao Logan Peng, Rita Pereira, Sílvia Pereira, Cenel-Augusto Perez, Natalia Perkova, Guy Perrier, Slav Petrov, Daria

Petrova, Andrea Peverelli, Jason Phelan, Claudel Pierre-Louis, Jussi Piitulainen, Yuval Pinter, Clara Pinto, Rodrigo Pintucci, Tommi A Pirinen, Emily Pitler, Magdalena Plamada, Barbara Plank, Alistair Plum, Thierry Poibeau, Larisa Ponomareva, Martin Popel, Lauma Pretkalniņa, Rigardt Pretorius, Sophie Prévost, Prokopis Prokopidis, Adam Przepiórkowski, Robert Pugh, Tiina Puolakainen, Christoph Purschke, Sampo Pyysalo, Peng Qi, Andreia Querido, Andriela Rääbis, Ella Rabinovich, Alexandre Rademaker, Mizanur Rahoman, Taraka Rama, Loganathan Ramasamy, Carlos Ramisch, Joana Ramos, Fam Rashel, Mohammad Sadegh Rasooli, Vinit Ravishankar, Livy Real, Petru Rebeja, Siva Reddy, Mathilde Regnault, Georg Rehm, Arij Riabi, Ivan Riabov, Michael Rießler, Erika Rimkutė, Larissa Rinaldi, Laura Rituma, Putri Rizqiyah, Luisa Rocha, Eiríkur Rögnvaldsson, Ivan Roksandic, Norton Trevisan Roman, Mykhailo Romanenko, Rudolf Rosa, Valentin Roșca, Paulette Roulon, Davide Rovati, Ben Rozonoyer, Olga Rudina, Jack Rueter, Paolo Ruffolo, Kristján Rúnarsson, Rozana Rushiti, Shoval Sadde, Pegah Safari, Aleksi Sahala, Shadi Saleh, Alessio Salomoni, Tanja Samardžić, Konstantinos Sampanis, Stephanie Samson, Xulia Sánchez-Rodríguez, Manuela Sanguinetti, Ezgi Sanıyar, Dage Särg, Marta Sartor, Albina Sarymsakova, Mitsuya Sasaki, Baiba Saulīte, Agata Savary, Yanin Sawanakunanon, Shefali Saxena, Kevin Scannell, Salvatore Scarlata, Emmanuel Schang, Nathan Schneider, Sebastian Schuster, Lane Schwartz, Djamé Seddah, Wolfgang Seeker, Sven Sellmer, Mojgan Seraji, Syeda Shahzadi, Mo Shen, Atsuko Shimada, Gyu-Ho Shin, Hiroyuki Shirasu, Yana Shishkina, Muh Shohibussirri, Maria Shvedova, Janine Siewert, Einar Freyr Sigurðsson, João Silva, Aline Silveira, Natalia Silveira, Sara Silveira, Maria Simi, Radu Simionescu, Katalin Simkó, Mária Šimková, Haukur Barri Símonarson, Kiril Simov, Dmitri Sitchinava, Ted Sither, Aaron Smith, Isabela Soares-Bastos, Per Erik Solberg, Barbara Sonnenhauser, Shafi Sourov, Rachele Sprugnoli, Vivian Stamou, Steinhór Steingrímsson, Antonio Stella, Abishek Stephen, Milan Straka, Omer Strass, Emmett Strickland, Jana Strnadová, Alane Suhr, Yogi Lesmana Sulestio, Umut Sulubacak, Hakyung Sung, Shingo Suzuki, Daniel Swanson, Zsolt Szántó, Chihiro Taguchi, Dima Taji, Luigi Talamo, Fabio Tamburini, Mary Ann C. Tan, Takaaki Tanaka, Dipta Tanaya, Mirko Tavoni, Samson Tella, Isabelle Tellier, Marinella Testori, Guillaume Thomas, Tarık Emre Tıraş, Sara Tonelli, Liisi Torga, Marsida Toska, Trond Trosterud, Anna Trukhina, Reut Tsarfaty, Utku Türk, Francis Tyers, Sveinbjörn Hórðarson, Vilhjálmur Horsteinsson, Sumire Uematsu, Roman Untilov, Zdeňka Urešová, Larraitz Uria, Hans Uszkoreit, Andrius Utka, Elena Vagnoni, Sowmya Vajjala, Socrates Vak, Rob van der Goot, Martine Vanhove, Daniel van Niekerk, Gertjan van Noord, Viktor Varga, Uliana Vedenina, Giulia Venturi, Eric Villemonte de la Clergerie, Veronika Vincze, Anishka Vissamsetty, Natalia Vlasova, Eleni Vligouridou, Aya Wakasa, Joel C. Wallenberg, Lars Wallin, Abigail Walsh, John Wang, Jonathan North Washington, Leonie Weissweiler, Maximilan Wendt, Paul Widmer, Shira Wigderson, Sri Hartati Wijono, Vanessa Berwanger Wille, Seyi Williams, Miriam Winkler, Shuly Wintner, Mats Wirén, Christian Wittern, Tsegay Woldemariam, Tak-sum Wong, Alina Wróblewska, Qishen Wu, Mary Yako, Kayo Yamashita, Naoki Yamazaki, Chunxiao Yan, Koichi Yasuoka, Marat M. Yavrumyan, Arife Betül Yenice, Enes Yılandiloğlu, Olcay Taner Yıldız, Zhuoran Yu, Arlisa Yuliawati, Zdeněk Žabokrtský, Shorouq Zahra, Amir Zeldes, He Zhou, Hanzhi Zhu, Yilun Zhu, Anna Zhuravleva, Rayan Ziane, and Artūrs Znotiņš. 2024. Universal dependencies 2.15. LINDAT/CLARIAH-CZ digital library at the Institute of Formal and Applied Linguistics (ÚFAL), Faculty of Mathematics and Physics, Charles University.

A Appendix: Prompt templates and examples from the parallel dataset

Here we show examples of sentences from our dataset, as well as the prompts 1 through 6, as defined in section 2 and Table 1.

(3) **Ko.**: Митяяслöн керкаыс бокынджык грездса мукöд керкаясысь , но зэв гажа местаын , неуна кыр горув лэччыштан — Эжва визувтö .
Pol.: Dom Mitji jest oddalony od reszty domów w wiosce , ale w bardzo miłym miejscu , dołem stromego zbocza płynie Eżwa .
Eng.: Mitya's house is remote from other houses in the village, but in a very pleasant place, slightly down a steep slope - the Ezhva flows.

(4) **Ko.**: — Эн тэрмасьöй , Аннаыд ачыс бöръяс , кодi колö , — дорйис пöдругасö Зоя .
Pol.: - Nie pospieszaj , Anna sama zdecyduje kto jest potrzebny - Zoja wsparła swoją przyjaciółkę .
Eng.: "Don't rush, Anna will choose who is needed herself," Zoya supported her friend.

System: You are a multilingual personal information detection tool. Personal information is information that can lead to someone in the text being reidentified, like their name, surname, middle name, patronymic, nickname, where they live, address, city, country, zip code, where they work, study, or spend a lot of their time, what unique lines or modes of transport they travel with, their age, any dates mentioned in the text, phone numbers, personal identity numbers, bank account numbers, other number sequences, e-mail addresses, urls, their work titles, education, types of family relations, information about faith, political beliefs, sexuality, ethnicity, unique achievements, etc.

User: For each token in the given text, determine whether it is a piece of personal information. Return the text with "PI" replacing every instance of personal information.

Example:
Text: I'm from Slovakia , but one of my best friends , Marie , is from Norway .
Result: I'm from PI , but one of my best friends , PI , is from PI.

Text: [PLACEHOLDER]
Result:

Figure 2: Prompt 1, [PLACEHOLDER] is replaced with an actual text.

System: You are a multilingual personal information detection tool. Personal information is information that can lead to someone in the text being reidentified, like their name, surname, middle name, patronymic, nickname, where they live, address, city, country, zip code, where they work, study, or spend a lot of their time, what unique lines or modes of transport they travel with, their age, any dates mentioned in the text, phone numbers, personal identity numbers, bank account numbers, other number sequences, e-mail addresses, urls, their work titles, education, types of family relations, information about faith, political beliefs, sexuality, ethnicity, unique achievements, etc.

User: For each token in the given text, determine whether it is a piece of personal information. Return the results in a JSON format.

Example:
Text: I'm from Slovakia , but one of my best friends , Marie , is from Norway .
Result:

```
{
  "1":{"I'm":""},
  "2":{"from":""},
  "3":{"Slovakia":"PI"},
  "4":{",":""},
  "5":{"but":""},
  "6":{"one":""},
  "7":{"of":""},
  "8":{"my":""},
  "9":{"best":""},
  "10":{"friends":""},
  "11":{",":""},
  "12":{"Marie":"PI"},
  "13":{",":""},
  "14":{"is":""},
  "15":{"from":""},
  "16":{"Norway":"PI"},
  "17":{".":""}
}
```

Text: [PLACEHOLDER]
Result:

Figure 3: One of the prompt templates used in this study. When fed to a model, [PLACEHOLDER] is replaced with an actual text.

System: You are a multilingual personal information detection tool. Personal information is information that can lead to someone in the text being reidentified, classified according to the following pattern:
<firstname_female> — women's given names
<firstname_male> — men's given names
<firstname_unknown> — given name that does not have an obvious binary gender
<surname_female> — women's surnames
<surname_male> — women's surnames
<surname_unknown> — women's surnames
<patronymic_female> — a woman's patronymic
<patronymic_male> — a man's patronymic
<street> — street names, names of squares, avenues, etc.
<city> — cities, villages, towns
<region> — regions smaller than a country
<country> — countries
<geo> — other geographical elements, such as mountains, lakes, rivers
<age> — age in digits or words

User: For each token in the given text, determine whether it is a piece of personal information. Return the text with an appropriate tag replacing every instance of personal information.

Example:
Text: I'm from Slovakia , but one of my best friends , Marie , is from Norway .
Result: I'm from <country> , but one of my best friends , <firstname_female> , is from <country>.

Text: [PLACEHOLDER]
Result:

Figure 4: Prompt 3, [PLACEHOLDER] is replaced with an actual text.

System: You are a multilingual personal information detection tool. Personal information is information that can lead to someone in the text being reidentified, classified according to the following pattern:
<firstname_female> — women's given names
<firstname_male> — men's given names
<firstname_unknown> — given name that does not have an obvious binary gender
<surname_female> — women's surnames
<surname_male> — women's surnames
<surname_unknown> — women's surnames
<patronymic_female> — a woman's patronymic
<patronymic_male> — a man's patronymic
<street> — street names, names of squares, avenues, etc.
<city> — cities, villages, towns
<region> — regions smaller than a country
<country> — countries
<geo> — other geographical elements, such as mountains, lakes, rivers
<age> — age in digits or words

User: For each token in the given text, determine whether it is a piece of personal information and assign the appropriate tag. Return the results in a JSON format.

Example:
Text: I'm from Slovakia , but one of my best friends , Marie , is from Norway .
Result:

```
{
    "1":{"I'm":""},
    "2":{"from":""},
    "3":{"Slovakia":"<country>"},
    "4":{",":""},
    "5":{"but":""},
    "6":{"one":""},
    "7":{"of":""},
    "8":{"my":""},
    "9":{"best":""},
    "10":{"friends":""},
    "11":{",":""},
    "12":{"Marie":"<firstname_female>"},
    "13":{",":""},
    "14":{"is":""},
    "15":{"from":""},
    "16":{"Norway":"<country>"},
    "17":{".":""}
}
```

Text: [PLACEHOLDER]
Result:

Figure 5: Prompt 4, [PLACEHOLDER] is replaced with an actual text.

System: You are a multilingual personal information detection tool. Personal information is information that can lead to someone in the text being reidentified, classified according to the following pattern:
<birth> — characteristics true of a person at birth, most of which are difficult or impossible to change, such as nationality, gender, caste, etc.
<society> — include characteristics that commonly develop throughout a person's life and are defined in many countries as a specially designated "status", such as immunization status.
<social> — categories corresponding to social groups such as teams or affiliations – e.g. member of the women's softball team, student of Carnegie Mellon University.
<character> — sequences of letters and numbers that can often uniquely identify a person or a small group of people; they change relatively infrequently and can therefore persist as sources of identification for years or decades – e.g. a name, surname, social security number, credit card number, IBAN, or e-mail address.
<records> — information typically consists of a persistent document or electronic analog that is not generally-available, but can allow for the (reasonable) identification of an individual – e.g. financial or health records.
<situation> — uniquely identify an individual, but that is restricted to a given context or point in time – e.g. date, time, GPS location, place of residence.

User: For each token in the given text, determine whether it is a piece of personal information. Return the text with an appropriate tag replacing every instance of personal information.

Example:
Text: I'm from Slovakia , but one of my best friends , Marie , is from Norway .
Result: I'm from <birth> , but one of my best friends , <character> , is from <birth>.

Text: [PLACEHOLDER]
Result:

Figure 6: Prompt 5, [PLACEHOLDER] is replaced with an actual text.

System: You are a multilingual personal information detection tool. Personal information is information that can lead to someone in the text being reidentified, classified according to the following pattern:
<birth> — characteristics true of a person at birth, most of which are difficult or impossible to change, such as nationality, gender, caste, etc.
<society> — include characteristics that commonly develop throughout a person's life and are defined in many countries as a specially designated "status", such as immunization status.
<social> — categories corresponding to social groups such as teams or affiliations – e.g. member of the women's softball team, student of Carnegie Mellon University.
<character> — sequences of letters and numbers that can often uniquely identify a person or a small group of people; they change relatively infrequently and can therefore persist as sources of identification for years or decades – e.g. a name, surname, social security number, credit card number, IBAN, or e-mail address.
<records> — information typically consists of a persistent document or electronic analog that is not generally-available, but can allow for the (reasonable) identification of an individual – e.g. financial or health records.
<situation> — uniquely identify an individual, but that is restricted to a given context or point in time – e.g. date, time, GPS location, place of residence.

User: For each token in the given text, determine whether it is a piece of personal information and assign the appropriate tag. Return the results in a JSON format.

Example:
Text: I'm from Slovakia , but one of my best friends , Marie , is from Norway .
Result:

```
{
    "1":{"I'm":""},
    "2":{"from":""},
    "3":{"Slovakia":"<birth>"},
    "4":{",":""},
    "5":{"but":""},
    "6":{"one":""},
    "7":{"of":""},
    "8":{"my":""},
    "9":{"best":""},
    "10":{"friends":""},
    "11":{",":""},
    "12":{"Marie":"<character>"},
    "13":{",":""},
    "14":{"is":""},
    "15":{"from":""},
    "16":{"Norway":"<birth>"},
    "17":{".":""}
}
```

Text: [PLACEHOLDER]
Result:

Figure 7: One of the prompt templates used in this study. When fed to a model, [PLACEHOLDER] is replaced with an actual text.

Multi-label Scandinavian Language Identification (SLIDE)

Mariia Fedorova*, **Jonas Sebulon Frydenberg***, **Victoria Handford***,
Victoria Ovedie Chruickshank Langø*, **Solveig Helene Willoch**, **Marthe Løken Midtgaard**,
Yves Scherrer, **Petter Mæhlum**, **David Samuel**

Department of Informatics, University of Oslo

{mariiaf,jonassf,vlhandfo,victocla,solvehw,marthemi,
yvessc,pettemae,davisamu}@ifi.uio.no

Abstract

Identifying closely related languages at sentence level is difficult, in particular because it is often impossible to assign a sentence to a single language. In this paper, we focus on multi-label sentence-level Scandinavian language identification (LID) for Danish, Norwegian Bokmål, Norwegian Nynorsk, and Swedish.[1] We present the Scandinavian Language Identification and Evaluation, SLIDE, a manually curated multi-label evaluation dataset and a suite of LID models with varying speed–accuracy trade-offs. We demonstrate that the ability to identify multiple languages simultaneously is necessary for any accurate LID method, and present a novel approach to training such multi-label LID models.

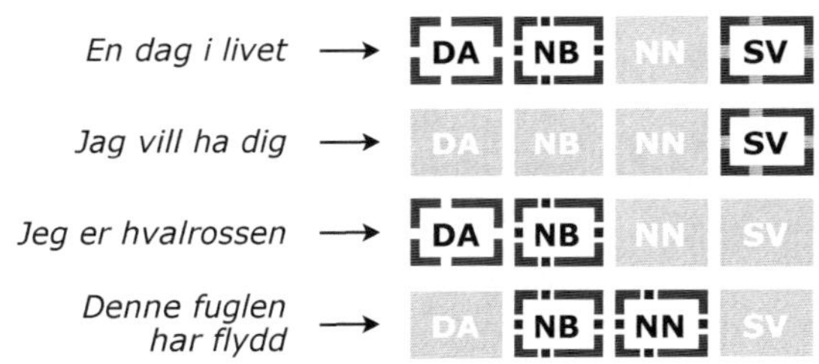

Figure 1: **Scandinavian similarity** Accurate language identification has to necessarily be multi-label when discriminating between closely related languages.

1 Introduction

Correctly identifying the language of a short piece of text might seem like a simple (and possibly already solved) task. While differentiating between two distant languages might be straightforward, we show that, when focusing on a group of closely related languages, this task becomes substantially more challenging. This is especially true when we consider the fact that language identification (LID) tools have to be fast and efficient, as they are often used for preprocessing large quantities of texts.

In this paper, we focus on the four closely related Scandinavian languages: Danish, Norwegian Bokmål, Norwegian Nynorsk, and Swedish. In order to accurately differentiate within this group, we move away from the standard single-label (multi-class) language identification and instead treat this problem as multi-label classification task, allowing for the identification of multiple languages simultaneously as illustrated in Figure 1. Sentences valid in multiple Scandinavian languages are fairly common—they account for about 5% of our evaluation dataset and 16% of the sentences shorter than 6 words. If not accounted for, these examples can skew evaluation of existing systems. The three main contributions of SLIDE (Scandinavian Language Identification and Evaluation), are as follows:

1. **A multi-label evaluation dataset** We have created a manually corrected multi-label LID dataset for four Scandinavian languages. We present two evaluation methods using this dataset: one designed for a more accurate evaluation of traditional multi-class LID methods, and a second for assessing the performance of multi-label methods.

2. **A suite of LID models** We train a family of language identification models of varying complexities. The best performing models are

*Equal contribution.

[1]While acknowledging that the term *Scandinavian* in English sometimes also includes Icelandic and Faroese, we use the term Scandinavian in the sense of *Mainland Scandinavian*, in accordance with established and legal usage of the term in these languages. We also consider Swedish as a single language, overlooking the nuances between Finland-Swedish and Sweden-Swedish.

Proceedings of the Third Workshop on Resources and Representations for Under-Resourced Languages and Domains (RESOURCEFUL-2025), pages 179–189, March 2, 2025 ©2025 Association for Computational Linguistics

based on fine-tuned BERT models and smaller, substantially faster models based on FastText embeddings. The source code, datasets and models are released at `https://github.com/ltgoslo/slide`.

3. **A novel multi-label LID method** Manual creation of a clean multi-label LID dataset is costly. Instead, we present a novel method of silver-labeling such a dataset by utilizing existing machine translation models.

2 Related work

Language identification The task of identifying the language of a text is an "old" NLP task dating back to the 1960s. Simple but relatively powerful tools have been available since the 1990s (Jauhiainen et al., 2019).

In recent years, the main focus of NLP research has shifted towards large language models, and especially towards extending their coverage to an increasing number of languages. As training data for underrepresented languages is mostly found in web crawls, reliable LID systems covering a large number of languages are more important than ever. While the earliest LID systems were restricted to a dozen languages, recent systems cover hundreds (Joulin et al., 2017; Grave et al., 2018; Burchell et al., 2023; Jauhiainen et al., 2022a) and even thousands (Kargaran et al., 2023) of languages.

In terms of methods, simple linear classifiers with character-level and word-level features have often outperformed more sophisticated neural models (Jauhiainen et al., 2019). Most currently available large-coverage LID models are based on the FastText architecture (Joulin et al., 2017), a multinomial logistic regression classifier with character n-gram embeddings as input features. These include FastText-176 (Joulin et al., 2017; Grave et al., 2018), NLLB-218 (NLLB Team et al., 2022), OpenLID (Burchell et al., 2023) and GlotLID (Kargaran et al., 2023). Different approaches are used by HeLI-OTS (Jauhiainen et al., 2022b), which bases its decisions on a combination of character n-gram and word unigram language models, and `gpt2-lang-ident`[2], which is a fine-tuned decoder-only model (Radford et al., 2019).

In practice, LID is most often applied to individual sentences, even though the tools can work with longer or shorter segments of text.

[2] `https://huggingface.co/nie3e/gpt2-lang-ident`

LID for closely related and Nordic languages To our knowledge, the only publication focusing specifically on LID for Nordic languages is Haas and Derczynski (2021). They compile a dataset for the six languages (including both Norwegian standards) from Wikipedia and evaluate a range of LID models on it. They find that the languages mostly cluster into three groups: Danish–Bokmål–Nynorsk, Swedish, and Icelandic–Faroese. Their models were not available online as of writing this paper. Besides this, de la Rosa and Kummervold (2022) present two FastText-based LID models: one containing only the 12 most common languages of the Nordic countries (including several Sámi languages, Finnish, and English), and one with an extended coverage of 159 languages.

Futhermore, the previously mentioned off-the-shelf LID systems (NLLB-218, OpenLID, GlotLID, HeLI-OTS) cover all six Nordic languages, with the exception of FastText-176, which does not include Faroese.

Multi-label language identification Most existing LID training and evaluation corpora are not manually labeled. Instead, they are based on the assumption that the language is determined by the source it is retrieved from. If a sentence is retrieved from a Danish newspaper, it is assumed to be only Danish. But when dealing with closely related languages, it is often the case that an instance cannot be unambiguously assigned to a single language (Goutte et al., 2016; Keleg and Magdy, 2023).

Recent proposals address this issue by framing LID between similar languages as a multi-label task (e.g., Chifu et al., 2024; Abdul-Mageed et al., 2024) and by manually annotating the evaluation data (e.g., Zampieri et al., 2024; Miletić and Miletić, 2024). However, these works do not include studies of Scandinavian languages.

3 Data

One of the main contributions of this paper is the release of manually and automatically annotated multi-label datasets. In Section 3.1, we introduce the sources from which we compile our datasets. We then present our manually annotated multi-label evaluation dataset (Section 3.2). Next, we describe a way to obtain multi-label annotations automatically for the larger training set in Section 3.3. Lastly, we outline different approaches to data augmentation in Section 3.4.

3.1 Data sources

As a starting point, we use the Universal Dependencies 2.14 treebanks (UD; Nivre et al., 2016, 2020), keeping their train/dev/test splits intact.[3] For each of the four languages, we associate each sentence in the treebank with the language tag corresponding to that treebank's language. This results in a foundational single-label dataset with the following language tags: Danish (DA), Norwegian Bokmål (NB), Norwegian Nynorsk (NN), and Swedish (SV). We further incorporate examples labeled as `other`, drawing random samples from other UD treebanks to represent other languages.

As the UD treebanks are manually annotated, we assume that the texts accurately reflect their corresponding languages. Additionally, the treebanks cover multiple genres, improving the robustness of the models to different text varieties. However, while the resulting dataset is clean, it is not disambiguated. For example, a sentence labeled as Nynorsk is almost guaranteed to be in Nynorsk, but it could also be a valid Bokmål sentence.

3.2 SLIDE dataset: manually multi-labeled evaluation data

Manual inspection To identify multi-label instances in the validation and test splits, we performed a combination of automatic filtering and manual annotation. Automatic filtration was done by removing frequent words that unambiguously define a language (e.g. 'ikkje' is only valid in Nynorsk; the full list is to be found in our Github repository).

After filtering, we split the remaining instances among a group of annotators to manually check for cases of multilingual acceptability. All annotators were native or near-native Norwegian speakers. Annotation tasks were delegated depending on the speakers' knowledge and exposure to Swedish and Danish (all native speakers have received education in or about other Scandinavian languages through the public curriculum or university classes).

Unclear instances Most cases of multilingual acceptability involved short sentences with proper names, numbers, or words that are acceptable in multiple Scandinavian languages. Instances consisting of only proper names were annotated with all Scandinavian languages, even if more common in one language than another. Numerical values were treated similarly as they are universally acceptable across the languages.

[3] Specifically, we use the following UD treebanks: `no_bokmaal`, `da_ddt`, `no_nynorsk`, and `sv_talbanken`.

Language	Train split	Validation split	Test split
Bokmål	23 120	2 543	2 098
Danish	5 977	563	677
Nynorsk	21 587	2 031	1 628
Swedish	6 911	553	1 250
Other	8 360	1 124	1 745
Total	61 406	6 433	6 950

Table 1: **Dataset sizes** Number of sentences per language. Multi-label samples are reported once for each language, while the summary row shows total number of unique sentences.

Non-Scandinavian instances Sentences from other languages that are not valid in the Scandinavian languages retain the `other` label, and we set restrictions on when this label is used. This distinction is crucial as it ensures that the `other` label exclusively identifies non-Scandinavian sentences, setting it apart from the potential multi-label nature of the remaining labels. For example, this instance from the Danish treebank, "- Gerne.", is labeled as only Danish, despite it also being acceptable in German. This approach allows us to evaluate a model's ability to handle ambiguity and focus on the sentences that could belong to multiple Scandinavian languages, without having to consider all possible languages.

Punctuation errors We found several sentences that were orthographically identical in Danish and Bokmål, where commas were the sole distinguishing factor. When a subordinate clause occurs in the first position of a sentence, both languages include a comma at the end of the clause. However, if the subordinate clause does not occur in the first position, Danish can include a comma before that clause[4], whereas Norwegian cannot[5]. The optional comma, in this case, means that Danish can follow the same punctuation rules as Norwegian but does not have to, making differentiation difficult.

Such a sentence is shown in example (1) from the Danish treebank. The words in this sentence are

[4] https://ro.dsn.dk/?type=rulesearch&side=49

[5] https://sprakradet.no/godt-og-korrekt-sprak/rettskriving-og-grammatikk/kommaregler/

written the same in Danish and Bokmål however, the comma introducing the subordinate clause *at hun skulle havne på et teater* is technically not allowed in Norwegian.

(1) Der stod ingen steder i Mai Buchs eksamenspapirer, at hun skulle havne på et teater.
It said nowhere in Mai Buch's exam papers that she would end up in a theater.

We decided to annotate such sentences as both Danish and Bokmål, thereby focusing on lexical information rather than punctuation. This is due to Norwegians' challenges with following comma rules in general (Michalsen, 2015, pp. 37-39), perhaps due to Norwegian earlier having Danish comma rules (Papazian, 2013). We also find 29444 examples of a comma preceding *at* 'that' in the Norwegian LBK corpus, keeping in mind that some of these might be examples of other usage (Fjeld et al., 2020).

Code switching There were also sentences in the dataset that included more than one language. One such example is:

(2) Låten heter "The spirit carries on."
The song is called "The spirit carries on."

For these sentences that include non-Scandinavian words, we annotated them for the Scandinavian languages only. In cases where a sentence had words from different Scandinavian languages, e.g. a Nynorsk quote in a Bokmål sentence, we made small changes to make the sentence monolingual.[6]

Number of multi-label instances The statistics of the validation and test sets are shown in Table 1. The resulting shares of multi-label instances in the validation and test sets are 6% and 5% respectively.

3.3 Automatically multi-labeled training data

As there is no available multi-labeled training dataset for any subset of the Scandinavian languages, and manually annotating a large-enough dataset would be out-of-scope for this project, we decided to silver-label the UD training split automatically. To do so, we converted the task of machine translation into the task of language identification. This conversion then allows us to utilize existing high-quality resources for multi-label language identification.

[6]There were few instances of this, however, it is important to mention that there is not a complete 1-to-1 correlation between the source material and our dataset.

Alterations	Loose accuracy	Exact-match accuracy
Augmentation + Regex	98.6	**96.4**
Augmentation	98.4	96.3
Regex	98.4	96.2
NER	**98.7**	95.5
Base	98.3	96.2

Table 2: **Ablation study** Impact of data augmentation and regular expression normalization on SLIDE-base measured by test set performance. "Augmentation" refers to punctuation augmentation, "Regex" refers to regular expression normalization, "NER" refers to named entity swaps and "Base" is neither of the above.

Machine translation conversion The method relies on our observation that machine translation models tend to stay conservative and minimize the changes between the source and target texts. Thus, if the translation of a sentence does not lead to any changes, we label it as a valid sentence of the target language. This means that the machine translation model can only add additional language labels to a sentence as a result; we do not use the translated sentences in any other way.

Specifically, we use `NorMistral-11b` to perform the translation (Samuel et al., 2024). While this large language model is able to translate in a zero-shot manner, we increase its reliability by fine-tuning it on the small high-quality Tatoeba evaluation set (Tiedemann, 2020) in all translation directions between Bokmål, Danish, Nynorsk and Swedish.

3.4 Data augmentation

Punctuation augmentation To prevent our models from relying too much on punctuation, we augment the training data with random punctuation. This is especially important for disassociating punctuation from the `other` tag, for which the training data exhibits punctuation noise to a higher degree than the Scandinavian language examples. We randomly add either (i) a period, an exclamation point, or a question mark to the end of the sentence or (ii) a hyphen, dash or comma at the beginning of the sentence. Additionally, there is a $1/3$ chance of including an intervening space. This augmentation scheme is chosen to try to mimic punctuation variance that is present in sentence-level (parallel) corpora.

This method is only applied to instances not labeled as `other` and is performed on about 7.5% of the training data. This value is heuristically chosen.

Regular expression normalization We normalize URLs, email addresses, and numbers into the following special symbols: ⟨URL⟩, ⟨mail⟩ and ⟨num⟩. These elements are not informative for language identification, and we do not want a model to associate them with a certain language.

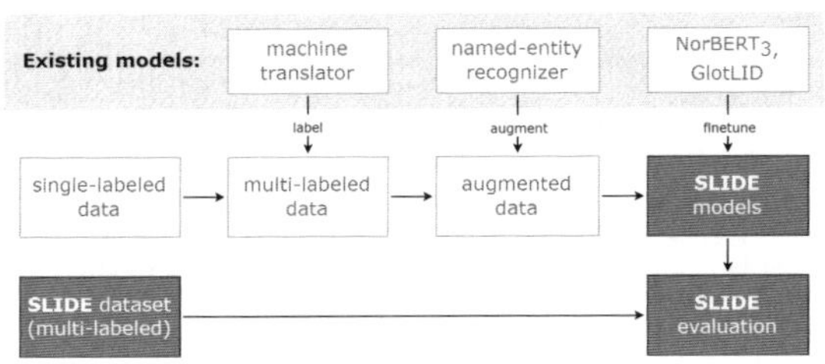

Figure 2: **Training pipeline** A diagram that illustrates the flow of the full training pipeline. We start with a high-quality, single-labeled training dataset, then extend it with multi-label annotations using a strong machine translation model. The dataset is further augmented by randomly swapping named entities identified by existing NER models and through other rule-based augmentations. We use the (augmented) data to fine-tune strong tranformer-based models from a family of NorBERT_3 models (Samuel et al., 2023), a fast model from the GlotLID static word embeddings. Finally, the manually-annotated multi-label dataset is used to evaluate the resulting models.

Alphabet variations The alphabet of the four Scandinavian languages differs by the usage of the letters *ä, ö* (in Swedish) and *æ, ø* (in Danish and Norwegian). To ensure that the model does not learn to associate the presence of these letters solely with their corresponding languages, we augment the training data by adding Swedish sentences containing the Danish–Norwegian letters and Danish and Norwegian sentences containing the Swedish letters (e.g., in proper names and in the context of quotations).

We use the NPK parallel corpus[7] containing translations of news texts from Bokmål to Nynorsk to extract texts containing *ä* and *ö*. For Swedish, we use the EU Bookshop corpus (Skadiņš et al., 2014) to extract Swedish sentences containing *æ* and *ø*. Together, this yielded 10,262 sentences, which are included in Table 1.

Named entity swaps We also want to prevent a model from associating named entities with a given language. Although named entities are unequally distributed across languages, they are not necessarily language-dependent. We perform named-entity recognition (NER) on the training data using the spaCy[8] to identify and extract persons, organizations, locations, and miscellaneous entities. We randomly swap the recognized entities with other entities from the same category to try to break up any connection between entity name and a given language.

4 SLIDE evaluation

We introduce two evaluation metrics in our comparison: *loose* and *exact-match* accuracy.

Loose accuracy This evaluation metric is designed for models that output only one language label per input, which is common for off-the-shelf classifiers like FastText and NLLB. According to this metric, a prediction is considered correct if the single predicted label is among the gold labels. This metric is unreliable for multi-label models, since a model that always predicts all four languages would get 100%.

Exact-match accuracy This evaluation metric is more strict and requires an exact match between the predicted and gold labels sets, making it more appropriate for models capable of predicting multiple labels.

Per-language scores Additionally, we report the F_1-score for each individual language to measure the quality of classifications for each of the four languages separately. Here, a true positive prediction happens if and only if the respective language is present both in the set of predicted labels and in the set of gold labels.

5 SLIDE training methodology

In this section, we present our approach to training the SLIDE models. We explore two main direc-

[7]`https://www.nb.no/sprakbanken/en/resource-catalogue/oai-nb-no-sbr-80/`

[8]`https://spacy.io/` pipeline. We use the large language-specific models, where the Norwegian model is used for Bokmål and Nynorsk.

tions: transformer-based models that achieve high accuracy but require more computational resources, and a fast model based on static word embeddings that trades accuracy for faster inference times.

5.1 Transformer models (SLIDE x-small, small and base)

Fine-tuned masked language models are nowadays the most popular sequence classification solution for problems that require accurate solutions and reasonable inference time (Devlin et al., 2019).

Selection of BERT family We assessed massively multilingual, Scandinavian, and Norwegian BERT-like models with comparable number of parameters in order to choose a model to focus on for further optimizations.

We test two massively multilingual models: *XLM-RoBERTa-base* (Conneau et al., 2020), which is trained on a corpus containing 100 languages (including the Scandinavian languages) and has a total of 278M parameters, as well as *DistilBERT-multilingual-base* (Sanh et al., 2019), which is a distilled version of the multilingual BERT base model trained on Wikipedia data from 104 languages (including all the Scandinavian languages) with 135M parameters. The Scandinavian model we use is called *ScandiBERT* (Snæbjarnarson et al., 2023); it is a BERT-like model with 125M parameters trained on Icelandic, Danish, Norwegian, Swedish and Faroese data. Finally, *NorBERT$_3$-base* (Samuel et al., 2023) is a masked language model trained mostly on Norwegian data.

Preliminary experiments showed that the NorBERT$_3$ models performed the best on our dataset, as shown in Table 3. We thus use the NorBERT$_3$ models for further experiments and consider the following sizes from this family of models: *xs* (15M parameters), *small* (40M parameters), and *base* (123M parameters). This allows us to train SLIDE models of varying accuracy-to-speed trade-offs.

Training details Fine-tuning is done using the `transformers` library (Wolf et al., 2020) and the `PyTorch` framework (Ansel et al., 2024). We use binary cross-entropy as the loss function to train the model for multi-label classification.

To find our final hyperparameters, we perform a simple grid search. The models are fine-tuned with a learning rate of $5 \cdot 10^{-5}$, a batch size of 64, 1% warmup steps with a linear scheduler together with the AdamW optimizer. We train the models for 3 epochs (2,877 steps) and load the best checkpoint at the end based on metric performance (weighted multi-label accuracy). Model evaluation is performed on the validation set every 100 training steps. We fine-tuned the three NorBERT$_3$ models in this way and release them as SLIDE-xs, SLIDE-small and SLIDE-base.

Model	Loose accuracy	Exact-match accuracy	Macro F_1
XLM-RoBERTa-base	96.8	94.6	95.4
DistilBERT-base	96.5	94.5	95.2
ScandiBERT	97.6	95.9	96.6
NorBERT3-base	**98.6**	**96.4**	**97.0**

Table 3: **Base model selection** We made our choice based on the validation data split, the metrics in this table, given in percent, are for the test split. F_1 is per-language exact match. NorBERT3 refers to the same model as SLIDE.

Various training set compositions were evaluated; the best model was trained on the multi-label UD dataset combined with the 'alphabet variations' dataset using the punctuation augmentation approach and regular expression normalization described in Section 3.4. We also observe that lowercasing the training set leads to slightly better performance. Therefore, we applied lowercasing to all the training data. While performance typically improves with more training data, this was not observed on our validation set. The final training set has a skewed label distribution: 35% Bokmål, 33% Nynorsk, 13% other, 11% Swedish, and 9% Danish. The validation and test sets reflect similar skews (see Table 1). We briefly tested both upsampling and downsampling to balance labels, but the multi-label nature of the data made this challenging, and it ultimately yielded no improvement.

5.2 Static-word-embedding model (SLIDE-fast)

Since our dataset is smaller than that used to train baseline FastText models, we train a tiny multi-label model instead of concentrating efforts on pre-training a model on our dataset. The model is based on GlotLID sentence embeddings and has 20.9k parameters, not counting the input embeddings. It uses a feed forward network with 1 hidden linear layer of size 64 and a ReLU activation function between it and the output linear layer, and is trained with a regular binary cross-entropy loss. We selected the 0.5 sigmoid threshold to accept a class based on the validation data split. The `other` class is selected only if all other classes are below the threshold. Reducing number of classes from 2,102 to 4 explains faster inference (Table 4) than that of original GlotLID.

Additional Scandinavian data Since a SLIDE-fast model trained on the same training dataset as the larger model does not correctly discriminate Bokmål from Nynorsk and Danish sentences, we enhance the training dataset with additional Bokmål, Nynorsk, Danish and Swedish sentences from the Tatoeba evaluation dataset (automatically labeled in the same way as the UD-based training dataset). NER, punctuation augmentation and regular expression normalization are not applied to the resulting training split.

6 Experiments

We evaluate our SLIDE models against several established LID baselines, comparing both prediction accuracy and speed. Our evaluation focuses on two key aspects: performance on our manually annotated multi-label test set, and generalization to out-of-domain data. We first describe the baseline models used for comparison, then present our main results and the results of our out-of-domain experiments.

6.1 Baselines

We compare against LID models available at the time of writing that support the four Scandinavian languages: FastText-176 (Joulin et al., 2017), NLLB-218 (Grave et al., 2018), NB-Nordic-LID (de la Rosa and Kummervold, 2022), OpenLID (Burchell et al., 2023), GlotLID (Kargaran et al., 2023); Heliport, a faster version of HeLI-OTS (Jauhiainen et al., 2022b)[9], and `gpt2-lang-ident`.

While top-k prediction with confidence scores is possible for the FastText and GPT2-based models, we observe that the confidence scores are unreliable, i.e. there is no consistent threshold value that improves performance, and for all baseline models, except Heliport, the best results are achieved when they are used as single-label classifiers.

6.2 Main results

Table 4 presents the main results of our experiments on the manually-annotated SLIDE test set. We report loose accuracy and exact-match accuracy as overall metrics, along with per-language exact-match F_1 scores for each of the four languages and the 'other' category. Additionally, we measure inference speed in milliseconds per sentence, averaged over three runs[10].

6.3 Out-of-domain test set

Haas and Derczynski (2021) provide two test sets with single-label annotations, extracted from Wikipedia. In order to evaluate our models on an out-of-domain dataset and compare them with previous work, we use their two test splits containing 3 000 and 14 960 samples respectively and map Icelandic and Faroese to the 'other' label. We present the results on these test sets in Table 5.

7 Discussion

Performance of baseline models The baseline models exhibit varying levels of performance, see Table 4 for detailed metrics. These results demonstrate that, while most FastText-based models offer speed advantages, they fall short in accuracy for closely related languages such as Norwegian Bokmål and Norwegian Nynorsk. GlotLID, though slower (0.51 ms/sentence), provides the best performance among the baseline models, with Heliport being a close contender while being significantly faster (0.02 ms/sentence). `gpt2-lang-ident`, originally pretrained as a monolingual English model, fails to tell Danish and two Norwegian languages from each other, while being able to detect Swedish and 'other', which again highlights the importance of a dataset focused on Scandinavian languages.

Performance of SLIDE models Our three BERT-based LID models SLIDE-xs, SLIDE-small and SLIDE-base perform the best on our test set, with the `base` version reaching an exact-match accuracy of 96.4%, while the `small` and `xs` both reach 95.7%. This comes at the cost of significantly longer runtimes compared to the static embedding models. These models are suitable when high accuracy is of most importance. However, it is worth noting that we measured inference speed solely on a CPU, one sentence at a time, to ensure a fair comparison with the faster baseline models intended for CPU usage. Using a GPU with larger batch sizes would result in significantly faster runtimes for the transformer models.

[9] `https://github.com/ZJaume/heliport`

[10] Measured on an AMD EPYC 7702 CPU, with a batch size of 1.

Model	Loose accuracy	Exact-match accuracy	NB F_1	DA F_1	NN F_1	SV F_1	Other F_1	Runtime ms/sample
BASELINES								
gpt2-lang-ident	61.2	58.9	47.0	24.0	36.9	83.6	86.2	52.07
FastText-176*	80.5	77.7	72.6	66.0	55.7	92.7	93.5	**0.01**
NLLB-218*	95.3	91.6	93.0	85.9	89.0	96.8	93.6	0.08
NB-Nordic-LID*	83.3	80.6	85.0	67.0	84.8	89.7	70.2	0.02
OpenLID*	94.2	90.2	91.5	82.6	88.7	95.7	93.3	0.08
GlotLID*	97.2	93.4	93.5	89.5	89.4	97.9	98.1	0.51
Heliport (HeLI-OTS)	96.5	92.6	90.9	89.0	91.2	97.6	97.2	0.02
OUR MODELS								
SLIDE-fast	95.7	93.4	94.5	90.2	92.4	97.5	96.4	0.16
SLIDE-x-small	97.8	95.7	97.5	90.4	96.2	98.0	98.7	13.22
SLIDE-small	98.1	95.7	97.7	89.9	96.3	98.0	99.1	19.70
SLIDE-base	**98.6**	**96.4**	**98.1**	**92.0**	**97.1**	**98.6**	**99.4**	38.41

Table 4: **Detailed results on the manually-annotated multi-label SLIDE test split** The best result for each metric is typeset in bold; higher values are always better, except for the runtimes. * shows which baselines use FastText.

While our SLIDE-fast model reaches the same exact-match accuracy as GlotLID, 93.4%, it performs better on Nynorsk, Bokmål and Danish, with Nynorsk performance increasing by 3%.

Overall, performance on Danish is consistently the lowest—the best model reaches 92% F_1. Our models have been trained on more Bokmål than Danish data, and we observe a slight tendency to predict only Bokmål instead of both Bokmål and Danish for multilingual samples. We do, however, notice the same trend with lower Danish performance across all evaluated models, see Table 4.

As seen in Table 2, the punctuation augmentation led to minor performance improvements. The main motivation behind this approach, however, is increased robustness to noisy data. While the model trained with named entity swapping (see Section 3.4) gained the highest loose accuracy performance, 98.7%, it performed poorly on exact-match accuracy, 95.5%. We therefore decided not to include this in the final SLIDE models.

Error analysis Common error sources are proper names (half of 'other' instances misclassified as Scandinavian contains proper names (e.g. 'kruvi: *Karl Marx*'), instances in English (30% of 'other' instances misclassified as Scandinavian), and loanwords ('- Ta avisa *Kommersant*.', 'Server med pastasalat med bakte grønsaker og *tsatsiki* til', 'Men Anne Linnet - *oh la la*.') Bokmål and Nynorsk are confused most often. If a sentence valid both in Bokmål and Nynorsk contains irregular Bokmål spelling like 'høg' instead of 'høy', and 'tjuvfiske' instead of 'tyvfiske', it is likely to be misclassified as Nynorsk only. Some errors imply that particular tokens influence the prediction more than a sentence representation as a whole: 'høyre' is a valid word both in Nynorsk ('hear') and Bokmål ('right'), but the sentence 'I alle år har vi fått *høyre* at med dagens forbruk er det olje nok for mange tiår.', which is Nynorsk because of 'høyre' used as a verb, is misclassified as Bokmål, while a both Bokmål and Nynorsk sentence 'I den nye designen er *høgre* og venstre spalte på framsida til nettavisa fjerna.' is misclassified as only Nynorsk because of the spelling. Additionally, some 'other' instances containing subwords matching those in Scandinavian are misclassified, although the whole sentence semantics does not make any sense: 'Va shiaulteyr *er ny* skeabey harrish boayrd.' (Manx).

Out-of-domain evaluation In order to ensure that we do not overfit to the UD data, we evaluate our models on the out-of-domain test set presented in Section 6.3, which was the only LID dataset specific for Scandinavian languages available at the

Model	3K test split	15K test split
SLIDE-base	92.7	95.3
SLIDE-fast	85.4	88.5
GlotLID	**93.0**	**95.7**

Table 5: **Performance on an out-of-distribution single-labeled datasets** Accuracy on the test sets from Haas and Derczynski (2021). As this dataset is single-label, we consider a prediction to be correct, if one of the predicted languages is correct.

time of writing. While SLIDE-base reaches lower performance than GlotLID on this test set, we must add that this dataset is heavily preprocessed: lowercased and stripped out of numbers, punctuation signs and some accented characters. We also noticed a fair amount of mislabeled sentences in the dataset, with sentences like "ou di be t aatm ne en wadi", "atahualpa yupanqui" and "tromssan ruijansuomalainen yhdistys" being labeled as Swedish, Danish and Nynorsk, respectively. Furthermore, this dataset contains Icelandic and Faroese as the `other` languages, which are similar to Nynorsk in many cases. In short, we cannot draw confident conclusions from this result, but it hints at the worst-case performance of our models on out-of-distribution inputs.

8 Conclusion

We release a novel multi-label LID dataset for Danish, Norwegian Bokmål, Norwegian Nynorsk and Swedish with manually annotated validation and test splits. Using machine translation for creating a silver multi-label training dataset from a single-label one has proved to be efficient.

Although fine-tuning models for a specific data source may be helpful to obtain high performance on a selected test set, such models (especially the FastText-based ones) may be not robust towards the test dataset change. Also, excessive training data preprocessing may lead to performance degradation on data from unknown domains compared with training without any preprocessing.

Limitations

We limit ourselves to the larger Scandinavian languages, and include neither the other closely related Nordic languages Faroese and Icelandic (also known as Insular Scandinavian), nor the smaller Scandinavian varieties with a limited written tradition, such as Scanian, Elfdalian and Bornholmsk. We also do not look at other sources of variation, e.g., dialectal, diachronic or otherwise different varieties found in literature or social media.

Another limitation is that while all Norwegians generally understand Swedish and Danish well, as these languages are a compulsory part of the public curriculum, and also teaching languages of Norwegian universities, their productive capabilities are much lower, and there might be cases of mislabeling.

Acknowledgments

We would like to thank Helene Bøsei Olsen and Karoline Sætrum for their work on annotating the initial version of the test set. Some computations were performed on resources provided by Sigma2 – the National Infrastructure for High-Performance Computing and Data Storage in Norway.

References

Muhammad Abdul-Mageed, Amr Keleg, AbdelRahim Elmadany, Chiyu Zhang, Injy Hamed, Walid Magdy, Houda Bouamor, and Nizar Habash. 2024. NADI 2024: The fifth nuanced Arabic dialect identification shared task. In *Proceedings of The Second Arabic Natural Language Processing Conference*, pages 709–728, Bangkok, Thailand. Association for Computational Linguistics.

Jason Ansel, Edward Yang, Horace He, Natalia Gimelshein, Animesh Jain, Michael Voznesensky, Bin Bao, Peter Bell, David Berard, Evgeni Burovski, Geeta Chauhan, Anjali Chourdia, Will Constable, Alban Desmaison, Zachary DeVito, Elias Ellison, Will Feng, Jiong Gong, Michael Gschwind, Brian Hirsh, Sherlock Huang, Kshiteej Kalambarkar, Laurent Kirsch, Michael Lazos, Mario Lezcano, Yanbo Liang, Jason Liang, Yinghai Lu, CK Luk, Bert Maher, Yunjie Pan, Christian Puhrsch, Matthias Reso, Mark Saroufim, Marcos Yukio Siraichi, Helen Suk, Michael Suo, Phil Tillet, Eikan Wang, Xiaodong Wang, William Wen, Shunting Zhang, Xu Zhao, Keren Zhou, Richard Zou, Ajit Mathews, Gregory Chanan, Peng Wu, and Soumith Chintala. 2024. PyTorch 2: Faster Machine Learning Through Dynamic Python Bytecode Transformation and Graph Compilation. In *29th ACM International Conference on Architectural Support for Programming Languages and Operating Systems, Volume 2 (ASPLOS '24)*. ACM.

Laurie Burchell, Alexandra Birch, Nikolay Bogoychev, and Kenneth Heafield. 2023. An open dataset and model for language identification. In *Proceedings of the 61st Annual Meeting of the Association for Computational Linguistics (Volume 2: Short Papers)*, pages 865–879, Toronto, Canada. Association for Computational Linguistics.

Adrian-Gabriel Chifu, Goran Glavaš, Radu Tudor Ionescu, Nikola Ljubešić, Aleksandra Miletić, Filip Miletić, Yves Scherrer, and Ivan Vulić. 2024. VarDial evaluation campaign 2024: Commonsense reasoning in dialects and multi-label similar language identification. In *Proceedings of the Eleventh Workshop on NLP for Similar Languages, Varieties, and Dialects (VarDial 2024)*, pages 1–15, Mexico City, Mexico. Association for Computational Linguistics.

Alexis Conneau, Kartikay Khandelwal, Naman Goyal, Vishrav Chaudhary, Guillaume Wenzek, Francisco Guzmán, Edouard Grave, Myle Ott, Luke Zettlemoyer, and Veselin Stoyanov. 2020. Unsupervised cross-lingual representation learning at scale. In *Proceedings of the 58th Annual Meeting of the Association for Computational Linguistics*, pages 8440–8451, Online. Association for Computational Linguistics.

Jacob Devlin, Ming-Wei Chang, Kenton Lee, and Kristina Toutanova. 2019. BERT: Pre-training of deep bidirectional transformers for language understanding. In *Proceedings of the 2019 Conference of the North American Chapter of the Association for Computational Linguistics: Human Language Technologies, Volume 1 (Long and Short Papers)*, pages 4171–4186, Minneapolis, Minnesota. Association for Computational Linguistics.

Ruth Vatvedt Fjeld, Anders Nøklestad, and Kristin Hagen. 2020. Leksikografisk bokmålskorpus (LBK) – bakgrunn og bruk. *Oslo Studies in Language*, 11(1):47–59.

Cyril Goutte, Serge Léger, Shervin Malmasi, and Marcos Zampieri. 2016. Discriminating similar languages: Evaluations and explorations. In *Proceedings of the Tenth International Conference on Language Resources and Evaluation (LREC'16)*, pages 1800–1807, Portorož, Slovenia. European Language Resources Association (ELRA).

Edouard Grave, Piotr Bojanowski, Prakhar Gupta, Armand Joulin, and Tomas Mikolov. 2018. Learning word vectors for 157 languages. In *Proceedings of the Eleventh International Conference on Language Resources and Evaluation (LREC 2018)*, Miyazaki, Japan. European Language Resources Association (ELRA).

René Haas and Leon Derczynski. 2021. Discriminating between similar Nordic languages. In *Proceedings of the Eighth Workshop on NLP for Similar Languages, Varieties and Dialects*, pages 67–75, Kiyv, Ukraine. Association for Computational Linguistics.

Tommi Jauhiainen, Heidi Jauhiainen, and Krister Lindén. 2022a. HeLI-OTS, off-the-shelf language identifier for text. In *Proceedings of the 13th Conference on Language Resources and Evaluation*, pages 3912–3922, Marseille, France. European Language Resources Association.

Tommi Jauhiainen, Heidi Jauhiainen, and Krister Lindén. 2022b. HeLI-OTS, off-the-shelf language identifier for text. In *Proceedings of the Thirteenth Language Resources and Evaluation Conference*, pages 3912–3922, Marseille, France. European Language Resources Association.

Tommi Jauhiainen, Marco Lui, Marcos Zampieri, Timothy Baldwin, and Krister Lindén. 2019. Automatic language identification in texts: A survey. *Journal of Artificial Intelligence Research*, 65:675–782.

Armand Joulin, Edouard Grave, Piotr Bojanowski, and Tomas Mikolov. 2017. Bag of tricks for efficient text classification. In *Proceedings of the 15th Conference of the European Chapter of the Association for Computational Linguistics: Volume 2, Short Papers*, pages 427–431, Valencia, Spain. Association for Computational Linguistics.

Amir Hossein Kargaran, Ayyoob Imani, François Yvon, and Hinrich Schütze. 2023. GlotLID: Language identification for low-resource languages. In *The 2023 Conference on Empirical Methods in Natural Language Processing*.

Amr Keleg and Walid Magdy. 2023. Arabic dialect identification under scrutiny: Limitations of single-label classification. In *Proceedings of ArabicNLP 2023*, pages 385–398, Singapore (Hybrid). Association for Computational Linguistics.

Bård Borch Michalsen. 2015. *Komma. Kommategnets personlighet, historie og regler*. Juritzen forlag.

Aleksandra Miletić and Filip Miletić. 2024. A gold standard with silver linings: Scaling up annotation for distinguishing Bosnian, Croatian, Montenegrin and Serbian. In *Proceedings of the Fourth Workshop on Human Evaluation of NLP Systems (HumEval) @ LREC-COLING 2024*, pages 36–46, Torino, Italia. ELRA and ICCL.

Joakim Nivre, Marie-Catherine de Marneffe, Filip Ginter, Yoav Goldberg, Jan Hajič, Christopher D. Manning, Ryan McDonald, Slav Petrov, Sampo Pyysalo, Natalia Silveira, Reut Tsarfaty, and Daniel Zeman. 2016. Universal Dependencies v1: A multilingual treebank collection. In *Proceedings of the Tenth International Conference on Language Resources and Evaluation (LREC'16)*, pages 1659–1666, Portorož, Slovenia. European Language Resources Association (ELRA).

Joakim Nivre, Marie-Catherine de Marneffe, Filip Ginter, Jan Hajič, Christopher D. Manning, Sampo Pyysalo, Sebastian Schuster, Francis Tyers, and Daniel Zeman. 2020. Universal Dependencies v2: An evergrowing multilingual treebank collection. In *Proceedings of the Twelfth Language Resources and Evaluation Conference*, pages 4034–4043, Marseille, France. European Language Resources Association.

NLLB Team, Marta R. Costa-jussà, James Cross, Onur Çelebi, Maha Elbayad, Kenneth Heafield, Kevin Heffernan, Elahe Kalbassi, Janice Lam, Daniel Licht, Jean Maillard, Anna Sun, Skyler Wang, Guillaume Wenzek, Al Youngblood, Bapi Akula, Loic Barrault, Gabriel Mejia Gonzalez, Prangthip Hansanti, John Hoffman, Semarley Jarrett, Kaushik Ram Sadagopan, Dirk Rowe, Shannon Spruit, Chau Tran, Pierre Andrews, Necip Fazil Ayan, Shruti Bhosale, Sergey Edunov, Angela Fan, Cynthia Gao, Vedanuj Goswami, Francisco Guzmán, Philipp Koehn, Alexandre Mourachko, Christophe Ropers, Safiyyah Saleem, Holger Schwenk, and Jeff Wang. 2022. No language left behind: Scaling human-centered machine translation.

Eric Papazian. 2013. Moltke moe og norsk språknormering fram til 1907. *Språklig samling*, pages 69–104.

Alec Radford, Jeff Wu, Rewon Child, David Luan, Dario Amodei, and Ilya Sutskever. 2019. Language models are unsupervised multitask learners.

Javier de la Rosa and Per Egil Kummervold. 2022. NB-Nordic-LID.

David Samuel, Andrey Kutuzov, Samia Touileb, Erik Velldal, Lilja Øvrelid, Egil Rønningstad, Elina Sigdel, and Anna Palatkina. 2023. NorBench – a benchmark for Norwegian language models. In *Proceedings of the 24th Nordic Conference on Computational Linguistics (NoDaLiDa)*, pages 618–633, Tórshavn, Faroe Islands. University of Tartu Library.

David Samuel, Vladislav Mikhailov, Erik Velldal, Lilja Øvrelid, Lucas Georges Gabriel Charpentier, and Andrey Kutuzov. 2024. Small languages, big models: A study of continual training on languages of norway.

Victor Sanh, Lysandre Debut, Julien Chaumond, and Thomas Wolf. 2019. DistilBERT, a distilled version of BERT: smaller, faster, cheaper and lighter. *ArXiv*, abs/1910.01108.

Raivis Skadiņš, Jörg Tiedemann, Roberts Rozis, and Daiga Deksne. 2014. Billions of parallel words for free: Building and using the EU bookshop corpus. In *Proceedings of the Ninth International Conference on Language Resources and Evaluation (LREC'14)*, pages 1850–1855, Reykjavik, Iceland. European Language Resources Association (ELRA).

Vésteinn Snæbjarnarson, Annika Simonsen, Goran Glavaš, and Ivan Vulić. 2023. Transfer to a low-resource language via close relatives: The case study on Faroese. In *Proceedings of the 24th Nordic Conference on Computational Linguistics (NoDaLiDa)*, pages 728–737, Tórshavn, Faroe Islands. University of Tartu Library.

Jörg Tiedemann. 2020. The tatoeba translation challenge – realistic data sets for low resource and multilingual MT. In *Proceedings of the Fifth Conference on Machine Translation*, pages 1174–1182, Online. Association for Computational Linguistics.

Thomas Wolf, Lysandre Debut, Victor Sanh, Julien Chaumond, Clement Delangue, Anthony Moi, Pierric Cistac, Tim Rault, Remi Louf, Morgan Funtowicz, Joe Davison, Sam Shleifer, Patrick von Platen, Clara Ma, Yacine Jernite, Julien Plu, Canwen Xu, Teven Le Scao, Sylvain Gugger, Mariama Drame, Quentin Lhoest, and Alexander Rush. 2020. Transformers: State-of-the-art natural language processing. In *Proceedings of the 2020 Conference on Empirical Methods in Natural Language Processing: System Demonstrations*, pages 38–45, Online. Association for Computational Linguistics.

Marcos Zampieri, Kai North, Tommi Jauhiainen, Mariano Felice, Neha Kumari, Nishant Nair, and Yash Mahesh Bangera. 2024. Language variety identification with true labels. In *Proceedings of the 2024 Joint International Conference on Computational Linguistics, Language Resources and Evaluation (LREC-COLING 2024)*, pages 10100–10109, Torino, Italia. ELRA and ICCL.

Federated Meta-Learning for Low-Resource Translation of Kirundi

Kyle Sang
University of Maryland
ksang@umd.edu

Tahseen Rabbani
Yale University
tahseen.rabbani@yale.edu

Tianyi Zhou
University of Maryland
tianyi@umd.edu

Abstract

In this work, we reframe multilingual neural machine translation (NMT) as a federated meta-learning problem and introduce a translation dataset for the low-resource Kirundi language. We aggregate machine translation models ($\rightarrow$ en) locally trained on varying (but related) source languages to produce a global meta-model that encodes abstract representations of key semantic structures relevant to the parent languages. We then use PerFedAvg to fit the global model onto a specified target language in a few-shot manner. The target language may live outside the subset of parent languages (such as closely-related dialects or sibling languages), which is particularly useful for languages with limitedly available sentence pairs. We first develop a novel dataset of Kirundi-English sentence pairs curated from Biblication translation. We then demonstrate that a federated learning approach can produce a tiny 4.8M Kirundi translation model and a stronger NLLB-600M model which performs well on both our Biblical corpus and the FLORES-200 Kirundi corpus.

1 Introduction

The federated learning (FL) paradigm has drawn great interest for its inherent privacy, scalability, and performance across myriad vision and language tasks. Recent works have proposed federated learning as a solution for low-resource machine translation (Tupitsa et al., 2024; Moskvoretskii et al., 2024a). Centralized federated learning often focuses on optimizing a global model by aggregating weights over a cluster of clients trained on identical tasks (with varying local datasets). Current literature suggests a global model can also be used as a meta-model to increase model performance and convergence speed (Fallah et al., 2020; Chen et al., 2018). In the meta-learning setting, clients train on similar, but heterogeneous tasks, enabling few-shot adaptation to new tasks of the same flavor.

In this paper, we attempt to utilize federated learning, viewed through the meta-learning lens, to produce a seq2seq translation model for Kirundi, which despite having 11.2 million speakers, is rarely considered in literature and lacks translation resources. Here, the meta-task is $\rightarrow$ en machine translation, with varying source language. We aggregate a global model over a small cluster of parent seq2seq models. The parent models train higher-resource Bantu languages, specifically Luganda, Bemba, and Kinyarwanda.

To the best of our knowledge, the FLORES-200 dataset (Costa-jussà et al., 2022) is the only publicly-available parallel translation corpus of Kirundi, containing roughly 2000 sentences (aligned with 200 other languages). We produce a novel corpus of 29,506 English to Kirundi sentence pairs by scraping pairs from parallel corpuses of the New and Old Testament produced by The International Bible Society (available at `bible.com`). We demonstrate that the federated meta-learning strategy can boost performance on both the FLORES-200 Kirundi and our Bible corpus. We use our approach to construct a tiny, but performant 4 million parameter run $\rightarrow$ en model and to improve the performance of NLLB-600M, which has already been trained to translate Kirundi (among many other languages).

2 Algorithm and Preliminaries

The PerFedAvg algorithm combines FedAvg (McMahan et al., 2017), Reptile (Nichol et al., 2018), and personalization to increase convergence speed and stability. To rapidly adapt to a new language for a machine translation task (in our case,

Proceedings of the Third Workshop on Resources and Representations for Under-Resourced Languages and Domains (RESOURCEFUL-2025), pages 190–194, March 2, 2025 ©2025 Association for Computational Linguistics

`run` $\rightarrow$ `en`), we split our approach into 3 steps, similar to PerFedAvg (Fallah et al., 2020).

1. **Global Model Training**. Using the FedAvg federated learning algorithm (McMahan et al., 2017), we aggregate gradients across multiple clients. Each client holds data for a language exclusive to them. Training is performed, and gradients are aggregated to update the global model, which is used by clients for the next epoch of training. It is well-known the heterogeneous weighting of gradients during aggregation is required to achieve optimal performance (Moskvoretskii et al., 2024a; Fallah et al., 2020; Tupitsa et al., 2024; Kairouz et al., 2021). We use the Optuna library to fine-tune gradient weighting rather than using an even average (McMahan et al., 2017) or weighing by the the amount of client data (Fallah et al., 2020).

2. **Reptile Meta-Learning**. The fine-tuning is tested against a subset of Kirundi training data. We run the Reptile algorithm (Nichol et al., 2018) 10 times on our model after training the global model to improve model performance as outlined by PerFedAvg. Reptile enables our meta-model (i.e., federated global model) to quickly adapt to `run` $\rightarrow$ `en` translation by repeatedly sampling other parental translation tasks and performing SGD on each parent task, then updating the initialization parameters in the direction of the of the `run` $\rightarrow$ `en` loss minima. This will prepare our global model for rapid personalization towards our full Kirundi training sets.

3. **Kirundi Personalization**. We take our fine-tuned, Reptile-optimized global model and then perform full training over our Kirundi datasets.

3 Experiments

3.1 Kirundi Dataset

While machine translation work has been performed for other African languages(Vegi et al., 2022; Emezue and Dossou, 2022; Omwoma et al., 2024; Nyoni and Bassett, 2021), besides FLORES-200, there are no other widely-known parallel corpora for Kirundi. Despite having 11.2 million speakers, it is underrepresented in the machine translation community. One of the initiatives of this work was to curate a new dataset of sentence pairs to stimulate further work on this language.

Using the Kirundi Bible we were able to directly translate English sentences to their Kirundi counterparts. The Kirundi verse pairs were extracted and cleaned from the Kirundi Bible found at `https://www.bible.com/`. The dataset itself contains 29,506 sentence pairs. For training purposes, we truncated the full set down to sentence pairs with token lengths $<=11$ (for a total of 1317 pairs) during training with a train dev/test of 80%/20%. We intend to release these sentence pairs on GitHub following the deanonymization of this submission.

3.2 Training

Small seq2seq model. For our tiny model scenario, we use 4.8M parameter Seq2Seq torch models with Bahdanau attention (Bahdanau et al., 2014), Adam optimizers, and NLL loss (Sutskever et al., 2014). Learning rate is set to $1e-5$, weight decay to $1e-4$. FedAvg for our global model is run for 50 communication rounds where every client participates in 1 local epoch per round. After 25 communication rounds, Optuna is used to finetune the gradient weights (i.e., model mixture) every 5 rounds. Reptile is run for 10 rounds. After the global meta-model is prepared for knowledge transfer, we run local Kirundi training (i.e., personalization) for 100 epochs. We source Luganda-English pairs from a published Zenodo set (Kimera et al., 2023) and Kinyarwanda-English pairs from a biblical translation.

NLLB. For federated training of NLLB-600M Kirundi, we adopt the same hyperparameters as the tiny model scenario, but we do not perform Optuna finetuning due to the sheer size of the model. That is, we use equal weighting of the parent Luganda, Bemba, and Kinyarwanda models, with all training and test data sourced from FLORES-200.

3.3 Translation Tasks

3.3.1 Kirundi Bible Corpus

In Table 1, we record the BLEU scores of various models on our Bible corpus. PerFedAvg refers to parental model weighting N_k/N where N_k is the number of training samples for client k and $N=\sum_k N_k$. Equal weighting sets federated weights equal to $1/k$ (in our case $k=3$). Frozen weights applies an Optuna fine-tuned, Reptile-optimized global meta-model directly on the Kirundi bible test set. No global model trains the tiny seq2seq

Model	BLEU Score
Fine-Tuned FL + Personalization	**20.67**
PerFedAvg Weights	17.66
Equal Weights	17.89
Frozen Weights	17.01
No Global Model	17.70
NLLB-600M	23.85

Table 1: **Kirundi Bible Dataset.** Highest achieved BLEU scores of different algorithms averaged over 3 runs on our Kirundi Bible Corpus. NLLB is also included as a baseline.

model from scratch (no federated learning). Fine-Tuned FL + Personalization weights refers to Optuna+Reptile global model fine-tuning in addition to Kirundi bible train set personalization. We observe that a federated model with fine-tuned parent model mixtures can achieve the highest performance – lagging only the NLLB-600M model which is roughly 125x its size.

3.3.2 FLORES-200 Corpus

Model	BLEU Score
Fine-Tuned FL + Personalization FL	19.26
NLLB-600M (Unchanged Default Weights)	23.46
NLLB-600M (No FL + Personalization)	23.45
NLLB-600M (FL + Personalization)	**25.51**

Table 2: **FLORES-200 Dataset.** Highest achieved BLEU scores of different algorithms averaged over 3 runs on the FLORES-200 Kirundi dataset.

In Table 2, we study how our various models perform on the FLORES-200 Kirundi corpus of roughly 2000 sentence pairs (approximately 1000 pairs for train/test). Fine-tuned FL + Personalization performs respectably on FLORES-200 with no personalization the FLORES train set, indicating the Bible training corpus imbues our tiny model with general knowledge of modern Kirundi. We observe that federated learning is able to improve the performance of NLLB-600M, which is already pre-trained on massive web corpora of Bantu languages (Costa-jussà et al., 2022).

3.3.3 K-shot Learning

We can see across all of our ablation training curves, depicted in Figure 1, using a global model (Fine-Tuned FL) for pre-training leads to an increase in performance. It maintains this improvement in all k-shot tasks. We found that improvement was especially impressive in few-shot learning environments, with consistent increases despite a low amount of accessible training data.

In addition to this, we can also observe a much faster convergence for the pre-trained model in Figure 1. The pre-trained model can be seen converging 5 to 10 rounds before a model trained without a meta-model.

These improvements in training speed and accuracy can be explained by the pre-trained model having already seen similar examples during the training of the global model. With this in mind, using a global model as a meta-model presents an avenue for improving model performance when target language data is low, but data from related languages is available.

3.4 Weighting Algorithms

In Figure 2, we review different weighting strategies and their performance compared to our algorithm. Compared to the PerFedAvg strategy (weighting proportional to size of training data), we can see increased performance in our algorithm. PerFedAvg weights on sample count, but in our case, we have a low number of clients with differing amounts of data. As a result, PerFedAvg weighting results in overfitting to a specific language which is detrimental in obtaining optimal meta-model weights.

We also compare our algorithm to equally weighting gradients from all clients. If finding the truest average of our client languages during our global model training was the most effective for personalization, this strategy would yield the highest performance. However, during our weight tuning, we found that oftentimes certain languages would be weighted as more important to personalization. For example, during training, we found that weights from our Kinyarwanda client would be weighted slightly higher than other clients. Intuitively, this is because Kinyarwanda has a closer lexical similarity to our target language of Kirundi compared to Bemba or Luganda.

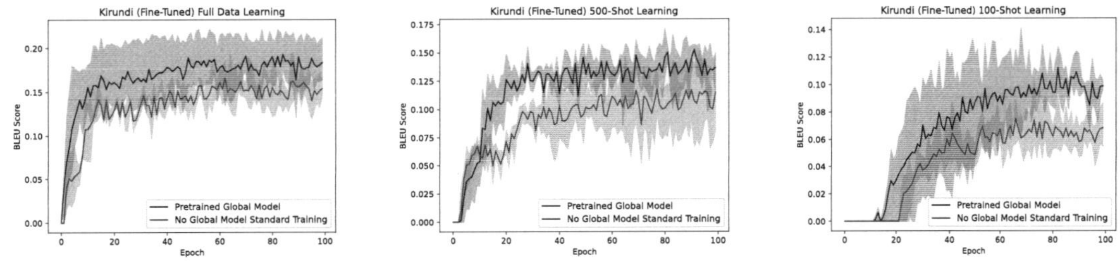

Figure 1: Comparing performances of fine-tuning from a pre-trained global model and training from scratch in different k-shot settings.

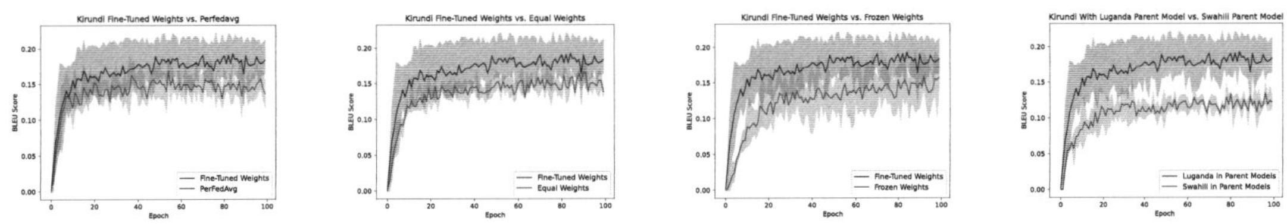

Figure 2: Comparing the performance of different weighting strategies applied during training of the global model.

We also analyze the performance of personalization with frozen intermediate weights. Again, our algorithm outperforms this setting. This demonstrates the task as more than a fine-tuning task, but a more complex meta-learning problem.

From these results, we can surmise that there exists a most optimal set of weights for each client that is based on the lexical similarity of the parent languages used in training the global model to our target languages.

3.5 Parental Model

We also explored the impact of other Bantu languages on our personalization step, replacing Luganda in our parent languages with Swahili. We previously discussed the correlation of lexical similarity to a target language and the importance of a parent language. Other studies have claimed unrelated parent models should not have an impact on the personalization step (Moskvoretskii et al., 2024b). However, from our experiment illustrated in Figure 2, we can see that an unrelated language has deleterious effects on performance. Despite being a Bantu language, Swahili is much less lexically related to Kirundi than Luganda. As a result, the drop in performance can be associated with our Swahili client effectively poisoning the weights of global model with an unrelated task.

4 Conclusion

In this work, we curate a dataset and develop an algorithm for English to Kirundi translation. Despite being a widely spoken Bantu language, there were no previously existing translation resources for Kirundi. Despite limited sentence pairs, our work shows a translation model can be developed with certain federated learning techniques to provide support for an underrepresented language.

References

Dzmitry Bahdanau, Kyunghyun Cho, and Yoshua Bengio. 2014. Neural machine translation by jointly learning to align and translate. *arXiv preprint arXiv:1409.0473*.

Fei Chen, Mi Luo, Zhenhua Dong, Zhenguo Li, and Xiuqiang He. 2018. Federated meta-learning with fast convergence and efficient communication.

Marta R Costa-jussà, James Cross, Onur Çelebi, Maha Elbayad, Kenneth Heafield, Kevin Heffernan, Elahe Kalbassi, Janice Lam, Daniel Licht, Jean Maillard, et al. 2022. No language left behind: Scaling human-centered machine translation. *arXiv preprint arXiv:2207.04672*.

Chris C. Emezue and Bonaventure F. P. Dossou. 2022. Mmtafrica: Multilingual machine translation for african languages. Proceedings of the Sixth Conference on Machine Translation (2021) 398-411, Association for Computational Linguistics.

Alireza Fallah, Aryan Mokhtari, and Asuman Ozdaglar. 2020. Personalized federated learning with theoretical guarantees: A model-agnostic meta-learning approach. *Advances in neural information processing systems*, 33:3557–3568.

Peter Kairouz, H Brendan McMahan, Brendan Avent, Aurélien Bellet, Mehdi Bennis, Arjun Nitin Bhagoji, Kallista Bonawitz, Zachary Charles, Graham Cormode, Rachel Cummings, et al. 2021. Advances and open problems in federated learning. *Foundations and trends® in machine learning*, 14(1–2):1–210.

Richard Kimera, Daniela N Rim, and Heeyoul Choi. 2023. Building a parallel corpus and training translation models between luganda and english. *arXiv preprint arXiv:2301.02773*.

Brendan McMahan, Eider Moore, Daniel Ramage, Seth Hampson, and Blaise Aguera y Arcas. 2017. Communication-efficient learning of deep networks from decentralized data. In *Artificial intelligence and statistics*, pages 1273–1282. PMLR.

Viktor Moskvoretskii, Nazarii Tupitsa, Chris Biemann, Samuel Horváth, Eduard Gorbunov, and Irina Nikishina. 2024a. Low-resource machine translation through the lens of personalized federated learning. *arXiv preprint arXiv:2406.12564*.

Viktor Moskvoretskii, Nazarii Tupitsa, Chris Biemann, Samuel Horváth, Eduard Gorbunov, and Irina Nikishina. 2024b. Low-resource machine translation through the lens of personalized federated learning.

Alex Nichol, Joshua Achiam, and John Schulman. 2018. On first-order meta-learning algorithms.

Evander Nyoni and Bruce A Bassett. 2021. Low-resource neural machine translation for southern african languages. *arXiv preprint arXiv:2104.00366*.

Vincent Omwoma, Lawrance Nderu, Kennedy Ogada, and Tobias Mwalili. 2024. Neural machine translation for low resource bantu languages in east and southern africa. *Research Square*.

Ilya Sutskever, Oriol Vinyals, and Quoc V. Le. 2014. Sequence to sequence learning with neural networks.

Nazarii Tupitsa, Samuel Horváth, Martin Takáč, and Eduard Gorbunov. 2024. Federated learning can find friends that are advantageous.

Pavanpankaj Vegi, Sivabhavani J, Biswajit Paul, Prasanna K R, and Chitra Viswanathan. 2022. ANVITA-African: A multilingual neural machine translation system for African languages. In *Proceedings of the Seventh Conference on Machine Translation (WMT)*, pages 1090–1097, Abu Dhabi, United Arab Emirates (Hybrid). Association for Computational Linguistics.

Author Index

Association for Computational Linguistics
209 N. Eighth Street
Stroudsburg, Pennsylvania 18360

ISBN 979-8-3313-1889-5

CURRAN ASSOCIATES INC. proceedings.com